W9-AUG-059

MONOLOGUE
TO
DIALOGUE

Prentice-Hall Series in Speech Communication
Larry L. Barker and Robert J. Kibler, Consulting Editors

136718

HM
258
.B76
1979

SECOND EDITION

MONOLOGUE
TO
DIALOGUE
An Exploration
of
Interpersonal Communication

Charles T. Brown
Western Michigan University

WITHDRAWN

Paul W. Keller
Manchester College

PRENTICE-HALL, INC., Englewood Cliffs, New Jersey 07632

GOSHEN COLLEGE LIBRARY
GOSHEN, INDIANA

Library of Congress Cataloging in Publication Data

BROWN, CHARLES T
  Monologue to dialogue.
  Bibliography: p. 315
  Includes index.
  1. Communication.   2. Interpersonal relations.
3. Nonverbal communication.   I. Keller, Paul W.,
joint author.   II. Title.
HM258.B76 1978   301.14   78-16541
ISBN 0-13-600825-9

Prentice-Hall Series in Speech Communication
Larry L. Barker and Robert J. Kibler, Consulting Editors

© 1979 by Prentice-Hall, Inc., Englewood Cliffs, N.J. 07632

All rights reserved. No part of this book
may be reproduced in any form or
by any means without permission in writing
from the publisher.

Printed in the United States of America

10 9 8 7 6 5 4 3 2 1

PRENTICE-HALL INTERNATIONAL, INC., *London*
PRENTICE-HALL OF AUSTRALIA PTY. LIMITED, *Sydney*
PRENTICE-HALL OF CANADA, LTD., *Toronto*
PRENTICE-HALL OF INDIA PRIVATE LIMITED, *New Delhi*
PRENTICE-HALL OF JAPAN, INC., *Tokyo*
PRENTICE-HALL OF SOUTHEAST ASIA PTE. LTD., *Singapore*
WHITEHALL BOOKS LIMITED, *Wellington, New Zealand*

Contents

Preface, ix

1   **Relatedness,** 1

Communication
What is a Relationship?
A Definition of Feelings
How Our Feelings Work in Interaction
How Feelings Bond Us
How Feelings Change the Quality of Relatedness
The Kindred Spirit
Trust
Relatedness Shapes Identity

2   **The Self-Concept and Self-Esteem,** 28

The Self in Motion
Enter Self-Esteem
The Depressing Backdrop for the Evolving Self-Concept
The Self-Concept and its Growth Process
The Present Self Versus the Ideal Self
Disparities in the Self-Concept that Create Fear
Two Communication Processes that Bear on the Self-Concept
Conclusion

3   **Both Sides of Silence:**
            The Nature of Communication, 58

            The Impact of Both Sides of Silence on Life
            The Meaning of the Stories
            The Silent Side of Communication
            The Noisy Side of Communication
            Communication: The Interactive Results of Listening and Speaking
            Conclusion

4   **Feelings, Energy, and Values in Process,** 82

            Feelings
            Energy
            Information: The Key to Power
            Behavior
            The Role of Values
            Values and the Ultimate Bond
            The Four Ultimate Values
            Patterns of Communicating
            Conclusion

5   **Meaning: What Language Does To Us and For Us,** 110

            Myth: The Meaning is in the Words
            The Domain of General Semantics
            Meaning and the Act of Translation
            The Languages of Belief, Value, and the Self-Concept

6   **Meaning: Nonverbal Messages,** 140

            The Inescapability of the Nonverbal
            Nonverbal Messages that Affect Communication
            Nonverbal Messages that Do Not Fit the Words Spoken
            The People Who can Best Read Nonverbal Messages
            The Ultimate in Self-Awareness: Reading Your Own Nonverbal Messages
            Breaking the Code

7   **Emotion and Communication,** 164

            The Price of Language Without Emotion
            Emotion and Words

Language Cleanup Time
Listening and Emotion
Speech and Emotion
Despair—Anxiety—Hope
Conclusions

8   Judgment, 188

Descriptions and Analyses of Judgment, Criticism, and Discrimination
The Need to Judge
The Results of Being Judged
The Results of Making the Judgment
A Case for Critical Listening
Nonjudgmental Discrimination

9   Power, 212

Tomorrow's Probable Power Problem
Summary

10   Conflict, 240

A Definition of Conflict
How Conflict Works in Interpersonal Communication
The Forms of Communication Conflict
What are Patterns For?
Conclusion

11   Ethics, 274

A Snapshot of Past Thought
An Interpersonal Ethic
Support for the Argument
The Interpersonal Ethic Restated
Factors that Make an Interpersonal Ethic Hard to Apply
Implications of the Interpersonal Ethic
The Sixty-Four-Dollar Question
The Ethic Illustrated
Contempt and Ethics
Summary

12   **From Monologue to Dialogue,** 294

Monologue
Technical Dialogue
Resistant Communication
Confrontation
Dialogue
The Language of Dialogue
Conclusion

Selected Readings, 315

Index, 323

Preface

Of the writing of communication books there seems to be no end. Flood level, the potential reader must feel, was reached long ago. From his perch in the highest tree, surveying the rising tide around him, he has every reason to ask, "Why should there be still another book?"

When we were at work on the original edition of this book we thought the answer was clear: "Because someone ought to view the communication process through the eyes of the listener rather than, as traditionally, through the eyes of the message-sender." We dedicated ourselves to that focus. And now, six years later, that still looks like a worthy goal to us.

But in the flood of writing one thing is becoming crystal clear: Communication is a complex, intricate, multifaceted, indivisible set of acts. Faced with that knowledge, some writers have chosen an orientation and stuck with it—for example, all of communication is viewed as a subtle application of the art of persuasion; all communication is explained in terms of a cost-benefit analysis; or all communication is seen as the development of self-esteem. Other writers have selected some topics, out of the infinite number available, and have dealt systematically with them. Still others have taken the view that the topic is too big to encompass anyway, and that the best we can do is expose people to selected experiences (exercises, simulations, games, etc.) in the hope that useful insights will emerge in the process.

All of these approaches, we think, make their contribution. But they have convinced us that if communication does, indeed, have so many parts, the search should sometimes focus on the connections between them. "How," the question might be put, "does communication hang together?" If the pieces are inseparable, what are the strands that bind them? That kind of question became the springboard for this second edition. And what began as a process of updating and enriching the original volume turned into what almost amounted to the building of a new book.

We begin, in this edition, with the idea that relationship and human bonding are fundamental to life, and that communication is the means by which they are realized. We go on, then, to identify the foundation features of relationship-communication. These features are shown in a unified model to which all later material is related. In short, we present a unified theory of relationship-communication. In the latter part of the book, by which time the reader has had the model fleshed-in with explanation, we provide an Instrument (at the end of Chapter 10) with which s/he can measure how the elements hang together in his or her own communication.

To attempt this new, more inclusive view of communication has required the addition of four chapters, and the extensive re-writing of most of the others. Instead of beginning with "A Point of View," the revision devotes its first chapter to the analysis of relationship and human bonding.

Then Chapter 2 explores how the self-concept, which governs the way we communicate, is shaped in the bonding process.

Chapter 3 picks up parts of the former beginning of the book, showing, again, how the speaking-listening union in each of us is deep in the very process by which we form our identity in communication.

Chapter 4 is entirely new, and is the spearhead in thinking that brought the development of relationship in Chapter 1 and the conflict data in Chapter 10 into focus. It was not that we did not know the social psychology research from the 1940s to the early 1970s when the first edition was written. It was Robert Freed Bale's *Personality and Interpersonal Behavior* in 1970 that started to crystalize our thinking. The union of his work with that of Charles Osgood's semantic differential and the values research that has permeated much of the literature in education in recent years formed the thinking of the chapter, "Feelings, Energy, and Values in Process." The chapter is a statement of the basic dynamics of the human communication process.

It is easy to discuss language at fairly superficial levels, but harder to understand how it really functions in communication. In the first edition, in the language chapter, we tried to explain how language works in us to make us human. In the new edition (Chapter 5) this is matched with a beginning section on how language can get in the way of communication—a section devoted to principles of general semantics and their application in everyday interaction.

The chapter following on nonverbal language is revised and con- fined to those features of nonverbal research that bear most directly upon interpersonal communication. We were tempted to follow up the exciting research in all facets of nonverbal communication, but to do so with other than an outline would end in a book on nonverbal communi- cation.

Chapter 7, on emotion, is essentially unchanged, except for the section on anxiety. The chapters on judgment and power have been altered only to relate them better to the focus of the beginning chapter on human relationship.

Chapters 10 and 11 are cornerstone additions, as we view this edi- tion. How conflict is touched by communication, and how communica- tion can function constructively or destructively in conflicted moments, is a topic creeping into an increasing number of interpersonal communi- cation books. We treat conflict as an inescapable and potentially creative part of interaction rather than as communication out of order.

With the role of values seen as one of three basic forces shaping communication, it seemed wise to add a chapter on ethics. That chapter, Chapter 11, is a description of ethics as a phenomenon of human rela- tionship, rather than the traditional catechism of ethical prescriptions.

The book concludes with a revised statement of the former last chapter "Monologue to Dialogue," eliminating dated examples, includ- ing new ones, and hopefully sharpening the concept of human dialogue.

This is not a skills book, in the usual sense, but it is deeply concerned about the improvement of interpersonal skills. It works from the as- sumption that skill changes are significant only insofar as behaviors are coupled with understanding. As one comes to understand, he tends to build his own skills from a formula custom-built. The reader should always be asking how theory works out in life. To aid him or her we have created instruments at the end of each chapter, tools for applying the principles to oneself. More needs to be said about this feature.

There are one or more instruments for each chapter, thus providing a way of letting the student measure himself on the key concepts in each chapter. In the instrumentation we have tried to keep the design similar from instrument to instrument, so that one does not weary of learning how to use the instruments, and yet varied enough so that the student does not grow weary of a format. The tests are original, although we have studied the literature of several hundred instruments presently pub- lished. We have not scrambled the items of a given test in order to camouflage its purpose, except in the instance of the Communication-Conflict Instrument at the end of Chapter 10, which is being developed for research purposes. We sacrificed that feature in order to have instruments that would not require a complicated key for scoring. As a consequence of the transparency of purpose, students, we have learned, may say to themselves, "I would be expected to react as I am reacting to this item, so I had better be careful." Students should be encouraged to respond as they are inclined to, not as they think would make them appear the way they wish they were. (Instrument 1 of Chapter 2 is designed to measure that disparity, which is in all of us.) That is, in part, the reason that the writers have, following some instruments, given their own scores and interpretations. We were sometimes disappointed with our scores. There is little purpose in studying interpersonal communication if we refuse to look at our communication as it is. In our judgment, to make instruments for such a study, which by subtleness causes the person to reveal himself unwittingly, is of little value, for the person who will not reveal himself will interpret the scores in ways to defend what he is set on defending.

There is another reason for the transparency of the instruments. A book built around the significance of human relationships, in which the authors and instructors have instruments intended to cause students to reveal more than they intended, is not cricket. Besides, it won't work. Most of us know how to defend ourselves.

Many persons will not fully comprehend a given instrument, however, for in it is often a complicated analysis. Even the early makers of authoritarian tests did not realize that there are authoritarian liberals as well as authoritarian conservatives. As the student comes to understand an instrument in this respect, s/he will better understand the process and structures of human communication. While we have tried to keep the instruments as simple as we know how to, we tried, at once, to avoid oversimplicity—washing away the excitement of human intricacy. We hope we hit the midpoint between simplicity and complexity.

Obviously the instruments have not been subjected to statistical analyses, though we are in process of analyzing the data from several hundred subjects on the Communication-Conflict Instrument. It may be that we shall analyze certain of the other instruments as we begin to collect the data from classes. But these are teaching instruments, not research instruments.

Our interest in instruments came as a consequence of making some in recent years for class use; we found that they gave the student a direct way of internalizing concepts, by experimenting with the items of the tests. Moreover, we found that the discussions sparked by differences between students in their answers had a vitality to them that cannot be gained by questions about text material, or even exercises.

Finally, we have conceived of these instruments as perhaps the most direct way of integrating subject matter and skills training, though there are exercises at the end of each chapter, as in the previous edition. The instruments are added to move the book more to a skills orientation, without any sacrifice in content-understanding.

Our experience makes us expect that at least some, and often many, students will complain about an instrument, much as they do about dormitory food in every college or university. Forced choices create resistance. But we also find that once the test is taken, new insights evolve and teaching falls into place. It is the instrumentation of workshops that makes workshops so much more effective than the usual classroom.

Our debt to other writers, both in the profession and in related disciplines, is clearly seen in the footnotes and index. What is harder to see is the impact of one's colleagues and one's students. We deeply appreciate the many research seminars and the endless sessions in offices and hallways. Such statements of appreciation seem inadequate, but we do not know how to do better.

At the close of the preface of the first edition, we observed that "we have been teaching the perceptions of this book for some years and have noted that our students have discovered new ways of seeing themselves . . . ways that enriched their lives . . . we hope we may do the same for the reader." The reward has been that many readers have told us the book has made a difference in their lives. We hope the second edition is even more effective in this way.

Charles T. Brown
Paul W. Keller

MONOLOGUE
TO
DIALOGUE

1

Relatedness

The longing for interpersonal intimacy stays with every human being from infancy throughout life;
and there is no human being who is not threatened by its loss.

*Frieda Fromm-Reichmann**

The first human need, beyond survival and safety, is the need for relationship. Life styles may change, institutions may fade, but the urge to belong—to be related—remains the center of the human universe, reaching back into the very roots of life.

Charles Ogburn, in *The Adventure of Birds,* tells about a "birder" who took over 400 sparrows from San Jose, California to New Orleans and released them. Next winter he recaptured 26 of them in San Jose. Though frail and indifferent in flight power, these birds had found their way back home in an 1800-mile flight. The birder, curious devil, then transported the unsuspecting sparrows to Maryland, 2400 miles away. Next winter, in San Jose, he recaptured 6, almost one-fourth of the Maryland transplants. The story is impressive. But beyond the mystery of how birds know how to get home and know when they have arrived, is the deep, deep awareness of the hunger for attachment in life, for belonging.

We are not birds—although we are flighty enough sometimes to join them. We are humans. However, if the psychologist Abraham Maslow is correct, the bonding "instinct" is just as strong in us as in any animal. When that need is met, the human flourishes and develops. When it is not met, loneliness and alienation spawn problems without end.

*Frieda Fromm-Reichmann, "Loneliness," *Psychiatry,* 22 (February 1959), 3. By permission of William Alanson White Psychiatric Foundation, Inc.

We live now in a period accented more by "splitting" than by "joining," more by separation than by a sense of community. And the view from our moment in time often creates a despair born of the conviction that there is nothing we can do about it. But there is evidence that new understandings of communication can help make human interaction healthier than it often is.

Happily, where nature has planted a need it has provided the tool with which to meet it—in this case, communication.

Communication between people involves, in its essence, two things—relationship and information; the former determines the latter. Both of them end in human bonding and personal identity. This is too much to understand in two sentences. The rest of the chapter will, we hope, reveal their meaning.

Any relationship between people, casual or important, always involves (1) feelings of varying intensity—loving or hostile; (2) some sort of authority arrangement between the participants; and (3) at its heart, the self-image of the people involved, each created by interaction with the other.

Machines do not have feelings, authority problems, or conflicts of self-image, or even images of any sort involved in their communication. If you tune your radio to a given frequency, you almost always get a given station. You can predict, with almost total accuracy, that whatever information is available on that carrier wave will come through. You do not have to worry that the station will sometimes be found at some other frequency. As long as you stay with that channel, the information of that channel comes through, except under the rarest atmospheric conditions.

Not so with people. They are constantly shifting their carrier waves, their emotions, their attitudes[1] toward authority, and their images of self and others—the stuff of a relationship. Sometimes they broadcast to one person in such a way as to exclude another. At other times they are preoccupied and thus indifferent to others, sending information only to themselves. Many times they are anxious in their relationship with the other person and, for that reason, distort both the information received and the information sent. They may not even hear some information. Thus even two scientists differ in their reception of the information about, say, pollution, because their basic relationships with people, things, and ideas, built up over a lifetime of communication with other people, things, and ideas, determine their interpretations of a given bit of data. Consider the debates about nuclear power plants in this context.

Though we might wish it otherwise, the most critical factor in human communication is the relationship produced by interaction. As

[1]An attitude is a sustained feeling.

you read the following, play it back against your more unsettling experiences with people. Imagine that a student committee is gathering to develop a proposal for an overseas study program. The meeting is called because each of the participants has some specialized knowledge that the others do not have. If the knowledge is pooled successfully, there is a good chance that the proposal will be accepted. But at a crucial moment one student, who is the only one familiar with the intricacies of financing such a program, has nothing to say. The committee struggles and finally breaks up, having decided that there is no way to make the plan financially practical.

What fails in this communicative exchange? The information necessary for a workable plan is present. Mary Jones, the student who did not speak up, is an excellent communicator. She listens accurately, speaks clearly. But something breaks down. A little history sheds light on what has happened. Mary has been abroad several times on her own. She sees herself as something of an authority on foreign travel. She had tried, just the year before, to organize a student tour under her management. No one responded. She was hurt and took it as a personal affront. Now she sits and smiles in the committee meeting, knowing that she has the knowledge, but knowing that even if she provides all the information she will not be chosen to manage the tour. She says the necessary, superficial things but withholds the information the committee needs. Inwardly she says, "I am not going to be used by them." The committee is identified, for her, with those who snubbed her—it is now the enemy. Change that part of her relationship with the committee and her information could become available. The story is a parable of human interaction: Information is dependent on relationship.

Every person's life, at all its depths, is a collage of relationships. The picture of a life dulls or brightens in terms of the quality of those relationships. Socrates glowed, even in the face of death, because there were enlivening human beings with whom he shared the search for ultimate answers; Van Gogh watched his human ties disintegrate one by one— and yielded, finally, to the disintegration in himself.

Indeed, a person or personality is not some entity separate from his or her relationships with other people but, rather, a self-picture and a set of associated behaviors determined by relationships with the others in his or her life. Harry Stack Sullivan, the famous American psychiatrist, described a person as the sum of his or her interpersonal behavior—his or her relationships with other people.[2] The sociologist George Herbert Mead, reasoning in much the same way, saw society as held together by

[2]Calvin S. Hall and Gardner Lindzey, *Theories of Personality* (New York: John Wiley and Sons, Inc., 1957), p. 134.

the mirror image of the self that each person must have and that is provided for each person by the others with whom he or she talks.[3] Each person he or she meets helps shape his or her identity. Thus a person *is* and *behaves* as a consequence of his or her relationships with others. A star in a cluster of stars has its own motion, but the change in that motion is determined by the location and mass of every other star in the cluster. Like that star, the person, as Harvard psychologist Henry A. Murray has observed, is also a compromise between his or her impulses and the demands of other people.[4]

Thus relationships do not occur capriciously or mysteriously. They occur as the very process of communication. No communication, no relationship—and the reverse. To communicate is to make contact, to inspire and receive a response. So the act of communication nurtures relationship and, in turn, is fed by it.

COMMUNICATION

Let us look at our basic terms and how they connect. First, *communication,* for our purposes, should be conceived of as *symbolic interaction.* By interaction we mean what happens when one person says something and the other responds to it. Then the first may respond to what the second said, back and forth, on and on. Our best conversations are essentially a flow of interactive responses. But, at the very minimum, we have to have at least *one response to one initiation* before we can say we have established a connection, a hookup, a relatedness—a tie of communication.

Indeed, some theorists say there has to be an initiation, a response of the other, and a response by the initiator to the response of the responder—so that we have a response to a response—before a "bit" of relatedness is set up. To illustrate:

Initiation:	"Looks like Jackson will get the election."
Response:	"Yea, I thought all along it wouldn't make any difference whether I voted."
Response to Response:	"Sounds like you aren't very high on Jackson."

For our purposes, it is not important whether we define a unit of communication as involving an initiation of some line of thought and a

[3]George Herbert Mead, *Mind, Self, and Society* (Chicago: University of Chicago Press, 1934).

[4]Hall and Lindzey, *op. cit.,* p. 190.

response to it, or as an initiation-response-response, though certainly the latter, a response to a response, ensures that *speaking is tied into listening and one life tied* (in some small measure) *into the other.* But for us the critical point would be this: One response is necessary in an exchange before communicative interaction has taken place. An unrelated series of statements does not constitute communication. Consider the following:

"Looks like Jackson will get the election."
"I have to go to the dentist this afternoon."
"Five dollars does not buy very much these days."

The only way one can conceive of that exchange as an interaction is to note that each of the speakers waited until the other had stopped talking before starting to talk. There is no interaction because there is no listening—and thus there is no relatedness. Interaction requires a response because communication is the instrument of relatedness.

Symbols

But we have said that communication is *symbolic* interaction. What is a symbol? A *symbol* is something that suggests, represents, or stands for something else. The words you are reading are symbols standing for meaning in the experience of the writer. To the degree that these words represent your experience, the author is communicating with you. So communication is symbolic interaction. And interaction takes place as you read, for out of the words on this page, the way they are arranged, their choice, and the emotional tone they arouse in you, you conjure the author. In short, these words even *stand for* me, the author. You *conjure a relationship* with me. You read what I write because in my writing I attract or repel you. I arouse feelings in you about me and about what is said. If your feelings are not aroused, you lay the book aside. It puts you to sleep because the author—as far as you are concerned—"has nothing to say." He has not been able to establish an emotional connection. Symbols make connection. Communication is *symbolic* interaction.

Relationship as a Social Function of Communication

Communication has many functions, but as suggested earlier, its primary one is connecting—relatedness. No relatedness, no community; no social life. No relatedness, no work, no food, no babies, no future. In short, one cannot conceive of a system—a marriage, a school, a government, a factory, a society—without relatedness and its instrument, communication. Relatedness is thus the basic social function of communication.

WHAT IS A RELATIONSHIP?

As we need to have communication clearly described in our minds, so we need also to be precise in talking about "relatedness." Let us put it in abstract terms first. A relationship is a kinship of some sort. Brothers and sisters have common parents. Friends are people who are mutually attracted. Lovers are connected by amorous feelings. Even passers-by on the street have a kinship by way of space and time.[5]

Relationship Begins with Feelings

If, however, humans are related by more than the accidents of their movements through time and space, they experience feelings for each other. Thus feelings are the stuff of human relationships. As we talk face to face, we tend to experience the feelings of liking each other or of disliking each other or of becoming indifferent to each other, as mentioned earlier. The nature of these feelings describes the character of the relationship. Any given relationship is to be described by the feelings that connect the people in the relationship. So basic are the feelings aroused in our talk with each other that *these feelings become the very stuff by which we sketch the perceived faces of the people we are connected to.* This is why humanistic psychology emphasizes the here-and-now feelings.

Indeed, all human relationships, all human associations, intellectual or physical, are built on feelings.[6] Einstein parted with those who would build a theory of the nature of the universe on the mathematics of probability. Such thinking aroused repulsive feelings in him. He said, "God does not play dice with the Universe."[7] Thinking is association among perceived facts. But the perceived facts and the logic are formed in the feelings of experience. "It is also clear that the desire to arrive finally at logically connected concepts is the emotional basis of this rather vague play . . . ," said Einstein.[8] He went on to say that new awarenesses of the nature of the universe came to him in either visual images or muscular feelings.

[5]Gerald Miller and Mark Steinberg, *Between People* (Chicago: Science Research Associates, Inc., 1975), Chap. 2.

[6]Brewster Ghiselin, *The Creative Process* (New York: Mentor Books, 1955).

[7]Ronald W. Clark, *Einstein, the Life and Times* (New York: Avon Books, 1971), Chaps. 3, 10.

[8]Ghiselin, *op. cit.*, p. 43.

Let us stop here a moment and examine what we are doing as we build this case for communication on the foundation of the feelings of human relationships. Historically, because our view of man has come from Athens, we have conceived of human life as split into two worlds— the rational and the irrational, the cognitive and the affective, the logical and the emotional. Greek education was designed to sharpen the logical and to tame the passionate. And we have learned that split view all too well. Even at this instant, in the arguments that pervade life in Western culture hundreds of people are saying, "My feelings aside, I think that..." With due respect for Aristotle, the main voice of the past to which we are responding, the fact remains that this tendency to categorize, putting things in one bin or another, does not explain how all the things in all the bins work together in one world. We hold the view that the logical processes of argument are not detached from our feelings, following the dictates of cold fact. Arguments between people, even arguments about what is logical or is a fact, are verbal chess games directed by perceptions that are shaped by the feelings involved. We opt for the view that we have a feeling-thinking system founded on our sensory world.

As Descartes, taking the Greek view, arrived at the conclusion "I think, therefore I am," we would say, "I feel, therefore I am." Those who are inclined to think that their thought is unguided by feeling obviously have little faith in the whole organism as a processing system.

Let us ask the critical questions. How do you know which of two items of contradictory data is better? How do you know how to spend your life, what to do as a career, where to live, whom to trust, what to trust, what to believe, what to value, how to live?

God knows, the challenge of every human is to live a rational life, but one will not do it by sorting out his or her verbal processes but by sensing his or her inclinations and conflicting inclinations, by calling to the verbal level the data that will allow the whole organism to do its will. Nobody knows the process that leads to wise decisions, behavior, and talk. But the whole thrust of social-psychological research and therapy of the past thirty years indicates that it is futile to ignore or try to beat one's feeling world. Thought does not have to give in to every feeling, but in the end, one way or another, verbalization will be the servant of our deepest feelings. People cannot successfully disengage their verbal world from the imprint of the millions of years of life from which they have emerged as conscious creatures to spend a few moments of time. Nor is it intelligent to do so.

This book attempts to build a view of communication on the foun-

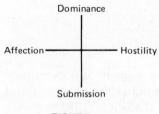

FIGURE 1-1

dations of life. As feelings are the foundation and the director of our verbal thought, they are basic to the understanding of human communication.

A DEFINITION OF FEELINGS

Using the approach of Albert Ellis, we understand feelings to be the description of the arousal generated by whatever or whomever we are involved with.[9] Feelings are simply what we say to ourselves about our experiences. As suggested earlier, this description becomes the very tool with which we sketch the players in our life's drama. "He is a good guy" means "I like him."

HOW OUR FEELINGS WORK IN INTERACTION

Patton and Giffin[10] say that "as people disclose bits of information to each other—information about themselves—they tend to reach agreements on what matters and what does not... They tend to develop a working consensus..." They quote Erving Goffman's statement in *Behavior in Public Places,* which argues that this interacting forms an agreed-on, though often unspoken, definition of the participants' relationship, their contract. They label such a defining process *involvement.* They then go on to describe the Timothy Leary model of interpersonal involvement,[11] which is perhaps best seen in Figure 1-1.

In this model one can plot any behavior as a mixture of the relational feelings and the amount of control exercised. In our judgment, the Leary model is clear but not quite accurate. It says that the two basic dynamics of behavior are relational feelings and the degree of authority exercised. But authority, or power-over, important as it is in human interaction, is the consequence of a more basic process, described as

[9]Albert Ellis, *Reason and Emotion in Psychotherapy* (New York: L. Stuart, 1962).

[10]Bobby Patton and Kim Giffin, *Interpersonal Communication, Basic Text and Reading* (New York: Harper & Row, 1974), p. 346.

[11]Timothy Leary, *Interpersonal Diagnosis of Personality* (New York: Ronald Press, 1957).

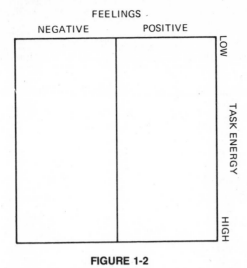

FIGURE 1-2

follows. The expenditure of energy in doing something is basic to doing that thing well. By doing well we make an impact on others and as a consequence are looked to for leadership. So the forerunner of domi- nance (basic in the Leary model) is the energy that produces competent action. When dominance or power over other people is the focus in an interaction, it reflects somebody's inability to settle for the power he or she can assert by way of competence.

"OK," said one bright student, "do I understand you to say it is incompetent for the boss to give an order?" If the house is on fire or the boat is going down there is no time for discussion. Or if things have been talked out and people do not agree, a person in charge may have to make a decision that some will not like. Sometimes the power of compe- tence is the assertion of authority. But the fine line between competence and power does not negate the fact that they are different and that competent action is the forerunner of authority.

In the past twenty-five years Blake and Mouton, as well as others, have moved to the model that replaces dominance with task energy.[12] This thinking is seen in the model shown in Figure 1-2.

When our feelings for each other are positive, our actions in a relationship can be located in the upper half of the model in Figure 1-2. All our behaviors (or the things we say about the relationship) are de- signed to preserve the relationship. Each person who is a party to such a relationship will exercise a positive impact on the other, as is dictated in order to get the tasks done in the prized relationship. The people belong to each other. They have a community bond. They have defined their

[12]Robert R. Blake and Jane S. Mouton, "The Fifth Achievement," *The Journal of Applied Behavioral Science,* 6 (1970), 413–426.

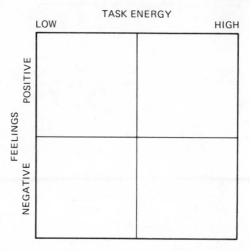

FIGURE 1-3   Task Energy Devoted to the Maintenance of a Relationship

relationship, unconsciously or in discussion, as an end in itself. Individual differences must be ironed out *in* the relationship.

Conversely, if their feelings for each other are essentially negative, encompassing all behaviors below the middle horizontal line of the model, they will exercise their own drives to get the others to bend to their will. If they fail, they will withdraw from the relationship. They have defined the relationship as secondary to their *individual* needs.

Thus when our interaction creates deeply stressful feelings the critical question emerges, "Shall each of us make our individual needs the first priority, or shall the relationship become the first priority?" When the latter is the focus, the task to which we devote our energy is the relationship itself, as suggested in Figure 1-3.

In short, returning to the thinking of Goffman, when the defining of our relationship is *the conscious task,* we see in the model that positive feelings are the dynamic force and that any differences that arise about what is to be done will be adjusted so as to preserve the relationship.

HOW FEELINGS BOND US

If we use Everett Shostrom's breakdown of feelings in his *Caring Relationship Inventory,* we can recognize seven kinds of feelings that work to bond us to each other:[13]

[13]Everett Shostrom, *Caring Relationship Inventory* (San Diego, Calif.: Educational and Industrial Testing Service, 1966).

1. Commonality of perception
2. Affection
3. Empathy
4. Kinlife
5. Self-feelings
6. D-feelings
7. B-feelings

Let us define each of these items and discuss them briefly.

Commonality of Perception

We are attracted to people with whom we share common perceptions. Shostrom calls this the *character* of friendship. It seems to us that all of the seven kinds of bonding can go into friendship. By whatever name, however, commonality of perception means we are interested in the same things and have the same vision of those things. One may be interested in politics, ideas, football, research, music, and so on and on. We tend to talk best to people who are interested in the same things and who tend to perceive them as we do.

Studies in the development of a relationship indicate that there are stages in the exchange of information of a personal character.[14] As strangers meet, there is a certain wariness, a primitive fear of the unknown. At first we note the other person's state of emotional being. Most of this is determined by the ease of the other person and his or her recognition of the rules of politeness. Then, in stage two, we will tend to get biographical data from each other, where we have come from, what we do, where we are going. If those perceptions are mutually agreeable, we pass on to stage three, in which, the literature says, we are concerned about the other person's attitudes about himself or herself, about other people, and about what is socially right. As we will see in later chapters, human beings who hang together do so essentially because they share common values. At the bottom of it all, they share common feelings about what is right and wrong. But after a person decides that the other person's codes fit his or her own, then, in stage four, he or she wants to talk about "content and structural dimensions"—how the other person thinks about the things he or she thinks about. We feel good about sharing our perceptions with people who are interested in the things we are interested in and whose views of these things are agreeable to us.

[14]Charles R. Berger and Richard Calabrese, "Some Explorations in Initial Interaction and Beyond: Toward a Developmental Theory of Interpersonal Communication," *Human Communication Research*, 1 (1975), 99–112.

Affection

Affection refers to the most direct way people are bonded in interaction. It refers specifically to the degree of attractiveness of each for the other. It is a common temptation to think that relatedness is based entirely on degrees of personal attraction. Such an idea clearly overstates the matter, but all ways of bonding do bear upon affection.[15] The more ways we are pleasantly bonded, the more we feel affection for the other person.

One can scarcely think of affection without the concept of intimacy, though each term conjures a different set of images. In using the term *intimacy* we refer to the distance between people, and distance can be measured both physically and psychologically. Edward T. Hall classes 6 to 18 inches as intimate, 18 inches to 4 feet as personal, 4 feet to 12 feet as social, 12 feet to 25 feet as public.[16] Equally significant is the fact of psychological distance, and a number of personality instruments measure this. Two people can be side by side in an automobile, at a party, or in bed and yet be many miles apart as spiritual creatures. Conversely, people can be miles apart and spiritually together. Consider the distance, at this moment, between you and those you love dearly.

Strange as it may seem, some people can feel intimate only at a distance. We have known people who are most comfortable with intimate verbal exchanges on the telephone or in a letter.

Intimacy of distance and spirit causes people to be deeply affectionate—or the reverse. It is true that we often hurt the ones we love the most. Nonetheless, the degree of affection is in essence the degree to which one person is attracted to be close and open to another, spiritually and/or physically.

Empathy

By definition, we use the term *empathy* to refer to the capacity to understand with appreciation the feelings functioning in a person as he or she is experiencing them.[17] Through empathy, then, we know what it is to be the other person. For a second we stand in the other's shoes. Above all other means of bonding, perhaps, empathy provides tolerance for differences in a relationship. If our feelings make us perceive and act as we do, the capacity to accept another person so different from our-

[15]Ellen Berscheid and Elaine Walster, *Interpersonal Attraction* (Reading, Mass.: Addison-Wesley Publishing Company, 1969).

[16]Edward T. Hall, *The Hidden Dimension* (Garden City, N.Y.: Doubleday, 1966), pp. 117–125.

[17]Gerald Miller and Mark Steinberg, *op. cit.,* pp. 167–174.

selves depends on understanding the feelings that make him or her perceive differently. Let it be clear that empathy is more than just understanding another person's feelings. We have to appreciate them, or feel them as he or she feels them.

Kinlife [18]

Kinlife feelings are those that create and nurture relationships. Kinlife feelings evolve when the task of interaction is the relationship itself. When we feast, sing, laugh, or pray together we ritualize and celebrate our belongingness, our community. Even when we talk out our conflicting feelings with others, in search of reconciliation we pay homage to the kinlife. Kinlife came more naturally and more unconsciously, perhaps, when people were born and died in the same house, having known the same neighborhood of people throughout their lives. But with the coming of trains, planes, and cars we are all more or less on the move, and in our mobility we have forgotten that man does not live by transportation alone. Something there is in life that grows between people and takes time to grow—and that we desparately need in order to achieve the security basic to the development of self-esteem (discussed in the next chapter). W. C. Schutz uses the word *inclusion*. Kinlife feelings, in essence, are the celebration of our belonging, our inclusion. It is kinlife that washes away estrangement, alienation, and loneliness.

In *Bridges, Not Walls* John Stewart talks about relationship as a spiritual child, which is to say that any relationship that is of consequence to the lives of the people involved actually has a life of its own.[19] One of the authors recently spent a weekend with his grown son at the family cabin. Though now they seldom see each other, each has a deep regard for the other and a deep appreciation of the many ways that they have known each other over a span of thirty years. When they meet, what happens is more than each bringing the other up to date with what has been and is happening in his life, exchanging points of view on a variety of things of common interest. It is also a caring for and an adding to a mosaic of memories that tie their lives together, making each present to the other even at a distance.

As they parted each spoke of the beauty of the fall woods. "This place has been good for all of us," said the son. They walked away from

---

[18]Shostrom uses the term *Eros* at this point and in his test of caring he conceives of Eros as erotic experience. Freud, Rollo May, and others have conceived of Eros more broadly. We have discovered, however, in discussions with students that the story of Eros is for many a story of sexual, even selfish, and punitive love. Thus we devised a new term.

[19]John Stewart, *Bridges Not Walls*, 2nd ed. (Reading, Mass.: Addison-Wesley Publishing Company, 1973).

each other, preparing to go their separate ways. Then together they stopped and turned toward each other and smiled. In that exchange each knew that the other made a toast to a relationship as significant to their lives as the lives themselves. That is kinlife.

In *Who's Afraid of Virginia Woolf,* a play about a man and woman wedded to the destruction of each other, Albee creates the third party in a two-person world by having the couple make intermittent references to their son, who in fact exists only in their fantasy. Thus even a sick relationship has its own being, living as a vital part of each person, helping them carry out their attack on each other.

Each person is an entity, but an entity that is composed in part of ties to all his or her significant relationships with other people. The other part of the being of relationship resides in other people. When any of these people meet, the being of the relationship between them is re-united and is nurtured by some ceremony, some ritual, some form of celebration—some gesture with deep meaning for those involved. Kin-life is the being of our union with all the people who count in our lives. It is kinlife that protects us from sinking into loneliness.

Self-Feelings

One of the more commonly held perspectives about feelings is that every person is responsible for his or her own feelings. Equally well recognized today is the fact that we project our feelings. If we think this through, we come to the difficult truth that our feelings are statements about our perceptions of ourselves, stimulated to be what they are by our interaction with ourselves and others.

Thus our feelings about ourselves and our relationships with others are in fact two ways of talking about the same thing. As feelings about the self wax or wane, so our relationships prosper or fail.

The virtue of separating out the self feelings for analysis is this. If we are upset by our present interaction, we can keep from wallowing in despair when we think and talk *about* the conditions and situations that "cause" the distress. We can "by the heave of the will" (that William James conceived to be the heart of freedom) change what we can and accept with grace what we cannot change. In almost any plight we can restore good feelings for the self if we *will*. Then other healthy relationships with people are nurtured. This heave is possible only because the misery of self-hate is in the end a despair that we cannot stand.

D-Feelings

Maslow, Shostrom, and others have made the term *deficiency feelings* or "deficiency love" common parlance. What is being referred to is the need of one person that is satisfied or cared for by another person. "Deficiency" is a way of saying that a person is not complete as an entity separate from other people. It is the deficiency of any one person that necessitates kinlife. One cannot make love without a lover. One cannot play tennis without a partner. One cannot be a father or mother without having children. *Doctor* implies a relationship with a sick person. Without *student* there is no teacher. A seller cannot do business by selling to himself or herself. Transactional and transpersonal psychology are in fact explorations of what happens between people because of their deficiencies as individuals.

Take a different view. There is interdependence among all things and people if the world is a system. Lewis Thomas, a biologist, has written a fascinating book called *The Lives of a Cell* in which his central view is this.[20] In the genetic code are the links with all past life, back to the beginning. And since life is of the universe, in each life, in each organ of life, in each cell of each life is the print of the whole system—the lives of a cell. The cell is the universe in miniature yet, at the same time, no cell, organ, person, animal, vegetable, planet, or star can exist alone. If all things are part of the whole thing, then each part alone is deficient.

In a very real sense each of us alone cannot survive. In all our interactions, each of us is drawing on the energies of the others we interact with. So communication is a transaction of different kinds of energy. In the highly independent value system of the democratic view of life, we like to conceive of ourselves as "self-sufficient." And the view is extremely contagious. We are everlastingly amazed by the way our foreign students from authoritarian nations all over the world are, within less than a year, captivated by independence from authority. They assert that it gives them a sense of strength and maturity.

It is becoming increasingly clear to the authors that, though independence is an illusion, dependence, except in the beginning of life, is the measure of a sick relationship. The women's movement, uneven in course, is a cry against the low self-esteem imposed by dependence. We are all deficient, but the exchanges of energies of a relationship must be on an interdependent base if the relationship is to foster growth.

To be dependent in all or most ways is to feel small. To be dominant in all ways related to another person is to feel bigger than one is in fact. And if one needs to be so dominant as to maintain the relationship exclusively on his or her own terms, he or she is as dependent as the nondominant friend. The boss and the bossed exploit each other.

Some people persisted in holding the view that (1) we need to be unconditionally supportive in order (2) to move toward being self-supportive. But this view, almost correct in our judgment, is still

---

[20]Lewis Thomas, *The Lives of a Cell* (New York: Bantam Books, Inc., 1974).

spawned by the illusion that ultimate freedom is independence. Actually, the ultimate freedom attainable is equality of interdependence. The great challenge of humanity is not to stand independent but to establish relationships on the basis of equality of dignity.

It is true that nobody can learn to be self-supportive without being unconditionally supported. But people need to belong to others in order to feel self-supported. We are all, by ourselves, deficient. Thus the issue at stake is the quality of the interdependence. Do we as we grow up feel more and more equal in our interdependence? In the power chapter we explore the issue in some depth. Here we leave it with the observation that perhaps we fail to celebrate our union with each other essentially because, on our road to freedom, we have come to fear and despise the deficiencies that make us interdependent.

B-Feelings

Almost sounding like a contradiction of what we have just said, "B-feelings" or "B-love" refers to feelings of integrity, uniqueness, and individuality. A person can feel identity not by describing what he or she belongs to but by separating out what he or she is. One has a self-awareness, and that awareness, while sensed in relationship, feels itself only in terms of its impact, its own doing. Thus a person, by the demand of identity, must have will, freedom, assertiveness. If we really feel close to a person, then we have feelings of caring for that kernel or center of his or her self that calls for feeling his or her own powers. That is, we have a feeling for the other person's being—B-feelings.

Summary

There are, then, seven ways in which we are bonded. With such varied ways to bond, one is amazed that the glue of relationship dissolves or dries out—until we sense, again, that its stuff is feeling and that feelings vary from pleasant to unpleasant, from attractive to repulsive. The quality of relationship is a reflection of our pervading feelings. The quality of any group or organization is a reflection of the pervading feelings of its members.

HOW FEELINGS CHANGE THE QUALITY OF RELATEDNESS

Roger Brown says that the feeling that we belong to a group, and our differing individual status in the group—which work against each other—"appear to govern much of social life. They lie behind the great regularities of everyday behavior."[21] But status difference and mutual

[21]Roger Brown, *Words and Things* (New York: Free Press, 1958).

attraction live together precariously. When there is any intense or prolonged struggle in the social hierarchy, attraction can soon fade and
change to repulsion. Any kind of diminution, any kind of one-
upmanship in a phrase or a look, begins to alter the quality of the bond
between people.

What Is Relationship with Good Quality?

Bennis and his colleagues say that a healthy relationship is one in
which all parties recognize the following:[22]

1. *The interdependence of all parties.* Influence is balanced among the parties.
   This means that all parties to the relationship talk to each other, but also
   that they listen to each other. Otherwise status difference erodes the bonds
   between people of different status.
2. *The need for each individual to choose, without pressure from another, whom to
   depend on and to what degree.* Conversely, this implies that each person, without pressure from another, decides who shall depend on him or her and to
   what degree.
3. That *differences of feelings and opinions should be settled by consensus.*
4. That *differences that escalate to real conflict should be settled or managed with a
   sensitivity that allows all parties to feel dignified.*

It is obvious that these stipulations are ideals seldom achieved, particularly item number 3. Majority vote seems the best we can do. But
difference in viewpoint and conflict are just a part of human life, for
reasons we shall see in the chapter on conflict. Yet we have to know the
ideal relationship in order to keep from wasting ourselves in unproductive conflict.

The Process

The way quality alters in communication can be seen vividly if we
relate the essentials:

1. Interaction stimulates emotional involvement.
2. Positive emotional involvement stimulates the exchange of more and more
   personal information.
3. The more open two people become, the more they enhance the ability of
   each to empathize with the other.
4. The more empathic response they achieve, the more fully they accept each
   other unconditionally.
5. The more fully they accept each other, the more they trust each other (we
   will say more about this in a moment).

[22]W. G. Bennis *et al., Interpersonal Dynamics,* rev. ed. (Homewood, Ill.: Dorsey, 1968), p.
663.

6. The more fully they trust each other, the deeper the bonds of relationship—the greater the kinlife.
7. The deeper the bonds of relationship, the more positive the emotional involvement.

This cycle can be seen vividly in Figure 1-4.

As you will recall, the quality of relationship has been described in terms of reciprocity within the relationship, the degree of *freedom from coercion* provided for all parties. If you return to the description of Figure 1-2, you will note that power over others is a function of negative feelings. Thus it is that the quality of relationship must be seen as a function of the rise and fall of good feeling. So a deteriorating relationship may be seen as a cycle of negative feelings, as illustrated in Figure 1-5. Note the fact that negative feeling reverses the flow of process and that indeed the order of events changes.

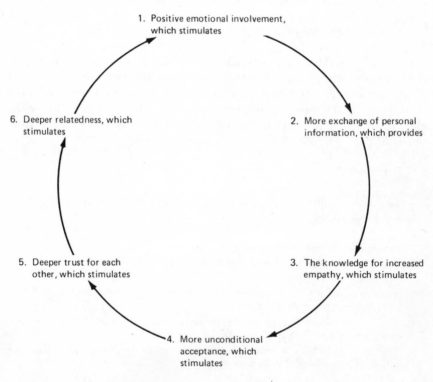

1. Positive emotional involvement, which stimulates

6. Deeper relatedness, which stimulates

2. More exchange of personal information, which provides

5. Deeper trust for each other, which stimulates

3. The knowledge for increased empathy, which stimulates

4. More unconditional acceptance, which stimulates

FIGURE 1-4 The Cycle of Positive Feelings

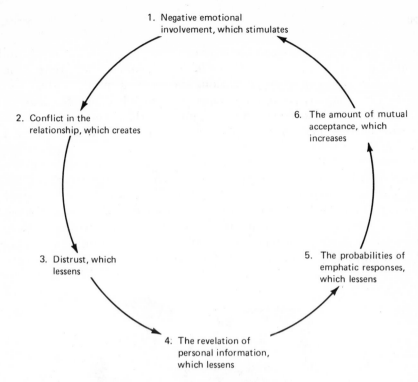

FIGURE 1-5 The Cycle of Negative Feelings

Summary

At point 3 in the cycle of negative feelings, one of two things eventually happens. If *distrust* leads to less and less emotional involvement or interaction, the two people finally fail to see each other any more, in which case the relationship dies, for there is no feeling left. The people drift apart. Or, the havoc of the conflict of profoundly negative feelings will ultimately lead to the violent death of the relationship. The circle is broken. The function of bad feelings is a mutual effort to control, leading to withdrawal or violent struggle. The function of mutual good feelings is understanding, acceptance, and the development of kinlife, or commitment to the union.

THE KINDRED SPIRIT

At the beginning of the chapter we quoted Frieda Fromm-Reichmann: "The longing for interpersonal intimacy stays with every human being from infancy throughout life, and there is no human being who is not threatened by its loss." Those who know us most deeply and appreciate us the most become our lifelong friends. They are the ones whose feelings in all seven dimensions and whose aspirations (dealt with in the next chapter) give them perspectives much like our own. You will find only a few kindred spirits in a lifetime, perhaps your mate and one or two friends, perhaps a child or two, perhaps a brother or a sister, perhaps a parent.

The kindred spirit has two dimensions. First, it knows life as you know life. Your kindred spirit has the same or a similar heartbeat. Second, as a consequence the relationship of kindred spirits persists through time. He/she shares your joys and sorrows, the ups and downs of life, and you two repeat many handshakes, laughs, exchanges of information, sharings of feelings and observations, feastings, and goodbyes. Fondness, belonging, like the making of all good things, is a func-

Fraternity. From Carl Zigrosser, *Prints and Drawings of Kathe Kollwitz* (New York: Dover Publications, Inc., 1951, 1969). Reprinted through the permission of the publisher.

tion of time. Novelty is exciting, but repetitions are required if one is to know the meaning of "coming home."

We, in America, are not doing very well on this score at present. Skipping around, we have much coming and going, much kissing and hugging of virtual strangers, "Yes, darling." The authors have been surprised to find that in some interpersonal communication classes, composed of people in their thirties, dyadic exchanges have gone to depths of personal involvement that these people said they had not known before. Their talk had always before been locked into superficial and safe exchange. The course gave them an excuse for experimenting, for breaking the habit of evading the search for the kindred spirit.

Indeed, the sensitivity and encounter groups that have been so popular in recent years are actually explorations in coming to know people, in becoming related. Now the move is toward couples teaching couples how to get acquainted. All this makes sense to the extent that the people involved search for ways to put the practice to work every day so that they may find and nurture their relationships with the significant others of their lives.

TRUST

If kinlife is the present great need of humanity, its condition is trust. What do we mean by *trust?*

Credibility

It is common to think of trust in terms of credibility. Credibility means you can believe what another person says. Aristotle said that we are persuaded by logical argument, emotional appeals, and the *ethos* of the person, his or her credibility. He noted that of these three factors ethos is the most powerful. A good doctor in our eyes is one who is well informed and cares enough for us to try to help us. We believe in such a person. We entrust our lives to him or her.

Predictability

But trust also has the dimension of predictability. Every time our faith in a person is shaken we are shocked in the interaction; the other person has done what we did not expect. Youth tends to shun this definition. Predictability sounds boring. The culture's emphasis upon individuality and freedom makes predictability seem dull. But this rejection is not real. We all want to put our money in a bank where we can get it when we want it. We all prize the automobile that starts at the first turn of the key, no matter what the temperature outside. We throw away the pen that sometimes writes and sometimes does not. How can we have friends we cannot depend on?

Again the factor of time comes to bear on relatedness. If you depend on another, you have learned that you can predict how he or she is going to respond to you.

Confidentiality

Unconditional confidentiality is at the heart of trust. If you trust a friend you give your friend information about yourself—thereby deepening the relationship. You trust your friend will not exploit you or use the information in ways injurious to you.

A girl dating two men may all too easily, in order to enhance one relationship, tell one of the men how much more interesting he is than the other. She cannot reveal the same information in the other relationship unless she wants it to decay. That is a confidence she should probably keep to herself, at least until one relationship comes to an end. Back in the Forties, Secretary of Agriculture Henry Wallace gave a speech in Europe criticizing America. President Truman fired him. George Bach, in *The Intimate Enemy,* talks about fighting fair with your mate. The essence of fair fighting, he says, is to keep the fight between the two of you. You break confidentiality when you try to marshal the support of children or to hurt the relationship of your mate with a child.

Martin Buber in *I and Thou,* a book that has found its way into almost all the languages of the world, says that when we take our stand in relationship with another there can be no deception. Though it is extremely difficult to be confidential, this is the ultimate measure of our trustworthiness.

Confidentiality Versus Openness

Confidentiality is a "must" if people are going to be open and really come to a full understanding of each other—and this applies to all relationships, from the dyad to international involvement. Yet confidentiality by its very nature implies secrecy, closed walls around the relationship.

Complete	Confidentiality	Complete
Openness		Closedness

FIGURE 1-6

In a day of open personal files and insistence on agreements arrived at in open meetings we have made a legal move, in the form of "sunshine" laws, away from secrecy. We are caught in contradictions, or at least apparent contradictions. We understand the movement toward openness. The FBI and CIA, because of the secrecy allowed them so that they might protect the government, have become involved in activities dangerous to the government, some of which may yet not be known. Thus complete secrecy can be a problem.

But so can complete openness. In our social design the press is the agent that protects the people from governmental corruption. But the fact is that responsible writers and broadcasters do not *always* tell *all* they know, because those who leak information, on which the press in part depends, are disloyal people, at least to the relationship in which they gain the information they give to the press. And disloyal people often have destructive feelings. The member of the press or of a governmental agency who would leak national data that endanger our relationship with, say, Russia is a disloyal citizen. Not all things can be known by all people in this world; wisdom dictates a position between total openness and total secrecy (see Figure 1-6). The central point is that a certain amount of information in a relationship is private to that relationship, depending on the way the parties have consciously or unconsciously defined the fence that sets the relationship apart from others.

In Figure 1-7 we have three people who know each other because they directly share what for the three we call "public information." When all three are together they determine, usually unconsciously or at least in only an informal way, what they can share of their personal worlds and

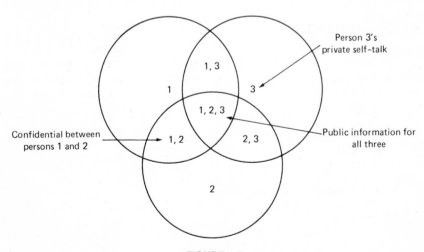

FIGURE 1-7

their mutual worlds. The larger the area of public information, the more deeply involved the three are as a group. But if the three are a strongly knit group, 1 does not, in talking with 2, say things to 2 about 3 that he or she cannot say to 3. Confidentiality does not refer to the need for secrecy so much as it does to caring and loyalty. The more open we are, to a certain point, the more we can understand each other. But we do not give of ourselves to be used by others. Careless use of others lessens our faith in self and in humanity, closing us off from both. That is loneliness indeed.

RELATEDNESS SHAPES IDENTITY

These words signal chapter 2: "To understand himself man needs to be understood by another." And "To be understood by another he needs to understand the other." Each of us talks and looks out from a face that cannot see itself. Thus each of us, in that empathic union, is mirrored by the other person. If relatedness is the first function of communication, then the first function of relatedness is the development of self-identity.

The development of self-identity will be explored in the next three chapters.

INSTRUMENT 1-1

WHAT'S BETWEEN US?

Arrange a conversation with a person you are at least relatively well acquainted with on the topic "What's Between Us?" The device can work even if you are casually acquainted, provided that you are comfortable with each other.

1. *Common Perceptions*   *List Here*
   What topics do you usually talk   _____
      about?   _____
   How similar are your views?   _____
   What common values make you   _____
      appreciate each other?   _____
2. *Affection*
   List the reasons you are mutually   _____
      attracted to each other. (This   _____
      will spill over into the others.) _____

One of the discrete things you
can share is your feeling about
the degree of affection between
you and how that affects your
life. (We all need warmth for
the spirit, as we need clothing
for the body.)

3. *Empathy*

   How much do you understand
   each other's feelings right now?

   Do you approve or disapprove of
   each other's feelings?

4. *Kinlife*

   You are actually creating or de-
   stroying kinlife in this conversation. Is this conversation a celebration of your relationship?

5. *Self-feeling*

   What feelings about yourself are
   you experiencing?

   Are they stimulated by your relationship with each other?

6. *Deficiency Feelings*

   In what ways do you satisfy each
   other?

   In what ways are you dependent
   on each other?

7. *Being Feelings*

   In what ways do you each sense
   the separateness of the other
   person?

8. What did you learn?

INSTRUMENT 1-2

A TRUST-IN-RELATIONSHIP SCALE

I

List *seven polar adjectives* that you think describe the various ways one
might talk about *the character of human nature.*

The following are provided as an illustration:

1. Beautiful–ugly
2. Warm–cold
3. Tall–short
4. Healthy–sick

5. Dependable–undependable
6. Open–closed
7. Honest–dishonest

II

Now place each pair of polar adjectives on a seven-point scale as follows:

Beautiful						Ugly
7	6	5	4	3	2	1

(Place the *adjective* that is *attractive to you* at the *high* end of the scale.)

III

Now circle the number on each scale that best represents your feeling about human nature as reflected by the adjectives of that scale.
For example:

Beautiful						Ugly
7	(6)	5	4	3	2	1

IV

Now go back over the scale and put a square around the number that represents your response to the way you wish human nature really was. For example:

Beautiful						Ugly
[7]	6	5	4	3	2	1

V

Now add all the circled numbers and put the score here:_____.

VI

Now add all the numbers with squares around them and place that number here:_____.

VII

Finally, subtract the total of the numbers in circles (V) from the total of the numbers in squares (VI). Place that number here:_____. This score might be called your trust-in-relationship score or your trust in community score. (The lower it is, the more you trust.)

    A. Compare your score with that of a classmate; compare it with the mean of the class.

    B. Discuss the polar adjectives chosen by different people.

EXERCISES

1. Arrive at estimates for each of the following: (a) "healthy" marriages you know about in your own experience; (b) marriages that have been dissolved, or are in the process of dissolution, in your experience; (c) cases in which students are well related to their parents; (d) cases in which students are in tension with their parents. Talk about (or make a journal entry about) the conclusions you draw regarding relationships today.

2. In groups of four or six discuss the meaning of the words *intimacy* and *loneliness.*

3. Draw two circles representing the way you and your parents are related now. Draw another pair of circles representing that relationship four years ago. Draw still another pair of circles representing the relationship as you believe it may be in another four years. Orally interpret the circles. The circles might look like this:

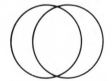 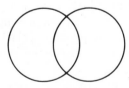 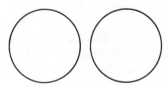

2

The Self-Concept
and Self-Esteem

To understand himself man needs to be understood by another.
To be understood by another he needs to understand the other.

*Thomas Hora**

When you are dead set on getting a four-point average for the semester, preparing for a camping trip, saving money for a new automobile, getting acquainted with a new lover, becoming competent in a new job, losing weight, or whatever, you are happiest and most integrated. When you are in limbo—you do not know whether to complete the semester, drop out of your love affair, quit your job, change your curriculum—you suffer most. Indeed, the greatest burden we carry is ourselves—when our goals are unclear. Yet the central problem is not that the goals are unclear. That is but a symptom. The problem is lack of clarity about the self.[1] The self-concept is a description of the self. When we do not know who we are, we cannot establish goals.

During the periods when you are at your best, eager to get things done, even if it is just to have a good time, the subject matter of this chapter may seem unimportant. Indeed, the questions about *who you are* and *whither you tend* are not even interesting. Your self-concept is virtually lost in what you are doing. But in times of indecision the topic of self-concept is totally absorbing, if a shade depressing, for you find that you cannot answer the questions *Who am I?* and *Who am I becoming?*

*Thomas Hora, "Tao, Zen and Existential Psychotherapy," *Psychologia,* 2 (1959), 236–242. By permission.
[1]William Glasser, *Schools Without Failure* (New York: Harper & Row, 1969).

THE SELF IN MOTION

All of which is to say that the self-concept, one's identity as a person, is not a snapshot of oneself that one carries in his or her head. Rather, it is something like a (poor) television picture, something moving but also involving its ghost images. You are what you have been, what you are, and what you hope to be. Thus the self-concept is at best a motion picture, for it is a picture of a person in process.

We are healthiest when we are caught in a beautiful balance between ourselves as we are and the ghost images of our future. It is our image of our future that motivates us to seek goals. We feel like a going concern; our energy flows freely; we discipline ourselves and do not let ourselves slip into overeating, overdrinking, oversleeping, over-sexual involvement, over-anything. The "temptations" or extravagances that make us feel lousy about ourselves are simply not a problem.

ENTER SELF-ESTEEM

We observed in the preceding chapter that the basic factor in our existence and in our relating to ourselves and other people is the way we feel about ourselves—our self-esteem. We also noted that the way we feel is not to be separated from the way we perceive. We see ourselves as we feel about ourselves. We see others in accordance with the way we feel about them. What is more, *we are very likely to feel about them as we feel about ourselves.* Our perceptions are the *projections* of our feelings.[2] Thus when you feel good about yourself, you are essentially responding positively to the motivations you feel, your sense of what you are becoming.

Listen to this crucial conversation between a mother and her daughter:

> "I am going to say something, Jan, that is very dangerous, but somehow I cannot restrain myself. I see you and John moving toward marriage."
> "Well, maybe, what do you mean?"
> "For one thing the kind of gifts you gave each other for Christmas."
> "Hm."
> "Don't hear this wrong. I don't disapprove of the gifts. In a sense they are irrelevant."
> "What are you getting at, Mother?"
> "Look, Dear, I love you and I don't want to see you hurt."
> "You don't like John."
> "No, no, in fact I like the charming devil. Look, before I ever hear you

[2]Don E. Hamachek, *Encounters with the Self* (New York: Holt, Rinehart, & Winston, Inc., 1971), Chap. 1.

say, for sure, you are going to marry John, I have to say this, and then I'll never say anything more. I just do not believe John is capable of commitment."

"You mean he is what?"

"He's essentially a loner. I notice he always has other things to do when there is any stress—even just a little."

"You don't really know John, Mother. That's all on the outside. I know him very well. He's frightened and you frighten him. You don't understand that. I just want you to know I know what I am doing."

"I just had to make sure you consider what I have said."

"I have, and I know what you are saying, and I know what I am doing."

"Good. I shall not speak about it again."

The topic of this conversation is quite obviously "two views of John." But in fact, as in all conversations, the mother and daughter both perceive John partially *as he arouses them to see him,* but also as they each feel about themselves and each other.

In your hearing of the conversation how would you describe the daughter's feelings about herself? How does she perceive herself and how does she feel about herself? What kind of self-esteem does she reveal? On what are you basing your view?

How about the mother? What kinds of feeling about herself would impel her into this dangerous conversation?

Having just studied the chapter on relationship, it has probably occurred to you that these questions cannot be answered without an awareness of the relationship between mother and daughter. How do they feel about each other? How do those feelings tell you anything about the self-esteem (the self-feelings) of each?

Behind everything we say are the feelings we have about ourselves—our self-esteem and the self-image that arouses that esteem.

The success of any interaction depends on each person's understanding and respecting the self-image and esteem of the other.[3] To be taken as dishonest when you think you have been honest, as incompetent when you felt you were effective, is embarrassing and deeply upsetting. Wrecked relationships and unproductive conflicts are the consequence, in the main, of interaction in which at least one person ignores or refuses to confirm the self-image and esteem of another.

THE DEPRESSING BACKDROP FOR THE EVOLVING SELF-CONCEPT

However, these feelings cannot be separated from the feelings and perceptions of the social world of which we are a part.

[3]Michael Argyle, *The Psychology of Interpersonal Behavior* (Baltimore: Penguin Books, 1967), p. 129.

As a nation we are in limbo. Watergate has made us very skeptical of the politician and the capacity of the government to meet our mounting problems. The slang term *ripoff* has entered the language because it seems so appropriate as a description of too much experience of exploitation in business and in the everyday world. Though we have a gross national product almost twice that of Russia, four times that of Japan or Germany, ten times that of China or Canada, and twenty-five times that of Mexico,[4] because of inflation almost all the things we make are becoming cheaper in quality.

Further, it is common knowledge that at present rates of worldwide use there is (as of 1978) enough oil to last 25 years; natural gas, 20 years; uranium 235—for the atomic plants we fear—only 60 years. Tin, silver, gold, copper, zinc, lead, and mercury will be running out in 10 to 20 years. The iron supply is good for another 400 years. Coal, as it is currently used, is our most plentiful fossil fuel, good for another 800 years.[5] You may have read different estimates than these, and this is part of the problem. Who knows for sure how much of any fuel or mineral there is underground?

One should not read these facts to mean that the riches of the industrial age are over. The essential limitation is energy, but the sun is the basic source of all our energy, and it will not end until it grows cold, some 5 billion years from now. The essential question is, "How may the light and heat of the sun be translated into our needs?" Difficult as it may be to change light into electricity, inventing a television receiver is probably just as impossible—but you may have one in your room.

Consider this unsettling fact about the world to which we belong: 10,000 people die of starvation every day. Though the soil of the earth will not feed an unending increase in population, there really is no need for anybody to starve now. The great problem of our time, which damps the spirit of any sensitive person, is our present inability to marshal the energies and aspirations of the human family to meet the priorities of life. Great reservoirs of human energy are dissipated by competing for dwindling resources. In this kind of environment it is not easy to develop a positive self-concept.

THE SELF-CONCEPT AND ITS GROWTH PROCESS

"Humanistic psychology" is the branch of psychology most closely related to the concepts of interpersonal communication. The foremost leader of this movement has been the late Abraham Maslow, whose last

---

[4]These are 1970 comparisons.

[5]James G. Miller, "Living Systems: The Supernational System," *Behavioral Sciences*, 21 (September 1976), 346.

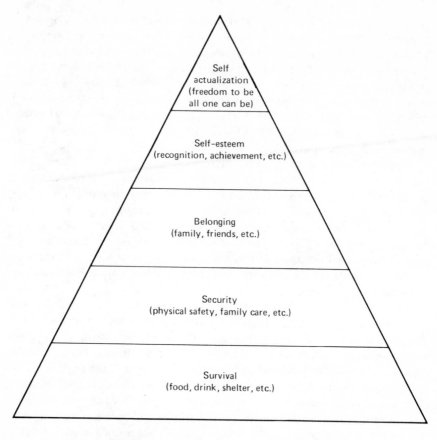

FIGURE 2-1   Maslow's Hierarchy of Human Needs

book, *The Farther Reaches of Human Nature,* was devoted to the self-concept.[6] Behind that work was Maslow's broadly accepted concept that people live according to a hierarchy of needs. This heirarchy is shown in Figure 2-1. Each of the lower levels holds a priority over one's capacity to be motivated at a higher level *when that lower level is challenged.* Note that the first two levels are in fact of little concern to most people reading this book except when they are ill, on a treacherous road, in a dark alley, or in fearful contemplation of the future. But esteem is intimately related to social and economic safety.[7] As you may know from your own observations, three dynamic relationships have been noted. A person with

[6]Abraham Maslow, *The Farther Reaches of Human Nature* (New York: The Viking Press, 1971).

[7]Abraham Maslow *et al.,* "A Clinically-Derived Test for Measuring Psychological Security-Insecurity," *Journal of General Psychology,* 33 (July, 1945), 24–41.

high self-esteem and low security (e.g., someone who has just lost a job or an election) will be hostile and even ruthless in attacking others. But a person of low self-esteem in the same circumstances will turn the attack inward and criticize himself or herself. Insecurity requires an immense amount of self-confirmation from others, particularly if self-esteem is low. Strikingly different, the person of low self-esteem who is in a very secure position will be quiet and most accommodating. "Don't blow a good thing" is that person's assessment of the situation.

The Role of Values

Within the hierarchy just presented the self has another dimension, and this is what we call *value.* The power of the self depends on what one considers to be of ultimate value.

In the heyday of industrial development the gravest error in our self-descriptions was the belief that a person's worth was his or her net worth. To live in a fine house, to have the best of clothes, to eat in the finest restaurants, to have wealth, indeed to leave money to one's children and perhaps, if rich, to a philanthropic fund in one's own name, as a monument to the self, was conceived as the ultimate in successful living. However, if Maslow understood the needs of human beings correctly, such aspirations for the self were in fact a neurotic tie to survival and security as the end goals of life.

The generation under thirty is not caught in this trap. This is not to say that you do not like the luxuries of industry. Indeed, you seem to like *things* more than your grandparents did. You enjoy them for their use to you, and for their beauty. You are less likely than the previous generation to tie your feelings of self-esteem to your ownership of things.

So you are freer to need to belong, freer to search for self-esteem in what you are as a person, and thus more driven to become what you may potentially become. At least in part, this is why the college students' self-value scores in the communication-conflict instrument (chapter 10) are so high. Indeed, the great value conflict of your generation is the conflict between autonomy and mutuality, the struggle between the prestige of uniqueness and the prestige of belonging to the groups you admire.[8]

"Low and High Grumbles" in the Search for Esteem

It should be clear that taking care of the needs in the hierarchy does not really bring less frustration and more contentment before one

[8]Argyle, *op. cit.,* p. 120.

reaches the actualization stage. In fact the reverse is true. There is no real sense of fulfillment until one gets beyond the fear of failure.

It is important to recognize, therefore, that the feelings of people are bound to be negative and destructive until they have almost achieved the "farthest reaches" of being. In his provocative exploration of people's search for self Maslow devotes a chapter to the topic of "grumbles."[9] Low grumbles are about survival needs. High grumbles are about the lack of freedom, prestige, and dignity of the self.

The Grumble About Power

What makes the movement toward a productive environment hard to accomplish is the fact that the movement toward freedom and dignified conditions of living not only fails to stop the grumbling but at one stage produces more intense grumbling and even catastrophic behavior.

The basic social improvement in the development of healthy self-concepts involves a changing of the conditions of authority. (This is why we devote a chapter to power.) If leaders of social institutions, parents or executives, are going to meet the high "grumbles" for a sense of belonging and self-esteem, they have to reduce their authority and arbitrary decision making. Those who make decisions for another person hold that person in psychological childhood.

But as we say, the immediate consequence of increasing freedom to make decisions is anxiety and fear and, thus, defensive exploitation. Perhaps this can best be understood as you reflect on your own struggle to gain your independence from your parents. No matter how gentle and understanding your parents may have been, at one point you had to find a reason to be angry with them in order to break the dependent relationship of your childhood.

We are discussing the inevitable growth problems of the self-concept. The road to actualization involves a regressive stage when the freedom for dignity is first provided.

"Meta-Grumbles" in the Development of a Self

But once we live out our rebellion and grumbling about not being treated with dignity, we move on to a stage characterized by *meta-grumbles. In short, self-esteem does not stand alone on being treated with respect.* The question put to the self upon gaining dignity in a relationship is,

[9] Abraham Maslow, *The Farther Reaches of Human Nature* (New York: Viking Press, 1971), Chap. 18.

"Am I worthy of it?" There is only one way to find out, and this is to attain a competence that establishes one's own esteem. Does that mean developing a skill—social, mechanical, artistic, mathematical, or whatever? Well, yes, but only if "skill" is taken broadly. It means "getting good" at something about which one can reward oneself. Being able to grow plants successfully brings deep satisfaction to one person we know; learning the language of the railroad engineer stirs another. Self-esteem is not a gift to the self; it is the interest on an investment of time and energy.

Peak Experiences for the Meta-Grumbles

Maslow says that the movement from the sense of belonging to self-actualization hinges on the capacity to achieve peak experiences.[10] A peak experience is a momentary fantasy, a moment when one loses consciousness of self (past, present, and future) and becomes absorbed or identified with some thing, some person, or the physical environment. Some people have many such experiences; others not so many. For some these experiences are vivid, for others the self intrudes and the experience is faint.

One of the authors had one memorably vivid experience that he can relive in memory with varying degrees of intensity, sometimes as if it were just happening. He was hiking alone in the northern wilds and came upon a lake he had heard of but had not seen before. It was like a star flashing through the trees ahead. He pushed through the brush and stood on a high shore marveling at its beauty. The south shore was a huge granite wall. As he stood there recovering his breath and resting, he seemed to become part of the silence of the trees and the timelessness of the granite. It was as if for a few seconds he *was* the scene. As he came back to self-awareness he had the feeling that he had for moments known, for the first time, the meaning of eternity.

He cannot know whether in the effort to recapture that moment he has conveyed anything significant to the reader. Such an explanation can only point. If it arouses the memory of a similar experience, the reader will know that there is an ecstasy in being something beyond the self. You will also know that the physical tone and the overall feelings about one's life, surrounding this peak moment, are positive and self-affirming. These priceless moments happen to people of all ages when the emotional state of being invites them—and only then.

[10]Abraham Maslow, *Religions, Values, and Peak-Experiences* (New York: The Viking Press, 1970).

A Peak Experience?

The Peak Experience of Childhood

Way back in childhood other things have happened, long forgotten, that are important to the development of the self-concept. According to a study of 300 creative lives, it was noted that in moments of doubt, while working through a project that tests his or her competence, the creative person tends to call forth the feelings of peak experiences of childhood.[11] The childhood experience was of the following character, at least as it is remembered: The child might have been lying on the ground on a beautiful summer afternoon looking up into the clouds, watching them change their forms from, perhaps, a mountain into a face, and then into some animal. He or she may have heard some expla-

[11]Edith Cobb, "The Ecology of Imagination in Childhood," *Daedalus*, 88 (1959), 537–548.

nation of the immensity of the universe and may have tried to conceive of the distance to the sun, our closest star and a minor one, 92 million miles away. Perhaps he or she recalled being told that if on the day Christ was born, almost 2000 years ago, a train had started to the sun at 90 miles an hour, it would not yet have reached its destination. The child was overwhelmed by the feeling of the immensity of a universe in which he or she must be only a speck—but a "considerable" speck that, amazingly, has at least some comprehension of this immensity.

Though contemplating narrowing options as he or she works with a difficult problem in later years, the person, tempted to quit and fail, plunges forward with the feelings about the self sparked by that moment of fantasy that changed his or her being years and years before on an aimless, sunny afternoon. These moments in our childhood are the cradle of our growth.

Alexander Bickel was one of America's greatest jurists. As a boy of 14 he immigrated to the United States from Rumania. Among his fondest memories throughout his life were those of the summers he had spent on his grandfather's farm back in Rumania. Note the significance he attributes to the following experience:

> Just before dusk, . . . the village street would be full of these [wagons], rows of them coming along, everybody going to the barn to unload the hay. . . . To be hoisted and riding on top . . . was unforgetable, an indescribably joyful experience. . . . If you've had in boyhood . . . [an] experience of . . . heroic and great, great pleasure, I think your expectations in life . . . [are] enhanced. . . . I don't doubt that my experience on the Schaefer farm gave me as much of a sunny outlook on life as I managed to sustain . . . [a feeling] that life holds pleasures, that it isn't a vale of tears . . . [To] sit there surveying the world from this mountain of hay is as if early in life I'd been shot to the moon and had a moon walk. . . . It gives you a sense . . . that extraordinary things [are] possible in life, [and that] they can be done. . . .[12]

Growth springs from the pleasure of living, and thus the source of our power as people is the ecstatic moment Maslow calls the peak experience.

The Power to Belong and Empathize

The peak experience is crucial to the development of a person in two dimensions. First, it is the way of achieving stage three in the hierarchy of growth. It is what belonging is. Belonging is that strange experi-

---

[12]From the remarks of Abraham S. Goldstein, Dean of the Yale Law School, at a Memorial Service for Alexander Bickel.

ence of letting go and losing oneself in the beautiful sunshine as you walk out of a class building, feeling the swoop of a hawk overhead, feeling ecstatic when watching the stumbling walk of an infant. Belonging is trustingly giving oneself up. It is incorporating the essence of the other and momentarily obliterating one's own essence.

The second thing we achieve in a peak experience is the power to empathize, to feel as the other person does, with appreciation for that person. Peak experience, belonging, and empathy are all interactive forces hinging on the feeling level discussed in the previous chapter.

In Sharp Contrast

One of the authors spent a memorable weekend in a workshop on the education of feelings sponsored by the Danforth Foundation. At one point the participants, all college honor students, talked about their feelings. The thing that came crashing through was the degree to which they felt and feared despair. They talked of their distress. They spoke of feeling that they did not belong to anyone, of their fear that they might not be able to establish a lasting relationship with a person of the opposite sex. We heard nothing of their joys, though indeed they were a select group of young, handsome people in good health, bright, effective, and loving. They were too energetic to have known no ecstacy. But they cannot leap to their full powers while doubt and caution restrain them from moments of losing themselves in an identification with something other than the self. They too persistently see the world through their own eyes.

If, however, our observations as professors are accurate, the college age period is one of doubt. In a number of studies of moral development, researchers have seen the person as moving from a sense of being a dependent victim of authority, to self-assertion, to relationship with other persons, to the development of the basic principles of ethical behavior, all by the time he or she has reached the age of 18 or 20.[13] But then a regression sets in, a period when one again becomes involved with individual relationships and concerns rather than being immersed in the development of moral principles. As the authors see it, in the college years people become overwhelmed, or at least completely absorbed, in trying to work out their relationships. One has been disappointed in a love affair; another has been used in ways he or she did not expect. Trust drops, and the desire to rise above a world that Tennessee Williams sees

---

[13]Irwin L. Child, *Humanistic Psychology and the Research Tradition: Their Several Virtues* (New York: Wiley, 1973), pp. 32–41.

The Self of the Moment

as a world of "mendacity"—a world that never tells it quite like it is—causes them to feel that the highest aspirations of the self are probably only impractical fantasies. Thus, in defense they settle for an emotional tone that screens them from their potential. The years from 16 to 22 are years of identity crisis.[14] In some future day, as the person reaches for achievement, he or she may crash through and recapture the energy and guidance of the peak experience.

THE PRESENT SELF VERSUS THE IDEAL SELF

It is clear that we cannot draw upon an arid past, though the most successful lives, at least as judged by productivity, contain deep pain and

[14]Erik Erikson, "The Problem of Ego Identity," *American Journal of Psychoanalysis,* 4 (1956), 56–121.

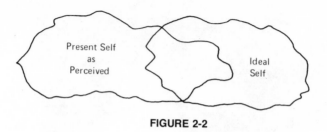

FIGURE 2-2

sorrow too. Indeed, one's capacity to feel the peak is in part dependent on having known the pit.

But what is the appropriate tension between the self as currently perceived and the "idealized" concept—the person we would like to become? From therapeutic research we have learned how the present self-concept and the ideal self are appropriately related. In his research at the University of Chicago Carl Rogers did some comparisons of the relationship between these two self-concepts by means of an instrument known as the Q-sort.[15] In this device one arranges a set of statements about the self, as currently perceived, in rows ranging from least like the current self to most like the current self. Then the statements are arranged in rows from the least like the ideal self to the most like the ideal self. A statistical device is then used to measure the degree of similarity between the self as perceived and the self aspired to. Rogers found that the correlation between the two images, on the average, changed in therapy from −.01 to .31. For healthy people the correlation would be higher. There is a considerable overlap of the two images, as seen in Figure 2-2. Yet there is much difference too. One may note that there are two unhealthy states: (1) Some people aspire to be what they feel they are not at all like, and (2) some people feel that they are perfect and do not need to change. In the first case, you dislike yourself—all that you are is unworthy compared with what you want to be (Figure 2-3). In such cases the correlations between present and ideal self run from very low to actual minus correlations. In a high minus correlation, say −.75, you conceive of yourself, in most respects, as nearly the opposite of what you would like to be.

Something very important must be understood here. In cases in which such people were in therapy, the two concepts began to overlap as they improved, and the concept that changed was *not the ideal self but the*

---

[15]Carl Rogers, *On Becoming a Person* (Boston: Houghton Mifflin Company, 1961), Chap. 10; *Psychotherapy and Personality Change* (Chicago: University of Chicago Press, 1954), p. 61.

FIGURE 2-3

perception of what they were like. In short, they began to see themselves as more like their ideal than they had formerly perceived themselves to be. They did not alter their ideals. They became more accepting of their imperfect selves.

At first blush this acceptance of weaknesses in the self, as measured against the ideal, would seem like some kind of a con job on the self, an inflation of one's self-esteem *without* improving one's performance. But this is not what happens. The person just becomes more realistic. According to some authorities, besides the powerful effect of rejecting parents, the main cause of low esteem is the choosing of too high a comparison group.[16] If you have to be the President of the United States, or even of a corporation, in order to feel good about yourself, you are probably in for a life of low self-esteem. You need not lower your ideals to feel good about yourself, but you must be realistic in evaluating your achievements.

The second unhealthy state about which Rogers talked is the one in which the person can find no reason to idealize; his or her present self is all one could hope for. But what appears to be serenity is in fact the *fear* that one cannot change one's behavior, that one has no choices. Or, if you can see yourself only as your ideal, you may *project* any "apparent" errors or weaknesses onto the conditions of life or onto other people, not accepting the responsibility for your choices. Or, indeed, we have still another deceptive way of dealing with the difference between the perceived self and what indeed is the feared ideal, and that is not to own up to the fear. Bonaro Overstreet, in her classic descriptions of the ways of fear, says, "Fear wears a thousand faces." One of them is a mask that allows us to play Halloween or Mardi Gras and travel incognito.[17] Those

[16]M. Rosenberg, *Society and the Adolescent Self-Image* (Princeton, N.J.: Princeton University Press, 1965).

[17]Erving Goffman, *The Presentation of Self in Everyday Life* (Garden City, N.Y.: Doubleday, 1959), pp. 6–14; P. Watzlawick, J. H. Beavin, and D. D. Jackson, *Pragmatics of Communication* (New York: Norton, 1967), pp. 62–67; H. Deutsch, "The Impostor: Contribution to Ego Psychology of a Type of Psychopath," *Psychoanalytic Quarterly*, 24 (1955), 483–505.

who, in this way, protect themselves from their own criticism lay themselves open to criticism from others. Unfortunately, they are sometimes called *impostors*. More gently (but not much), we sometimes charge such people with pretense. When we attack people for faking we usually drive them to defend their pretense. Thus they fake less guardedly, proving their pretense to everybody but themselves.

If you have been reading this closely you sense a close relationship between the terrible fear of the pretender and the indignant drive to destroy the pretender that lurks deep in all of us. If our perceptions of self and others are the product of our emotions (a basic thesis of this book, developed in the first chapter), then our terrible urge to rip the mask from the face of the impostor tells us that we too pretend, hate pretense in ourselves, and angrily discharge the feeling by projecting it. An understanding of our anger should help us comprehend the person who is so frightened that he or she puts together the two basic self-concepts by denying any disparity between them.

One More Use for Elmer's Glue

All this self-deception has in recent years come under the label of "self-defeating behaviors." The spread of the workshop on self-defeating behaviors is recognition that we are all a little like Humpty Dumpty—if we tell the truth about ourselves. It seems to these authors that the competently led workshops may help many people put together the present self and the ideal self a little better, allowing for another climb up the hierarchy of human possibility.

DISPARITIES IN THE SELF-CONCEPT THAT CREATE FEAR

Fear is such a basic component of life and so self-defeating that we often become numb to it. Thus a further sharpening of awareness is called for. There are basically four categories of fears about the self: body image, intelligence, the social self, and the moral self.

Body Image

The core of the self is the body image. When the body fails, we die. Little wonder that we are all concerned for our bodies. If we lack health we are hurt. But important as the health of the body is, the way others respond to our body is perhaps equally important. It is a fortunate person whose body attracts other people, especially early in life. Lewis

Terman, a psychologist, whose work we will refer to several times in this book, made a long-term study of 1000 highly intelligent people aged 10 to 35.[18] At the end of 25 years he compared the childhood records of the 150 most successful with the 150 least successful. Success was defined in terms of achievement. He found only one difference in the early records: The more successful were more commonly described as attractive.

Attractiveness has, of course, many components, but the first response we elicit in another cannot be separated from the way we look to them. Thus our power to achieve is related to our attractiveness to older people when we are a child. Throughout life our sense of well-being is always in part associated with the way we feel about our bodies. How strong are we? How skillful? How graceful?

Intelligence

Almost equally important in our perception of ourselves and our ideals for the self is our perception of our intelligence. Do we feel smart enough to cope? Almost all competence is in some measure tied up with intelligence. Given the fears generated in us when we are being educated, it is clear that many of our fears, *usually unfounded,* surround our perceptions of our intelligence. We will explore this more fully in Chapter 4.

The Social Self

The self-concept is in part a perception of the way we feel we are related to others. Do people in general like me? Do I like other people? How much at ease am I with others? With what kind of people am I most at ease? Why? Do I belong, or am I essentially a lonely person?

Much recent research bears on these questions. James C. McCroskey and others have found a high correlation between low self-esteem and "communication apprehension"[19] in the adult population. One might consider this research unrelated to our point until one examines the meaning of "communication apprehension." McCroskey and his associates point out that avoidance of interaction with others is the result of feeling punished in communication situations, distrusting the overtures

[18]Lewis Terman *et al., The Gifted Child Grows Up* (Stanford, Calif.: Stanford University Press, 1947).

[19]James C. McCroskey, John A. Daly, Virginia Richmond, and Raymond L. Falcione, "Communication Apprehension and Self-Esteem," *Human Communication Research,* 3 (Spring 1977), 269–277.

of others, wanting not to disclose oneself, feeling isolated, feeling ineffective in social activities and the ability to discuss one's problems with
others, especially parents and other significant persons in one's life. In
short, "communication apprehension" is a feeling that one is not socially
accepted, and low self-esteem is the self-confirmation of the fact that one
does not feel acceptable.

The Moral Self

Am I a good person? What is a good person? What is good and what
is bad? These are profound questions for all of us. As we will see, again
in Chapter 4, in large measure we hang the meaning of our life on our
values. Thus the degree to which we live out our values has much to do
with how good we feel we are. Indeed, the topic is so important that we
have devoted Chapter 11 to it and merely introduce it here. How do you
feel about your morals? How does the answer to that question bear on
your self-concept?

TWO COMMUNICATION PROCESSES THAT BEAR ON THE SELF-CONCEPT

1. We Come to Know Ourselves as We Are Reflected in the Eyes of Others

At the end of the first chapter we alluded to the fact that each of us
looks out through eyes that see many faces but never our own. This
perception is basic to understanding the self-concept. We are what we do
and are guided by what we aspire to do, but we know both only as they
are reflected to us. What one does is measured by its impact on others.
The validity of our aspirations is tested by the responses of others to the
way we express ourselves.

In a day of great individualism this dependence on others is not easy
to see or to accept. So while we know it as an abstract truth, we are likely
not to see it in our own experience.

This fact points to the power of the communication process. In any
conversation each person speaks from the residual self, that is, the self
he or she was at the beginning of the conversation. As each speaks, he or
she has an impact on himself or herself and on the other person. In
return, when the other person speaks that person has an impact on
himself or herself and on the first person. So each person changes,
perhaps minutely, sometimes greatly, as a conversation proceeds.

The degree to which one changes and is changed can be sensed as
follows:

1. I speak to you from the residual me.
2. You speak to me from your residual self plus my impact on you.
3. My residual self is now changed by your impact (involving my impact on you) as I interpret my impact on you and your impact on me.

This can seem too complicated unless you go back over the previous three steps carefully. What we are noting is the way communication fuses people into a system in which, in fact, it is very difficult to retain self-separation. It is like pouring water into a container from two separate pitchers. If you empty your pitcher and then dip the pitcher into the water and refill it, how much of its original water does it contain?

Yet, as one author notes, a person holds a certain separateness (in union) that can be seen in sensing the progress of thought in the following three statements about the nature of self-concept:[20]

1. I am *not* what I *think* I am.
2. I am *not* what *you think* I am.
3. *I am* what *I think* you think I am.

Thus the critical thing that gives a person freedom in the communication union is the fact that the impact of the other is made *in accordance with the receiver's interpretation.* Thus the degree to which you, the reader, interpret what is said in this book is the degree to which you are not being shaped by this book.

Of course you can become free by stopping your reading. But then what? The only way you can be completely free is to cease to communicate with all other people. But in that freedom you lose your identity, *for the self is a social creation.*

The authors have never seen this more vividly portrayed than in John Lilly's *The Center of the Cyclone,* a psychiatrist's explanation of his efforts to discover his ultimate powers through experiments in sensory deprivation, by cutting off the self from all external impact.[21] This led him close to suicide and then to a long, long search for deep, trusting relationships in which he could rediscover himself.

/ *Communication Process One: We come to know ourselves (past, present, and future) as we are reflected in the eyes of others.*/

---

[20] A. H. Bleiberg and H. E. Leubling, quoted in William W. Wilmot, *Dyadic Communication* (Reading, Mass.: Addison-Wesley, 1975), p. 42.

[21] John C. Lilly, *The Center of the Cyclone* (New York: Bantam Books, 1972).

GOSHEN COLLEGE LIBRARY

GOSHEN, INDIANA

KNOWN TO ME   NOT KNOWN TO ME

	KNOWN TO ME	NOT KNOWN TO ME
KNOWN TO OTHERS	Open 1	Blind 2
NOT KNOWN TO OTHERS	Hidden 3	Unknown 4

FIGURE 2-4 The Johari Window. Joseph Luft, *Of Human Interaction* (Palo Alto, Calif.: National Press Books, 1961). Adapted from *Of Human Interaction* by Joseph Luft by permission of Mayfield Publishing Company (formerly National Press Books). Copyright © 1969 by The National Press.

2. Self-Knowledge is a Function of Disclosure

By *disclosure* we mean revealing personal information about how we feel and perceive our personal experience. Sidney Jourard has observed that in order to have a sense of identity one must make oneself known to at least one other person.[22] This is the minimum. But in truth we should be known by many, for the confusion and mendacity that run through all of us make us need the responses of many people in order to determine the truth about ourselves. *Looking back over our lives, it is clear that the most significant responses have been those that told us the promise that others saw in us.* Thus our powers are dependent on our disclosure.

Easy to see, hard to do Why, then, should it be so difficult to reveal ourselves? At the bottom is the problem of distrust of both self and the other, for if in communicating we change ourselves with the aid of the other, what may be the result? The Johari Window (Figure 2-4) highlights the character of our problem. Several things stand out clearly:

[22]Sidney Jourard, *The Transparent Self* (Princeton, N.J.: D. Van Nostrand Company, Inc., 1964).

1. In certain ways we both know me. In this we are comfortable and open.
2. In some ways the other person knows things about me that I do not know or do not want to know.
3. In some ways I know things about myself that I have not felt free to tell the other.
4. In some ways we are both blind about what I am. The conscious self is but a ship in a great sea of unconsciousness. Perhaps something tells us it would be best to "leave well enough alone."

Several questions arise as to what will happen if I open up and give more information to the other person:

1. How will I then think or feel about myself?
2. Will the other person understand me as he or she does now, or will his or her perceptions of me change and will our relationship thus change in ways that are not satisfactory?
3. What will the other person *do* with this knowledge about me?

Disclosure and loneliness   This has often been called the Age of Alienation: People have been separated from their physical environment as a consequence of industrialism; they have been separated from each other as a consequence of the fears we have discussed; and thus they have been separated from their natural growth because they cannot know except through others. The result is loneliness.

It is odd how the interacting forces here have put us in a double bind. The great scientific drive that has made survival easier and has given us much safety has moved us along the hierarchy of needs to the point at which our primary need is to belong. Those very changes in our way of living have created the conditions that have alienated us from each other and made us fearful of belonging to each other.

There are two ways in which people respond inappropriately to these pressures. One is to devalue the self to the point at which one tries to escape despair and find himself or herself in relationship with others. The other is to become so self-oriented in one's values that one cannot relate effectively to others. Both result in loneliness (see Figure 2-5).

Some people become totally dependent on others, the victims of the latest fad, the joiners, the people whose whole life is their social life. They are the "other-directed people" that David Riesman wrote about in *The Lonely Crowd,* all huddled together but all terribly alone.[23] To have to be reassured that one really belongs is always to feel that one does not belong. One is driven to please. And the belonging such a person seeks is more a search for comfort in his or her relationship than a search for

[23]David Riesman, *The Lonely Crowd* (New Haven, Conn.: Yale University Press, 1950).

Two Kinds of Loneliness

Other	I–Thou	Self
Value	Belonging	Value
"I am nothing without you"		"I am nothing unless I am free of you"

FIGURE 2-5   Two Kinds of Loneliness

rich involvement with others. It has in it the same emptiness a person experiences when he or she is alone.

The French novelist Balzac is an interesting case in point. His life was a strange combination of living beyond his means, entertaining and feasting with the nobility to whom he desperately wanted to belong. He was born an illegitimate peasant. In order to get out of debt and continue his endless search, he worked from dawn to dusk writing novels that played on the duplicity, corruption, and phony relationships of the very people he so wished would accept him. Indeed, it is said that his novels became a powerful force leading to the French Revolution, which ultimately destroyed the society he wanted to be a part of.

He once said that his most terrible experience, which he faced each day, was that moment alone in the dark as he wearily gave himself to sleep. He died in his early fifties, an exhausted man.

Balzac was a lonely man because he could not accept his birth and lineage. He spent his life trying to be confirmed by the nobility and thus to prove to himself that he was a noble man. It should come as no surprise that he made a coat of arms for himself.

If fearful people must communicate with others in order to be accepted by them, they cannot disclose themselves, for that would make them unacceptable. They must play the role of the person they wish they were. *They cannot disclose and belong because the difference between their self-concept and their ideal self is too great.* If one cannot belong to oneself, one cannot disclose and come to belong to others. Conversely, if one does not trust others, one cannot reveal the personal information that, if acceptable to others, would allow one to accept onself. This series of sentences runs in the very circle that closes people off if they are driven to find themselves totally and only in their relationships.

The second kind of loneliness is the result of being so self-oriented that it is difficult to relate deeply with others. It is the consequence of a culture that has placed more and more emphasis on individuality. The Christian religion, which values each person and emphasizes the spiritual or inner life, has been a powerful force in the development of societies more responsive to the rights of individuals. Oddly, however, protecting individuals can also lead to a separating effect.

Legal protection of the second kind of loneliness   During the 1800s the American courts defended the "right of privacy" in the guise of property rights. The right of privacy was defined as the "right of an individual to be let alone, to live a life of seclusion, and to be free from unwarranted publicity."[24] In 1890 Louis D. Brandeis, later Justice Brandeis, was coauthor of an article in the *Harvard Law Review* entitled "The Right to Privacy" that set out for the first time a new category of legal rights and a new field of legal philosophy.[25] Thus it is that in the past 100 years the importance of personal privacy has been legally institutionalized.

A side effect of the human-potentials movement   In the past thirty or more years the "human-potentials movement" in psychology has emphasized the concept of "self-actualization." In this emphasis the question of whether personal growth takes place separately from relationships or within them has not been answered clearly. The concept of "commitment" to a relationship has become deeply troubling.

The so-called Gestalt Prayer, conceived by Fritz Perls as a way of urging people to take responsibility for their own feelings and decisions, is widely misinterpreted as the ticket to a life without regard for any other life. It goes like this:

I do my thing, and you do your thing.
I am not in this world to live up to your expectations
And you are not in this world to live up to mine.
You are you, and I am I,
And if by chance we find each other, it's beautiful.
If not, it can't be helped.[26]

The "privacy" emphasis has made its most troubling impact on marriage and other intimate relationships. In our efforts to understand the fear young people are experiencing, the central problem, as we see it, is the suffering, the feeling of inadequacy, the great emptiness, often the intense guilt, anger, and destructive urges that consume both people in a relationship when the break comes. We have seen people literally immobilized by deep depression for weeks and months.

How can one understand this?

The self-concept is developed in intimate interaction with others. The self is a social phenomenon. As one cuts away the other person in

[24]*Frith* vs. *Associated Press* (DCSC) 176 F Supp 671 (applying South Carolina law).

[25]*Hamberger* vs. *Eastman,* 106 NH 107, 206 A2d, 239, 11 ALR 3rd 1288.

[26]Frederick S. Perls, *Gestalt Therapy Verbatim* (Lafayette, Calif.: Real People Press, 1969), frontispiece. © Real People Press 1969. All rights reserved.

breaking the relationship, since the other was involved in his or her own self-making, that person must kill a part of himself or herself.

One of the authors talked to a minister in his late 30s who had recently been divorced. Since he had been a counselor for couples, he and his wife were determined to separate without hurting each other. "It was easy enough to see why we should end the marriage," he said. "I had become converted to a liberal view and she remained as conservative as our fundamentalists . . . But I am sick. At one point we just had to tear each other up. It was vicious. I guess I think now you can't get out without being hurt." He shook his head slowly and stared into space.

We have heard people in the communication profession talk about the possibility of "desensitization training" to help people break relationships as pleasantly as they engage in them. What this might do, if it is possible, is hard to know for sure. We suspect that if people can be saved from despair they will also be deprived of ecstacy. But in any case we deeply question whether such desensitization is possible. If one gives oneself to a relationship, one must be hurt when it breaks. One cannot half belong. It is like being a little bit pregnant.

But if we cannot belong—and we will not if we are afraid—then we must know the pangs of loneliness.

All this discussion of loneliness emerges as a part of noting how *Communicaton Process Two* bears on the workings of the self-concept: *Self-knowledge is a function of disclosure.*

So we are lonely if we do not disclose and perhaps hurt if we do. What is the answer? First, it is to understand. Not to understand is to be a helpless victim.

But to understand, alone, will not solve the problem. One has to decide for oneself which risk is the greater—loneliness or possible hurt. And one can experiment both ways. As we found earlier, self-defeating behaviors are the offspring of inertia and the inability to make choices. To make a choice and to be willing to pay the consequences takes courage—"the heave of the will." Courage comes when the pains we suffer are too great to bear.

As we review our own thoughts here it seems that we have presented a terribly stoic view. But we see no other way and certainly no easy way. Suffering is part of being fully human. And we live in a painful period in humanity's search for itself. The sad truth is that there is no communication without risk.

CONCLUSION

In this chapter we have explored several ways in which the self-concept develops. It would be hard to find a more crucial topic in the study of communication/In working with the children of Watts, California, William Glasser was able to demonstrate that people must know who they are, and what their potentials can lead them to be, before they can marshal the energy to establish and achieve goals. For the fully human person the development of an authentic, satisfying self-concept is the first order of business.

INSTRUMENT 2-1

SELF-CONCEPT INDICATORS
FOR PERSONAL GROWTH

Take each term separately and apply it to yourself by completing the following sentence:

I am a (an) ———— person.

In column I, decide how much of the time this statement is like you and rate yourself on a scale from one to five according to the following key:

1. Seldom is this like me.
2. Occasionally this is like me.
3. About half of the time this is like me.
4. A good deal of the time this is like me.
5. Most of the time this is like me.

In column II, using the same term, complete the following sentence:

I would like to be a (an) ———— person.

Then decide how much of the time you would like this trait to be characteristic of you and rate yourself on the following five-point scale:

1. Seldom would I like this to be me.
2. Occasionally I would like this to be me.
3. About half of the time I would like this to be me.
4. A good deal of the time I would like this to be me.
5. Most of the time I would like this to be me.

Start with the word *accepting* and fill in columns I and II before going on to the next word. Be honest with yourself so that your description will be a true measure of how you look at yourself.

	I	*II*
1. accepting	_____	_____
2. ambitious	_____	_____
3. dependable	_____	_____
4. affectionate	_____	_____
5. self-revealing	_____	_____
6. preoccupied	_____	_____
7. democratic	_____	_____
8. calm	_____	_____
9. helpful	_____	_____
10. judgmental	_____	_____
11. cruel	_____	_____
12. friendly	_____	_____
13. trusting	_____	_____
14. vague	_____	_____
15. logical	_____	_____
16. perceptive	_____	_____

	I	II
17. mature		
18. meddlesome		
19. aggressive		
20. broad-minded		
21. intellectual		
22. responsible		
23. fault-finding		
24. tolerant		
25. independent		
26. accurate		
27. competitive		
28. sarcastic		
29. confident		
30. cautious		

1. Count the number of instances in which the number in columns I and II is the same. Place that number here: _____.
2. Count the number of instances in which the difference between the two numbers is 1. Place that number here: _____.
3. Count the number of instances in which the difference between the numbers in columns I and II is 2. Place that number here: _____.
4. Count the number of instances in which the difference is three or more. Place that number here: _____.

The greater the disparity between the numbers in columns I and II, the greater your anxiety about yourself. Compare yourself with others and with the mean for the class. A certain stress is healthy. The amount that is healthy varies. The real test of the right amount for you is your health.

INSTRUMENT 2-2

TIME ORIENTATION (PAST, PRESENT, AND FUTURE) AND THE SELF-CONCEPT

The questions in this time orientation instrument are in the form of three statements. Each question has a total value of 5. The 5 points may be divided in whole numbers among the three statements as follows: 5, 0, 0; 4, 1, 0; 3, 2, 0; 3, 1, 1; 2, 2, 1; 2, 3, 0; etc.

A rating of 5 for a statement means (as compared to the other two statements) that this statement is "almost always like me."

A rating of 4 means "usually like me."

A rating of 3 means "often like me."

A rating of 2 means "occasionally like me,"

A rating of 1 means "seldom like me."

A rating of 0 means "almost never like me."

Here is a sample question:

__2__ A. I like to anticipate the future.

__2__ B. I like to spend my energy in the here and now.

__1__ C. I like to think of the past a great deal.

1. ____ A. I spend my time planning and preparing for the future.

____ B. I spend my time living my life right now.

____ C. I spend my time contemplating my life in the past.

2. ____ A. In working through a problem I consider the impact of the decision on my future.

____ B. In working through a problem I let my feelings about what is right for me guide me.

____ C. In working through a problem I keep trying to remember how I have most successfully acted in the past.

3. ____ A. The future keeps worrying me.

____ B. I am more likely to worry about what I am currently involved in.

_____ C. I spend considerable energy wishing my past might have been better.

4. _____ A. People who stay future oriented are likely to be effective.

_____ B. My experience suggests that the effective person lives fully in the present.

_____ C. I am impressed by the fact that the effective person remembers his or her history very vividly.

5. _____ A. I think a lot about the future.

_____ B. I take care of things right now, knowing that this is the best preparation for the future.

_____ C. I think about the past as important preparation for both the present and future.

6. _____ A. I often find myself trying to justify my plans.

_____ B. I am often making excuses for my present use of my time.

_____ C. I am often trying to defend my past actions.

7. _____ A. I spend a lot of energy trying to predict how things will turn out for me.

_____ B. I spend a lot of energy trying to figure out what decision to make now.

_____ C. I spend a lot of energy trying to figure out how I have gotten into the problems I get into.

8. _____ A. One should be somewhat afraid of the future.

_____ B. We should live with considerable caution.

_____ C. To feel bad about the past helps one in both the present and the future.

9. _____ A. When I listen to a person I keep figuring out how I want to respond.

_____ B. I just speak out spontaneously when I am in a conversation.

_____ C. In listening I am inclined to try to remember how I have responded in the past.

10. _____ A. I frequently talk about the future with my friends.

_____ B. My conversations with friends are almost always on whatever subject comes up.

_____ C. I talk about the past considerably with my friends.

Add the numbers in the ten A's and place the sum here:_____.

Add the numbers in the ten B's and place the sum here:_____.

Add the numbers in the ten C's and place the sum here:_____.

Now add those three numbers here:_____.

Divide the A score by the total of A + B + C. Place the percent here:_____.

Divide the B score by the total of A + B + C. Place the percent here:_____.

Divide the C score by the total of A + B + C. Place the percent here:_____.

To test your arithmetic, add the three percentages. They should add up to 100 percent.

The future, present, and past percentages provide a way of looking at your time orientation. This makes for a productive class discussion and gives you an opportunity to assess the uses of your energy.

EXERCISES

1. Talk with a friend about ideas in this chapter that have personal meaning for you. This is likely to lead to an exchange about yourself. Here are a number of topics that you may explore:
   A. Self—past, present, and future
   B. Belonging
   C. Where I am vulnerable
   D. My hangups
   E. My kind of loneliness
   F. What I want
   G. My grumbling
   H. A peak experience
   I. How I got the way I am

2. Of all the things we have encouraged students to do, nothing more consistently has paid off in student growth so much as the journal. Write about yourself, on one or more of the preceding topics or other things that concern you, for a half-hour a day for a week. If you have never done this before it is just a matter of writing yourself a letter.

   If you have trouble keeping a steady course in your college work, for instance, a good start would be some letters to yourself about what you want to make of your life. Where to begin?

   What do you do well?
   What do you like to do?
   Of what do you have fantasies?
   What do you yearn for?

   Most people spend their adult lives doing what they dislike in order to pay the bills. That's a hell of a note and a sad commentary on education. This journal writing can lead you to a life in which you get paid for doing what you want to do.

3. What do you own that you are particularly fond of? Write those things down. Prepare to talk with your class about those things and why you feel you are very fond of them. After telling this to the class, ask others to tell you what information about yourself as a person you have revealed. To illustrate, one of the authors has a four-wheel-drive vehicle. It sits up high, gives a good view, rides hard, and goes lumbering almost any place off the beaten path. He knows the thing uses too much gas for these times, but how he would hate to give it up! What do you know about him?

4. Do the following operations with the Johari window (see page 46). Step 1: Draw a Johari window to represent a way you relate to people in general; that is, not all four windows are necessarily the same size, depending on your openness. Step 2: Draw a pair of Johari windows, one to represent the way you relate to a certain friend, the other showing how you think he or she relates to you. Step 3: Invite the friend to draw a pair of windows showing the relationship from his or her point of view. Step 4: Trade the pairs of windows and discuss. Step 5: Report your conclusions or observations to the class.

3

Both Sides of Silence: The Nature of Communication

Mankind craves definition as he craves lost innocence. He simply does not know what his life means until he says it.*

Melvin Maddocks

One of the more important perspectives of this book is that to understand human communication one must erase the concepts of "speaking" and "listening" as separate or wholly different acts. We are trapped by our usual language into thinking that there are in the communicative act a speaker and a listener, and that the speaker speaks and the listener listens. But the stage-frightened "speaker," as we all know from experience, is listening as he or she speaks. And the significance of this fact, that the "speaker" and the "listener" are the same person as well as two separate individuals, brings us closer to the description of communication on which this book rests. Put in the form of a proposition, the view could be stated as follows:

> Human communication revolves chiefly around two kinds of speech: silent speech (listening) and overt speech (talking). Silent speech is the necessary preliminary to overt speech, and the quality of overt speech cannot be better than the quality of the silent speech from which it springs. One's expressive powers can never exceed one's silent powers.

Viewed this way, speech is at the very heart of communication. The

*Melvin Maddocks, "The Limitation of Language," *Time*, March 9, 1971, 36–37. Reprinted by permission from *Time*, the Weekly Newsmagazine: Copyright Time, Inc. *

flow of communication within a person and between people is an intricate, indivisible process featuring only listener-speakers interacting.

Further, a study of the speech act cannot lead to an understanding
of communication—as an act of establishing and understanding
relationship—unless it concentrates on silent speech, the source from
which overt speech emerges.

THE IMPACT OF BOTH SIDES OF SILENCE ON LIFE

What is more, human growth depends on the listening–speaking
cycle. People are made or broken by the kind of relationships that
evolve, and both silent and overt cues shape those relationships. If one
acknowledges the centrality of communication in human life, one senses
that there are no "self-made men" who have grown by themselves into
their potential. Students have been our teachers here. As they verbalized
the forces that had shaped them, they shed eloquent light on their
silent-overt worlds. Perhaps the reader can best gain the "feel" for what
we sensed if we share two of the many stories students have told us about
the impact of a communication. As you examine these vignettes, you
may find it difficult to determine whether you are being told a story
about the power of listening or the power of speech.

"IN A WAY I AM LIKE THAT OLD SHACK"

When I was a boy of about eleven or twelve, I had a strange urge to be
alone. I just didn't want to be with anyone at times. Around our house there
wasn't much of a chance of me being alone, so I had to go out and find a
place. It was by accident that I found it. I was a paperboy. I walked down
this highway named Woodward, which was made up of eight lanes. Just
before I got where I picked up my papers on the left side of this block
was—I even remember the name—the GMC Truck and Coach Warehouse.
There were trucks coming in and out of that place all the time. Machines
and men were working like crazy. Across the street was this huge block of
rotting buildings. . . . And next to another trucking company was a lot full
of brush. And to the back of this lot was an old shack. I guess it must have
been an old railroad watchtower.

One day I went up to the door of the shack and pulled off the boards that
were locking the door and walked in. It was dark, so I broke out all of the
glass in the windows and pushed out all of the boards blocking the light. I
picked up an old crate, placed it next to one of the windows and sat down.
Then the funniest thing happened. With all the noise coming from the
warehouse and the trucking company and cars passing on the highway, it
was quiet. It is hard for me to explain, but with all the noise going on
outside, it was really quiet here. I must have sat for two hours, and all I did
was think. For a kid of eleven I thought of some of the weirdest things. I
thought about if I would ever make it to college; if I would ever marry; I

even thought about what I was going to do with my life. And while I was thinking about all of this, it was silent. I just couldn't hear a sound.

I must have gone to my place every few weeks for maybe two years, until the inevitable happened. A local businessman bought that sacred lot. He tore down the shack and he built a gas station.

In a way I am like that old shack. I am that person in the middle of all the noise and racket who just isn't noticed. I just sit back there and watch all that is going on. I sit back and think to myself. You know, I looked and looked for another place to go and think, but I guess that old shack was a one-in-a-lifetime thing for me.

"YOU'RE JUST LIKE YOUR MOTHER"

"You're just like your mother. She was no good and you'll grow up to be just like her." Repeated over and over, this phrase has done more to affect my personality than any other utterance I've ever heard. Along with that favorite of my grandmother's went such ego-building statements as "Nobody else wanted you, so I had to take you. Your father can't be bothered with you. He won't want anything to do with you until you're old enough to work."

Grandma Field wasn't really such a witch. She was basically a good Catholic woman who, at age 65, found herself burdened with the care of an active, troublesome four-year-old. This child was the product of a broken marriage of which grandma had thoroughly disapproved from the start but had no power to prevent. My parents were hastily and secretly married when my impending arrival was realized. Grandma learned of the marriage by reading it in the newspaper.

For all of this messy background, I had a very uncomplicated childhood. I remember feeling sorry for myself occasionally, but what child doesn't? I remember saying to a high school friend that, considering the crazy-mixed-up family life I'd had, I was a remarkably well-adjusted person. Perhaps I was, at that time, but I think that marriage and the responsibilities of a family were the catalysts of change. I was no longer responsible only for myself but for others. I had no emotional framework within which to react to this responsibility. After having three children in three years, I felt that I had to give up my religion in order to maintain my sanity. This was the turning point in my life. It's been downhill ever since. I started working in a bar and that was the beginning of my drinking problem and the marital problems that went along with the drinking.

Perhaps it was a curse, perhaps it was a prophecy, but my grandmother's repeated phrase did come true. I am just like my mother. She is fat; I am fat. She drinks too much; I am an alcoholic. We are both opinionated and argumentative. She was pregnant when she married and so was I. She has been married three times. I have only one husband, but there have been numerous emotional involvements with other men. My mother is a nervous person; so am I. My mother is oversensitive to criticism; so am I. I never really got to know my mother until I was fifteen, but we cannot get along together because we are too much alike.

Those two phrases echo in my mind as I think of listening experiences that shaped my life. "You're just like your mother" and "Nobody wants you."

I am sure that unless I am strong enough, I am doomed to continue suffering the guilt of my birth. I have spent the adult years of my life in a frenzied effort to prove my grandmother right. When I look at myself now, all I see is a person without worth. A person nobody should want. A person the world would never miss. Yet even as I write this, I know that through all of this pain and confusion, one person wants me and thinks me worthy. My husband has stayed with me when no other man would have. He has heard my inner screams for help. Maybe through this excruciating experience I can find the person within me that he thinks I am. Maybe I can find the person that I want to be.

THE MEANING OF THE STORIES

Hundreds of stories like these have come to us from students (the reader could probably add others). What they tell us is (1) that human growth is closely tied to human speech, and (2) that to study only how messages are sent is to limit one's capacity to understand communication.

How is one to understand that boy sitting in the old railway shack except in terms of the way he listened to himself and to the others in his life? Somewhere, somehow, he had learned to make extensive private commentary on his experience. Clearly, that realm of silent speech is important to him, as is his comment about the value of telling his story to others—a matter of no small consequence, as we will see in the pages ahead.

It would be equally futile to try to understand speech in the life of the alcoholic woman by fastening onto the mechanics of her overt speech, her voice, and her organization of ideas. Overt speech has had and will have a controlling impact in her life, but this is so because of the echoes that keep reverberating in her silent world—the thousands of things she has said to herself as a consequence of those words she has heard far too often: "You are just like your mother."

With this perspective, we need to discuss three things in this chapter: (1) the nature of listening and its functions; (2) the nature of speaking and its functions; and (3) how the two work together to produce communication and its functions.

THE SILENT SIDE OF COMMUNICATION

No feature of everyday existence is more misunderstood than is listening. Common sense tells us that listening is the receiving of information by ear. We shout to a small boy as he crosses the street, "Watch out!" The boy looks up, jumps appropriately out of the path of the automobile, and reinforces the age-old illusion: A speaker sends a message; the listener receives the message; communication is a game of verbal *give and take*. Even sophisticated scholars use language that helps fix the misconception. J. P. Hughes, in his *Science of Language,* for instance, says that speech is a system of symbols "by which thought is *conveyed* from one person to another."[1] And M. Pei in his *Story of Language* says that speech is "produced by the human voice, received by the human ear, and interpreted by the human brain."[2] However, a second reading of the latter statement suggests the weakness in the "conveyed and received" view. If a message is conveyed, it arrives in its own right. Why must it be interpreted?

Even the popular communication models of the day help sustain the illusion that the speaker *sends* and the listener *receives.*

Encode____Transmit____Channel____Receive____Decode

But such models contradict the overall conception of sending and receiving, too, for they entail *encoding* on the sending side and *decoding* on the receiving side, suggesting that the meaning, if received, is not necessarily the meaning sent. One may note that the act of assigning meaning to a "received" message is labeled *decoding,* not *re-encoding.*

What is listening, then? Listening, or decoding, is speech, a verbal response to what is heard. It is, to put it another way, silent speech. When it is defined that way, an important distinction between hearing and listening emerges. Hearing is the recording of sound waves; and this, plus the memory of those recordings, allows us humans and several species of birds to repeat words and songs. But listening is not recording. Listening is the speech excited by that recording. Therefore, while the fundamental requisites for listening are hearing and memory, it does not follow that if a person can hear and remember he or she will listen. If no verbal response is made to what is registered in the ears, there is no listening. And this happens. How often have you sat through a lecture to which you made no verbal response? You may even have repeated some of the words, or taken notes. But the speech had no meaning for you because you did not listen; you did not say to yourself, "Now let me see. She says, 'History is the ethical struggle of man.' I thought history was a story of the past. Well, not all of the past or we couldn't study it all in one lifetime. History is selective—the selection of some people. Maybe she means it is the selection induced by the struggle of humans to conquer

[1]J. P. Hughes, *The Science of Language* (New York: Random House, 1962), p. 6. ((Italics added)

[2]M. Pei, *The Story of Language* (Philadelphia: Lippincott, 1949), p. 100.

the evil in themselves." Now such an interpretation may not be what was meant by the speaker. And certainly a listening response is telegraphic, being developed into the communications of interpersonal statements, as in the preceding examples, only as needed. But the point is that listening is a talking back to the recording that one hears and remembers. Listening is the response to reception.

The question still remains, "How do we gain any degree of commonality of meaning, which of course we do, when we cannot transmit meaning?"[3] How do we understand each other if we cannot receive meaning from each other? The answer is that we all live in the same physical universe with its common stimuli for sense organs. And although the studies in perception—the way we see and hear—do show that our personal needs often distort, the fact remains that we are all earthlings and thus we do have some commonality of basic experience. We walk, we eat, we joy, we pain, on the same earth, under the same sky. "Doth not a Jew bleed?" asks Shylock in his plea to be understood as a member of the human race. Much experience is common to all of us.

In addition, any social group whose members try to communicate has a common linguistic structure that allows its users to point to things in the physical world, to smile or frown, to shake their heads. In short, there is enough of the commonness of earth experience and similarity of basic design in all languages (which scholars like Noam Chomsky and others are trying to discover and describe) for even a German and a Chinese on their first meeting to achieve some identity of meaning at the more primitive levels. The commonness of experience breeds commonness of meaning.

The key fact remains, however, that as far as meaning is concerned, each of us is encapsulated in his or her own experience. We do not, because we cannot, transmit the meanings of our experience. Thus listening is the silent speech aroused by the words recorded in our brain cells when we hear.

Nature's Provisions for the Listening Act

Nature has provided at least three basic conditions for listening as here described.

Shift of attention   Attention is not a continuous thing, but broken. Research by the psychologists Woodworth, Pillsbury, and others, who followed up William James's emphasis on consciousness and attention, has demonstrated that we can attend one source of stimuli for only

---

[3]See Jon Eisenson, J. Jeffrey Auer, and John V. Irwin, *The Psychology of Communication* (New York: Appleton-Century Crofts, 1963), p. 118.

a few seconds at a time. Apparently, attention is an on–off mechanism, which means that in our recording of a speaker we do not behave as the electrical tape recorder does, registering a continuous flow of the incoming words. Rather, we hear a discontinuous flow. So our hearing and recording of another is an alternating of recording and listening. We hear, we make comment, we hear, we make comment; thus nature's shift of attention provides the basic condition, the gaps needed for response.

Language and attention shifts   But these shifts of attention alone would not be consequential in designing the character of listening as described earlier. Animals also demonstrate the shifts of attention, but, without language, their shifts are a series of diversions. Not so with humans, for language, carrying the burden of past association, when excited generates new patterns of association. And so we are induced, as soon as we learn to use language, to hear the other's speech, and in the gap of attention to comment, at first aloud, as children do, and then gradually to ourselves. Lev Vygotsky calls what we are talking about "inner-speech," a "fluttering between word and thought," or truncated speech. It is similar to making a note to remind yourself of something. Some speech professors call it self-talk. Laymen call it listening.

In large measure the speaking–listening process may be explained in terms of social reinforcements received throughout a lifetime, beginning in infancy; the baby is loved and coddled as it exchanges nonsense sounds with its mother. As speech structure is learned, it continues to be conditioned by interaction with other people. Thus children of five or six will verbalize six times as much in the presence of others as when alone.[4] Because of the gaps in attention and the impulse to verbalize, triggered by the speech of others, we learn to listen—to make commentary on what we hear.

The linguistic causal system   Nature's third provision for inducing listening may be so deeply imbedded in the growth mysteries that we can never know the mechanism and how it works in full detail. But it is quite obvious from common experience that in the nature of humans is some kind of energy that emerges in the response, "What does that mean?" and this is also basic to an understanding of listening as described here. The mockingbird sings only in deathless repetition; we humans translate; we say something else. It is as if each utterance heard arouses the commentary, "As the echo of that thought fades I am inclined to say. . . . And having said that I am reminded of this. . . ." A string of associations is unraveled until we hear or remember something unrelated, or perhaps something we cannot or will not associate with the words just released.

[4]A. R. Luria and F. J. Yudovich, *Speech and the Development of Mental Processes* (London: Staples Press, 1959).

Self-Listening

Thus far we have discussed listening, in the main, as a verbal response to what is said by the other person. But we also hear, as we talk silently or aloud, our own speech, and so listening is also a response to ourselves. In truth, "self-understanding" depends on developing the power to *explore the meaning of our own speech.* Indeed, all that we call well-organized speech, and more important, what we call wisdom, is the product of hearing our speech as we speak, assessing—saying to ourselves, "And what does that mean?"—matching what we said with our purpose, and then proceeding.

We often call this the act of thinking, but it is profitable to conceive of the act as a self-conversation, an exchange between *called-up experiences and the commentary thereon.* Self-listening, like conversation with other people, is directed and determined by the feelings aroused in the exchange. And thus it is the feeling of freedom to call up thoughts, and the freedom to comment in new and often surprising ways on them, that shapes our growth.

Of course, there is no good self-listening that does not also involve good listening to others. The two cannot, in fact, be separated. But this is all in the abstract. Let us examine the meaning of what we say here by looking at several lives that illustrate it.

The Good Listener—to Both Self and Others

The life of an older student, among many that might have been chosen, illustrates the productive balance between listening to self and to others, a mixture that releases powers.

This man had lived, he said, on an Arkansas plantation the first fifteen years of his life. His recollection of those years was that it was like living in a prison. He was, in fact, a black youth trapped in a white society. But his parents, both very religious, taught him to accept the conditions of this life and to love all people, black or white. If he did that, they told him, he would get his reward in heaven.

So at that point the pressure to "listen" to the voices from outside the self was very strong. But silent speech, the voice of the self, was already stirring to restore the balance:

> I thought I loved everybody, but as I look back on it, I remember a mixture of hate and envy for the white man and his automobile and his big white house. And I hated my father's high laugh and loud talk in the presence of white men. When there were no white men around, he often sat silent and dejected or talked arrogantly to us children. I thought I loved my father, but actually I felt he was weak.

From age fifteen onward, the inner-outer mix of messages was vigorous, if often baffling:

> When I was fifteen some relatives from the North came to visit and one uncle said, "There are no signs. You can eat where you want." The wildest statements came, however, from my peer group in Arkansas and my imagination led me to believe that Michigan was a heaven on earth. I went to Lansing, where I spent three miserable and confused years. I couldn't find out what to believe. Some people said you couldn't get served in that restaurant. So I would go in and order a meal and they would serve it to me. Then they would tell me, but you can't get fitted to a suit of clothes in that store. So I saved my money and went in there and they sold me a suit of clothes. But I'd often walk into an employment office and ask for a job, and they would say there was no work. They'd tell me to come back later. I would wait and watch and the next white man would get a job. I knew where I stood in the South and couldn't find out where I stood in the North. The northern white didn't play it straight with me, and my northern black peer in most ways was worse than the country hicks from the cotton sticks. I got full of hate and frustration. I got into fights. I spent much of my time complaining to friends who felt like I did.
>
> Two of the most important things in my life happened the summer I was eighteen. I returned home and I found, for the first time, how deeply I loved my father and mother, my sisters and brothers. That was good, to have the love wash through me. And the other thing: I had an aunt who I had never liked. She talked too much and too self-righteously. She said something one day and I spoke mean back to her. Then I heard myself say something I had never before said to anyone. I apologized. "I shouldn't have said that. I'm sorry. Forgive me." That was the first time in my life I had ever apologized to anybody. I don't know why, but I know that was the beginning of the most important change in my life. Gradually over the next ten years, at first dimly, I began to see the hate in me, and to see that the hate was eating me up. I'm 34. Three years ago I told my wife, "I've hated all my life. I'm done with that."

The revelations of profound internal changes taking place in this student's life appear to show him moving toward introspection, toward the painful effort to conquer a seemingly unconquerable feeling. But his final statement shows him still aware of the messages from outside, and still willing to accept them as part of his reality:

> But I am still a frightened man. I am now a college senior. I am six-feet-five, weigh 220 pounds and quake inside with fear on examination days, like a boy. That's weakness. I don't want to be weak. I want to be a counselor of the young. You aren't ready to counsel until you are strong.

Here, then, is a man who has learned something about who he is, who has been able to stay tuned in to his silent messages even when they are frustrating, and who has made the invigorating discovery that he can sort out the worth of the messages he gets from the outside: He approaches the next stage in life with his eyes and ears open.

All sense of direction in life comes from remembrance of the imaginings of childhood.[5] In short, one can listen to oneself only if one *has* listened to oneself. And one can do nothing socially constructive with one's self-awareness if one does not understand others. Self and other listening are appropriately balanced when the person grows and is productive.[6]

Tuned to the Voice of Others: Turned Off from the Voice of Self

A very different story emerges in the case of the legendary Jimi Hendrix and Janis Joplin. Talented, charismatic, endlessly energetic, they both became singing stars—more than that, symbols of the "now" generation. There were not enough superlatives to describe the musical magic they were able to work.

Then, suddenly, they were dead—first Jimi (from too many sleeping pills); three weeks later Janis (from an overdose of drugs). Age for both—27. Why the passion, exhibited by both, for drugs? Why the readiness to quit, so soon, a life they seemed to love?

The answers cannot be known with confidence, but much of the evidence adds up to something like this: Jimi Hendrix and Janis Joplin were tuned to the voices from outside themselves so completely that they could not hear the inner messages that could have told them they were losing control of their lives. They were, from an early age, people who knew they had exceptional powers for entertainment. Someone noticed them. They got contracts. They got money. They made hit records. The voices from outside were strong and clear. Like moths drawn hypnotically toward the light, they were tuned to applause, recognition, reputation. And the more those messages flooded in, the more they gave. Toward the end they were performing with a transcendent kind of frenzy few people had ever seen.

Then they were dead. At least one interpreter of their early deaths saw in them an inability to accept the reality of change that faced them and to accept their limitations within that change. At the very least, we seem to see here two lives enslaved by the messages from outside and shut off from the messages from within. They could communicate with thousands. They could not make sense to themselves.

[5]Best seen from in-depth interviews with creative people.

[6]See Emil Ludwig, *Genius and Character* (New York: Harcourt, Brace and Co., 1927), for biographies illustrating this point.

Heard Who?

Intelligent speech depends on intelligent listening, and listening is always a verbal response to what we hear from ourselves as well as from our conversant. Whether we focus on what we ourselves said or what the other person said—or both—is of critical concern. We have said that the energy that propels speech, whether it be silent or aloud, is "and what does that mean?" This question, however, seldom stops with the word *mean* but is followed by "to him or her" and/or "to me." These differences in listening orientation are profound. Let us illustrate with an incident from one of our classes.

A young man, fulfilling a communication assignment, took a book to the student center, sat down near people in conversation, opened his book, and proceeded to listen to the conversation. Two girls were talking and he tuned in. One was doing most of the talking, and she was saying, according to his report,

> I don't know why I stay in school. I'm not getting anything out of my classes. I don't study. Last semester I almost dropped out. I don't know why I stay. I guess because I don't want to go home and I don't know where else to go. Nobody cares. Maybe I'll go away tomorrow. It really doesn't seem to matter. . . .

The young man said:

> My commentary to myself at this point was, "An awful lot of people just let their speech be a funnel for their bad feelings. Listening to the girl I began to feel uncomfortable. I wanted her to quit talking. I decided I was not going to spend my life pouring my complaints into the ears of other people."

In the class in which the preceding report was made a girl said,

> I didn't hear the same thing in that story. I wish I knew the girl you refer to, her name and where she lives. I want to listen to her. I am pained too by what she said. But she is crying for help and I have the urge to sit down and listen to her. Somehow I know it would be good.

The point is this: The boy was asking as he heard, "What is the meaning of this girl's speech *to me?*" The girl in the class was asking, "What is the meaning of that girl's speech *to her?*"

And if one follows through the implications of this story, one sees that each of us makes the twists and turns of our growth in accordance with the questions we ask ourselves as we listen. The possibilities are as follows:

1. What does his (her) comment mean to him (her)?
2. What does his (her) comment mean to me?
3. What does my comment mean to him (her)?
4. What does my comment mean to me?

If we ask only what his (her) and my comments mean to *me,* our silent speech tends to make us highly egocentric, with several possible turns. We may withdraw from people if the meanings are generally painful. If we find great pleasure in the meanings for ourselves, we can grow narcissistic as we study the mirror. If we are suspicious of others, we become hostile as we listen to them. The results of finding only meanings for oneself in what we hear are many and varied.

On the other hand, there are some people who are incomplete because they respond almost exclusively to speech with the question, "What is the meaning of this to him (her)?" While these listeners are always the more sensitive among us, they also include the conformists, the weak, the gullible, the purposeless, the celebrity lovers. Add to this second orientation a noncritical listening to one particular group and an occasional, "What is the meaning to me?" and you have the person with missionary zeal, driven to be the instrument of social change. Mix in hatred and you have those who like to do battle for great causes. As we increase self-hearing to meet the power of listening to others there comes a balance between listening to self and to others—a balance about which we know little—where the product is the evolution of the wise and calm person. Note the union of the two in Abraham Lincoln's description of his own evolvement.

In 1860, on a train near New Haven, Lincoln fell into conversation with a Rev. J. P. Gulliver of Norwich, Connecticut, who asked him how he got his talent for "putting things." Lincoln's reply is reported as follows:

> Well, as to education, the newspapers are correct—I never went to school more than six months in my life. But, as you say, this must be a product of culture in some form. I have been putting the question you ask me to myself while you have been talking. I say this, that among my earliest recollections, I remember how, when a mere child, I used to get irritated when anybody talked to me in a way I could not understand. I don't think I ever got angry at anything else in my life. But that always disturbed my temper and has ever since. I can remember going to my little bedroom, after hearing the neighbors talk of an evening with my father and spending no small part of the night walking up and down, trying to make out what was the exact meaning of some of their, to me, dark sayings. I could not sleep, though I often tried to, when I got on such a hunt after an idea, until I had repeated it over and over, until I had put it in language plain enough, as I thought, for any boy I knew to comprehend. This was a kind of passion with hand-

ling a thought, till I had bounded it north, and bounded it south, and bounded it east, and bounded it west. Perhaps that accounts for the characteristic you observe in my speeches, though I had not put the two things together before.[7]

Bounding a thought on all sides is saying the thought for oneself in ways that are meaningful to all concerned.[8]

The Functions of Listening

What, then, are the contributions of the listening act to the communication process? Essentially, listening serves two purposes: (1) to establish empathy and (2) to acquire information. Each is important, though they operate together and have little meaning independently. We are aware that other writers describe listening functions more exclusively as listening for information. We feel, however, that the functions of empathy and information acquisition work together in the priority given here.

Empathy Empathy is the act of imagining the universe of thoughts and feelings out of which a statement emerges. In short, it is (1) the ability to perceive from the standpoint of the speaker (2) with appreciation. Without appreciation, good listening can be exploitive. Listening with appreciation is probably the most sophisticated and the most imaginative act a person performs. The effect is something like the reperception of instant replay on television, *experienced* (as it usually is) *from a different camera position.* One senses that one sees the same action and interaction that one just experienced, and yet it is different, seen as it is from a second cameraman's "point of view." Empathy thus provides the perspective of two or more observations of an interaction. In the end, it is this that provides the data necessary to internalize the whole of a communication exchange. Thus empathy is the basic ingredient of what we call understanding.

The way language permits us to empathize and to get meaning is

[7]From *New York Independent*, September 1, 1864.

[8]The question quite naturally arises, "But what is the difference between listening and thought?" The answer we offer is this: listening is verbal thought, but not all thought, for the human thinks in nonverbal symbol systems too. People count, sing, dance, paint, sculpt, make homes, public buildings, and cities. And then there is body English—the skills of the athlete, the automobile driver, the mechanic. Thinking goes on in many language systems. But the native tongue, which Pavlov significantly called the secondary signal system, is the one kind that is self-reflective. By the association of person with person and the language symbols that attend these human relationships each of us has learned to use language as a mirror of others and of ourselves. Thus while verbal language is not the only symbol system, and therefore is not the only kind of thought, it is the most important one to personal evolvement and, thus, the most important of all symbol systems.

the burden of the next chapter. Here it is perhaps enough to note that understanding springs from the ability to speak for two people at once. As we become the other, as well as the self, three things happen: Relationships with the other improve; understandings about others increase, and remarkably, self-understanding, the sense of identity, increases. In recognizing how empathy works we learn why we have to lose ourselves to find ourselves. Empathy is, thus, the central skill in growth. In large measure this book is designed to increase the perspectives achieved by empathic response.

Acquiring information   The second function of listening is to recognize and acquire information. As we hear words and later state and restate them in different words, we are trying to isolate the significant points. The Lincoln story reveals the boy of his past who paced the floor trying to probe the dark sayings of older people, searching for the basic information in their interaction. In order to know what they said he had to remember how they spoke, too. One must remember the stammerings, the tonal quality of a critical word, the expression of the face, the tension of the body, a constellation of detail discussed in the chapter on the nonverbal code. Lifting out the important information is the ultimate test of our listening, for this, as Lincoln suggests, is the way we develop our thinking powers. Nobody can reach beyond his or her ability to select a perspective in listening and to store the pertinent detail accurately. Even if we listen just to enrich our relationship with another, it is what we listen to that makes the difference.

Yet we shall not analyze the process of gaining and storing information as our central focus because it is our view, as we said in Chapter 1, that the dynamics of information acquisition rest in the factors that shape our relationships. One perceives, accurately or inaccurately, what one must in order to satisfy one's needs. Thus whatever bears on relationship is central to understanding the role of listening. But while we do not study the acquisition and storage of information in a book concerned with the dynamics of interpersonal communication, we should recognize the importance of acquiring information, for this is usually if not always the ultimate purpose of listening.

The contributions of listening to the communication act are empathy and the acquisition of information.

THE NOISY SIDE OF COMMUNICATION

Communication takes place between people—as well as within them. It thus requires overt speech as well as silent listening. And while no one can speak more intelligently than he or she can listen, overt talk is different from silent talk and has functions that the latter cannot serve.

The Functions of Speech

First, it is through talk that we may be transparent to each other. "A penny for your thoughts" says, "I know something about you as a consequence of your nonverbal behavior. I sense that you are experiencing thought that is deeply significant to you. Tell me about it." Speech is the window that reveals the person within. Through speech we can be transparent to one another. This is its first function.

Second, speech permits us to test the accuracy and reasonableness of our silent, and more telegraphic, speech. Only as we openly say what we think can we find out if we believe what we think.

Thus overt speech is a test of covert speech. The therapy session is probably our most dramatic example. But business conferences, family discussions, and the pervasive bull session, or "rap" session, to mention a few speech situations, all illustrate the testing function of speech. Most of the decisions and plans of action in this world are hammered out in the speech exchange.

As egocentric individuals, we are likely to see group decision making as a personal sacrifice of truth, not a test of truth, especially if we are emotionally involved. But group judgments in distinguishing small differences in objective things like weights or sizes of objects tend to be more accurate than individual judgments. Although there is no objective measure of what is true socially and morally, this very fact makes the decision of the group, arrived at through talk, the only socially acceptable position. So talk is a test of truth—as well as the way we may reveal ourselves to each other.

Common Resistance
to Verbalizing Our Listening

In spite of, or perhaps because of, the values of overt speech, many college students resist the translation of experience into verbal terms, at least for the ears of others. Instructors know well the vacant look and passive attitude of a class the moment the lights are turned on after an emotionally packed film. An attempt is made to arouse the class to discussion. "Why do we have to talk about it?" one will ask, and the rest will join him or her. They are saying that there is a world beyond words that words profane.

We can in part appreciate this view. Much of our most delightful experience is like the whisper of the wind or the tingling sensation of music surging gently over us. If the very words just written are a poor translation of some experience that was deeply moving to you, you can only resent us. Who wants to hear, "Now ain't that pretty" upon first viewing the Grand Canyon? Bad commentary on a peak experience is an abomination. Better depend on imagery and sensations, and just say to onself, "I'll do this again." But we will try to win the argument by saying that at least you have to listen this much; that is, verbalize to yourself, "I'll do that again." Long-term memory is verbal.

Humans simply cannot build a unified and powerful life without words. Words must be found for an experience or the experience soon dies within us, as does the very process of giving our life meaning. We build into our lives a quality equal to the words that form the commentary on experience. That is to say, all experience is best when turned to the verbal, at least to the self.

Consider the words of Gibran on that miserable word *work:*

> Often have I heard you say, as if speaking in sleep, "He who works in marble, and finds the shape of his own soul in stone is nobler than he who ploughs the soil ... I say, not in sleep but in the overwakefulness of noontide, that the wind speaks not more sweetly to the giant oaks than to the least of all the blades of grass; And he alone is great who turns the voice of the wind into a song made sweeter by his own loving ..."[9]

To make no commentary—at least to self—is to be empty. In the end, escape from comment to others is an escape from the opportunity to make ourselves available to ourselves and others, and to test our listening.

In reflecting on the analysis of these pages one will note that the line between the functions of overt speech and silent speech is as faded as the hour between day and night. But the fact remains that the difference is real. The person who listens and will not talk is an enigma and seldom finds his or her greatest powers. And the person who talks and will not listen seldom makes sense. It takes both silent and overt speech in union to produce the effective communicator.

COMMUNICATION: THE INTERACTIVE RESULTS
OF LISTENING AND SPEAKING

The bulk of writing in humanistic psychology, psychotherapy, religion, and sociology in our times has led us, and many others, to place communication at the center of human concerns. The role of communi-

---

[9]Kahlil Gibran, *The Prophet* (New York: Alfred A. Knopf, 1968), p. 27.

cation is seen for what it is if we note the matching functions of speech and listening. The two together produce our capacity to know ourselves and to think through our problems, as suggested in Figure 3-1.

Open talk and empathic listening help establish mutually trusting relationships. As we will see, out of such talk and listening a person grows to understand and to accept his or her identity. The testing function of honest speech is matched with the urge of the listener to discover the pertinent information. Thus thought in both speaking and listening remains fluid and subject to change. These are the functions of communication—to enhance a sense of identity and to maintain an evolving flow of creative thought. Of course we can conceal and fail to test; we can reject the imaginative use of the ears of others, and even our own. Many people are confused about themselves and cannot think clearly.

Communication Functions:
(1) To Produce Identity in Relationships

Many of us would like to know our identity more clearly. By *identity,* as defined in the preceding chapter, we refer to the need to feel some sense of direction in our lives. And this is the primary function of the relationships that evolve out of our speaking and listening.

How does an open and empathic relationship between people carve out their identity? Each person is caught behind his or her own eyes, in his or her own bag of skin, looking out at others. By ourselves we cannot see and hear and know ourselves, as we learned in Chapter 2. Even that loner, Thoreau, intimated his dependence on others for capturing a concept of himself, saying, "It is as hard to see oneself as to look backwards without turning around."

We have stressed the role of listening to others in achieving identity. What about the role of speaking? The importance of the act of speaking

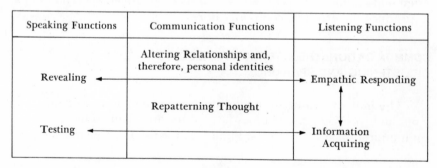

Speaking Functions	Communication Functions	Listening Functions
Revealing ◄—	Altering Relationships and, therefore, personal identities	—► Empathic Responding
Testing ◄—	Repatterning Thought	—► Information Acquiring

FIGURE 3-1

may best be seen by looking at the strange world of the psychotic child, who listens but does not speak. One guess is that such a child develops this self-imposed mutism because in early efforts to interact with others he or she has been traumatically frustrated (by an abusive or insensitive parent, perhaps). Perhaps the child discovers that crying can bring swift and unexpected punishment, so he or she gradually ceases to cry or use the voice—and in the process learns not to speak. Indeed, the child may cut off all expressive communication, verbal and nonverbal. But he or she continues to listen, and that listening, without the balancing corrections of speech, may lead him or her into a world of fantasy.

A report by Dr. Richard D'Ambrosio describing his efforts to teach a 12-year-old girl to talk gives a vivid picture of what it means to speak.[10] Wan, weak, and without any sense of direction, the girl had learned to dress and eat. She could be led from place to place, but she did not initiate any behavior except to cry silently on occasion, unpredictably, and usually at night when alone. She gave no sign of being aware of the world of things or people around her.

In their weekly meetings the therapist spoke kindly and intimately about the flowers and toys they both could see in the immediate surroundings, working for hours to prove that he could share and be trusted. Her first response, an isolated one, came one day as they were walking together. A group of hilarious children on roller skates came rushing upon them and Laura threw her arms around the doctor in terror.

Over the subsequent months he became aware that she was gradually and occasionally responding internally to his talk. An idea occurred to him. He built a house of blocks as he talked about it and its decorations and the people who would live there. During one session, he fumbled in trying to arrange the furniture, she reached out and arranged some pieces, then retreated to complete passiveness again for weeks.

Knowing the story of her life, the doctor placed a father and a mother and a baby in the house and developed a quarrel between the parents that ended in a vicious beating of the child. As the story developed, he sensed the girl's intense watching and heavy breathing. When he reached the climax, in which the parents turned on the crying baby, she screamed "No! No! No!" and grasped the parent dolls, beat them furiously, and tore the house apart. At length she fell into convulsive sobbing as the therapist comforted her. All this pent-up terror, hostility, and revulsion was understood. This child had literally been terrorized by drunken and psychotic parents.

[10]"No Language But a Cry," *Good Housekeeping*, August 1970, 64.

For a week Laura retreated again to silence and despair. But, and here is the significant perception for us, as she began to talk (for the first time in her life) to the doctor in their next session she grew confused and lost orientation. She could not remember whether she had ever been in the room before—though they had been meeting there weekly for years.

What this means is not easy to pin down, but our hunch would be that her world of awareness was so shocked by overt speech that her perceptions became strange and unreal to her. Her previous world had been touched and stirred by the words of others but never tested in the crucible of her own spoken language.

We who have had our mouths open most of our waking hours probably can understand this by alerting ourselves to the way we react upon coming out of a good novel in which we have been buried for half a day. As we leave the book and take up life at the dinner table we may feel like strangers to the people beside us. So Laura may have felt, most shockingly, as for the first time she entered the world where she heard her own voice.

We have been discussing the functions of speech and listening in forming the way we feel and relate to ourselves and others. And we have been saying that the critical thing for each person is this, that in these relationships one finds one's identity. Speech and listening together, two-way communication, produce relationship. Out of our relationships emerges our identity—limited only by our ability to make sense to ourselves.

Communication Functions:
(2) To Repattern Thought from New Information

Just as the physical person is something in process, so the cognitive person is something in process. Children think and speak as children. As they pass through the stages of life, from the "mewling and puking" infant to the old one whose very senses fade, their ways of thinking also change gradually. In these changing patterns it is basically the self-perceptions and relationships with others that produce new forms. When people are open and accepting with each other, they test what they think against each other's responses and thus produce self-changing awareness. As they change in their perceptions of themselves, they see and hear new and different things. The creative repatterning of the virile mind is the product of eyes and ears that remain open, seeing and hearing as freshly as the child does.

Until recent years the educational system has operated on the assumption that its province is the dispensing of information and the training of rational processes, as if the very emphasis on intellectual processes would free the learner's thought from wants, feelings, authority struggles, self, and other perceptions. But that is not the way it works. We all think as our ego needs direct us to think. We are as intelligent as the stuff that builds our relationships will let us be. Thus we are as intelligent as our listening and speaking are responsive to the new information that our constantly changing environment provides.

CONCLUSION

The essence of the chapter is this: We speak, we hear, we listen. Listening is silent telegraphic speech. Interactive *open* speech and *empathic* listening together produce relationships that allow an exchange of accurate information, the results of which are a clearer identity and more creative thought for the participants.

INSTRUMENT 3-1

WHO AM I?

Note: Do not read through this instrument before you begin. Go step by step.

A

Following are 20 "I am ____" statements. Complete each one with *the first thing* that comes to mind. It may be a word or several words.

1. I am _____.

2. I am _____.

3. I am _____.

4. I am _____.

5. I am _____.

6. I am _____.

7. I am _____.

8. I am _____.

9. I am _____.

10. I am _____.

11. I am _____.

12. I am _____.

13. I am _____.

14. I am _____.

15. I am _____.

16. I am _____.

17. I am _____.

18. I am _____.

19. I am _____.

20. I am _____.

B

Now count the number of classifications or roles identified, such as *I am a woman, a student, a daughter,* and place the sum here:_____.

C

Then count the self-descriptive words or phrases, such as *I am attractive, pleasant, worried, somewhat tall,* and place the sum here:_____.
Now divide each number by 20.

Place the B (group identity) percentage here:_____.

Place the C (individual identity) percentage here:_____.
What do you want to say about yourself?

EXERCISES

1. This exercise tailgates Instrument 3-1. Choose a partner who also has completed Instrument 3-1.
    A. Exchange the completed "I am_____" statements.
    B. Tell the other person what you learned about his or her self perceptions that you did not know before.
    C. Also tell him or her which of those self-perceptions stand out clearly to you.

    D.   Also tell the other person your perceptions of him or her.

    E.   Now reverse roles so that the other person responds to your "I am
_____" statements.

2. Try the exercise on simultaneous feedback. On television you may have seen a person who can speak in unison with another person no matter what the other person says. This involves an uncanny ability to anticipate the speech of another.

    Give a slow, short speech to the class instructing everybody to silently say the same thing with you as you go. Give a short listening test to the class over the material to see how much they remember and to test their understanding of the speech. Discuss the results with the class.

    How does this demonstrate that listening is not passive reception but active response?

    How does it demonstrate the shift of attention?

3. Tell the class a fascinating story. Have it understood that a colleague will ring a bell without notice and you will stop talking. Everybody is to write down what he or she was thinking just as the bell sounded. Compare the responses.

    What conclusion does the data support?

4. Keep a journal of your responses (a) to yourself and (b) to what other people say that impresses you. Write in the journal three times a week.

    Write the thing you are going to respond to, then respond. As the weeks pass, note that gradually you learn not only to respond but also to respond to your response and then to respond to that response. On a good day there is no end except in exhaustion.

    This is the essence of the process of creative thought.

    What conclusion does it support?

5. This is a zero-feedback exercise. Have a person go to the blackboard and draw a geometric figure as you describe it. Pass out the figure to the class. Without any questions from the person at the board, tell him or her what to draw, sentence by sentence. Compare the figure on the board with the one the students have at their seats.

6. Go to the back of the room or get behind a screen (the latter is better) and give a short speech to the class. Come before the class and tell them the difference between talking "behind their backs" and talking to them face to face.

7. Study for an hour with earplugs in your ears. Then study for an hour without them. Report to the class the difference in your comprehension and productivity.

8. Arrange to have a person in the class be interviewed twice for a position, say, as a high school teacher. He or she will be interviewed by two superintendents. One is secretly told to feel superior to the candidate and to act accordingly. The other "superintendent" is told to feel that the candidate is a very superior person and to act respectful.

9. Go as long as you can without talking or listening to anybody. Note your feelings and thoughts. Report the experience to the class.

10. Go away for twenty-four hours to a place where you do not speak to anybody. Report to the class what happened to you internally.

11. If it is available, take and have scored the Everett Shostrom Personality Orientation Inventory. One of the most important items is the support

index. It tells how much you are "inner" and "other" directed, relatively how much you listen to yourself and to others.

Report to the class or write a paper on your interpretations of the score.

12. Tell about a person you know who had to have approval from others so much that he or she became confused and no longer recognized his or her own private needs.

    What conclusions do you draw from this that relate to the chapter? State these conclusions.

13. Tell about a person you know who is so self-absorbed that he or she does not listen to others. Discuss this person's personality and its impact on you.

    What conclusions do you draw from this that relate to the chapter? State these conclusions.

14. All of us who have prepared speeches carefully, especially in our early training, have been shocked by the difference between the prepared speech and the one given, even if the prepared speech was memorized.

    a. Prepare a speech carefully, recording it at least once.
    b. Now give the speech to the class, recording it.
    c. Compare the two recordings and report the difference to the class.
    d. What conclusions do you draw from this experiment?

15. For twenty minutes talk to a person in the class whom you have not previously known—on any subject.

    Then, either by guess or actual data that came out, let each of you fill out the following form on the other person:

    a. His(her) age_____.

    b. He(she) is one of_____children.

    c. He(she) is_____in the order of siblings.

    d. He(she) comes from a community of_____(number of people).

    e. He(she) is closer to his(her) father, mother. (circle one)

    f. His(her) father had_____years of education.

    g. His(her) mother_____years of education.

    h. His(her) political sympathies lie with the_____party.

    i. He(she) is a liberal, conservative, reactionary in social issues. (circle one)

    j. He(she) is

	1	2	3	4	5	6	7
	relaxed						tense

    in social situations. (circle one number)

    k. He(she) is usually

	1	2	3	4	5	6	7
	moody						cheerful

    l. He(she) is emotionally

	1	2	3	4	5	6	7
	stable						unstable

m. He(she) is athletically	1	2	3	4	5	6	7
	inclined					not inclined	

n. He(she) is interested in:

Athletics	1	2	3	4	5	6	7
	very much					not much	

Art	1	2	3	4	5	6	7
	very much					not much	

Music	1	2	3	4	5	6	7
	very much					not much	

Drama	1	2	3	4	5	6	7
	very much					not much	

Philosophy	1	2	3	4	5	6	7
	very much					not much	

Religion	1	2	3	4	5	6	7
	very much					not much	

Travel	1	2	3	4	5	6	7
	very much					not much	

People	1	2	3	4	5	6	7
	very much					not much	

Our conversation	1	2	3	4	5	6	7
	very much					not much	

Having filled out this form, now have the other person correct it. The fewer the corrections, the more perceptive a listener you are.

From your own correction of the other person's awareness of you, what do you learn? How revealing are you? How hard are you to read?

Write a short paper on what you have learned or, if you are keeping one, make an entry in your journal.

4

Feelings, Energy, and Values in Process

The central concern of the field of communication . . . is to understand what is fundamental to all acts of communication.

C. David Mortensen*

An odd feeling about the nature of social connectedness is gained by going alone to a large city for the first time. One is totally disoriented by both the locale and the buzz of activity. Cars flow or spurt in all directions and planes thunder in and out overhead. People, with places to go and apparent reasons for going there, criss-cross each other in the airports, hotels, and streets. Nobody seems to be related to anybody, yet it is clear that some relationship of one to another, and of one to all, is at work.

High up in a hotel room minutes later one may hear and feel the rumble of the city that drones on relentlessly all day and all through the night. A city is a living, interactive system of people, a system with immense energy. This chapter is concerned with the basic sources of life in the communication flow within a person, between people, in the activity of a city.

The basic sources of life in communication are (1) feelings, (2) the sheer energy to do, and (3) the values of human life. The first two, feelings and energy, are the very wellsprings of our behavior.

*C. David Mortensen, *Communication, the Study of Human Interaction* (New York: McGraw-Hill Book Company, 1972), p. 22. By permission.

FEELINGS

Animals are sensory creatures, tasting, smelling, seeing, hearing. We, *homo sapiens,* are sensory creatures *with language,* so that our feelings, as indicated in the first chapter, are the ways we describe, for ourselves and others, the way we are responding to and perceiving the meaning of our sensations. The quality of our relationships with ourselves and others is, then in effect a result of our happiness, and the reverse is also true. In a sense we are all hedonists, pleasure seekers, expending energy from the time we wake until again we fall asleep, searching for ways to feel good or to escape from feeling bad, or sometimes giving up and wallowing in our bad feelings.

/Cognitive creatures (that is, language creatures) that we are, we tend to develop a kind of philosophy out of the memory of all our feelings. In varying degrees and hues, each of us sees life and people as essentially good and benign or as dangerous and exploitive/ Some of the widely used personality tests measure one's perceptions of human nature, the way one feels about the human race. The trust instrument at the end of Chapter 1 is designed to test these perceptions. One young woman in our class recently showed a thirty-five-point difference between her evaluation of the human race and the way she thought it ought to be. It is little wonder that in Instrument 4-2 she revealed that she paid little attention to others when they spoke and revealed little personal information to others. To all appearances she interacts pleasantly and easily with others. In fact, however, as she revealed in a journal, she has devised a way of encapsulating herself. At the least threat of an unpleasant relationship with another person, say a customer in a bank where she is a teller, she tunes out the other person.

The guiding force at the bottom of all the forces that bear on our interaction is our feelings. The ancient Greeks classified people on a continuum stretching from sanguine to melancholy, and attributed bad feelings to the flow of liver bile. There may be something to that. Certainly some of us are basically more optimistic, hopeful, and even trusting than others.

So primary is the power of our feelings in determining what we do, and indeed what we value in doing, that we have set aside a chapter simply for the exploration of what we know about emotions. But in this chapter, designed to discuss the dynamic process of communication, it is enough to grasp the centrality of feelings in communication and how they work in our interactions with self and others. Again using the grid cited in Chapter 1, we want to emphasize the dividing line between the feelings that bond one person to another and those that cause one to

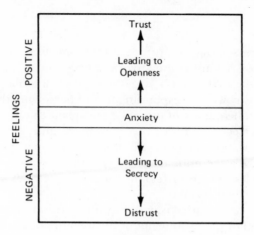

FIGURE 4-1

dominate another or to withdraw. Anxiety, a kind of general uneasy and unsure state, divides attraction to self and others from distrust of ourselves and others (see Figure 4-1).

Let it be clear that we are describing trust and distrust not as kinds of feelings but as the product thereof. When you feel comfortable with yourself and your conversant, you tend to reveal information about yourself. That is trust, and trust breeds trust. The converse is also true—when you feel uncomfortable with a person you guard what you say and the other person begins to guard himself or herself and to distrust you.

ENERGY

Electrical energy is the flow of electrons in a wire. It may culminate in heat, as in a toaster, or mechanical power, as in a motor. Human energy is an electrochemical state of the body. It may culminate in thought (the gathering and ordering of information) or in the mechanical processes of talking, walking, writing—in short, doing.

In the broadest sense, any kind of doing is a communication act, for it has a meaning for both the doer and the observer. Chopping down a tree, for instance, involves an intention, and the observed act may excite a variety of responses. But we will confine our definition of communicative energy to the acts of talking, the interaction of speaking and listening. Of course, this includes silent talk, that is, thinking.[1]

---

[1]We are not suggesting that verbal thinking is the only kind of thinking. Humans think in all their symbol systems—mathematics, music, painting, etc.

The first and basic factor that determines the flow of energy is a person's physical state of being. Rest and health are requisites. Among people who are healthy and rested there is an immense difference in the flow of energy, however. Figure 4-2 shows the continuum of energy from low to high, which we observe in any person as he or she interacts with another person. A second factor about the flow of energy that we must consider is what we may call *commitment*. Commitment is the focus of energy, the stick-to-it-iveness that varies so much from one person to another. Thomas Edison is said to have tried some 2200 different filaments before he came upon tungsten, which glows brilliantly for months before it burns out. Many of the filaments he tried would not glow at all; some flashed and were gone. How many of us would have tried 25 filaments, or even 200, and upon failing with these have become convinced that it was all a crazy idea in the first place? Single-purpose attention and focus is probably a *function* of unwavering, confident self-esteem. Lewis Terman, in his class study of the lives of 1000 geniuses (referred to earlier) compared the 150 most successful with the 150 least successful as they were at age 35. We find it significant that two of the three differences between the most successful and least successful were in the capacity to *conceive a life plan* and *stick to it*. Commitment is, as we see it, a function of confidence—high self-esteem—and confidence was the third difference Terman found.

Energy → Learning → Intelligent Action

Let us look at this flow of energy from the growth or learning perspective. How do people learn? Actually, we know little about the

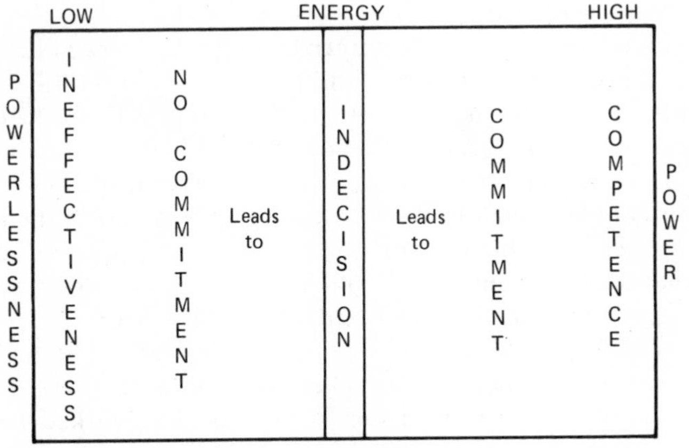

LOW			ENERGY			HIGH	
POWERLESSNESS	INEFFECTIVENESS	NO COMMITMENT	Leads to	INDECISION	Leads to	COMMITMENT	COMPETENCE	POWER

FIGURE 4-2

processes that go on inside a person. But it is not hard to understand what goes on in behavior. *People learn to do what they try to do.* If you want to listen better, listen and take a listening test. You will usually get a higher score on the second attempt. You try, note when you succeed or fail, pay attention appropriately when you try again. This applies to every skill.

With the coming of the intelligence tests early in this century we may have begun to overemphasize natural talent in achievement. The authors do not underestimate the significance of intelligence. Dull people are seldom accomplishers. But the world's greatest accomplishments do not correspond at all with intelligence levels higher than just above average.[2] Indeed, there is a much greater correspondence between *wanting* and *doing.* An old adage says that significant achievement is "one percent inspiration and ninety-nine percent perspiration." Down through the centuries keen observers of the process of invention have noted two things: that discovery is usually a happy accident, but also that the happy accident occurs for the prepared mind. By the "prepared mind" they mean that the person sticks to the task of observing and studying whatever will sharpen his or her powers of observation. George Hegel's philosophical system was so broad and all-encompassing that almost all historical, economic, political, sociological, and philosophical thinking since his time (the early 1800s) has in some way been related to his thought. Yet notes on his college record indicate that his philosophy professors considered him deficient in the capacity for philosophical thought. Albert Einstein was dismissed from the *Gymnasium* as an ineffective and troublesome student. He failed the entrance examinations the first time he tried to get into the technical college in Switzerland. He was the only person in his graduating class who was not assigned a position in the school. For seven years he was employed in a patent office. In his spare time, and long into the night, he worked first on the paper that earned him a doctorate and then on papers on the nature of light and the special theory of relativity that led him to world recognition. These stories may strongly suggest that teachers do not know their best students, and sometimes this is true, for it is very difficult to evaluate the strength of *want* and *tenacity.* That can be known only in the living of a life. But given the blessing of a good brain and good health, it is *wanting* that leads to competence and its result, *impact,* more than any other thing. Our faulty view of the dynamics at work comes from attributing a brilliant accomplishment too exclusively to native talent. What the person produced, we conclude, was brilliant; therefore he or she was basically brilliant. The fact is, that person worked hard and

[2]Ellis Paul Torrance, *Gifted Children in the Classroom* (New York: Macmillan, 1965).

became brilliant. Niels Bohr, a Danish physicist, conceived the design of atomic structure, thus advancing the work of Einstein. But Bohr was slow and had to work for years before he could comprehend Einstein's theory of relativity.

What we are focusing on is the *power of energized interaction* with the self and others as a basic factor in the growth of people or groups of people.

INFORMATION: THE KEY TO POWER

It is common in sociological history to state that power was once a result of position and rank. Then, with the development of trade and agriculture, money and property became the sources of power. Probably most people today would think of wealth as the source of power. But among social scientists there is a growing view that it is the *information of interaction* that is the key to power.[3] Those who were born to royalty in completely authoritarian societies were the only ones who had the information of power, all based on one piece of information that they were happy to share: "The blood in our veins is royal." With the transfer of ownership into the hands of nonroyalty, power spread. But the power was not in the money. It was in the information that let people know how to get money and property. *It is the degree of secrecy that surrounds information that determines the distribution of power.*

As the world has become more democratic, information has spread, though unevenly, among more people. An informed electorate, we say, is necessary in order that democracy may work. This view holds that the basis of power is information. Power, then, is essentially what you know. And what you know is interlocked with whom you know. Power is the information that flows through the central communication network of a family or a business or any group or institution. Those who are privileged to know the most important information hold power.

Information is the material of power, and power is the result of expended energy.

BEHAVIOR

What the mosaic shows so far is diagramed in Figure 4-3. Translated into the simplest terms, its message might be as follows: If you are willing to put your energy into doing something, you can become skilled at it

---

[3] R. B. Ritchie and Paul Thompson, *Organization and People* (New York: West Publishing Company, 1976), conversation with Warren Bennis, pp. 335–349.

(and, in the process, raise your self-esteem), through the information you receive from others. But whether others are willing to give you the information will depend on the relationship between you and them, and that will depend on whether their feelings toward you are positive (in which case information will flow freely) or negative (in which case information will be distorted or closed off). If information flows freely and clearly, the "power to do" will come to you. And as you recognize this growing competence, you will gain the courage to find your destiny.

The Chemistry of Behavior

Behavior is what a person does. The two basic dynamics of behavior (the way we express ourselves and the way we communicate) are the range of our feelings that bond people or turn them against each other and the degree to which they express their feelings in interaction with others. Our behavioral expression is, thus, shaped by whom we relate to and how, which will determine what we do with what we know.

The basic information about the behavioral grid was presented in Chapter 1. That chapter was concerned only with the way the two dynamics (feelings and energy) bear on human relationship; *this chapter is concerned with the way these two variables bear on any task.* The way positive

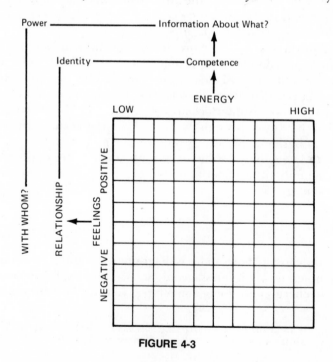

FIGURE 4-3

feelings work with low and high energy was explained on page 9. The way distressing feelings work with low and high energy is the same. What we have done here that adds to the explanation in Chapter 1 is to explain more fully the character of both feelings and energy, showing how feelings are rooted in sensation, expressed in words reflecting relationship, and how power is rooted in energy, expressed in information.

H. S. Lasswell, a communication theorist, called attention to these important variables in the simple statement, "Who said what, in what channel, to whom and with what effect?" Thus he pointed out that *who* speaks to *whom* is significant and that what is said makes a difference. The dynamics that create the scenario, we are saying, are the feelings that govern *who* speaks *to whom* and *how,* together with the concentration of energy that marshals the information that has impact.

Application: The Jimmy Carter Case

We now have a behavioral grid, with its parts identified and its usefulness described. What we need is a public figure most readers of

Jimmy Carter Time Magazine Cover: Copyright © 1976 by James Wyeth; and TIME, The Weekly Newsmagazine, © Time, Inc.

this book are likely to know about, a person we can use as a part-by-part example of how behavior can be illuminated through the grid. The number of individuals whose ongoing behavior can be observed by most people is very limited. We have decided that President Carter will provide a useful example. We are aware that some readers are not tuned to politics and may not be interested in the fine points of Presidential strategy. But we hope that they will focus on Jimmy Carter for a moment for the sake of understanding communication and, indeed, themselves.

Warning   As we move through an analysis of Mr. Carter with you, we will be attempting to discriminate between the way he works and the way other public figures work. Our statements are not presented as facts. They are the subjective inferences of two people trying to understand a third person. And we hope that watching us risk such guesses will encourage you to risk your own.

"Jimmy what?"   As of this writing, Mr. Carter has been generally seen as a man of contradictions. He talks in terms of love, of serving the people whom he loves because they are basically "good and decent" under God. Some people say, "It is good that the country now has a president with human feelings—the man is a person with a sense of the significance of the way we feel and relate to each other." Others say, "That's not true. He's a con artist or a Sunday School teacher. You can't run a nation with love. The business of a President is to care for the economy, to get an energy program, to stabilize our foreign relationships. He's not clear on issues or he is shifty; maybe both."

In addressing the issues, Mr. Carter says that inflation must be checked, the economy stimulated, the bureaucracy in Washington streamlined, the energy problem solved. And he says with a smile to those in Congress who show signs of opposing him, "I'll go to the people, your constituents—and I have more ready access to them than you do." In response, some people say, "The man's potentially dangerous. He talks love and doesn't give a damn about people. Look at his cabinet, not much in the way of minority representation, either blacks or women. Noble promises, but the choice of the same tired people who have been around Washington a long time." Others respond, "The man is going to be efficient. After all, he's been an engineer, a farmer, and a businessman. He is basically a conservative man, and his 'populist' talk is just designed to get the vote of the poor man."

Four years ago this man was not known to many of us. He has had no previous experience in Washington. Culturally, he springs from the Old South, and his family has only recently become affluent. At this hour his *behavior* is an enigma.

The criticism may spring from Mr. Carter's inability to communi-

Leadership Styles

1	2
Developer–Missionary	Executive–Compromiser
Mixing good feelings for people with low energy for output, he, in trust, arouses and develops good relationships with people.	Mixing good feelings for people with highly energized output, he, in turn, arouses and exercises imaginative cooperative behavior.
4	3
Bureaucrat–Deserter	Benevolent–Autocrat
Mixing negative feelings for people with low energy for output, he, in low trust, withdraws from the struggle.	Mixing negative feelings with highly energized output, he, with low trust, arouses and exercises competitive power to get the job done.

FIGURE 4-4

cate a coherent leadership style composed, as it must be, of a set of relationships with people and an expenditure of energy focused on given tasks. However, the criticism may also spring from the fact that people cannot really imagine the style of a man who says, "Let us, in love, bind up our wounds, and take care of the needs of the people. Let us be efficient. Bad management dissipates our riches that belong to the people."

Is there a way to understand a man in such a public leadership post and thereby add to our understanding of ourselves? Fortunately, the behavioral grid we have just described can be used for the purpose. Labels taken from an excellent organizational study fit the quadrants in our grid as shown in Figure 4-4.[4]

Leadership style no. 1—the developer-missionary When things are going well, resources are plentiful, and good will is the order of the day, perhaps the most successful leader is the "developer." Trusting people, his or her goal is to develop their powers. He or she tends to work as a member of a team, giving the other members considerable authority—and the society or organization thrives. President Eisenhower was inclined to function this way, and he was reasonably successful because the times fit the style.

At the 1976 Democratic National Convention Mr. Carter acted this way, and his acceptance speech was in this style. It was appropriate. But as described in Chapter 2, the nation at large is divided, and times are stressful. This kind of leadership, in which the purpose would be to keep

[4]W. J. Reddin, "Management Style Diagnosis Test," 2nd ed., Organizational Tests, Ltd., 1972, Box 324, Fredericton, N.B., Canada.

everybody happy, will not work now. Our dwindling resources are a real problem that we must begin to solve if we are to lift ourselves to an energized state in which we can act effectively to solve our other problems. This is no hour for the "developer."

If the "developer" cannot adjust to the mood and needs of the hour, others take over who have more know-how and the assigned or elected leader preaches the good gospel of love and/or decries the conditions produced by evil people. He or she becomes the missionary.

The authors are of the opinion that Mr. Carter could be a developer; that is, he has the disposition. But he is too aware of the depression of the times to fall into this trap. How do you see Mr. Carter on this point?

When you assert leadership in a group, are you inclined to be a developer? How much of the missionary style do you hear in your language?

Leadership style no. 2—the executive-compromiser The executive develops a team but stays very much in charge. He or she tries to devise innovative programs to solve knotty problems. Exercising immense energy, such a leader arouses faith but expects productive results. He or she must have immense charisma if times are tough, and must not only gain respect for his or her integrity but also demonstrate great capacity to help the team members solve their problems, social and technical.

We would wager that Mr. Carter will begin in this style, and he doubtless has the traits of spirit and habit to function in this way. The questions are, Will his team members be good enough? Will he be able to arouse great aspirations in the cabinet, in Congress, in the people? Good management means efficiency and orderly thinking. But good team leadership is the power to arouse the emotions and dreams and faith of people. In political action, the leader must feel heroic and have the rhetorical power to arouse people to action. In the terrible depression of the 1930s it was the voice of Franklin D. Roosevelt on the radio that stirred the nation out of its despair and lethargy.

Mr. Carter has the capacity to feel deeply, and he is not afraid to express his feelings. In hours of anguish he will surely be stirred to speak with great feeling and aspiration. At such a time you may assess whether he has touched the people, at the right hour, with a perspective that is turning things around. Perhaps you will see it as an uneven performance: sometimes "right on" but at other times faltering.

Any person without a power base, who with only family and friends sets out across the nation on a two-year search for the Presidency, has the feelings and energy that go with this style. We would not predict where

Carter's stint as President will take him, for we cannot know the dramatic depth of his powers or the challenges that the times may bring.

If Mr. Carter is rigid and this is the only style he can develop, and if he fails in his timing or in the strength of his persuasion, he must become the "compromiser." The compromiser gives all the appearances of being the innovative leader in tough times, but such a person gives in on too many principles and thus ends up with proposals that have given up too much and are therefore too weak to be effective.

Do you ever show the characteristics of an innovative leader? Is there something of the heroic in your communication? How much do you compromise?

Leadership style no. 3—the benevolent autocrat-autocrat   The benevolent autocrat dictates with the needs of others clearly in mind. Being of kindly disposition, he or she does not sink to great distrust of others, and yet runs the show. "Give 'em hell Harry" Truman presided in this style. Usually this style is effective when times are particularly good or particularly bad. And it works best, in American culture, if the leader can be somewhat humorous as well as tough.

Mr. Carter has some inclination to be a benevolent autocrat. He is an ethically sensitive man, and he is repelled by injustice and hypocrisy— "The present income tax is a disgrace." But as Truman's public style was tough, so Carter's *public* style is gracious. His style when he is autocratic will probably be kindly, though righteous: "You can depend on that." This will make some people angry. To many people it is immoral to be moralistic. Moreover, righteous talk is always aimed *at* and *against* somebody.

When the benevolent autocrat begins to feel power slipping away he or she is inclined to drop the benevolence. An autocrat, thus shorn of benevolence, acts with distrust, in ways that ensure his or her own authority, regardless of the value of those actions for others. When a President does this he usually protects his office but fails to gain a favored place in history. In our judgment Mr. Carter is not likely to adopt the autocratic style.

How aggressive are your efforts at leadership when you are trying to persuade another person or group?

Leadership style no. 4—the bureaucrat-deserter   The bureaucratic leader has a rule for every case. As problems come up, he or she looks up in the rule book to find out what to do and then functions according to the rule. As the person who chooses this style is a person of negative feelings and low energy, the rule book is a haven. Obviously, people will try to put the heat on such a person, and that person will not have to defend himself or herself because all he or she was doing was carrying out the rules that everybody (at least those in power) agreed to in the first place. There is only one hitch in the bureaucratic style: Leadership means working with people in solving problems. And the ornery thing about problems is that they are very often newborn things. Thus no rule applies exactly. Decision making almost always requires judgment, and judgment cannot be written out in rules and regulations.

Bureaucratic leadership is appropriate when the rule book has been designed for times that are well stabilized and repetitive—more circular than spiral in character. President Coolidge probably represents this style, which was effective in a relatively undramatic day.

Obviously, bureaucratic leadership is most appropriate to large organizations that take care of the routine of daily living. Certainly in our times the nation does not need this kind of leadership, and there is nothing in the Carter personality to suggest that he would be attracted to the Presidency if this style was called for.

To complete our analysis, when the bureaucratic leader is caught in changing times and cannot shift his or her style, that leader becomes a "deserter." He or she sticks to the rules but lets subordinates meet the angry people pounding on the door.

Applying the behavior grid to the actions of Mr. Carter, we have confined his likely style to the feeling and energy ranges of quadrants 1, 2, and 3. He will show concern for relationships when the job will get done without his supervision. He will use the executive style of leadership most of the time, if possible. If he fails to inspire, he will be tempted to compromise. *If he sees* the failure of his compromise, he will become a benevolent autocrat, because he is above all a man of good will with *immense energy.* If he becomes a self-serving autocrat, it will be because the pressures of the Presidency have destroyed his faith and broken his spirit.

A person who works with people to get things done stands a good chance of being seen, sooner or later, as characterized by duplicity. To be successful, a person must be task oriented. If the job cannot be done with good relationships, he or she is forced into bad ones. In short, behavior is a product of feelings and energy mixed in a variety of ways.

And now, what about you? How much of the bureaucrat is in your style of communication? Do you like to write the rule book? Which of the four quadrants of behavior are more natural to you?

Play it again, Sam   Dr. James David Barber, a political scientist, has evaluated presidents from three standpoints: style, world view, and character.[5] *Style* refers to the way they speak, negotiate, and prepare

---

[5]James David Barber, "President Nixon and Richard Nixon, Character Trap," *Psychology Today,* October 1974, pp. 113–118: *The Presidential Character, Predicting Performance in the White House* (Englewood Cliffs, N.J.: Prentice-Hall, Inc., 1972).

their proposals. *World view* refers to the way they respond to life and to the human race. Barber analyzes *character* on a grid composed of a scale from positive to negative feelings about experience and an active-passive scale of energy expenditure. Actually, he depends more on "character analysis" than on style and world view. His character grid uses a different terminology than the analysis we have been using here, but it is getting at the same thing. And indeed, his style analysis, though separate from the character analysis, is, in our judgment, an analysis of his active-passive scale or our energy expenditure scale. His world view analysis comes very close to an end-values perspective. So in effect Barber is using a set of concepts close to the design of this chapter.

It is fascinating to note, in his application to specific persons, that Barber finds a "worrisome" similarity of character among Nixon, Johnson, Hoover, and Wilson—highly active but essentially negative. It would be our judgment that they ran into dark days, in large measure, because by their own dark vision they darkened the skies we all live under.

To use the language of Professor Barber, Mr. Carter is an active-positive person like the Roosevelts. The results remain to be seen.

THE ROLE OF VALUES

A woman in one of our classes was disturbed that this explanation of communication placed so much importance on feelings.

She said, "Sometimes I get very angry with my parents and I want to tell them off. But I know deep down I love them and I must be careful I don't hurt them. See, I can't be governed by my feelings. I have to think."

This impressed us, essentially because this student was lifting out so vividly the reason she is troubled by the theory. Our culture says that one has to be rational and that feelings are irrational. But Aristotle, from whom our student inherited her view of feelings, observed with some disapproval that logic for most people has little power. And indeed, if one examines the woman's statement one notes that she is saying, "I want to tell my parents off, *but* I love them too much to do that." In effect, she is saying that she must follow the more powerful of two conflicting feelings. In addition, she observes that in moments of intense anger she is greatly tempted to quarrel with her parents but does not. Why does she not let her anger take over? She explains that "as much as I am angered and frustrated by them, I know deep down I love them."

One could say that "deep down" means that she loves her parents more than she hates them. But it means more than that. It means she has decided that her relationship with her parents is very important. She is placing a *higher value* on that relationship than the value of her own assertion when she and her parents clash. So what governs the expression of conflicting feelings is the dominant value called up when she is in conflict. That is the role of values.

What is a value? A value is a basic feeling about what is important, what counts. We call it a feeling because "what is important" is simply what we are attracted to. The student referred to earlier is attracted to maintaining a loving relationship with her parents and is repelled by the prospect of placing her personal feelings above that relationship.

Perhaps above all else the authors call a value a guiding feeling because there is no way to determine the worth of a value except on ethical grounds. An ethic is a "should." A "should," or value, is a compass needle directing us on our road or *way* of life. It is not insignificant that the words *ethic* and *ethos* are fundamentally related. An ethic distinguishes what is good from what is bad. Ethos, as indicated in Chapter 1 in connection with the discussion of trust, is the persuasive effectiveness of a person by virtue of his or her character.

VALUES AND THE ULTIMATE BOND

One of the bonding feelings you may recall from our earlier discussion is *affection*, the simple attraction of one person for another. The research of the past thirty years shows that "the more people associate with one another under conditions of equality, the more they come to share values and norms and the more they come to like one another."[6] In one study of the feeling of satisfaction with the relationship among the professors of college faculties, the greatest satisfaction was found to exist among professors in institutions where the atmosphere was essentially permissive and where the values were essentially conservative.[7] Several things run together here that we need to sort out and look at. The more people interact with each other, the rule is, the more they come to like each other. In addition, people who come to like each other do so most easily where relationships exist on an equality basis; thus the initiation of relationship is felt as self-motivated and without power strains. Further, the more conservative group values are, the less likely they are to change or, if you like, the more stable they are. Stability or predictability is a basis for trust.

But the central thing we see in the examination of the conditions under which people bond with other people is that people like people

[6]Bernard Berelson and Gary A. Steiner, *Human Behavior* (New York: Harcourt, Brace and World, Inc., 1964), p. 327.

[7]Paul F. Lazarsfeld and Wagner Thielens, Jr., *The Academic Mind* (New York: Free Press, 1958), p. 147.

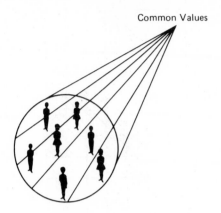

Common Values

FIGURE 4-5

who share the same values. "Friendship is more frequently based on similarity of ideals than on similarity of personality."[8]

Figure 4-5 illustrates what we are saying: that the study of groups shows that people like each other and are bonded together essentially on the basis of their shared ideals, their ultimate values. Bernard Berelson and Gary A. Steiner, whom we cited a moment ago, say that people come together in order to share their ideals. The process is unconscious. The directive force, or cause, is the search for comfort. We seek out people with our own values "in order to feel assured of the correctness of our own behavior."[9] That is why some students flock to fraternities while others gravitate to the corner of the Student Union reserved for "radicals."

As we learned in our discussion of the self-concept, the prevailing anxiety of the human race concerns self-esteem. Or maybe it should be put this way: The prevailing question of humanity is, "What is right?" Is what I am doing right?

Why this concern? The authors have given the communication-conflict inventory at the end of the chapter on conflict to almost 700 students. Two-thirds of the behavior scores fall into the shaded blocks of Figure 4-6. This means that the vast majority of those tested assessed their prevailing feelings as existing at this anxiety borderline between positive and negative feelings. They are also not too sure about their commitment to getting the job done with people. The closer one gets to the compromise point where the two center lines intersect, the more readily a person is "tempted" (1) to feel good about his or her fellows and

[8]Josephine Klein, *The Study of Groups* (New York: Routledge and Kegan Paul, 1956), p. 106.

[9]Berelson and Steiner, *op. cit.*, p. 328.

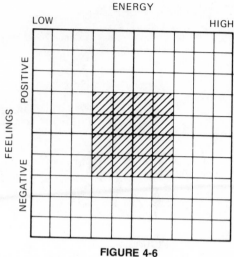

FIGURE 4-6

to cooperate; (2) to distrust them and try to dominate them (or, failing that, to give up in shame or feigned grace); (3) to distrust them in fear or contempt and thus to withdraw from them; or (4) in high faith in self and others, to submit for the sake of the relationship. Positive feelings lead to mutual confirmation in submission or cooperation. Negative feelings lead to a *zero sum* contest in which what one person wins another loses. The ethical issue at the heart of human behavior is the *human use of human beings.* What should one have at another person's expense? And if one is to have something at another person's expense, the central issue is power, or power-over. If all of us adopt the ethic of "get what you can," society becomes a jungle. Nobody belongs to another. For the sake of self-esteem via the prestige of power we have violated the first need, to belong, and have replaced the self-esteem derived from feeling—one's impact-resulting-from-competent-skill—with the esteem that comes from sensing one's power over another, and thus have denied ourselves the possibility of finding creative fulfillment.

The reason people must rest their behavior in values is the temptation to exchange the search for the power-to-know-and-do for power over other people. Power was central in Christ's three temptations, a dramatic parable about every person's basic problem:

1. Turn this stone into bread if you are the Son of God.
2. You can have all the kingdoms of the Earth if you will worship me.
3. Test the protection of your God by leaping from the pinnacle of the temple.

The answer that Jesus gave to each temptation is significant:

1. A life is made of more than bread. It is based on words of truth.
2. I shall worship the truth.
3. I do not doubt the truth.

Jacob Bronowski,[10] an atomic scientist and mathematician turned anthropologist in later life, concluded a book about the role of values in science and human life as follows:

> The values by which we are to survive are not rules for just and unjust conduct, but are those deeper illuminations in whose light justice and injustice, good and evil, means and ends are seen in fearful sharpness of outline.[11]

Throughout his book runs this thread: The central theme of value is Truth. The truth is not some fixed fact that anybody can know but a search for more accuracy in the facts that we now know, a dedication therefore to the unfolding of life, to creativity, which is the very essence of life.

Bronowski finds the great works of art and science to be the products of people dedicated to the value of aspiring. At one point he vividly reflects the "deeper illuminations" that may govern life as follows:

> In the museum at Cracow there is a painting of Leonardi da Vinci called "Portrait of a Lady with an Ermine": it shows a girl holding a [weasel] in her arms. The girl was probably a mistress of Ludovico Sforza, the usurper of Milan, at whose court Leonardo lived from about 1482 to 1499, amid the violence and intrigue which all his life drew him and repelled him together. The [weasel] was an emblem of Ludovico Sforza, and is probably also a pun on the girl's name. And in a sense the whole picture is a pun, if I may borrow for the word the tragic intensity which Coleridge found in the puns of Shakespeare. Leonardo has matched the [weasel] in the girl. In the skull under the long brow, in the lucid eyes, in the stately, brutal, beautiful and stupid head of the girl, he has re-discovered the animal nature; and done so without malice, almost as a matter of fact. The very carriage of the girl and the [weasel], the gesture of the hand and the claw, explore the character with the anatomy. As we look, the emblematic likeness springs as freshly in our minds as it did in Leonardo's when he looked at the girl and asked her to turn her head. "The Lady with the Ermine" is as much a research into man and animal, and a creation of unity, as is Darwin's *Origin of Species*.[12]

[10]Narrator in *The Ascent of Man*, a series replayed many times on public television.
[11]Jacob Bronowski, *Silence and Human Values*, (New York: Harper Torch Books, 1956), p. 94.
[12]*Ibid.*, p. 36.

Here is Leonardo's painting:

Portrait of Lady with an Ermine by Leonardo da Vinci. From Jacob Bronowski, *Science and Human Values* (New York: Harper & Row Publishers, Inc., 1956).

We take these devious routes to make vivid the significance of value in life because the word *value* itself is so abstract. Yet it is in accordance with the prevailing values or feelings of our lives that we live, die, and often destroy each other.

THE FOUR ULTIMATE VALUES

The behavior grid and Bronowski's concept of the fearful interplay of good and evil point in the same direction as one of the most remarkable pieces of research in social science.[13] Robert Bales and Arthur Couch assembled as many value statements as they could, taking them from value inventories, from personality inventories, from literature, from the statements of their acquaintances, even from passers-by on the street. The intention was to see if they could find the essential themes running through human values by means of a statistical analysis rather than by philosophical exploration in the manner of both Leonardo and Bronowski. Bales and Couch ended up with 872 value statements. They examined these statements for identical or similar statements; they thus reduced the number to 252 different value statements. Then they asked students to respond on a scale to those statements, indicating their attractiveness or unattractiveness as guides for life. In so doing, they were searching for the underlying themes of human aspiration.

A factor analysis determines the degree of association of each statement with each other statement and, once the clusters of association have been found, determines the strength of association between each statement in a cluster and the cluster itself. The Bales-Couch factor analysis set out four clusters of values. Translated into the terms we are using in this book, they are the following:

1. The importance of adopting the central values of the groups we associate with (*community values*).
2. The importance of appreciating the unique values of the individuals we are related to (*other person's unique values*).
3. The importance of making an effort to persuade others or to control others in a situation (*control values*).
4. The importance of asserting one's own individual and unique values (*own unique values*).

It should be relatively easy to see two things: First, human values, when reduced to the four basic themes, all become communication values or, if you like, relationship values. If Bronowski is correct in saying that value is the creative search for the truth about the means and ends of living, then the ultimate values are different ways of perceiving what is good and bad in human relationships. The second thing that becomes clear is that the four values of communication are the values placed on the four ways of behaving with people. Thus values and their support of the four categories of interaction with others may be seen as presented in Figure 4-7.

[13]Robert F. Bales and Arthur S. Couch, "The Value Profile: A Factor Analytic Study of Value Statements," *Sociological Inquiry*, 39, 1, 1969, 3–17.

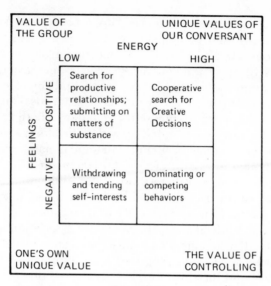

```
  VALUE OF                        UNIQUE VALUES OF
  THE GROUP                       OUR CONVERSANT
                         ENERGY
            LOW                          HIGH

              Search for
              productive          Cooperative
        POSITIVE
              relationships;      search for
              submitting on       Creative
              matters of          Decisions
  FEELINGS    substance


              Withdrawing         Dominating or
        NEGATIVE
              and tending         competing
              self-interests      behaviors


  ONE'S OWN                           THE VALUE OF
  UNIQUE VALUE                        CONTROLLING
```

FIGURE 4-7

Community value is the treasuring of kinlife.

Other value is the treasuring of other people as unique individuals.

Control value is the treasuring of one's own power in interaction.

Self-value is the treasuring of one's own individuality.

The treasures of life bear on our relationships with self and others and on what we do in life. Our treasures may be contradictory.

PATTERNS OF COMMUNICATING

Having given the communication–conflict inventory to many students, we have noted several styles or patterns of behaving and valuing. Two will be discussed here. Others will be discussed in the chapter on conflict.

The instrument provides a scale from 10 to 70 for each of six measures. The six items measured are (1) feelings, (2) task energy, (3) group or community values, (4) regard for the unique values of individuals, (5) the value placed on control of others, and (6) the focus of attention on one's own values. One may take the inventory as an evaluation of one's responses in any number of situations. The patterns we will discuss have emerged as a consequence of having students respond as they think they generally do in communication with people.

1. *The Zestful Participant* (see Figure 4-8)

Because one has to think here in patterns and relationships, the scores selected for the discussion, though appropriate for the pattern, are chosen so as to emphasize the relationships. The first thing to note is that the feeling score is generally positive and relatively high among the scores and that the commitment to expending energy is about average. These two scores locate behavior in the upper two quadrants, indicating that the person under the pressure of the situation moves back and forth between cooperatively finding creative ways to care for whatever is being done and tending the quality of the relationship. Also note that of the four values, the score for the "other" value is the highest. There is no conflict between behavior and values.

The more zestful communicators thus *empathize* in their listening and learn that though "every human being is an improbable combination of absurd contradictions," as somebody has noted, they need not be threatened. Indeed, they come to understand these contradictions in people. Such people have little trouble accepting and trusting. They know how much to invest in the relationship because they know who they are dealing with. Their tendency to support the other person's uniqueness, as a primary value, is reinforced by a strong group or community score, and they have little need to control, nor do they fear being controlled. The self-values (note the score) are high enough for them to

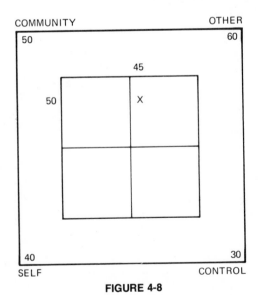

FIGURE 4-8

insist on asserting the self and knowing its relationship with the other as well as its own impact and identity.

We have found people with this profile to be open, to react spontaneously, to give excellent attention, to smile readily and easily. They reveal a striking humor without barbs, and they are optimistic. They manage conflict effectively, creatively making appropriate adjustments when there is stress. They are highly self-reflecting and self-concerned, but not morbidly so. They are just interested in the human condition.

2. The Aggressive Producer (see Figure 4-9)

In the psychological language of past decades we might call this person the extrovert. It may be noted that the peculiar character of this person's behavior is that it is "gung-ho" for getting things done. The feeling tone is essentially positive, though close to the border zone of doubt and bad feeling. The behavior is reinforced by a central value of competence, persuading, and controlling. People generally accept this person as a good leader. The self–other value scores indicate assertiveness value, but there is also high respect for sensitivity to others. The person generally, especially if young (25–35), is not highly responsive to group mores and community or authoritarian values. Thus the person is something of a rugged individualist. He (she) wins because he (she) wants to win. Whatever that person has in ethical guidance is not derived

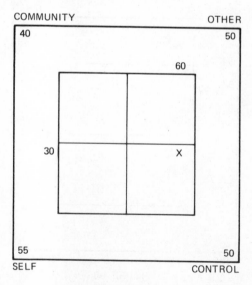

FIGURE 4-9

from community principles but from sensitivity to other people he or she knows and is attracted to.

We have discussed two patterns. One is marked by behavior that reveals positive feelings and an average amount of committed energy. This behavior shows sensitivity to others. Such people are usually service oriented. They are interested, usually, in being counselors, teachers, personnel agents—in working with people, in their behalf. The second behavior pattern is less sure of people, more committed to getting the job done, and oriented toward control. Such people are attracted to leadership and production careers. Among our students we find more in the former group than in this latter group.

There are several other very clear-cut communication patterns, but all of them involve considerable conflict either in the behavior or the values, so they will be discussed in the chapter on conflict.

In sum, the two communication patterns we have discussed here are (1) the openly and trusting cooperative person and (2) the openly competitive person—the less complicated persons in a society that is held together by improbable combinations of contradictory values.

CONCLUSION

Behavior is the expression of our feelings and energy. But a human is also guided by, or at least believes he or she is guided by, generalized feelings about what is right. Since these values are the flags under which we group together, they are basic to communication. One may ask, Does the behavior conform to values or is it the other way around? The truth is that they interact. When the values and behaviors conform, the person relates with others in one of the two styles just described. When the values and behaviors are in conflict—well, that's the topic of another chapter.

INSTRUMENT 4-1

COMMUNICATION ORIENTATION

For each of the following adjectives circle the number most like you:

> 5 means "almost always like me"
> 4 means "usually like me"
> 3 means "often like me"
> 2 means "occasionally like me"
> 1 means "almost never like me"

A

1. Careful	5	4	3	2	1
2. Reliable	5	4	3	2	1
3. Calm	5	4	3	2	1
4. Thoughtful	5	4	3	2	1
5. Passive	5	4	3	2	1
6. Steady	5	4	3	2	1
7. Agreeable	5	4	3	2	1

Add the circled numbers and place the sum here:_____

B

8. Talkative	5	4	3	2	1
9. Responsive	5	4	3	2	1
10. Uninhibited	5	4	3	2	1
11. Confident	5	4	3	2	1
12. Outgoing	5	4	3	2	1
13. Enthusiastic	5	4	3	2	1
14. Durable	5	4	3	2	1

Add the circled numbers and place the sum here:_____

C

15. Restless	5	4	3	2	1
16. Aggressive	5	4	3	2	1
17. Changeable	5	4	3	2	1
18. Impulsive	5	4	3	2	1
19. Active	5	4	3	2	1
20. Irritable	5	4	3	2	1
21. Adventurous	5	4	3	2	1

Add the circled numbers and place the sum here:_____

D

22. Reserved	5	4	3	2	1
23. Pessimistic	5	4	3	2	1
24. Quiet	5	4	3	2	1

25. Anxious	5	4	3	2	1
26. Inflexible	5	4	3	2	1
27. Moody	5	4	3	2	1
28. Disagreeable	5	4	3	2	1

Add the circled numbers and place the sum here:_____

"A" is a tendency to be *phlegmatic:* to be of good cheer but of low drive.
"B" is the tendency to be *sanguine:* to be ruddy and dynamic.
"C" is the tendency to be *choleric:* to be persistent and, if thwarted, moved to anger.
"D" is the tendency to be *melancholic:* to be pensive, saddened, and depressed.

The psychologists H. L. Eysenck and Sybil B. G. Eysenck devised a personality inventory around these ancient Greek descriptions. The following is a modification of their model.

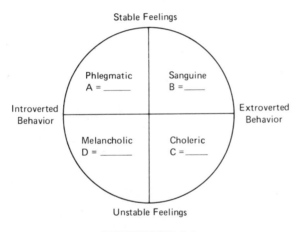

INSTRUMENT 4-2

LISTENING SCALE*

Name _____

Sex: M____ F____   Age _____

Person rated: M____   F____

On the following page you are asked to rate the person indicated as a listener. Please indicate your judgment of this person on the scales listed by placing a check mark on each scale.

*By permission of Dr. Richard Dieker, Department of Communication Arts and Sciences, Western Michigan University, Kalamazoo, Michigan.

For example, here is a single scale:

Rate the person indicated as a listener on the following scale:

Skilled: 7 : 6 : 5 : 4 : 3 : 2 : 1 :Unskilled

If you feel that the person is, in general, extremely skilled, you will circle the number closest to the word *skilled*. In general, consider the positions on the preceding scale to represent the following judgments:

Skilled:
  7. extremely skilled
  6. quite skilled
  5. slightly skilled
  4. neither skilled or unskilled; I cannot choose one alternative over the other
  3. slightly unskilled
  2. quite unskilled
  1. extremely unskilled

Be sure to circle only one number on each scale.

Do not omit any scales.

On each scale, the closer you place the mark to the adjective at the end of the scale, the more you feel that this adjective applies to the person rated.

Please rate the *person as a listener* on the following scales:

Responsive: 7 : 6 : 5 : 4 : 3 : 2 : 1 :Unresponsive

Concerned: 7 : 6 : 5 : 4 : 3 : 2 : 1 :Unconcerned

Closed-minded: 1 : 2 : 3 : 4 : 5 : 6 : 7 :Open-minded

Patient: 7 : 6 : 5 : 4 : 3 : 2 : 1 :Impatient

Interested: 7 : 6 : 5 : 4 : 3 : 2 : 1 :Uninterested

Inattentive: 1 : 2 : 3 : 4 : 5 : 6 : 7 :Attentive

Relaxed: 7 : 6 : 5 : 4 : 3 : 2 : 1 :Tense

Trusting: 7 : 6 : 5 : 4 : 3 : 2 : 1 :Suspicious

Warm: 7 : 6 : 5 : 4 : 3 : 2 : 1 :Cool

Rejecting: 1 : 2 : 3 : 4 : 5 : 6 : 7 :Accepting

Sincere: 7 : 6 : 5 : 4 : 3 : 2 : 1 :Insincere

Indirect: 1 : 2 : 3 : 4 : 5 : 6 : 7 :Direct

Friendly: 7 : 6 : 5 : 4 : 3 : 2 : 1 :Unfriendly

Domineering:_1_:_2_:_3_:_4_:_5_:_6_:_7_:Permissive

Detached:_1_:_2_:_3_:_4_:_5_:_6_:_7_:Involved

Personal:_7_:_6_:_5_:_4_:_3_:_2_:_1_:Impersonal

Inconsiderate:_1_:_2_:_3_:_4_:_5_:_6_:_7_:Considerate

Insensitive:_1_:_2_:_3_:_4_:_5_:_6_:_7_:Sensitive

Unreceptive:_1_:_2_:_3_:_4_:_5_:_6_:_7_:Receptive

Nervous:_1_:_2_:_3_:_4_:_5_:_6_:_7_:Calm

Unsympathetic:_1_:_2_:_3_:_4_:_5_:_6_:_7_:Sympathetic

Thoughtful:_7_:_6_:_5_:_4_:_3_:_2_:_1_:Thoughtless

Intolerant:_1_:_2_:_3_:_4_:_5_:_6_:_7_Tolerant

Encouraging:_1_:_2_:_3_:_4_:_5_:_6_:_7_:Discouraging

Mature:_7_:_6_:_5_:_4_:_3_:_2_:_1_:Immature

Add the numbers circled and place the sum here:____

EXERCISES

1. Discuss the relationships between the four quadrants produced by the two axes of Instrument 4-1 with the four quadrants of the grid used in the chapter. Each throws additional light on the other.

2. Compare your scores in Instrument 4-1 with the description of the communication inclinations of President Carter on page 94. What kind of President would you make? Do you think you will be elected? (Do not laugh. It is a very fine position.)

3. In light of the discussion on pages 90–95, how would you assess President Carter's leadership style or styles?

4. If you filled out Instrument 4-1, compare the scores for that instrument with your scores for Instrument 4-2. Are the scores complementary?

5. Thomas De Quincy once said "Dyspepsy is the ruin of most things: empires, expeditions and everything else." As applied here, "dyspepsy" means "gloomy, cross." What do you make of that in light of the point of view of the chapter?

6. Take one of the instruments (or both) and score it for some person that members of the class all know. It could be a political figure, a celebrity, or even your professor. Discuss the agreements and disagreements in your assessments.

5

Meaning: What Language Does To Us and For Us

The limits of my language mean the limits of my world.

Ludwig Wittgenstein*

People still communicate with words. But some, like Marshall McLuhan, talk about humankind standing on the edge of a new epoch in which speech will be replaced by wordless understandings sent and received with more completeness and accuracy than any language could hope to achieve. Some "postlanguage" addicts claim that it is much more "real" to hear someone like Janis Joplin growl[1] than to try to tune in to words. But to put it mildly, the death of language does not appear imminent. It is almost certain not to occur within the lifetime of this book. We need, therefore, to understand (1) what effect language has on the meaning we say is present in an act of communication and (2) how we go about wringing sense from the words we use.

MYTH: THE MEANING IS IN THE WORDS

The easiest thing to conclude about meaning is that it is somehow carried in the language. It follows that since all of us are able to use the language we must be constantly and automatically engaged in the trans-

*From the book *Ludwig Wittgenstein: An Introduction to His Philosophy* by C. A. Van Peursen. Copyright © 1971 by Faber and Faber Limited. Published by E. P. Dutton & Co., Inc. and used with their permission and by permission of Faber and Faber Limited.
[1]William Hedgepeth, "New Language," *Look*, January 13, 1970, pp. 46–48.

fer of meaning. And the fact that we *do* get a cup of coffee when we ask for one at a restaurant charms us into thinking that "meaning intended is meaning received."

Consider a simple but common exchange:

> **Traveler:** Where would I find a good restaurant in this part of town?
>
> **Filling Station Attendant:** Joe's Family Steak House. Two and one-half blocks down this street. On the right. Good food. Reasonable prices. Salad bar.
>
> **Traveler:** Thanks.
>
> **Traveler (1½ hours later):** I just stopped back to suggest that you quit recommending Joe's Family Steak House.
>
> **FSA:** I've always found it to be one of the best places in town.
>
> **Traveler:** I thought you said they had good food.
>
> **FSA:** And . . . ?
>
> **Traveler:** A mushy couple of crabmeat cakes—you call that good food?
>
> **FSA:** Nothing better than that crabmeat.
>
> **Traveler:** Well, for $5.95 it is hardly "reasonably priced."
>
> **FSA:** I don't know where you eat, man, but you can hardly get a full meal anywhere these days for less than $6.00.[2]
>
> **Traveler:** (stalking to his car): Have it your way. But you're going to lose a lot of business if you keep misleading people like that.

Surprising as it may seem, several worthy conclusions can be drawn from this unpleasant conversation:

1. Every message is received in a frame other than its own.
2. It is a myth to think that meaning can be found in words. Meaning can be found, ultimately, only in people.
3. While words do not "contain" the meaning, they help determine how a person will think. We start out, says one writer, "speaking as we think, and end up thinking as we speak."

THE DOMAIN OF GENERAL SEMANTICS

The study of the relationships between words, things, and human behavior is the concern of *general semantics*. Alfred Korzybski,[3] who first

---

[2] Add whatever is necessary to this hypothetical price to account for the impact of inflation by the time you read this.

[3] Alfred Korzybski, *Science & Sanity: An Introduction to Non-Aristotelian Systems and General Semantics* (Lancaster, Pa.: Science Press Printing Co., 1933).

put together a systematic way of looking at the connections between language and human behavior, asked himself as a beginning point, "What is the difference between a human and an animal?" He saw that the crucial difference lay in the fact that the human's destiny was profoundly affected by how he or she used language. Wherever there were problems between people, language was an invariable factor. When, and if, there were solutions to the problems, language provided the means of solution. As the semanticist S. I. Hayakawa puts it, "The functioning of society is of necessity achieved by language or else it is not achieved at all."[4] In subsequent years others[5] have elaborated Korzybski's system in a series of fascinating applications to life as we know it. Within this framework, then, we propose to have a more careful look at the three conclusions listed earlier.

1. Every Message Is Received in a Frame Other Than Its Own

Our rather rudely handled filling station attendant clearly sent a message (from his frame of reference) that was received in a very different frame by the traveler. Every human observation, say the general semanticists, is screened, inescapably, through a unique nervous system. Therefore any statements you make are bound to emerge from private perceptions and cannot, in a strict sense, carry the same meaning that someone else would assign to them. This process of screening experience is called *projection*.[6]

When *unawareness of projection* exists in an exchange, the potential for communication is dramatically reduced (as the filling station attendant discovered, to his sorrow). On the other hand, to be *aware of projecting* is to wonder what differences there might be between your perceptions and those of the other person. Such awareness is the beginning of empathy. As Figure 5-1 shows, if either A or B is unaware of the tendency to project his or her meaning on the other rather than search for the other's meaning, bypassing will occur. There is the *appearance* of communication without the actual contact.

Examples of this linguistic booby trap are legion; they plague the people who sit around the tables at international conferences, and they

[4]S. I. Hayakawa, *Language in Thought and Action*, 3rd ed. (New York: Harcourt Brace Jovanovich, 1972), p. 14.

[5]J. Samuel Bois, *The Act of Awareness*, 2nd ed. (Dubuque, Iowa: Wm. C. Brown Co., 1973); John C. Condon, Jr., *Semantics and Communication*, 2nd ed. (New York: Macmillan Publishing Co., Inc., 1975); William V. Haney, *Communications and Organizational Behavior: Text and Cases*, rev. ed. (Homewood, Ill.: Richard D. Irwin, Inc., 1967).

[6]Note that the word as used here has a broader meaning than it often has in psychology, where it refers to assigning characteristics to someone else that one does not want to admit in oneself.

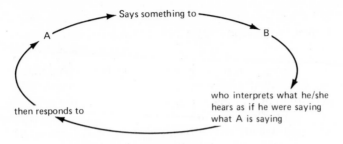

Says something to

A

B

then responds to

who interprets what he/she
hears as if he were saying
what A is saying

FIGURE 5-1

plague the ordinary person who is trying to make and maintain relationships. Two days before Jimmy Carter's election as President of the United States a news story reported that four black people had sought to become members of the Baptist Church in Plains, Georgia. They were refused membership, and the doors of the church were locked against them. Since this was the church of which Mr. Carter was a member, the story was considered to have very negative potential among black voters. But Mr. Carter asserted that he did not agree with the policy of his church, and he charged that the incident was engineered by his political opponents to damage him just before election day. When the story first broke, one of our students described the details to a group of fellow students. When he finished, a young woman who was present said, "I think that was awful!"

What did she mean? Did she mean, "Blacks should not be denied membership in any church?" Or did she mean, "Politicians should not resort to dirty tricks?" Or did she mean, "Mr. Carter shouldn't have charged that someone had done something underhanded?" A significant feature of the event was that *no one in the group asked her what she meant,* probably because they regarded their translation of what she meant as accurate. That is how the vital connections required in communication are often bypassed—with the easy assumption that the message received is the message that was sent.

The hope that we can make sense to each other rests in the fact that an awareness of the inclination to project meanings does help keep a person open to messages from outside. If, as Korzybski suggested, you mentally add "that is its meaning to me" when you make intense or categorical statements, the possibility exists that you will be able to live productively with people around you who hold different political views, who have different tastes, who follow different life styles, and the like. The key is the realization that no one else could filter the world of experience exactly as you do, even if they were trying to do so. If this attitude toward language is accepted, differences will be expected and agreement will be gratefully received as a bonus.

2. Meaning Is Found in People, Not in Words

There is, deep within us it seems, the conviction that words are containers, tubs filled with meaning. This idea is sometimes called the container myth. The hungry traveler referred to at the beginning of this chapter apparently believed in such a myth. He took the phrase "good food" and filled it with all the meaning he usually associated with that phrase—and assumed that it could have only the meaning contained in the words.

The dictionary would not have been very useful to him. It would have given him definitions for *good* and *food,* but putting those definitions together would not yield much. The question to be answered would still be, What does the user of the phrase mean? And not until that was searched out could the meaning be said to be known.

Dictionaries are, in any case, not the ultimate repositories of meanings. They are reports on how words are being used in the culture at a given time. In that respect they are general guides to where meaning might be located. But the meaning still cannot be known until the user lets you in on the private twists he or she is giving to a word that seems so obvious to you. And you will never know what those twists are unless you ask.

3. We Think as We Speak

"A word is to a thing," general semanticists are fond of saying, "as a map is to its territory." A map that tells you where the deer crossings are is no help if you want to get from Algora, Kansas to Beaumont, Texas. A map that shows 602 miles between Denver and Kansas City is considered unreliable if the distance turns out to be 590 miles when you drive it.

In short, a map is not much good unless you find what it says you will find when you examine the territory. And it cannot be predictable unless its structure (what it says about scale, topology, etc.) agrees with that of the territory. In the same way, the structure of the language must fit the structure of the world if it is to make sense.

There are several ways in which the very *structure* of the language seduces us into making and believing in bad maps. Let us take a look at three of those structural problems: (a) the monumental "is", (b) the polarizing trap, and (c) dividing the indivisible.

The monumental "is"   Most of the sentences in our language take the declarative form—"Something is something." This form gives us the capacity to connect or associate things, but its weakness is that it is a structure that implies more certainty than one finds when one examines the territory. Consider, for example, the following:

Chairman Mao is dead.
God is dead.
Chivalry is dead.

Each of those sentences is written in precisely the same form. Yet they exist at very different levels of certainty. The first is based on what is observable, the second on what is not observable, and the third on an abstract term almost impossible to pin down, much less observe. But all three have the ring of certainty because the monumental "is" has come to signify sureness in the language.

This feeling of certainty (where grounds do not exist for certainty) is called the "allness" attitude. Where both parties to an interaction carry the "allness" attitude, it is predictable that unresolvable conflict and disappointment lie ahead. It is therefore basic, if communication is to remain open and fruitful, that the participants recognize the limitations of the verbal maps they are drawing of the territory. They must develop the "non-allness" attitude—"Try as I may, I cannot say it *exactly* as it is."

The polarizing trap English, more than some other languages, is loaded with words that emphasize the extremes and ignore the middle ground (where virtually all of existence lies). Try the following simple demonstration:[7] For each of the words in the lefthand column, provide its polar opposite. For example if the word is *white,* you write *black.* Respond as quickly as you can to each of the following:

white	_____
success	_____
good	_____
honest	_____
polite	_____

This is clearly an easy exercise. But now let us try something else. You are given each of the polar pairs of terms, and you are to provide the middle term. Example: if you are given *white* and *black,* you will write *gray.* Now continue with the following:

white	_____gray_____	*black*
success	_____	*failure*

[7]Adapted from William V. Haney, *Communication and Organizational Behavior,* rev. ed. (Homewood, Ill.: Richard D. Irwin, Inc., 1967), p. 312.

good	_____	*bad*
honest	_____	*dishonest*
polite	_____	*impolite*

If you respond the way most people do, you will find that you can think of opposite terms easily and quickly but that when you try for the "middle" terms it takes much longer and you experience uncertainty, frustration, and even some anguish. The language is stacked against you. It is full of polar terms and slim on "mid" terms.

Much in nature encourages a two-valued language. There is, after all, either pushing or pulling; either coming or going; either up or down. But Korzybski pointed out that in the "real" world almost every class of phenomena shows graded variation. Any pool of motorists seeking to renew a driving license will show, when tested, degrees of difference in reaction time. To refer to them as "fast" or "slow" is to distort, and oversimplify, reality. So when the two-valued view is internalized we tend to overlook important features and assume that we are perceiving accurately.

Another aspect of the two-valued psychology is that it leads one to think one has to *accept something absolutely or reject it absolutely.* A particular student, for example, is an avid user of the library on her campus, enthusiastic about its resources. Then she is charged an overdue fine on a book that she allegedly did not return on time. She protests that she did return it. The library assistant insists that the book is not in the library and that the fine must be paid. The student reacts by vowing that she will not use the library again. That is the mechanism of oversimplification. It draws a verbal map that says, in effect, "The territory is entirely good or it is entirely bad."

Dividing the indivisible Finally, the language has built into it a tendency to talk about parts of actually interrelated wholes in such a way that we are seduced into feeling and thinking that those parts are separate. Since they can be talked about as if they were separate, why not deal with them as if they were separate? The fooler, of course, is that the very interaction of elements makes an element, when separated out for discussion, something other than what it is. This is an involved sentence. Let us illustrate.

The words *sensation, perception,* and *conception* appear to be so clear that it is easy to assume that each can be isolated and thought about in solitary form. But is this really possible? Examine Figure 5-2. Does it mean anything to you? Do you "see" anything in it? Do you have a label for it? Now let us suggest that what you are looking at is "Four Elephants Inspecting a Grapefruit." Suddenly you "see" what is there—and in that

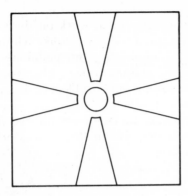

FIGURE 5-2 Permission of Price/Stern/Sloan Publishers, Inc., from *Droodles,* copyright 1953 by Roger Price, $1.50, 14th Printing, 1978.

act sensation (registering the marks on the page), perception (interpreting those marks as having some organization), and conception (relating the forms to labels that refer to similar forms) are all present.

This habit of thinking in terms of elements (separating elements that are indivisible) can be noticed in divisions like the following:

mind	body
thought	feeling
speaker	listener
religious	secular
thinker	doer
artistic	functional

All of those are elements that are interacting. The mind–body separation was rejected as false years ago by psychologists, but it still persists in popular thinking. Operations were sometimes performed, past reports tell us, on stutterers who "blocked." The operation consisted of cutting some of the muscles under the tongue in order to "loosen" the instruments involved in producing the sounds. Aside from the fact that this radical surgery did not work, the treatment overlooked the psychological elements, the neurological elements—and any number of additional elements that were interacting with the physical to bring on the stuttering. We have made progress in dealing with that problem today, taking a "nonelementalistic" view of it and recognizing how causes and solutions depend on interacting factors.

But consider the effort to eliminate accidents in a plant by putting safety devices in and around machines. The best of such designs cannot prevent the "accident-prone" worker from falling down the stairs. Such elementalistic thinking focuses on the physical without taking into account the psychological factors at work on the employee: motivation, self-image, desire for attention, and the like. Here is another example: we are beginning to recognize that our polluted atmosphere cannot be cleaned up just by antipollution devices. The problem, we are discovering, is not just an "engineering" problem. It is an engineering–moral–political–economic–etc. problem.

So an awareness that the language can lead us to overlook crucial relationships between elements in the "real" world becomes a way to more adequate thinking.

Summary

It is true that we often speak as we think. But it is just as true (more true?) that we learn to think as we speak. The directions this kind of learning takes are determined by some of the important features of the structure of the language we use: its way of appearing to be certain when that certainty is not justified; its way of slicing phenomena into polar domains when most of reality lies in the degrees between the poles; and its way of dividing verbally elements that are totally married. Increasing our awareness of such forces is a way of opening up the possibilities for communication.

So much for structure. What is the process by which, within that structure, we give meaning to the words we use?

MEANING AND THE ACT OF TRANSLATION

Forewarned that language structure makes us more sure of what we say than we should be, the fact remains that the world is what we say it is. And although the reader may admit this, one likes to think that the words one uses are the symbols of an independent truth. One finds it hard to accept the fact that in the very process of formulating sentences one creates one's own reality. It is our purpose in this part of the chapter to bring the reader so close to his or her own basic experience that he or she senses this meaning-making process, sometimes accurate, sometimes inaccurate.

We have discussed listening (in Chapter 3) as silent speech, truncated as compared to overt speech, often telegraphic. A single word or phrase may carry the essence of a lengthy statement. It is in that which trips off a word or phrase that we discover the dynamics of meaning. Meaning is achieved in the response act, in listening. The response may be to what we ourselves have said or to what another has said. It is this responding act that we must examine if we are to comprehend comprehension. We will call this act *translation*.[8]

Translation Between Statements

The experience of feeling we understand something, that a statement makes sense, is not to be found *in* the statement itself. Working in a tantalizing way, meaning is outside of the statements to which it belongs. More specifically, meaning is that which happens between two statements. It is a kind of sensing of the identity between different statements. Meaning is the recognition of relationship. Let us illustrate:

Statement	*Translation*	*Listening Response*
(Child speaking) "All gone boat."		"Boats of greater weight than water sink."
"That's the way the ball bounces."		"It is foolish to buck the inevitable."
"Mike is not serious."		"Mike is avoiding an examination of this thing. Maybe he's frightened."

Neither the statement nor the listening response alone has meaning. It is that silence turned to awareness, the thing that takes place as we move from statement to statement, that constitutes meaning.[9] "That's it." It is this awareness that Charles Osgood's semantic differential points to: This that I contemplate is alive, compelling, and right. We are looking at a psychic process as simple and primal as the osmotic flow of solution in plant life or the bird's "awareness" of the lengthening day that sends it on its northern flight. Simple, basic to survival, difficult to understand because it is the essence of our psychic being.

Here is another way of examining the phenomenon. The feeling that what I am experiencing makes sense is a perception of the relationship between foreground and background. "All gone boat" is the *foreground,* which really has no meaning except as seen in conjunction with the *background:* For the adult, "Boats of greater weight than water sink." And the difference between the child speaking the original statement and the adult's response is the difference in the "backgrounds" of the

[8]For those who have studied language in some depth, this part of the chapter deals with our comprehension of the nature of *reference* as discussed by Ogden and Richards and the term *mediation* as discussed by Charles Osgood and others.

[9]This is probably what Ruth Anshen alludes to in the statement, "Meaning is what silence does when it gets into words." From *Language: An Inquiry Into Its Meaning and Function* (New York: Harper and Brothers, 1957).

two. Further, the child's own background response to "All gone boat" is, if Piaget is correct, "Magic!" Things come into existence and go into nothing at will. It is like closing and opening your eyes. The adult who does not know the difference between his or her background and the child's background simply cannot talk to and listen to a child.

As a consequence of self-talk or conversation with another, meaning is the perception that takes place when we capture the relationship between two statements. In everyday reference to this translation process, we often say that a person who is having difficulty understanding something "doesn't see the meaning behind the words" or "takes things too literally." Such a person cannot "speak back to a statement" and gain the perception of sensing foreground against background. He or she cannot translate. Meaning exists in the perception of difference.

In an effort to control our listener's translations of what we say, we keep making statement after statement—until we finally conclude that we have "bounded" our intended meaning. Successful or unsuccessful in the end, the ongoing feeling while en route is one of endless misunderstanding.[10] And the consequence of getting anything out of the confusions en route is a concluding sigh, "Oh, I see." We have performed the miracle act of translation. As Susanne Langer points out, understanding or comprehension is basically emotional; first anxiety and finally a feeling of satisfaction or dissatisfaction with the chosen response.

Translation Within and Between Language Levels

An understanding of the way translation works is confounded by the fact that our mental gymnastics allow us to make statements at one of six levels of "reality." Let us create a visual model (Figure 5-3) that may help us get an overall view of the way translation operates to give us meaning.

First, as sensual animals our primary reality is physical action. We eat, sleep, anger, laugh, make love. Physical experience is our first-order experience, and the language of first-order experience is composed of emotional grunts, curses, weepings, ejaculations of glee, and our commands, what B. F. Skinner calls *mands*—"move over," "quit," "kiss me, honey." One can and often does, of course, put the emotional response and the command together—"Damn it, get out!" The important thing to note is this: The language of first-order experience is that *of* action and interaction and thus *has no subject, no actor expressed.* It is a distinctly different experience to say "Stop right there" than to say "I *say*, stop right

[10]Susanne Langer, *Philosophy in a New Key* (New York: The New American Library, 1948), p. 123.

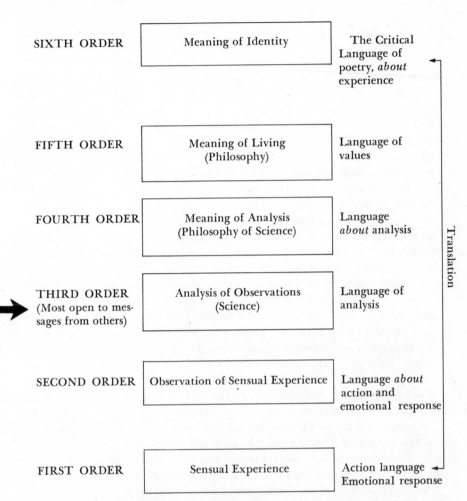

SIXTH ORDER	Meaning of Identity	The Critical Language of poetry, *about* experience
FIFTH ORDER	Meaning of Living (Philosophy)	Language of values
FOURTH ORDER	Meaning of Analysis (Philosophy of Science)	Language *about* analysis
THIRD ORDER (Most open to messages from others)	Analysis of Observations (Science)	Language of analysis
SECOND ORDER	Observation of Sensual Experience	Language *about* action and emotional response
FIRST ORDER	Sensual Experience	Action language Emotional response

Translation

FIGURE 5-3 Translation and Language Levels

there." The first is an unconscious or at least subconscious command; the second is a command and a conscious statement—"*I say . . .*" In first-order language there is no "I."[11] Emerging from feeling, vocal expression is as automatic as seeing and hearing. First-order language reveals our feelings and urges. But of itself it has no awareness.

As noted earlier, we do have an "I" available. Its use introduces us into the world of second-order language. The pronoun *I* is our doorway to awareness, and all the godlike experience of the human emerges from

---

[11]First-order language expresses, but does not describe, action and is thus very much like other animal and insect language.

the capacity of the "I" to make the "I" an object unto itself. Helen Keller, stricken blind and deaf at 19 months, learned language more painfully than most of us and thus achieved a peculiar perspective about that learning. She reports that she was a confused bundle of irritations until she gained the concept of "I," the self as an entity separate from all other things. It was, she said, in the gaining of a concept of self arising from the word *I* that she began to know the power of thought, of awareness. In speech that begins with *I* or any *subject* that *refers to* action or interaction, the perception of the speaker moves outside of first-order experience—like getting outside of a fence that surrounds a field—and he or she now talks about emotional expression and commands.[12] Second-order language makes comments on first-order experience. Here are some examples: "I feel good," "It is snowing again," "I wish that kid down the hall would turn his record player down." Each of these statements makes a comment about the self and/or other things observed. Note that the *tact*, as Skinner calls the language of commentary, shifts emphasis from action to things observed, not only by labeling a thing to be observed but also by replacing a strong verb of command such as *give, stop, strike* with some form of the intransitive verb *to be*.

Second-order language *translates* action and emotional response into concerns for study, and the translation process here is a capturing of the perception that takes place when one says, for instance, "Ah, nuts" (foreground) and then, perhaps to himself or herself, "I'm provoked" (background). The translation of the language of experience into the language of commentary on experience provides the barest rudiments of awareness, knowledge, or consciousness of experience. It is the beginning of the building of reality in abstraction and the beginning of making "I know" compete with doing. In essence, once again, it is achieved by creating a subject for a sentence, thus shifting the speaker from being an experience to being a commentator on experience.

Third, as creatures with the capacity to create worlds to explore within the frame of a language system, we have the capacity to talk about awareness, the very thing we are doing in this chapter. In this language, no translation is made from the language of action to the language of observation; rather, it is made within the language system of awareness itself. To illustrate, here is a continuous flow of third-level language: "The paper of this book is made of pine wood and the ink is an indigo which is made of herbs grown in India." And here is an example, without tangible references but still within the frame of the third order:

---

[12]Most of this explanation is similar to the reasoning of and the references in Paul Watzlawick, Janet Helmick Beavin, and Don D. Jackson. *Pragmatics of Human Communication* (New York: W. W. Norton & Company, Inc., 1967).

"College students today are trying to put together freedom, authority, responsibility, commitment, and love in a way that makes sense in their lives." Or, "A checking of differences in the positions of distant stars in subsequent photos suggests lines of force which, in turn, suggests that the universe is expanding."

Third-level language is the language of analysis. It takes things and ideas apart and puts them back together again. This is achieved by developing a vocabulary that labels details and relationships. The language of knowledge is the beginning of the designing of the world in words. The translation process in this language, as in the primary language of experience, is simply the foreground–background insight caught as one statement flows out of the one just made.[13] The peculiar perceptions we gain from analysis come from a verb change, from the verb *to be* to the verbs *to have* or *to be made of.* In short, analysis is the achievement of observing what *has* what, what belongs to what among our abstractions. Such is analysis, the language of science.

Fourth in the order of the human's ability to escape from sensation into flights of abstraction is the ability to create what we call a philosophical view, a structuring of the way the world works *for* us. In contrast, the scientist, as we have suggested, is concerned with making statements about the structure of the physical universe. The physical philosopher goes further and says, "In the light of what we know, here is what *I believe* we *can believe* about our experience." The translation is between the language of physical relationships (to have) and a language motivated by the urge to say "I believe." Its purpose? The philosopher is searching in his or her knowledge for a mirror for humanity. He or she wants to talk *about* the significance of the structures noted in scientific exploration. Just as second-level language constructs the rudiments of knowledge, so fourth-level language establishes the rudiments of a philosophy of human existence. It is the language of *awareness* of scientific thought, but it does not yet internalize that information and help people decide what to live for or how to establish purpose. That function is reserved for fifth-level language. Fourth-level language talks *about* scientific fact and organizes data amassed by the analysis of level three, which simply observes what happens. When we think and talk about "how things work out there," we are more than we were as collectors of data and less than we are yet to become when we abstract from the data some values by which to gauge our living.

[13]At this point this analysis parts company with Watzlawick *et al.* because of a somewhat different conceptualization of the linguistic character of identification. We conceive of identification as the phenomenon of translation between any two statements, whether within a language level or between language levels. And as we proceed it should become clear that we conceive of the greatest insights as the achievement of the greatest leaps of

The fifth step in the climb into a world of labels is the language of values. In it we assemble our beliefs into categories and arrange the categories into some rank order. As we leave the sensory world and climb the abstraction ladder, which we do when we are not hungry or driven by sex or anger or hate or any emotion that induces us to physical action, we begin examining our belief world, ourselves. We ask what we want, and what we want for tomorrow, and what, in the end, is the end of wants. We ask "Why?" We ask the "why" of our existence—and thus beliefs give way to values, and with this change a whole new concept of the word *meaning* emerges. When we think in response to a "Why?" the search for meaning goes beyond asking what goes with what to a search for the meaning of existence or, if you like, the meaning of meaning.

To restate, we have been talking up to this point about semantic meaning—how we make sense with language, and more important, how the translation process allows us to construct a world within a world within a world. But at the point where the semantic structuring begins to complete itself into a universe, we begin to ask the "why" of it all. We sense that we have built a world of symbols. But, like a man who works all his life to make a fortune, the main thing we have learned is the need to press on. We are forced to ask "And now what? Where does it all lead?" A person with many beliefs is a person of many planets without a universe, and such a person unites his or her beliefs by composing a cosmos of values. "Above all else," said Albert Schweitzer, "is reverence for life." Each of us evolves a holy of holies, and the statement that expresses it forms the center of our existence.

To repeat, at the fifth order of experience the peculiar thing about the language is that it asks the "why" of existence. All the "whys" in the lower orders are actually "hows"—how does something work? But at level five one is searching for a reason to justify one's existence. Such talk is aroused when we experience great tragedy—a loved one dies, a marriage or love affair goes on the rocks, we are caught in self-delusion or infidelity, we lose an eye or a leg. Something happens that severs *relationships* with former behavior or with people, and our daily existence is altered so radically that we question life—why live?

Probably no person has ever built a philosophy to justify his or her existence without contemplating suicide—why exist? And the forming of a set of values that in some degree affirms life involves a translation

---

identification between the most different levels of language. The ultimate achievement is Emerson's listening to the sermon of a stone.

process within the fifth level of language; that is, one puts one's values in clear order so that one knows what price one will pay for what when calamity strikes.

In *Man's Search for Meaning*, Victor Frankl talks of the way he and others learned to survive in a Nazi concentration camp. In story upon story, he shows that endurance depends on a "why" for existence, reaching Nietzsche's conclusion that a life with a "why" can endure any "how." A physician, Frankl observed that many of the prisoners with the strongest physical constitutions withered and died with little resistance and that often the frail people, like himself, who could verbalize at least to themselves some great meaning for their lives, persisted despite the horror and the toll of their daily experience. A "why" for existence, a religion, is not, it would seem, a luxurious fantasy but a basic need for human survival. It may be orthodox or unorthodox.

Let it be said this way. The common downgrading of abstract talk is based on an inadequate understanding of the nature of the levels of language and their roles in life. Abstraction at level five designs for a person his or her value scheme, which, if well built, maintains meaning for that person when tragedy strikes. A strong back and concrete talk are good only for sunny days. Hastily we concede that abstract language gives people the freedom to talk foolishly, too, but whoever does not enthusiastically take that chance does not build a value scheme to preserve him or her in the hour of darkness.

Basically, it is our belief in a myth that gives us the code by which we "put our stuff together." And as Rollo May points out, civilizations are composed and the lives of the individuals in those civilizations purposeful when the whole social order is directed by common myths.[14] The ages when humanity rises to great heights, such as the creative fifth century B.C. in Athens or the seventeenth century in Europe, which gave rise to the American Dream, are ages when a hopeful myth dominates the communication of the people. When such a common myth dies, despair, alienation, search for the doctor set in. As May points out, the listening professions are in great demand during those periods, as they are now. The death of a myth constitutes the death of a capacity to communicate adequately in fifth-level language (and above) and thus denies the power to become a whole human being. "Without myth we listen like a race of brain-injured people, unable to go behind the word and hear the person speaking," May said. "There can be no stronger proof of the impoverishment of our culture than the popular—though profoundly mistaken—definition of myth as falsehood."

[14]Rollo May, "Reality Beyond Rationalism," a speech at the Concurrent General Session II of the 24th National Conference on Higher Education, sponsored by the American Association for Higher Education, Chicago, March 3, 1969.

The myth is the story by which we interpret all that happens to us. The myth shapes our values and designs our responses to the messages that come our way. Myth is the master code that helps us translate. It is one thing to respond out of myth, "It is God's will." It is quite another— without myth— to respond "God, what a mess!"

In the shadows of the mind that hangs together is a myth.

Sixth and last, the human being, the symbol builder, reaches the highest level of existence and becomes completely organized only when his or her talk gives him(her) identity with many or all forms of existence. Lovers experience this ecstasy of identification, perhaps the most important contribution of the romantic experience—except for babies. A quarrel between people who eventually find the language "to comprehend" each other ends with words that permit a moment of identification, each with the other. Parents are likely to have this sense of at-oneness with life mysteries the instant they first behold their newborn baby. The second of awakening, having slept *on* the earth *under* the stars, or walking alone at the edge of the sea, sometimes will produce a moment of identification with seemingly everything. A person who ultimately arrives at reverence for all forms of life, as Schweitzer did, must ultimately feel an identification with a grain of wheat and a snail and the earth, as he did. Such a person cannot eat without offering up prayers of thanksgiving with feelings for the food that nurtures him or her similar to those for another person who has saved his or her life. With these feelings, that person nurtures life and in so doing *becomes* life itself. At this language level, we lose the sense of meaning as being "out there" and separate from us. "For all intents and purposes, our subjective experience of existence is reality—reality is our patterning of something that most probably is totally beyond objective human verification."[15]

Let us illustrate by using two stories from Frankl. He talks of attending a woman dying of diseases of malnutrition in a small hut in the camp. Though she knew she was dying, she was cheerful and peaceful; and she persisted even when he was sure she would be dead before his next visit. (The Nazis, having learned that Frankl was a physician, had put him to work in that capacity.) Just before the end, he asked her how it was that life was obviously sweet to her despite the horrid living conditions and the imminence of death.

> "I am grateful that fate has hit me so hard," she told me. "In my former life I was spoiled and did not take spiritual accomplishments seriously." Pointing through the window of the hut, she said, "This tree here is the only friend I have in my loneliness." Through that window she could see just one

[15]Watzlawick, Beavin, and Jackson, *op. cit.,* p. 264.

branch of a chestnut tree, and on the branch were two blossoms. "I often talk to this tree."[16]

Frankl's first silent response was, "She is probably delirious." But further probing indicated that in the long hours of waiting for the end she had seen the twigs and fluttering green leaves as symbols of life. They became exquisite to her and, in something of a trancelike state, she had felt her union with them and all that grows.

Frankl tells a story about his own experience that illustrates in a strikingly different way this phenomenon of identification and its resultant impact. He was marching in the snow to a work camp. His feet, clothed in rags, were swollen, wet, and bleeding. In his excruciating pain, his sense of immediate awareness gradually clouded, then faded. At that moment his consciousness (verbal behavior) was "transported" to a lecture hall in a medical school in Vienna where he delivered in fantasy a brilliant explanation of the nature of his emerging theory of the significance of identification with one's experience, documented by his very experience in the concentration camp. And when he ceased his translation and fell back into a consciousness of his marching, he reports that the fatigue and aching were within the bounds of endurance.

Language that performs the action of "peak experience,"[17] as Abraham Maslow calls these ultimate reaches of awareness, is achieved by a translation between the emotional expression of first-order sensual language and the value scheme of the sixth order of experience.[18] The language is poetic, for identities—"I am (whatever it may be)"—are not logical and therefore amenable to the treatment of semantic analysis. They are moments of transport of the self to something other than the self. This is the essence of all ecstatic experience, and it is achieved by the identity of "I" with something else beyond the physical self, achieved by the verb *to be*. Said Wittgenstein, "The subject (I) does not belong to the world, but it is a limit of the world."[19] The language of identification is poetry, is *analogical*, not analytical and logical. For the self "to be" something else other than itself is pure nonsense, except that it happens—and it happens because "being" is awareness, and awareness is the language

[16]Victor E. Frankl, *Man's Search for Meaning* (New York: Washington Square Press, Inc., 1963), p. 109.

[17]Abraham H. Maslow, *Values, Religion and Peak Experiences* (Columbus: Ohio State University Press, 1961).

[18]Helen Nierrell Lynd, *On Shame and the Search for Identity* (New York: Science Editions, Inc., 1965), pp. 179–180.

[19]Ludwig Wittgenstein, *Tractotus Logico-Philosophicus* (New York: Humanities Press, 1951), p. 151.

we are using at that moment. "Primary words do not describe something that might exist independently of them; but, being spoken, they bring out existence."[20] As suggested in earlier chapters, these moments are the source of the feelings that lead to depth of relationship and to self-actualization.

The capacities to express feeling, command, comment, analyze, believe, value, and transcend develop early in life.[21] The brain doubles in size during the first six months after birth and doubles again by age four. Psychologist Jerome Bruner believes his research shows that the child can be taught any concept as soon as he or she speaks in sentences, as long as the concept is taught in his or her vocabulary. We once heard a four-year-old tell how he had shot a bird with a wooden gun, stuck the bird on the end of the gun, and roasted it over a star. That takes some doing. Even more remarkable, we heard a five-year-old exclaim as he stood in awe of a fiery sky early one morning, "Nothing like that could be unless there was God," and then mumble seconds later, "But that doesn't make sense. Who made God?" The capacity to deal with questions of knowledge, value, and even existence are available to the child as soon as he or she has command of the syntax that does the job.

But, again the cruel paradox, our very power to build a universe in language is, at the same time, the power to fool ourselves. With the verb *to be* we glue together whatever we say.[22] The conceptualization of the self-image, including the value scheme, and one's image of the world are dependent, in the last analysis, on these identifications of the self with all sorts of things, only some of which need work to our advantage. The Who am I? test illustrates this point. One is asked to complete a series of "I am ____" statements. "I am brave." "I am nervous." "I am sarcastic." "I am a poor speller." "I am afraid of the older generation." "I am loved." Anything is anything I say it is.[23] It may well be that today's generation has sensed both the power and the danger in the identification experi-

[20]Martin Buber, *I and Thou* (New York: Scribner's, 1958), p. 1.

[21]For those who want to see the interlocking of the levels, this may be noted: In the languages of levels one, three, and five, experience is examined for the purposes of power and control. All things become an extension of the self. A command conceives of the other person as one's legs or hands. The ultimate purpose of science is to control physical nature or other people. A value scheme is designed in order to control oneself. Expression *of* and analysis *of* are made for "calculating" purposes. Conversely, the languages of self-awareness, belief, and transcendental experience in varying ways lose the power of being responsive to the physical reality of the moment for the achievement of insight gained by the quick shift of identification with that reality.

[22]For additional insights see Watzlawick, Beavin, and Jackson, *op. cit.*, Chap. 6.

[23]See Charles T. Brown, "An Experimental Diagnosis of Thinking on Controversial Issues," *Speech Monographs*, 17 (1950), 370–377. A simple assertion, "A thing is true because I say it is true," proved to be the second most attractive form of evidence to college students from freshmen through graduate school.

ence. Says nineteen-year-old James Kunen, "We youths say 'like' all the time because we mistrust reality. It takes a certain commitment to say something *is*. Inserting 'like' gives you a bit more running room."[24]

An Example of the Levels at Work

"Sounds fine," said the students in one of our classes when we had just gone through the preceding material, "but is it anything more than theory? Can it be used?" We suggested that they pick a word at random and see if we could apply it at each of the six levels. The word one student came up with was *sand*. Here is what we did with it:

Level 1 (control and feeling):	Out of my way! Damn sand in my eyes!
Level 2 (self-commentary):	Why did I scream, as if you and the wind were my enemy? I must understand my frustrations.
Level 3 (scientific observation):	Sand is the debris of the decaying earth, which is useful in the making of many things...cement, glass, molds. Fascinatingly, when mixed with oil or coal it forms silicon, a substance that is part inorganic and part organic.
Level 4 (meaning of observation):	What we can know about sand we can know about many other elements of the earth. We *can* predict what will produce silicon, and we can pretty well count on our prediction.
Level 5 (values; meaning of life):	Even in the sand I hear the sermons of the universe. Everything belongs together in a beautiful pattern if we can understand the formula. I must make my life one piece of the urge to live and the unavoidable need to die. The Trappist monks say that out of the desert of experience springs the life of understanding.
Level 6 (identity of the self):	I am willing to belong to the sand that lines the shores where life began, and of which I am a part. I am the sand.

The Role of Feedback in Translation at All Levels

As we have noted, self-talk, self-persuasion, and self-feedback are crucial in the reach for meaning. But so are the vibrations fed back to us

[24]James Simon Kunen, *The Strawberry Statement: Notes of a College Revolutionary* (New York: Avon, 1968), pp. 101–102.

by those who listen. We scan both our own words and our impacts on others for the assessment of meaning. In saying something we scarcely know what we are going to say until we hear ourselves saying it, and we search for its validity by looking into the eyes of our listener. The significance of feedback to meaning is seen in international conferences where the person speaking is the only person, other than the interpreter, who knows his or her language. The meaning of that person's statements is registered in a delayed translation and, for the speaker, a delayed feedback. As a communicator he or she is crippled because immediate feedback, so necessary to the effort to make sense, is lacking. Alex Bavelas suggests that in the future we consider a "member" of an international committee to be a pair of people speaking the same language—in order to ensure that the speaker has at least one person besides himself or herself to provide the dual feedback system so necessary to the functioning of a speaker.[25]

Here is another way of grasping the significance of feedback in the language process. In thinking to ourselves or talking with others, it is as if we were in a dark room with a flashlight, searching for the wall switch by which to illuminate the whole room. Failing in our search, we recognize that we are dependent on the small amount of data fed back from the focus of the light at the moment and that if we are to conceptualize the whole room we must remember, store away, and relate the information gained from the light as we move about.

Language is linear; words come one at a time. Attention is verbal awareness, and words are variable pinpoints of light, seldom global.

As you sit in your chair and read this, you are surrounded by objects and your ears are focal points in a sea of sound. You are aware of what you are aware of only in terms of the words that flash into existence. When your verbal response is reflecting details of sensory experience, of color, size, weight, heat, intensity, distance, awareness is a sharp pinpoint of light in a relatively darkened room. But words and the combinations thereof shift from one language level to another. When your language shifts to levels five and six—when you are sorting out the meaning of your existence or are identifying, in some transcendent moment, with a loved one, thing, place, or life itself—your language seems for the second to diffuse light so as to illuminate your whole internal being.[26] It is this momentarily diffused "comprehending" light that constitutes the deepest insight. And it is probably the feedback both within and between

[25]Mary Capes, ed., *Communication or Conflict* (New York: Association Press, 1960), p. 129.

[26]The catatonic is probably the example of pathological fixation of the identification experience. He or she cannot accommodate new information and so freezes on some comfortable identity, thus eliminating the data input of the scanning experience.

language levels that does the mechanical work for what we have been calling the translation process.

Confidence to Listen and Feedback Among All Levels

Only as we translate lower-order experiences into higher-order ones, and occasionally complete the cycle of translations by identifying our "why" of existence with first-order experience, do we gain the confidence to listen to new information without anxiety. Again, as language is linear, it picks up awareness in pieces. But we cannot tolerate a world in pieces. A world is one. Here we must resort to analogy again, as always when we want to ensure new comprehension. The operation of language is very much like watching life through a slit in a solid board fence—words and sentences coming one at a time. If a cat on the other side of the fence walks by the slit, we see its head first, then its body, and finally its tail. Only by "comprehending" that this is *one* thing, not a series of *unrelated* things, can we make sense of it. And we translate the parts into the whole with the word *cat*—the symbol encompasses all the separately perceived parts.

If the separate messages remain separate, they create great fear as to their meaning. Lacking sophisticated scientific data at language level three, primitive people live in terrible fear when the sky flashes fire and roars its thunder. Quaking, they identify their own fear and anger with the violence of the cosmos and thus imbue the universe with a personality very much like their own distraught selves. In confusion they ask, "Why is God vengeful? What have I done?" Even the father of one of the authors, though far removed from the cave dweller, was distressed by contemplations such as these. "It is dangerous to explore these things," he said. "We should have faith without question." Which, translated, says, "To ask about the nature of the abstract language we use to design and maintain our world in one piece is to look God in the face—and that might make Him angry."

Only as we create a God of our value scheme who engenders basic feelings of security can we permit any and all messages to be listened to. Thus the open mind must imagine the unknown plan, if plan it is, to be safe. Ultimately, it comes to this: The person who can listen fearlessly lives joyously in ambiguity, knowing that our lives are in a world where all is in flux—that each is a particle among particles forming a changing wave of particles in time. Learning to listen is like learning to feel safe in the womb of a ship that plunges and rolls and rumbles through the endless sea in the black night. It is this identification with the powers beyond ken or control that lowers anxiety and permits one to sense the verbal cues that lead into new states of awareness.

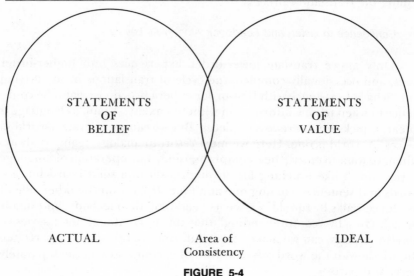

ACTUAL   Area of   IDEAL
                   Consistency

FIGURE 5-4

THE LANGUAGES OF BELIEF, VALUE, AND THE SELF-CONCEPT

Most of the listening-to-each-other problems of the human race involve the languages of beliefs and values—for here are the levels at which we create the verbal designs that hold us intact and steer our course.[27] If awareness is verbal behavior, then the *I* we are so fond of and about whom we each talk so much is a verbal image, a dual one involving the person I am and the one I want to be (a phenomenon discussed in Chapter 2). The basic tensions we feel concern the disparity between the perceived self and the ideal future self—and these tensions are aroused or allayed by our translations between the languages of belief and value.

It should be noted, as Figure 5-4 suggests, that what we call a belief is an abstraction that we feel we command, whereas a value is something we wish to attain. The statement "I believe in education" has a considerably different meaning than "I place a high value on education," for while the former says, "Education is indispensable," the latter suggests a

---

[27]Much of our thinking in this section has been stirred by the works of Milton Rokeach, most particularly *The Nature of Human Values* (New York: The Free Press, 1974). Rokeach identifies three kinds of beliefs: descriptive or existential; evaluative; and prescriptive or proscriptive. He sees value as a belief of the third type. "A value," he says, "is a belief upon which a man acts by preference" (see pp. 6–7).

priority and the willingness to pay a price for that priority. It sets the stage for decision behavior.

We are most shaken when the value scheme by which we govern our lives is reordered. Little wonder. Without this we are blown hither and yon by contradictory messages. It is not strange that studies of the self-concept demonstrate time and again that the value scheme of a person remains relatively fixed as he or she moves through life.[28] And the scheme of values stands firm when it is intimately related to the person's basic feelings. Sensual experience is always valid.[29] We can communicate without fear when our feelings and values work in harmony.

And, therefore, the most critical thing we do when we communicate is to check the incoming data against both our feeling world and our value world. If it fits both, we take it. If it fits one but not the other, we weigh it. If we take it something has to give.

We suffer intense stress when a message fits our feelings but upsets our value world. Tolstoy tells of his terrible urge to seduce a servant girl in his home after he had adopted a life of celibacy. If he gives in, his value world is shaken and he experiences deep emotions of confusion until some kind of value order is restored. It is just as bad if the message fits the value world but not the feelings. Consider the millions in the economic rat race who do what they hate to do because they value riches, position, or whatever. In the poem "Richard Cory," everybody in town admired and envied Mr. Cory, who went home one night and put a bullet through his head.

The message we listen to most easily comes to us with low emotional upheaval and without violence to our value scheme. In short, we can all handle information, and thus we are most open at language level three. Light travels at 186,000 miles per second, we are told. And probably not even a physical scientist would be disturbed at the prospect of finding out that it might be something different. What we cannot tolerate, without great confusion, is the likelihood of discovering that life is something different from what we imagine it to be—that either our basic feelings or the values that form our identity must change.

Each of us lives within his or her own Tower of Babel. Forming the highest reaches is the myth through which we look out on life. To evolve

[28]Richard Dieker, Loren Crane, and Charles T. Brown, "The Effect of Repeated Self-viewing on Closed-Circuit Television, or Changes in the Self-concept" (Washington, D.C.: U.S. Dept. of Health, Education and Welfare, Office of Education, Bureau of Research), Final Report, Project No. 7-E-198, Contract No. OEC-0-8-070198-2807, September, 1968; Carl Rogers, *On Becoming a Person* (Boston: Houghton-Mifflin Co., 1961); Ruth Wylie, *The Self Concept* (Lincoln: Nebraska University Press, 1961); Dean Barnlund, *Interpersonal Communication* (Boston: Houghton-Mifflin Co., 1968), p. 635.

[29]Richard S. Crutchfield, "Conformity and Character," *American Psychologist,* 10 (1955), 91–98.

into something near our potential we must interlace this myth with the feelings that are our foundation—to let things reveal themselves to us, to "talk of their nature, and be able to respond to them, to answer."[30] Yet we cannot do this alone. To know what we mean we must talk and listen to others whose revelations are different. It is therefore the lot of humans to live in doubt, which is good—if matched with courage. Said Tennyson, "There lies more faith in honest doubt... than in all your creeds." Existential anxiety is every person's problem in every age. The search for meaning is humanity's everlasting first order of business.

INSTRUMENT 5-1

MEANING MAGIC

The following is a paragraph from a newspaper feature column.[31] Every fourth word is missing. Fill in the blank spaces with the word that seems to fit.

_____ woman next to _____ at dinner was
        1   2

_____ about her school _____, and mentioned that
        3   4

_____ one term she _____ a cheerleader. "But
        5   6

_____ was the worst _____ in the history _____ the
        7   8   9

school," she _____, "because when the _____ team was
               10   11

losing, _____ wanted to cheer _____ up, too." Her
              12   13

_____ struck a nerve _____ me. I have _____ felt
        14   15   16

myself an _____ duck because it _____ been impossible
                 17   18

for _____ to be blindly _____. Sitting in the _____,
        19   20   21

---

[30]From "A Conversation with Wedard Boss," *Psychology Today*, December 1968, p. 63.
[31]From *Strictly Personal* by Sydney J. Harris. Copyright 1977 Field Enterprises, Inc. Courtesy of Field Newspaper Syndicate.

even with one _____ my own sons _____ the field, I
              22   23

_____ always secretly rooting _____ the underdog,
  24   25

whichever _____ that may be. _____ am a rotten
           26   27

_____, in the sense _____ being a fanatic _____ my
  28   29   30

side. People _____ often cheer or _____ when the enemy
            31   32

_____ commits some gross _____; I feel sorry
  33   34

_____ them. I don't _____ my side to _____ by
  35   36   37

default, but _____ merit.
            38

The 38 words are listed at the bottom of the page. Check (√) the spaces that you could not fill in or in which you chose the wrong word. Give yourself half credit where the word you chose makes just as much sense in the context. (*These* for *there* or *a* for *the* do not alter meaning.) Add the number of errors and subtract it from 38; place that number here:_____. Compare your score with the mean for the class. Your score tells you your power to formulate meaning out of the structure of the language.

Key to Instrument 5-1

1. The	14. comment	27. I
2. me	15. in	28. "fan"
3. reminiscing	16. always	29. of
4. days	17. odd	30. for
5. for	18. has	31. will
6. was	19. me	32. applaud
7. I	20. partisan	33. team
8. one	21. stands	34. error
9. of	22. of	35. for
10. said	23. on	36. want
11. other	24. am	37. win
12. I	25. for	38. by
13. them	26. team	

INSTRUMENT 5-2

YOUR LANGUAGE LEVEL[32]

Following is a list of words. Circle the words that best describe the kinds of activities in which you prefer to engage. Do not worry about whether they are things you ought to do. Rather, think about the things you really like to do. Circle the words that "fit" your life and way of operating. React immediately and trust your responses.

analyzing	imagining
assessing	intuiting
choosing	labeling
classifying	naming
comprehending	outlining
deciding	perceiving
describing	ranking things
dreaming	seeing causes
fantasizing	sensing
feeling	structuring
generalizing	telling about
idealizing	understanding

Now check the words below that you have circled.

Language Usage Scoring Sheet

First Order
(language of action; emotional
response)

feeling
intuiting
perceiving
sensing

Second Order
(language about experience
and emotional response)

describing
naming
labeling
telling about

Third Order
(language of analysis)

classifying
comprehending
seeing causes
understanding

[32]By permission of Dr. Ernest Stech, Department of Communication Arts and Sciences, Western Michigan University.

Fourth Order (language about analysis)	analyzing generalizing outlining structuring
Fifth Order (language of values)	assessing choosing deciding ranking things
Sixth Order (language of poetry about experience)	dreaming fantasizing idealizing imagining

The results show you how you prefer to use language. The levels with the greatest number of words checked in the righthand column are your preferred levels of operation.

EXERCISES

1. D. David Bourland conceived the equation $E' = E - e$, in which E represents all of the words in standard American English and e represents all forms of the verb *to be*. Writing (or talking or thinking) in E' will, he believes, make one a little less dogmatic and a little more accurate. Think about something you believe very strongly, then try to write and/or talk about it in E'. Note what happens to the "certainties" in your thinking. (Note also that this paragraph appears in E'.)

2. Practice the use of a multivalued orientation in conversation with someone else who has been exposed to the same experience as you. Discuss, for example, a television program both have seen, or a movie, concert, new record, sporting event, political speech, campus event, or the like. Try to talk about the event, avoiding polar terms wherever possible, describing the thing in comparative degrees and specifying measurements wherever possible (e.g., "in nine of the past ten years"). Do not back away from your evaluations, but try to avoid making them in oversimplified terms.

3. The humanistic psychologist Carl Rogers emphasizes listening as an instrument, both for clarification of communication and for resolution of conflict. He suggests that the listener state and restate what the other person has said to that person's satisfaction. In effect, what happens is that clarity of meaning is achieved through the translation of two adjacent statements.

    Listen to a classmate talk about something that is a source of confusion (anxiety, anger, enjoyment) and say back to that person, to his or her satisfaction, what you think he or she has said.

Note what you have learned.

4. Watch a movie or listen to a speech in your class. Write a one-sentence comment on it. Classify it into one of the six language levels. Discuss it with the class.

   Write six statements related to the movie or speech, one at each of the six language levels.

5. Arrange in order of importance (from 1 to 17) the following values as you perceive them. Discuss differences among your classmates.

	In the life of the average American adult	In the life of the average college student	In your life now
Helping others	( )	( )	( )
Fame	( )	( )	( )
Food	( )	( )	( )
Wealth	( )	( )	( )
Self-esteem	( )	( )	( )
Love and affection	( )	( )	( )
Achievement	( )	( )	( )
Security	( )	( )	( )
Possessions	( )	( )	( )
Your potentials	( )	( )	( )
Reputation	( )	( )	( )
Status	( )	( )	( )
Self-understanding	( )	( )	( )
Emotional stability	( )	( )	( )
Making creative things	( )	( )	( )
Being ethical	( )	( )	( )
Competition	( )	( )	( )

6. In order to make sense of our lives it is necessary to keep all abstractions well related to experience. The following game illustrates this. Have all your classmates write an abstract noun (*beauty, honesty, justice,* etc.) on a slip of paper. Collect the slips. From the slips randomly fill in the blanks in the following statements:

   a. Where ____ begins ____ ends.

   b. If ____ leads to ____ you may expect ____ to follow.

   c. Greater than ____ is ____.

   d. When a person achieves ____ he(she) reveals ____.

   e. ____, ____, and ____ are the essence of ____.

   How can you determine the sense in any of these statements?

7. Explain an intrapersonal conflict in which you are engaged, showing how it is a struggle between feelings and conflicting values. If this is unclear, reread pages 132–34.

8. Tell about a peak or transcendent experience.
9. Discuss your peak experience with people, things, nature, ideas.
10. Listen to the "thousand voices" of the river. As you listen to the river (lake, rain), how does your experience change? At what language levels do you translate the experience for your understanding?

6

Meaning:
Nonverbal Messages

A man does not lay down his hat... or take it up... but something escapes, which discovers him.

Laurence Sterne

One cannot not communicate.

Paul Watzlawick*

Some fascinating discoveries have been made recently about the messages people send each other without words. Here is a sampler:

Married couples experiencing the most conflict tend to cross their arms and legs more, have less eye contact, and touch themselves more frequently than they touch each other.[1]

Teachers who habitually gesture more get better results from their students.[2]

Extroverts choose to sit opposite people they are talking to. They tend to pass up positions that would put them at an angle to the other person.[3]

Extroverts choose positions that put them close to the other person physically, while introverts choose positions that keep them more distant, both visually and physically.[4]

---

*Paul Watzlawick, *An Anthology of Human Communication* (Palo Alto, Calif.: Science and Behavior Books Incorporated, 1964), p. 2.

[1]Ernest G. Beier, "Nonverbal Communication: How We Send Emotional Messages," *Psychology Today*, October 1974, pp. 53–56.

[2]Albert Mehrabian, *Silent Messages* (Belmont, Calif.: Wadsworth Publishing Company, Inc., 1971), p. 67.

[3]Mark L. Knapp, *Nonverbal Communication in Human Interaction* (New York: Holt, Rinehart and Winston, Inc., 1972), p. 53.

[4]*Ibid.*, pp. 53–54.

Increasing the distance between yourself and the person with whom you are communicating will help create a negative impression of yourself and may help destroy interpersonal trust.[5]

The catalog of such findings is long and is rapidly getting longer. It would be sheer folly for us to try to somehow cover the whole field of nonverbal expression in this chapter. What we want to do, instead, is to highlight the features of nonverbal messages that have the greatest effect on interpersonal communication. Specifically, we are looking for answers to the following questions:

1. What nonverbal messages most affect communication?
2. What happens to communication if the nonverbal messages do not fit the words being spoken?
3. Who are the people who can best read and interpret nonverbal messages?

THE INESCAPABILITY OF THE NONVERBAL

Before we plunge into answers to the preceding questions, we need to underscore a basic truth about nonverbal messages: They are inescapable in communication. Verbal messages are always sent in a nonverbal context. Therefore messages cannot be translated except with the help of nonverbal cues. How do we know the other person knows what he or she is talking about? Or that he or she is being honest? Or that he or she cares whether we communicate or not? The answer is nestled in the web of words and nonverbal signals. "It's not what you do but the way that you do it," went a popular song of the 1930s. Physical appearance, distance between communicators, relative position, posture, hands, face, eyes, voice—all of these are guides to our interpretation of each other's words. It is a misconception, as we have pointed out several times throughout the book, to think that if I do not say anything I do not communicate. "Although an individual may stop talking," says Erving Goffman, "he cannot stop communicating through body idiom.... He cannot say nothing."[6]

As a matter of fact, there is increasing evidence that if we compare the verbal and nonverbal codes the latter is more significant than the former. According to Ray Birdwhistell, a careful student of nonverbal communication, 65 percent of the social meaning in a two-person communication is carried by the nonverbal band and only 35 percent by the words spoken.

[5]Dale G. Leathers, *Nonverbal Communication Systems* (Boston: Allyn & Bacon, Inc., 1976), p. 62.

[6]Erving Goffman, *Behavior in Public Places* (New York: Macmillan Co., 1973), p. 35.

At the close of Michael Argyle's summation of the psychology of communication, based on some 120 pieces of research, he writes,

> Not only public speakers, and professional social-skill performers, but anyone who takes part in social encounters, must present some kind of "face" or self-image. If he does not the others will have difficulty in behaving towards him. It does not help for him to be obsequious and self-effacing. On the other hand the image presented should be realistic or there is a danger of it collapsing, which is one of the main causes of embarrassment. He should not be primarily concerned about the image-projection and its success, but about creating the responses he desires on the part of others.[7]

No matter how little or how much we respect the integrity of our respondent, the fact is we do not communicate without the urge to make an impact. The basic question of every listening act is, What does that message mean? How much of the message tells me about the image making of the other person? What in the message reveals something about myself? These taken together, what does the message tell me about the *facts* being talked about?

The salesperson says to a potential buyer:

> I would say the land at present is worth $250 per acre. In fifteen years it will go for $1,000 an acre. I don't know how to evaluate the house. At the going cost of $40 per foot it cannot be replaced for $60,000. But few people today would build a house like that. What do you think it is worth?

The client stammers, "I don't know." She does so because she cannot determine whether the salesperson has lapsed into an economic question: "Let us try to decide in this unusual situation how to set a value on that place." Or is he asking, "What is it worth to you?" Or is he asking, "How much are you attracted to a bargain?" Or something else? The words themselves are a constant, no matter how they are translated. But the listener cannot translate them without placing an interpretation on the nonverbal cues. The question in the interpretation is, What does the salesperson want me to say to him? What feelings is he trying to induce in me? What are we talking about that we are not talking about? The marriage of the verbal and nonverbal, we are trying to say, is inevitable and absolutely necessary. Otherwise meaning becomes an orphan whose face we can never rightly see.

[7]Michael Argyle, *The Psychology of Interpersonal Behavior* (Baltimore: Penguin Books, 1967), p. 204.

NONVERBAL MESSAGES THAT AFFECT COMMUNICATION

For our purposes it may be useful to adopt the labels now attached to the major kinds of nonverbal messages:

1. *Body movement (kinesics)*—messages carried in bodily movement, including movements of the face, head, eyes, hands, and other parts of the body.
2. *Distance (proxemics)*—messages sent through the use of personal space, relative position, and the like.
3. *Voice (vocalics)*—cues and nuances of meaning and feeling conveyed in the features of the voice (inflection, volume, harshness-softness, etc.).
4. *Touch (haptics)*—messages conveyed through touch. Let us look at each of these.

Body Movement (Kinesics)

The eyes   It is hard to say with any certainty whether the eyes are the single most important feature of bodily movement in the conveying of interpersonal meaning, but everyday observation suggests that this is so. Each of us knows some people who are so furtive that their eyes hardly ever meet our own, and others who look at us so consistently that it makes us uncomfortable. And on the basis of these behaviors we make silent statements: "She is afraid of her own shadow"; "She doesn't trust me"; "She doesn't trust herself." It is pretty clear that the eyes are a major channel in the effort of two human beings to make contact.

Research confirms that two of the most essential uses of the eyes are (1) to get feedback and (2) to control the unit of communication.[8] Without feedback, as our early discussion of the communication process showed, there can be no ongoing communication process. And the eyes, perhaps even more than the ears, become the channel through which that feedback can come. Some of the exercises at the end of this chapter invite you to demonstrate for yourself how important eye information is.

How do we go about this search for feedback? Knapp[9] reports extensive studies by Kendon in which it was discovered that when person A begins talking to B he typically looks away. Then, as A comes toward the end of what he has to say, he looks at B and continues to look at him as he begins speaking. In turn, B looks away as he begins his response and looks back as he comes to the end of it. If the person doing the talking does not look away at the conclusion of his remarks, the other person either delays his response or does not respond at all. It is as though when we are thinking about what we want to say we do not want to be dis-

---

[8]Knapp, *op. cit.*, p. 131.
[9]*Ibid.*, p. 131.

tracted by looking at the other. Indeed, continuing to look at one's listener after completing a statement is like a demand for agreement.

If this research is supported in the future, it points to serious problems in our eye habits, because looking away *during* a verbal explanation deprives us of the very feedback we need to tell whether we are making contact and what kind of effect that contact is producing. To complicate things, Kendon discovered, in the research just referred to, that person A will look at B more if he is showing a positive emotional response than if he is showing a negative emotional response. This would seem to cripple the speaker, leading him to overlook the negative signals he needs if he is to improve and clarify his message. As a sort of compensation for this vulnerability, it has been discovered that when we are sensitive to and like the other person we hold eye contact with that person. Any teacher or public speaker knows the value of the listener who meets and holds his or her gaze.

Interesting differences appear to exist between the sexes when it comes to use of the eyes. Argyle[10] found that women hold eye contact longer than men. There is more eye meeting between members of the same sex than between members of the opposite sex. This fits the much older observation that members of the same sex understand each other better than male and female understand each other. As we all know, much or prolonged eye contact between members of the opposite sex involves sexual attraction, and neither law nor mores have found a way to control the lovemaking of eyes that meet.

Women, more than men, search out the eyes of the other person as they speak. Indeed, women, it has been found, tend to talk less when they cannot see their conversant. Not so with men, who look more when listening and less when talking. Men can talk with ease to the back of their conversant. This probably means, as Argyle suggests, that women depend on the behavior of their listener to guide their speech. Men, who some studies show to be more independent and to have higher self-esteem, depend less on the response of their listener, and as listeners themselves they check out the veracity of their conversant more carefully than women do. Since self-esteem and independence are profoundly affected by the culture, it might be predicted that the changing role of women in our culture will reduce, and probably eliminate, the differences we have just reported.

Beyond sexual differences, what can we learn from the cases in which there is prolonged looking by one or both of the communicants? Long looking seems to be both a way of searching for affiliation and of attempting to control. The sergeant looks hard into the eye of his or her

[10]Argyle, *op. cit.,* Chap. 6.

subordinate when giving an order—and may step up close to do it. (Usually people hold longer eye contact at a distance than up close.) If the one so challenged wishes to meet the challenge, he or she holds to the eye contact as long as the other person is looking into his or her eyes. If he(she) weakens, his(her) eyes will drop. If he(she) withdraws—that is, ignores the challenge—he(she) looks away.

The eyes have their unconscious language, which has caused people through the ages to believe that a dishonest person cannot look you in the eye. But the sharp rascal knows this, so the most unscrupulous exploiters will feign honesty by means of intense, prolonged looking into the other person's eyes. Only their studied intensity gives them away— and it takes an extraordinary observer to sense this.

Here is an observation particularly relevant to the concept of this chapter. Prolonged looking at others on the part of a person, speaker or listener, indicates concern for the relationship. Short glances are in-

Five Grotesque Heads by Leonardo da Vinci. Reproduced by gracious permission of Her Majesty Queen Elizabeth II. Royal Library, Windsor Castle.

volved when people are more content oriented. These scanning glances, where content is the focus of attention, last from .25 to .35 of a second. This is what we do in monologue, just a quick glance to see if the other person is "with us." The fixations that attend the times when we are intensifying the relationship or are trying to determine what the other person really means will usually last from one to seven seconds—about as long as we can fix attention. Eye contact (looking when the eyes of both parties meet) ranges, depending on the nature of the conversation, from 10 percent to 30 percent of the time. And in most conversations fixations on the other person's face, eyes, or other features range from 30 percent to 60 percent of the conversation time. When we look at another person's face we look at his or her eyes more than at any other feature and, thus, more at the upper part of the face than at the lower part. We learn this early in life; studies by René Spitz show that the baby concentrates on the mother's eyes and is terrified when the mother wears a mask.[11] The lower part of the face may be covered without upsetting the child. The mask obscures identity, emboldens a person, and lowers his or her fears, as indicated by research at the University of Delaware.[12] Those who wish to live *incognito* wear dark glasses.

A potpourri of other findings about eye behavior throw light on the peculiar and significant role of the eyes in establishing the relationships of our conversations. As we come to the close of a comment we look at our listener in order to assess our impact, which at once—if we seem satisfied—signals our listener that he or she is free to speak. Conversants who like each other look more at each other than conversants who dislike each other. We all know the meaning of being avoided, especially if we look and the other person does not look back, for we know when that person's peripheral vision alerts him or her that he or she is being looked at. If we want to be believed, this urgent plea is registered in our prolonged and open look into our listener's eyes.

If we are looking at a person to whom we are listening, and we want to speak, we look away to signal our wish to take our turn. When we are giving longer comments, and thus want not to be interrupted, we look less at our conversant. And when the content of our speech grows more concrete, replete with metaphors and stories, we look less at our listener, unconsciously knowing that the vivid and dramatic impact of our words should act alone. As we shift to our thoughts and abstractions we look more and longer at our listener, apparently to compensate for the lowered power of abstract language. Just as we look less when we know our words are striking home, so we look less when smiling, apparently

---

[11]René Spitz, *The First Year of Life* (New York: International Universities Press, 1965).
[12]Argyle, *op. cit.*, pp. 114–115.

"knowing" that the smile is caring for the everlasting task of establishing and maintaining relationship.

Perhaps the degree to which we depend on our looking in figuring out the meaning of a conversation is best sensed by listening, with eyes closed, to a conversation. While some people, like the blind person, learn quickly how to interpret from sound cues alone, most people report feelings of irritation and confusion. Our students often report, "I heard the shuffling of feet, people moving in their chairs, people's breathing and sighing. I couldn't focus on the conversation. I got lost in a sea of sound."

Whether a person looks at someone or looks away; whether he(she) extends the duration of his(her) looking—these are matters of choice and can be changed by an act of will. But there are some eye messages that are beyond the control of the sender. And the more such nonverbal messages are beyond the control of the one sending them, the more the listener relies on them. So it is important to note one of them. Perhaps the least controlled of all our behaviors is the dilation of the pupils of the eyes when we look at a person we like. Studies at the University of Chicago with a sophisticated eye camera demonstrate this. Conversely, the steely-eyed look that we have all received from a person who dislikes us is in part due to constriction of the pupils.

The face   "The face," Dale Leathers points out, "can be used to communicate more emotional meanings more accurately than any other medium in interpersonal communication."[13] Studies by Ekman and Friesen[14] show that the face hardly ever carries just one emotional message. Rather, there are multiple emotions present at any moment, and the shift from one to another and then to still another occurs so rapidly that we find it easy to miss many of the signals that are there. Ekman and Friesen reported, for example, that a person saying nice things about a friend seemed to have a pleasant facial expression, but when a film of that expression was slowed down it could be seen that a look of anger crossed her face. The whole face apparently gets into the act, with one emotion shown in one portion of the face, another emotion in another portion. The face is, in short, a tremendously versatile tool for communicating emotional content and providing useful feedback. It may help you as a communicator to be aware that, whether you will it or not, your face is (1) communicating *evaluation,* telling the observer whether you regard a thing good or bad; (2) communicating *interest or disinterest* in what is happening; (3) communicating *intensity,* letting the other person know how much you are involved in the exchange; (4) communicating

[13]Leathers, *op. cit.,* p. 34.
[14]Reported in Knapp, *op. cit.,* p. 121.

the extent to which you have *control* over your own messages; and (5) communicating the degree to which you are *understanding* the exchange.[15]

The face is so mobile and so responsive to our moods and perceptions that over a lifetime it forms the lines, furrows, planes, and coloration that tell others about our stance toward life. Note the sketch from Leonardo da Vinci's notebook on page 145.

The hands   It is a funny thing about the hands. Very little research has been done on their effect on communication, but almost everyone agrees that they play a very important part in supplementing the verbal message. Many writers say that, next to the face, the hands are probably the most expressive part of the body. One writer hypothesizes that the face and eyes may carry clues to specific emotions, while the hands and other body cues may tell something about the intensity of those emotions.[16]

But the thing that is useful for anyone studying communication is the awareness that the body acts as a unit when it sends nonverbal messages, and the hands are a part of that unit. That means that *not* to use the hands is to send messages that signal fear or anxiety or determination to control the situation. Watching someone who is involved in an exchange and is seemingly unresponsive with his or her hands is a curious experience. If you watch closely, you will note the twitching of the fine muscles in the fingers and back of the hand, suggesting that impulses are there all right but are being restrained. It is "natural" to use the hands as a part of the total bodily reaction. Not to use the hands is unnatural.

We have already mentioned the study that showed that teachers who used more gestures are better liked by their students. Perhaps this is because hands, when freely used, help a listener know whether the speaker means what he or she says. Too often the hands send signals that belie the rest of the picture. A teacher sits "calmly" at a desk—constantly drumming his or her fingers. A speaker smiles while telling a joke—but his or her hands shake.

Communication improves as the hands are allowed to respond freely.

Posture   One's posture is a self-reflective statement. When we are determined, we lean into our task. Drooping shoulders indicate resignation. Standing tall suggests pride. Going limp indicates exhaustion. Re-

[15]Leathers, *op. cit.*, pp. 33–34.

[16]P. Ekman, "Differential Communication of Affect by Head and Body Cues," *Journal of Personality and Social Psychology,* # 2, 1965, 726–735.

searchers note that everybody has a characteristic posture "at rest to which he returns whenever he has deviated from it."[17] The word *return* is important here, for posture is not a static thing. And when the movement is restless or tense or deviates radically from its central tendency, the person reveals conflict and anxiety. Much of the research on posture is old; the most extensive work was done by the psychologist William James early in the century. This is what he concluded from his work:

> The posture as a whole is an ensemble or constellation of different parts. Of these the head and trunk are, as we have seen, the most significant for the generic expression of the total posture, and the hands and arms most important for the specification of the posture. The distribution of the weight of the body, the expansion or contraction of the chest, the raised or dropped shoulders are other factors which, each in its own setting, are important. Every one of these has in any particular position its own expression.[18]

He noted four postural attitudes: approach, withdrawal, expansion, and contraction. A second look at these categories indicates that James is talking about posture as an index of relationship. We approach or avoid—a person, a task, or ourselves—and we do so with assurance or with fear of defeat.

Distance-Personal Space (Proxemics)

When we talk to people we seek a distance from them that tells the degree of affiliation that is desired. Rosenfeld found that in American culture people wishing to be affiliated in a warm relationship with their conversant pulled their chair to about four and a half feet from the chair of the discussant.[19] Conversely, if they did not care to relate closely with the other person they pulled away to about eight feet. Edwart T. Hall's anthropological studies compare the distance factor from culture to culture.[20] In the Latin cultures, famous for intimacy as well as explosive temper, people get closer together in conversation. The more formal and less expressive cultures are marked by people who stand at greater distances from each other. Within our own relatively cool culture, intimacy can be induced by crowding people into small rooms or pulling the chairs together, for instance, in the circle of a class discussion. Again, in

[17]F. Deutsch, "Analysis of Postural Behavior," *Psychoanalytic Quarterly,* 16 (1947), 211.

[18]Dean C. Barnlund, *Interpersonal Communication: Survey and Studies* (Boston: Houghton Mifflin Company, 1968), p. 520.

[19]H. Rosenfeld, "Effects of Approval-Seeking Induction on Interpersonal Proximity," *Psychological Reports,* 17 (1965), 120–122.

[20]Edward T. Hall, *The Silent Language* (Greenwich, Conn.: Fawcett Publications, Inc., 1959).

recent years Hall has done research with the factor of distance to measure the violent urge of criminals. A violent person seems to be less able
to tolerate having another person close to him or her than a nonviolent
one.

As observed in the opening chapter, Hall identified four zones in
which our cultural habits regarding personal space could be observed:
intimate distance (0″ to 18″), *personal distance* (18″ to 4′), *social distance* (4′ to
12′), and *public distance* (12′ to as far away as it is possible for communication to exist).[21] Each of us learns (without being aware of it) what distance is comfortable. If we are empathic communicators, we also become
aware of what distance is comfortable for the other person.

Relative position   If distance is a measure of affiliation, then relative position is a measure of the quality of the intimacy.[22] Chairs placed
at an angle to each other suggest cooperative interacting. If we are
hostile or angry with a person, we are likely to select a position directly
opposite him or her and at a distance. Opposite, but not more than three
feet apart, seems to be a comfortable positioning for people in our culture, in a mutually cooperative attitude. Observers have noted that
people opposite each other are more likely to dominate the interaction
of a group of people than those who sit side by side.[23] Silent intimacy is
suggested and aroused by sitting beside a person. If executives want to
maintain an authoritative relationship, they may place their desk between themself and their subordinate or client. In more democratic relationships chairs at a round table or just chairs in a circle are often arranged to establish the desired atmosphere.

Among the places where the kind of nonverbal messages just discussed can be most abundantly found are classrooms and professors'
offices. What does it do to communication if the only face-to-face encounter possible in the classroom is between the teacher and the students
as a group? What is the impact of being in interaction with only one
other person in the classroom in spite of the fact that you are surrounded by peers? And what kind of feelings do you have when you go
to see a professor in his office? Does he place his desk between you and
him? Does that emphasize his position in the hierarchy? Or does he pull
up a chair within the range of Hall's "social distance" (4′ to 12′)? What is
the impact on you when that happens? And finally, when you visualize

---

[21]Edward T. Hall, *The Hidden Dimension* (New York: Anchor Books, Doubleday & Co.,
1966), pp. 111–129.

[22]Robert Sommer, "Further Studies of Small Group Ecology," *Sociometry*, 28 (1965),
337–348.

[23]B. Steinzor, "The Spatial Factor in Face to Face Discussion Groups," *Journal of Abnormal and Social Psychology*, 45 (1950), 552–555.

yourself getting into an occupation, do you imagine a desk, or space, or arrangement of your own in which you feel impressive and secure? Those are the questions we want to pose for you in this chapter in the hope that they will improve your awareness of the messages you send and receive via relative position.

Voice (Vocalics)

Other than the acts of the eyes and the hands, perhaps the most important nonverbal cues used in our interpretations are disclosed in the voice.[24] Every classroom has in it some students who speak in strong, clear, medium-loud to loud tones. It has others who speak in soft to very soft tones—sometimes so soft that the voice can hardly be heard. Can we generalize about what messages may be surmised from this nonverbal cue? Studies done by Mehrabian and Williams show that more submissive people speak in a softer voice when interacting with a stranger.[25] Have you ever listened to yourself when you walked into an office for the first time and asked for information? Does the softness of your voice (one of the vocalic elements) tell you anything about who you are? And does it tell the person to whom you talk anything about your level of confidence?

Vocal cues are prime message carriers. If the voice seems soft and easy or excited, we know that our partner likes us. When it is stern and harsh, we know the opposite. If the voice trails off, we know that our conversant could not care less. And then there is the voice we cannot figure out, and this is the voice of the person who chooses not to open up to us. In *The Voice of Neurosis,* Dr. Paul Moses, a San Francisco psychiatrist, has made a detailed statement about the meanings of various aspects of the voice, such as rate, quality, ranges of pitch, and volume.[26] And although his critics do not like the cataloging certainty of Moses's observations, many of us know from experience that we make important decisions in life precisely on these awarenesses. "I don't think I'll take the position. Why? I don't think I could get along with him." Or, "I liked her right away. I know we will be good friends." "I felt uncomfortable as soon as the salesperson spoke to me, so I decided to look elsewhere." "What's bugging you today, honey?" We choose and get along with our mates, and our Presidents, in considerable degree by interpreting vocal cues.

[24]Albert Mehrabian has evolved a formula: total impact = .07 verbal plus .28 vocal plus .55 facial. See "Communication Without Words," *Psychology Today,* September 1968, p. 53.

[25]A. Mehrabian and M. Williams, "Nonverbal Concomitants of Perceived and Intended Persuasiveness," *Journal of Personality and Social Psychology,* 13 (1969), pp. 37–58.

[26]Paul Moses, *The Voice of Neurosis* (New York: Grune & Stratton, 1954).

Some recent research indicates that in all the complexities of a voice that make an impact on us, in the main it is the character of the pitch features of the voice that we sense when we feel that we are attractive to the one speaking to us.[27] If we decide that our conversant does not like us, we note particularly the loudness features of his or her voice. And it is in the monotonous rhythms of his or her speech that we know our speaker is bored with us and thus signals cessation of relationship.

Touch (Haptics)

Sidney Jourard is reported to have counted the frequency of contact between couples in cafes in a variety of cities with the following results (number of contacts per hour): San Juan, Puerto Rico, 180; Paris, 110; Gainesville, Florida, 2; London, England, 0.[28] Aside from admiring the skill required to do this kind of watching, one can infer that touching may be one of the nonverbal channels that are clearly established within a culture. And if Jourard's observations have validity, Americans would seem to be rather aloof compared to other cultures. Indeed, there is some suspicion that the state of interest in encounter and human intimacy groups in this country is a symptom of our deep-seated need for physical intimacy in the face of cultural taboos against it.

Touch is the sense that develops first. An embryo less than an inch long from crown to rump and less than eight weeks old will bend its neck and trunk in response to light stroking.[29] And the evidence is impressive that infants and children deprived of touching are likely to be seriously impaired in their psychological growth.

The life script for most of us seems to run something like this: We give and receive touch messages from the moment of birth. For the first years of our life it is through touch that we gain a basic sense of security. But as we grow we are gradually removed from the physical presence of the parent and taught that touching must be limited to "proper" expression with all others. By the time we reach adulthood we have been conditioned to touch another only in terms of strict norms laid down by the culture and to be free only in terms of sexual intimacy. The reassurance and security provided through touch in infancy is now provided through words.

There is considerable evidence that this script is not enough—that words are often insufficient substitutes for touch. The story of a mother

[27]Frances G. Costanzo, Norman N. Marke, and Phillip R. Costanzo, "Voice Quality Profile and Perceived Emotion," *Journal of Counseling Psychology*, 16 (1969), 267–270.

[28]In Knapp, *op. cit.*, p. 109.

[29]Leathers, *op. cit.*, p. 142.

who is concerned about her withdrawn child is illustrative. The little six-year-old girl is withdrawing more and more. The mother becomes concerned. She spends more time with the child, reads to her, talks to her, listens to her. But the negative trend continues. As a last resort she seeks help from a counselor. The counselor senses a missing ingredient in the mother's obvious concern for the child, and his advice, in part, goes like this:

> Touch her every chance you get. Ruffle her hair when you go by her. Pat her bottom. Touch her arm when you talk to her. Caress her. Put your hand on her shoulder, your arm around her. Pat her back. Hold her. Every chance you get. Every time you talk to her.[30]

In this advice is the recognition that touching messages speak to some of our very deepest needs. But there is no intention to be prescriptive here. Every person has to find the touching behavior that is comfortable for him or her. Meanwhile, it may be helpful to be aware of how important physical reassurance is to us—and to those with whom we interact.

NONVERBAL MESSAGES THAT DO NOT FIT THE WORDS SPOKEN

If the nonverbal messages we send fit our feelings, and if our feelings fit the words we say, we are *congruent*—we are a harmonious whole, and the other person can know he or she is interacting with an authentic person. But our everyday experience tells us that we are frequently *incongruent,* and when this happens the nonverbal and verbal messages clash. We react in several ways:

If the nonverbal is compatible with what is said, we take the message as an honest one. We may or may not agree with it.

If the nonverbal cues conflict with what the words seem to say, we tend to resolve the conflict by accepting what the face or voice or body tells us. The nonverbal cues, for better or for worse, outweigh the words in such a situation.

If the nonverbal cues are uninterpretable, we do not know what to think. Some people are highly mannered in their speech and thus tell little about themselves. They speak in appropriate ways for the culture, but they do not let themselves show through. They have learned to play a communication game. But the players of communication games usually become very confused. Not knowing the true feelings of the conversant, the other person is not sure how to respond. Not knowing how to

---

[30]Ron Adler and Neil Towne, *Looking Out/Looking In* (San Francisco: Holt, Rinehart and Winston, 1975), pp. 229–231.

interpret that unclear response, the player is unclear about how to proceed and, therefore, unclear about himself or herself.

Let us think a moment about what has just been said and relate it to the significance of openness in communication. When we are open the nonverbal cues we send are not only congruent with the verbal message but supplement it in such a way as to make it clear and powerful. For the receiver of the message, a study of the nonverbal cues directs his or her interpretation of the message being received. The role of nonverbal communication is to provide the key for decoding. Or, if you like, it provides the information for getting inside the sender of a message and knowing the message as it is known by the sender.

Why do we send inconsistent messages? For a variety of reasons. Among them are the following: We are afraid to let the other know what we are really feeling. Or again, we have the feeling that dominating behavior would not be appropriate or persuasive (as when a parent says to a child, "You can take out the garbage if you would like to" while the tone of his or her voice is saying, "You had better take out the garbage if you know what's good for you"). Or again, we want to give a feeling of special emphasis by putting it into inconsistent form (as when an older sister watches her younger sibling make a perfect dive off the high board and says with obvious warmth and admiration in her voice, "I hate someone like that").[31]

Whatever the reasons may turn out to be, the evidence seems convincing that truly inconsistent messages play havoc with communication. If this is true, does the receiver of such a message have any hope of figuring it out? He or she can—and does. If the message comes in a setting in which the receiver feels the need to respond without uncertainty, he or she will take the nonverbal content over the verbal content and rely on it. The receiver will do this because (1) the visual is normally a more potent factor of attention than the auditory and (2) the nonverbal, much of which is known to be beyond the control of its sender, will be regarded as more authentic. There is research to support the view that when a listener is trying to decipher a feeling being sent inconsistently, the following equation applies:

$$\text{Total feeling} = 7\% \text{ verbal feeling} + 38\% \text{ vocal feeling} + 55\% \text{ facial feeling.}[32]$$

[31]For an excellent discussion of the functions of inconsistent messages, see Mehrabian, *op. cit.,* pp. 47–50.

[32]*Ibid.,* p. 44.

In a contest between the verbal and the nonverbal there is little doubt which will prevail!

THE PEOPLE WHO CAN BEST READ NONVERBAL MESSAGES

Sherlock Holmes was a remarkable fellow. He seemed to notice everything. And from the multitude of nonverbal messages that he caught (the length of the fingers, the slight turn of the head, the taut eyebrow) he deduced the conclusions that made him the envy of Scotland Yard. You may know someone who seems remarkably tuned to nonverbal messages that you have overlooked. The question that is more frequently being asked these days, however, is this: Is there a generalized ability developed in some people, and not in others, to notice and accurately interpret nonverbal cues? One hunch that is gathering increasing support is that children who grow up in an atmosphere in which they are encouraged to express themselves nonverbally will prove to be better readers of nonverbal signals than children who are taught early that nonverbal expressions are to be restrained. It is as though, having experienced the range of nonverbal expressions, the former have more chance for empathy than the latter.

THE ULTIMATE IN SELF-AWARENESS:
READING YOUR OWN NONVERBAL MESSAGES

If others decipher our meanings, they do so, in the main, by noting the way we say what we say. But we can read our own nonverbal cues too. The ultimate in self-awareness is probably attained by sensing the tensions of our own body, hearing the quality of our own laughter, and noting the nuances of our own voice. Again the camera and the tape recorder, now almost as common as typewriters, are available for our self-study, though much of our self-knowledge can be carried on by observing ourselves as we speak and listen.

In closing this discussion of the nonverbal statement, we are reminded of a haunting story we once read about the way the artist Rembrandt described himself to himself by visual cues. Among his 700 paintings and uncounted sketches, etchings, and drawings, Rembrandt made 84 self-portraits, 58 of which were paintings. No other visual artist has made such a close study of his or her own changing physical self as Rembrandt did. He began this work at twenty-one years of age and carried it on until his death at sixty-three, and he seemed to do the greatest number of these works in years of great excitement or turmoil in his life. In one year during his early romance and marriage with

Saskia he painted himself twelve times. Emil Ludwig speaks of the great composure that dominates these self-portraits. During the next few years Rembrandt became the most successful portrait painter in Amsterdam, but into his self-portraits creeps a certain melancholy.

Saskia died and the self-portraits stopped for five years. When they reappear we see mixed sorrow and bitterness. Then Rembrandt married again, but his fortunes dropped. He became less popular and ran into deep economic trouble. As if he was bracing himself with self-commands, his self-portraits take on a resolute aura, suggesting the military commander. And he holds a grip on himself throughout the remaining years of his life, though he ages fast. The self-portraits take on many wrinkles, and then the flesh becomes flaccid. In this period, however, there appears for the first time a self-portrait of the painter painting. He knows who he is, despite his falling fortunes.

Then his second wife and his beloved son Titus, born of his first wife, died. Two more self-portraits appear, of the face alone, the aging body omitted. In one he laughs. In the last a great pallor is more noticeable than the wrinkles. The eyes and mouth are deep. But the lips remain firmly closed, as in the portraits of his earlier youth.

In pictorial symbols Rembrandt made a detailed commentary on his own life. Here was a man alive to the meaning of the messages from his own body.

BREAKING THE CODE

The language scholar Edward Sapir once said that nonverbal communication is "an elaborate code that is written nowhere, known by none, and understood by all." It is its very elusive complexity that, at least in part, causes us to depend so much on it. One can monitor one's words a good deal more easily than the way one says them. The elusiveness and the fascination are also a consequence of the fleeting character of the nonverbal statement. A word is said and held in memory, but a glance, a tilt of the head, and the intonation of a word is like the flickering flame in a fireplace. It comes from nowhere, flashes into its unique form, and goes to nowhere. In its moment of being it leaves its impression. And competence in reading the impression may, we suspect, be in large measure the consequence of being fascinated by it.

With the tape recorder, the moving picture, and the television camera we now have ways to record nonverbal conversation. It would be strange if, having found ways to capture the nonverbal statement, we would not learn how to analyze it and perhaps even to break the code.

THE FACIAL MEANING SENSITIVITY TEST, PART ONE[33]

Part I of the FMST contains ten photographs representing the ten basic classes of facial meaning. Study the ten photographs and place the numbers in the appropriate blanks of the accompanying chart.

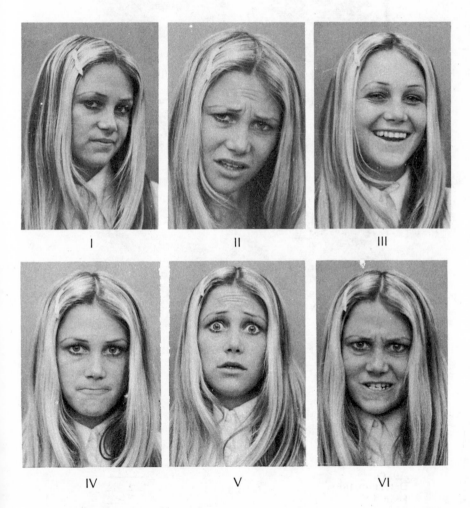

I	II	III
IV	V	VI

[33]From Dale G. Leathers, *Nonverbal Communication Systems* (Boston: Allyn & Bacon, Inc., 1976). By permission of Allyn & Bacon, Inc.

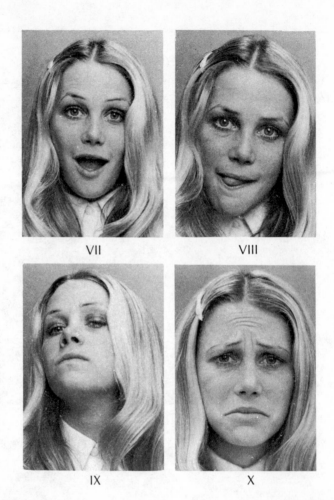

VII   VIII

IX   X

CLASS OF FACIAL MEANING	NUMBER OF EXPRESSION
Disgust	I
Happiness	III
Interest	VIII
Sadness	X
Bewilderment	II
Contempt	IX
Surprise	VII
Anger	VI
Determination	IV
Fear	V

The correct answers for Part I of the FMST are: disgust = I; happiness = III; interest = VIII; sadness = X; bewilderment = II; contempt = IX; surprise = VII; anger = VI; determination = IV; and fear = V.

On the following pages you will see thirty more photographs of facial expressions. Your task in Part II of the FMST is to group these facial expressions by class of meaning. Three of the photographs, for example, are intended to convey meanings that express some specific kind of disgust and, hence, should be perceived as part of that class of facial meaning. Likewise, among the thirty pictures are three expressions that may be classified as specific kinds of happiness. Your task, then, is to closely associate three photographs with each of the ten classes of facial meaning. Use each photograph only once.

FACIAL MEANING SENSITIVITY TEST, PART II

CLASS OF FACIAL MEANING	EXPRESSIONS THAT ARE PART OF EACH CLASS (No. of Expression)		
Disgust			
Happiness			
Interest			
Sadness			
Bewilderment			
Contempt			
Surprise			
Anger			
Determination			
Fear			

1

2

3

4

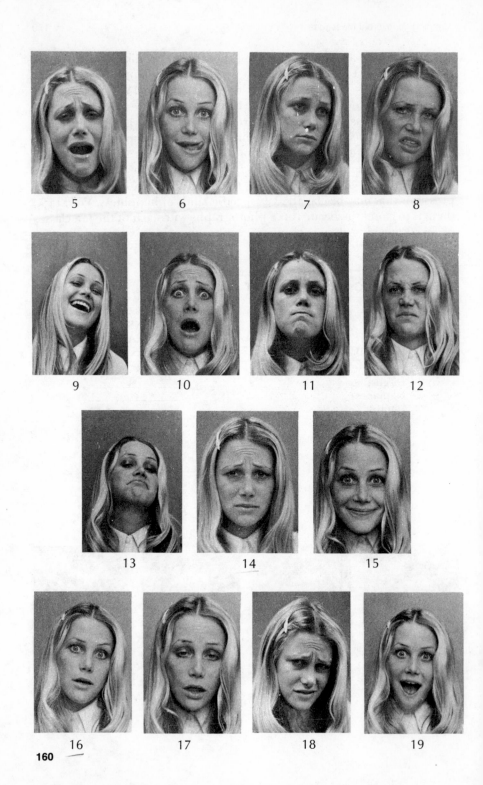

5   6   7   8

9   10   11   12

13   14   15

16   17   18   19

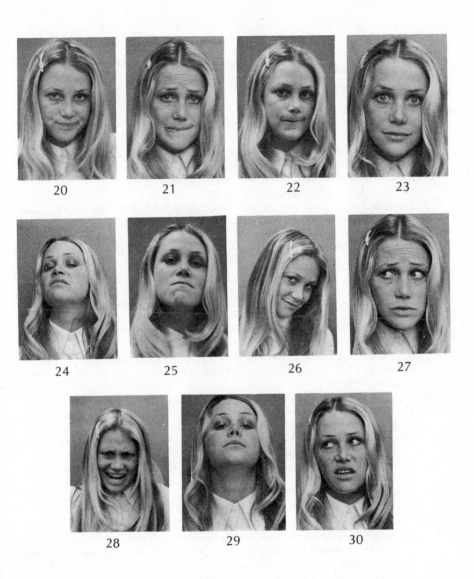

20   21   22   23

24   25   26   27

28   29   30

The correct choices for Part II of the FMST are: disgust = 8, 12, 30; happiness = 2, 9, 26; interest = 6, 15, 23; sadness = 5, 7, 14; bewilderment = 4, 17, 18; contempt = 13, 24, 29; surprise = 3, 16, 19; anger = 1, 20, 28; determination = 11, 22, 25; and fear = 10, 21, 27.

EXERCISES

1. Sit opposite another person at a distance of not more than two feet. Agree that you will look into each other's eyes for one minute without speaking. Have a third person monitor this experience so that the rules are not broken. Note the effect of the message sending of the eyes on both yourself and the other person. As a variation, you might try the exercise first with a person of the same sex; then try it with a person of the opposite sex.

2. With everyone in your group blindfolded, discuss a topic of mutual interest for 30 minutes. Does the blindfold free you or inhibit you? Is it a help not to have to deal with the nonverbal messages normally available to you, or do you find it threatening?

3. Blindfold half of the members of your group and allow the others to look around as usual. Discuss a topic of mutual interest for 30 minutes. What differences show up in terms of fluency, openness, and the like? As a variant on this exercise, blindfold the males and let the females remain sighted, then reverse that condition. Discuss the effect of the blindfolding in each case.

4. Make a survey of the physical arrangements in the offices of three or four of your professors. Does the arrangement require that you sit across the desk from the professor? Is the chair in which you sit "lower" than the one in which he or she sits? Does it *feel* lower? Does the office send formal or informal messages?

5. Repeat the preceding exercise with contrasting classrooms in which you are a student. Try to verbalize the feelings created in you by the different environments.

6. If you are adventurous enough, try the following: (a) Dress very convention-ally (suit, coat, tie, etc. if male; dress, high-heeled shoes, etc. if female); go to a downtown corner in your city and hand out nickels to ten pedestrians who come along. (b) On a subsequent day dress in hippie fashion, go to the same location, and do the same thing. Note the differences in your own feelings on the two occasions, and note the differences in the reactions you get from pedestrians.

7. Read for an hour wearing earplugs. Remove the earplugs and study for another hour. Report the differences between the two reading experiences.

8. The telephone distorts the sense of distance between the two conversants. Although the other person cannot see you or touch you, he or she is in your ear and this is closer than any other person in any other situation. Call one of your classmates, both recording the conversation. Get together, play the recordings, and discuss them. What did you learn?

9. The next time you are visiting, go sit in your host's favorite chair. Observe his or her behavior. What cues do you depend on to interpret the meaning of this act to him or her?

10. Give a short speech to the class in which you believe part of what you say and part you do not believe; in short, part of the speech is a lie. Have the class try to detect which part you believe and which part you do not believe. What cues did the people who read you correctly use?

11. Select a short section of a videotape of a person speaking. (a) Play only the visual. Then have each of the viewers in the group write whether the feel-

ings expressed by the speaker were generally affectionate, indifferent, or aggressive. Use a scale for this as follows:

			Affectionate			
1	2	3	4	5	6	7
slightly						highly
			Indifferent			
1	2	3	4	5	6	7
slightly						highly
			Aggressive			
1	2	3	4	5	6	7
slightly						highly

(b) Let the class read a typed script of what was said. Again let them write down whether the speaker is expressing affection, indifference, or aggression, and to what degree.

(c) Play the sound alone and have the class judge again as before.

12. To sense the impact of physical conditions, carry on parts of a discussion under three different conditions. Try ten minutes in chairs arranged in rows, ten minutes in chairs close together in a circle, and ten minutes in chairs far apart in a circle.

13. Engage in a conversation with one other person, changing position as described here following two minutes in each position: (a) opposite the other and within three feet; (b) opposite each other but with chairs placed at an angle; (c) side by side. Note how these variations alter your feelings, interaction and productivity.

14. Bring pictures of yourself at various ages to the group and talk about the perceptions, feelings, and memories aroused by the pictures.

15. Draw a picture of yourself and discuss the features that dominate as you try to draw. What pleasant or unpleasant feelings emerge as you engage in thinking about your physical image?

16. Look into a mirror and talk about what you see and feel.

17. Tell two stories, one entitled "I Was Fooled" and another entitled "I Fooled Them." In the first, tell about an incident in which another person said things so convincingly that you accepted them as his or her true feeling, only to discover later that he or she felt very differently. As you tell the story, try to understand why the nonverbal messages did not tell you to reject the verbal messages. In the second story, recall an occasion on which you succeeded in covering up, with words, how you really felt. Why did your nonverbal messages not give you away?

7

Emotion and Communication

Interaction has its basis in the underlying irritability of all living substance.

Edward T. Hall*

Men are disturbed not by things, but by the views they take of them.

Epictetus

Even when . . . communication is felt in silence . . . this silence is itself charged with the words that had been exchanged before it began.

Paul Tournier†

Emotion is inextricably intertwined with communication that changes a person in any way.

For too long, as observed earlier, emotion of any sort, or in any amount, has been thought of as troublesome to good communication. Anyone who wants to speak or hear a message right, we have been told, needs to keep his or her emotions out of it. He or she needs to act objectively, coolly, detachedly—unemotionally. The mature person, we have been led to believe, is a "rational" animal.

But emotion is a basic ingredient of life, and the belief that we can eliminate it from our communication leads to ludicrous behavior. You have doubtless heard a person say in a rising voice, "Now the only thing I'm interested in are the facts. I don't care how anyone else wants to go about it, but I'm not going to let emotion have anything to do with my part in it. Damn it, there's just too much sloppy thinking tangled up in this proposal." Pounding the table, this person shouts, "Now here are the facts . . ."

*Edward T. Hall, *The Silent Language* (New York: Doubleday & Company, Inc., 1959), p. 62. By permission of Doubleday & Company, Inc.

†Paul Tournier, *The Meaning of Persons* (New York: Harper & Row, Publishers, Inc., 1957), p. 130. By permission of Harper & Row, Publishers, Inc.

People have been tempted not only to separate emotion and reason but, having separated them, to argue that reason can "replace" emotion. The blind plight of the person in the preceding story is the booby trap of everyone at times.

The proposition this chapter seeks to develop is this: language that is rich in emotion accounts in large measure for the impact of communication. By definition, emotion is arousal, and the absence of arousal is indifference. Communication without emotional involvement is meager and indifferent. Emotion, it turns out, is the fuel with which communication is powered. Hence, vital communication invigorates both speaker and listener.

THE PRICE OF LANGUAGE WITHOUT EMOTION

Conversely, tepid communication exhausts the people involved. John Stuart Mill faced a nervous breakdown at age twenty. As he tried to think his way through the things that brought him to that pass, he concluded (1) that he was "suffering from an excess of analysis and a deficiency of feeling" and (2) that his father had been ineffective as a father because of his lack of tenderness. His father was, according to Mill, ashamed to show his emotions. Mill adds, "Absence of demonstrativeness in matters of affection and feeling is apt to starve the feelings themselves. If, for whatever reason, we habitually refuse to show our feelings, desuetude will eventually compel us to raise the question as to how real are feelings that are unable to address themselves to the person arousing them."[1] Emotion, Mill is saying, is one of the ingredients of life; it must be verbalized to find function, and it, along with relationships to ourselves and others, withers when it goes unverbalized.

EMOTION AND WORDS

Where there are emotions there are words. On occasion the authors have asked students to recall a moment when something of lasting consequence happened to them. In a remarkable number of cases, the students say they remember the words spoken in a situation saturated with feeling.

Here, for example, is what one student said:

> Our family has always thought of itself as close knit. I miss them when I'm at school, and I'm always glad to get home on vacations. Last year I was

[1] R. V. Sampson, *The Psychology of Power* (New York: Pantheon Books, 1965), pp. 70 and 87, from John Stuart Mill, *Autobiography*.

going with a girl who invited me home with her for the weekend. When we got there, she ran to her parents, and hugged them, and said, "I love you." It really hit me. It was so spontaneous and everything that I suddenly realized what a difference saying something like that out loud could make between people. It will sound corny, but I've found myself talking with my own parents ever since.

Or again, a father remembers a poignant experience that would have faded as most of our experiences do, except for the emotionally laden words in the encounter. One of his daughters, at age seven, had yet to master the art of riding a bicycle. It was a source of real embarrassment to her because virtually everyone her age in the neighborhood could not only ride but had already reached the "Look-Mom-no-hands!" stage. The father gave her the "feel" of balance, but to no avail. He finally decided that time would have to solve the problem and that he might as well relax and watch. Several days later his daughter marched solemnly into the house and said, "Come out here for a minute." It was clearly a command. As the father stood on the sidewalk, his daughter mounted the bicycle, rode the length of the block, made a smooth turn, rode back, dismounted, and threw the kickstand into position, saying "I did it because you thought I could." That simple statement, says the father, has echoed through his head ever since as a reminder of how little we are usually aware of the impact of words on our feelings and attitudes. The chief hallmark of the communication that hangs on, while so much of the flood of daily talk falls into some bottomless pit, is the emotional content.

LANGUAGE CLEANUP TIME

Throughout this book we have been talking about the feelings of people, and now a chapter devoted to a study of the *sentiments*, so important to the way we communicate, is called "Emotion and Communication." In general, the authors think that the term *feeling* arouses in you what we want to say better than the word *emotion*. If we should ask you what emotions you are experiencing now as you read, you would very likely say "None. I am not in an emotional state." But if we would ask, "What are your feelings about this?" you would probably have an answer. And a key point we have been trying to fix is this, that people are attracted or repelled as a basic response that so often is conceived of as an intellectual, cognitive, or logical process. So feeling, the disposition toward whatever you are experiencing, is basic to your response, and we like the word.

Yet we switch to the term *emotion* for this chapter because it is the more technical term. For instance, we want to discuss sensation and the chemistry of the body, which we must understand if, in turn, we are going to understand the differences between listening and talking. The word *emotion* should simply signal to you that we want to *analyze* the great sea of feeling that is so basic to life.

LISTENING AND EMOTION

Emotion and Distorted Listening

Perhaps the emotional aspects of communication have been discredited because of the distortions we note in the listening of the emotionally disturbed. A unique study done with paretic patients showed that when the patients were confronted with factual information they (1) replaced concrete concepts with generalities, (2) replaced concepts actually presented with more familiar concepts of their own, (3) diminished the significance of situations unacceptable to them, (4) found a motif and repeated it, and (5) showed an "insufficient" grasp of both the whole of the message and of its detail.[2] Governed by excessive feeling, they did not respond discriminatively to speech most of us would call rational.

Two other researchers, trying to find out the factors that are most mischievous in the thinking of college students, concluded that one of them was "permitting personal prejudices or deep-seated convictions to impair one's listening comprehension."[3] Aroused states in experimental subjects, it was concluded, create a significant disturbance in the listening process.

Emotion and Memory

But we should not conclude that some fixed amount of feeling is needed for good listening. Intense emotion, which may cause bad perception at the moment of occurrence, is also the character of memory that lasts for a lifetime. Walker and Tarte did an experiment in which it was shown that individual words associated with high arousal were rather poorly remembered when the subject was tested immediately and much better remembered on a test of long-term recall.[4] For words associated with the low arousal the pattern was reversed. It appears that

[2]P. Schilder, "Studien zur Psychologie and Sumptomatologie der Progressiver Paralyse," *Abhandle Neurolog, Psychat. Grenzgeb,* 58 (1930), 1–76.

[3]Clyde W. Dow, and Charles E. Irvin, "How We Teach Listening," *Bulletin of the National Association of Secondary School Principals,* 38 (1954), 137–139.

[4]E. L. Walker and R. D. Tarte, "Memory Storage as a Function of Arousal and Time with Homogeneous and Heterogeneous Lists," *Journal of Verbal Learning and Verbal Behavior,* 2 (1963), 113–119.

the "stirred-up" state may distort or block listening in the short run but aid it in the long run.[5]

An explanation of this finding has been evolving. Gerald Blum and his associates talk about an *amplification system*.[6] When experience comes to us from the outside, they think it puts nervous impulses to work. These combine with impulses already inside us, and in the process a closed loop of reverberating reaction is set up. It is like the sound that is made in a cave, seeming to increase as it echoes. The fact that the pattern is a closed loop, a phenomenon of "reverberation," helps explain why the message is kept from being immediately available to the consciousness. So reverberation, though divorcing the message from immediate consciousness, puts a heavy charge on the brain molecules, giving the message long duration.[7] You may draw a blank on what was actually said in the angry message your friend shouted at you earlier today but be able to recreate it in colorful detail as you reflect on it several days later.

How Emotion Works—A Theory

There are numerous theories about the way emotion works, and all of them in one way or another *relate chemistry* and words. What we present here is a theory, borrowing from many and accommodating itself to the nature of listening described in Chapter 3. We start with the common observation that the filtering of a message is determined, in part, by our state of arousal. This point of view dates back at least to the time of the Greeks, but the beginning of its refinement came in the latter works of Pavlov, and it has been developed into a comprehensive theory by William Sargent in *Battle for the Mind*.[8] Sargent points out that we listen to a message with an arousal that is located at some point on a continuum; one extreme of the continuum may be classified as hyperresponsive and the other end as phlegmatic. We all know what it is to be too sensitive to a series of messages, good or bad. Our common expression at such times is, "It was more than I could take." People who exist at the hyperresponsive end of the arousal continuum most of the time grow

[5]L. J. Kleinsmith and S. Kaplan, "Paired-Associate Learning as a Function of Arousal and Interpolated Interval," *Journal of Experimental Psychology*, 65 (1963), 190–193.

[6]Gerald S. Blum, P. James Getivitz, and Charles G. Stewart, "Cognitive Arousal: The Evolution of a Model," *Journal of Pesonality and Social Psychology*, 5 (1967), 138–151.

[7]Donald P. Spence, "Subliminal Perception and Perceptual Defense: Two Sides of a Single Problem," *Behavioral Science*, 12 (1967), 183–193.

[8]William Sargent, *Battle for the Mind* (Garden City, N.Y.: Doubleday & Company, Inc., 1957).

chronically irritated by that sensitivity and hence build barriers to messages.

Conversely, if we live at the other end of the arousal continuum, we are relatively impervious to messages. We are lethargic or phlegmatic. External stimulation must be intense in order to get through. A person who lives in this state most of the time may be described variously as thick-skinned, dull, or a Rock of Gibraltar, depending on the view of the observer.

Let us diagram the concept just explained.

Intermittently open and closed	Hyperresponsive Lively
Usually closed to messages	Calm Lethargic

What we note here, then, are two kinds of closedness, one at either end of the scale. People who are constantly open live for the most part at midpoints between the extremes. They change relatively easily, which is to say they do not need to experience deep and intense emotions in order to listen.

Body Chemistry and Listening

A number of researchers have discovered some of the chemical and physiological behavior related to the receptive state. When we are opening ourselves to external experience, adrenalin increases, noradrenalin decreases, and heart rate and blood pressure decrease.[9] Reaction time increases with increases of adrenalin, up to a point; then counteracting effects set in and as adrenalin continues to increase a great imbalance leads to passiveness, anxiety, and depression. So the very process that opens one to messages, when unchecked, leads to depression, and when pathological, to the depressive stage of manic depression. Unchecked openness is apparently self-defeating.

Conversely, as we close ourselves to sensory input, noradrenalin increases, adrenalin decreases, and heart rate and blood pressure increase. This is our self-assertive (and aggressive) state, in which we shift

[9]John E. Lacey, "Somatic Response Patterning and Stress: Some Revisions of Activation Therapy," *Psychological Stress,* ed. Mortimer Appley and Richard Trumbull (New York: Appleton-Century-Crofts, 1967), pp. 14–38.

attention away from external stimuli in order to do our arranging and patterning, our talking back, our interpretation of the information received. It is also, understandably, the state we adopt when we face unpleasant stimuli, when we fight, or when we reject the "pressures" from our world. Interestingly, this condition, characterized by the dominance of noradrenalin, slows down our reaction time; apparently this is necessary for thinking. Yet the increase in heart rate and blood pressure may slow reaction time to the point at which it blocks the flow of thought.

A number of researchers have observed the dynamics of the process just explained, and what they find is a network of feedback systems from heart to cortex (and other parts of the brain), from cortex to glands, glands to cortex, glands to heart, and heart to glands, so that all centers initiating processes send to other centers messages that set in motion the opposite processes.[10] At least two important implications can be drawn from these findings that bear on an understanding of listening. First, the emotional state in which listening is likely to be most productive is a state between extremes, for such listening depends on being open to our external world and yet at the same time not so overloaded by it that we cannot pattern its input. Because the cortex is involved in this network, the second implication is that language plays an essential role in determining human emotions. The two points together mean that while body chemistry influences talking, talking also influences chemistry.

The Role of Self-Talk in Our Emotions

As the therapist Albert Ellis points out so vividly in his works, there seem to be three stages in our response to a message.[11] Rather naively, we usually act as if the stimulus (A) is the cause and the response (C) the result.

A	B	C
Stimulus	What we say to ourselves about ourselves and the situation	Response

A report of an altercation between two people may go like this: "Then he snapped, 'O.K., take the day off,' and I said, 'No, if that is the way you

---

[10]Sanford I. Cohen, "Central Nervous System Functioning in Altered Sensory Environments," *Ibid.*, pp. 77–112. Also see Arnold H. Buss, *The Psychology of Aggression* (New York: John Wiley and Sons, Inc., 1961).

[11]Albert Ellis, *Reason and Emotion in Psychotherapy* (New York: Lyle Stuart, 1962).

feel about it, I won't.' I'll be damned if I am going to beg for any favors from him." The speaker will explain his or her responses (C) in terms of the language of the other (A).

Let us see this at work in a fairly typical student setting. Student X is about to leave her dormitory room when her roommate asks, "Where are you going?" And suddenly X turns on her roommate and rasps, "What business is it of yours? Why do you always have to be prying into my affairs?" And she stalks out. Trying, later, to figure out what triggered her emotional outburst, X says of her roommate, "I just can't stand her. She makes me so mad." Her analysis is based on the notion that her roommate does something to her (at point A) that inescapably makes her react with anger (point C). But the question "Where are you going?" does not necessarily have any kind of emotion *in it*. It has to have that assigned to it (point B); and student X does the assigning by saying things like the following to herself: "She wants to control me. She thinks I'm her little sister. Well, I'm not. She doesn't want me to have friends she can't have." On and on. It is the self-talk at point B, not the statement of the other person, that governs emotion.

No person other than yourself, Albert Ellis believes, can make you angry. Nor do the events of the day make you sad or happy or afraid. Events and other people stimulate you. But the stimulation has no determining power as to effect. What counts is *what you say to yourself* about that source of stimulation.

A comparison of humanity, the language maker, with other animals is of some aid in correcting our false view of our emotions. As far as we can tell, animals do not hate or love because they do not have the labels necessary to do so. Arnold Buss puts it like this:

> Since hostility develops on the basis of the verbal labels that identify and categorize stimuli, and since language responses exist only in humans, hostility occurs only in humans.[12]

The usual explanation is that animals react to *signs* while humans are able to react also to *symbols*. The chief difference between the two is that *signs* are words (or objects or events) that are *present to the senses* at the moment of reaction, while *symbols* are words (or things) that can stand for something not present. A snarling dog may associate the boy who wants to pet it with the salesperson who beat it yesterday, but its snarl response occurs only in the presence of a person and is limited to the moments of

---

[12]Arnold H. Buss, *The Psychology of Aggression* (New York: John Wiley & Sons, Inc., 1961).

that presence. The dog does not anticipate, with an increasing distaste, the coming of the boy. And when the boy is gone it does not continue to relish its "worked-up" state. But the boy can grow madder by the minute because of what he tells himself. Indeed, he can sustain his hostility throughout a lifetime. So there is a richness and extravagance in human emotion that does not exist for other animals. *Emotion, as humans experience it, occurs and is sustained in the symbols used in self-talk.*

The kind of emotion aroused is determined by the character of the self-talk It naturally follows, then, that our listening determines whether the emotions aroused are positive or negative.

> It would appear that positive human emotions, such as feelings of love or elation, are often associated with or result from internalized sentences stated in some form or variation of the phrase, "This is good for me!" and that negative human emotions, such as feelings of anger or depression, are associated with or result from sentences stated in some form or variation of the phrase, "This is bad for me."[13]

Positive emotions (love, courage, compassion) increase one's openness to messages The evidence summarized by Kenneth Gergen suggests not only that emotions can be induced by words but also that the "positive" emotions so induced are a significant aid to one's listening.[14] Having mastered sophisticated hypnotic techniques, Blum and his associates went one step further and carried out a study in which subjects were exposed to different degrees of "positive" (pleasure) arousal,[15] the state prescribed for the subject while he or she was hypnotized. The results showed that as subjects were exposed to higher degrees of pleasure they were able to react more alertly and that they committed fewer errors than they did when they were in neutral or negative states.

Goethe observed that we understand only that which we really love. To love involves the empathic ability to perceive through the eyes of the loved one. Could it be that any reservations or defensiveness we may have about the source of the messages leads us to make statements to ourselves that build barriers against understanding the message as it is intended by the other person? Could it be, in short, that the person whom we cannot accept unconditionally we cannot understand? If this is true, the emotion of love (defined as "unconditional" acceptance) may play a central role in our understanding of one another. Both theory and the data suggest this.

[13]Ellis, *op. cit.,* p. 51.

[14]Kenneth J. Gergen, "To Be or Not To Be . . .a Single Self," from *To Be or Not To Be . . . Existential-Psychological Perspectives on the Self* (Gainesville: University of Florida Press, 1967), pp. 22–23.

[15]Blum, *op. cit.*

We are dealing, here, with a challenge to the common belief that "love is blind." And there is no doubting that the sexual and social whirlwinds that catch up countless couples each spring excite "blind" response. But the love, romantic or otherwise, that endures into the summer and through the winter has to be built on the unconditional acceptance of another person in full awareness of his or her faults.

Havelock Ellis, a British physician, catches the point in a comment about romantic love:

> The women whom I have loved, and almost worshipped, are women of whose defects I have been precisely and poignantly aware. The lover who is not thus aware seems to me a crude sort of lover, scarcely even a lover at all, merely a victim of delusion . . . I feel contempt for the "love" that is blind; to me there is no love without clear vision, and perhaps, also, no vision in the absence of love.[16]

There seems some justice in paraphrasing his last sentence to read, "There is no love without listening, and perhaps, also, no listening in the absence of love."

But the listening that asks such openness has to be built upon another "postive" emotion—courage, the willingness to take a chance. Ross Snyder of the University of Chicago Theological Seminary sees communication as made up of the ingredients shown in Figure 7-1 and in the approximate proportions shown there. You will note that he assigns a significant role to the capacity to take risk. The risk involved for a speaker is obvious. He(she) may be misunderstood or rejected. He(she) may even be ignored. The risk for the listener is equally obvious. He(she) may be conned, exploited, and made to look ridiculous. Where is the person who has not been deeply hurt because he or she trusted another person without reservation? Hurt badly enough, a person may never

FIGURE 7-1   Ingredients in a Unit of Communication

[16]Havelock Ellis, in *Confessionals and Self-Portraits*, ed. Saul K. Padover (New York: The John Day Co., 1957).

again have the courage to accept another person sufficiently to understand him or her.

This happens in Edward Albee's play, *The Zoo Story*. Peter, a stereo-
type of the comfortable, middle-class, respectable family man, is sitting
on a park bench when Jerry, a dissipated, carelessly dressed ne'er-do-
well, walks up. Jerry tries to start a conversation with some questions
of the type, "Which-way-is-it-to-the-zoo-from-here?" Peter answers in
a perfunctory way. He has been brought up to be polite. But pretty
soon Jerry is talking about more important things, raising questions
about who Peter is, and launching into a detailed description of the
kind of grim, communicationless life he himself leads day in and day out.
At this point Peter senses the threat if he continues to listen, and he cries
out, "Stop it! I don't want to hear any more!" As it turns out, Albee is not
willing to let him escape, and the play roars on to its tragic climax. Peter
has not found the courage to listen, and as the play closes we suspect he
never will. Listening to understand another person requires courage.

Compassion is the third "positive" emotional state to be found in
those who can maintain openness in conversation. Courage, in its final
test, reflects a capacity to listen to criticism without vindictive reaction,
but compassion is a mirror of one's capacity to "keep caring" for the
person who is criticizing us. In an exchange of letters between the author
Sloan Wilson and his daughter, who had just dropped out of college, we
get the "feel" of compassion and the way it shapes communication between people. The father writes to his daughter, "I didn't want to spoil
the visit, but frankly I cannot yet learn to be happy about the fact that
you dropped out of college after only two and a half years." He goes on
to point out the practical values he sees in having a college education,
and he writes about the scorn he imagines his view might generate in his
daughter. But he closes his letter with the hope that he and his daughter
"can trust each other as individuals, not as representatives from the
enemy camp of another generation . . . Love, Dad."

His daughter writes with equal assertion and compassion. "I think
we ought to be open about it," she says. "You think I've made a rash—if
not stupid—move; one that I'll regret. But I think I *have* made the right
decision." She points out that if she had asked him before she dropped
out, her father would have told her bluntly not to do it. So, she argues,
she had to go ahead on her own. She gives her reasons for her decision
and closes her letter by writing:

> Never think that I left the home you worked so hard to create because
> I've lost respect for your opinions. It's just that I'm now gaining respect for
> my own opinions, too. My life may seem pointless and squalid to you, but it
> really is working for me. And no matter what you and I end up doing with
> ourselves, I don't think we could ask for more of each other than to believe

in our own ideas and to try to live by them. I know this is what you've always wished for me, and though you may be shocked by the way I've chosen to go about it, I love you for letting me go ahead. Much love, Lisa.[17]

Here are a father and daughter who listen to each other, even in an unalterable disagreement. Acceptance of another, "even knowing his faults," includes the courage to affirm that person when those "faults" lead to confrontation. Compassion is love when you cannot have your way. Compassion is a state of feeling that causes us to say to ourselves, "If I were he I would act as he does."

Negative emotions (fear, hostility, anger) cause a listener to close himself or herself to messages. The "negative" emotions, as most of us have discovered from experience, do drastic things to the organism.[18] We tend to quake and are inclined to action, either flight or attack (as suggested by the behavioral grid in earlier chapters), depending on the way we talk to ourselves about the experience we are involved in. If the emotional state is primarily one of anger, both adrenalin and noradrenalin are secreted; if the state is primarily fear, the changes produced by adrenalin alone seem more characteristic. But our concern is not so much with the physiological changes that take place as it is with their effect on behavior. Fear, in moderate quantities, often produces improvement in comprehension scores.[19] But the weight of the evidence shows that anger, hostility, and fear are disorganizing and disabling states. "An angry person," Buss points out, "finds it difficult to concentrate, to show skill in a task requiring attention and control.[20] And several studies conclude that subjects tend to recall material with which they are in agreement and to forget that with which they disagree. Listeners fearful of their own hostility will tend not to hear a hostile message, even when it is presented vividly.[21] Blum found that hypnotized subjects under the influence of increasing anxiety grow sluggish in response, become inaccurate, and report that their experience became "fuzzier and fainter."[22] Negative emotions, in the main, damp our intellectual powers and, thus, our capacity to listen.

Though it is rather difficult to build a thesis for aggressive behavior, it can be argued, however, that in a world unstabilized by struggle, anger

[17]Sloan Wilson and Lisa Wilson, "Father vs. Daughter: Two Letters That Crossed in the Mail," *Woman's Day,* March 1968, p. 50.

[18]Buss, *op. cit.,* p. 93ff.

[19]Charles R. Petrie, Jr., "The Listener," in Sam Duker, ed., *Listening Readings* (New York: Scarecrow Press, 1966), p. 340.

[20]Buss, *op. cit.,* p. 10.

[21]*Ibid.,* p. 110ff.

[22]Blum, *op. cit.*

and attack are to be desired over withdrawal and submission. This is seen when we examine the spectrum of emotions. On one end of the continuum is withdrawal and on the other is healthful acceptance, with aggression somewhere between them.

Withdrawal   Attack   Acceptance

Depression   Anger   Love

Translated for a discussion of listening, this means that in the withdrawal stage we do not listen. We close ourselves off because we do not have the strength to cope. At the anger stage we listen selectively. We listen for that by which to defend ourselves. As we move beyond anger we come to the healthy state of love and acceptance. Anger is closer to health than withdrawal.

Some people resent the labeling of "positive" and "negative" emotions. They feel that such labeling is the imposition of the author's value scheme on them. One student said, "There are some people I just don't like and I do not intend to like them. You say I cannot understand them because I don't like them. The truth is I don't like them because I do understand them." Probably nobody likes everybody he or she knows, and the authors do not feel disposed to preach the gospel of universal love. We do emphasize this, however: Whether we like it or not, fear and anger blunt our powers to perceive. Made indiscriminate by negative emotions, we perceive the world as a struggle between the "good guys" and the "bad guys." We know this view is inadequate, yet we nurture the emotions that sustain the view.

Emotions, Identity, and Empathy

The identity of a person comes essentially from seeing vividly the difference between his or her own view and that of the person with whom he or she talks. But if our emotions are negative, not only is our power to hear shades of difference dulled but our very pitting of ourselves against the other makes it impossible to adopt the posture of the other, so necessary to understanding. And when we do not really understand the other as he or she means to be heard we are unable to separate out from what he or she says that which tells about them and that which tells us about ourselves.

One can argue, like the student just mentioned, that "the truth is I don't like them because I do understand them." But such a position is taken without a clear understanding that our emotions make us what we become. The nurturing of our hostile feelings internalizes conflict, creates *an attack upon the self*. The injunction to "love thine enemy" is not moral because it prescribes the appropriate attitude toward others. It is moral because it states the conditions necessary to attain maturity. Anxiety, fear, and particularly hostility put cotton in our ears. Not hearing correctly, we design messages that impoverish and destroy the self. In all times, in all cultures, the most important and the hardest lesson to learn is that the emotions of divisiveness cut us off from listening to the information needed to give us coherent identity. This concept will be developed in full in the chapter on judgment.

Toward the Control of Emotion in Listening

If listening is, as it appears to be, so strongly influenced by emotion, the ultimate question is, "How far can we go in understanding and controlling our emotions?" Even supposing that we are able to recognize our temperament and our habitual response from the foregoing discussions, are we doomed forever to be as we are, to have no power to choose our emotions? Indirectly, all the research already cited, which links glandular response and words, gives a qualified no to the question. Steven Mattis[23] concludes that sensitivity to emotional expressions, both in the self and in others, can be increased by training. And the implication is that such increased sensitivity is the first step toward control. Davitz[24] points out that, unless severe obstacles appear *en route*, emotional sensitivity is a function of maturity and, thus, develops as the person grows up.

SPEECH AND EMOTION

We can assert direction over our emotions. And to this end overt speech has a distinct advantage over silent speech. Not too surprisingly, the research shows that the person who expresses emotion more freely, who can be emotionally involved, has a better chance for interpreting the emotional expression of others. Thus he or she gets the critical data for change. Levy, for example, found significant intercorrelations between (1) the ability to express feelings vocally to others, (2) the ability to identify feelings expressed vocally by others, and (3) the ability to iden-

[23]Joel R. Davitz, ed., *The Communication of Emotional Meaning* (New York: McGraw-Hill Book Company, 1964), p. 152.
[24]*Ibid.*

tify one's own vocal expressions of feelings.[25] Other research leads to the same conclusions.[26]

Verbalizing as a Key to Emotional Control

But awareness of the research alone is not enough to gain control. Nor is venting our emotions, helpful as that often is. One achieves the control one wants by *talking about* one's feelings and one's desired feelings, in addition to expressing them and understanding the theory. We are here noting that the power of control comes from learning to operate at a variety of language levels. Conversely, you can "blow your stack" repeatedly and get into deeper and deeper trouble, for while you get temporary relief you set the stage for the next blowup. If you stay at level one you achieve no perspective. First steps in learning to *control* emotion come as you develop the power to talk *about* your feelings.

As one talks about one's feelings two important things are achieved. First, one is not only sorting out those feelings (level two) but analyzing them (level three) and perhaps tying them to or throwing them out of one's beliefs, principles, and values. Thus one decides what feelings to build into one's universe. Then one can elicit some responses and inhibit others.

If I conclude, as I talk out an experience, that "nobody is going to take advantage of me!" I have not only talked *about* an emotional experience but am generalizing this experience into the language of my beliefs and values. I have, if only half consciously, shaped or reshaped and validated my perception of the universe: "It's every man for himself and an unsafe place for those who are not alert." I am setting myself up to respond with hostility to the next person who moves into my domain. So talk about emotion establishes for me the expectation that will determine future response. In short, freedom of choice is not a function of the moment of decision but a function of the talk carried on previously about past experience. Action comes close to being automatic. The moment of decision that cues action is designed in talk between moments of action. The psychiatrist Carl Binger, in telling about what he has learned in a lifetime, says:

> It is important to understand about luck or, better, chance and to realize that more often than not it is determined by the inner set of our personalities. There are some people who seem "to get all the breaks," just as there are some others who are constantly running head on into catastrophes

---

[25]Joel R. Davitz, *The Language of Emotion* (New York: Academic Press, 1969), Chap. 4.

[26]In G. Lindzey, ed., *Assessment of Human Motives* (New York: Grove Press, 1960), pp. 87–118. Davitz, *op. cit.*, Chap. 10.

of greater or lesser degree. The element of chance cannot be denied, but it plays less of a role in our fate than our private wishes do. In an uncanny way the outer world seems to conform to our inner needs, as though by some predetermined, almost inexorable mechanism. Many wise men know that luck or fate is much of our own making.[27]

Thus the great function of talk in regard to our emotions is that the *talking about* an emotional experience sets us up to respond as we predict we will.

Talk about an emotional experience internalizes conversation— builds into ourselves our own mirror—so that when we are unexpectedly faced with an emotionally arousing experience we are able to carry on self-talk that sorts out consequences while we are still living out the experience. This is particularly useful in interaction involving more than two people, where the sharing of the group talk is great enough to allow each person considerable time for his or her self-talk. One who has learned to talk about one's emotions to others now (having internalized the mirror) can note the activity and words being aroused in himself or herself. Imaginatively such a person can allow himself or herself to respond in action and words as he or she is tempted, to consider the impact on others, to consider the consequent impact on himself or herself. Who has not had the impulse to walk out of a meeting in disgust but has decided instead that the consequence would be more troublesome than bearing the talk of the group? In silent speech we check out an emotional response against our value scheme, a lesson we learn by internalizing overt talk about our feelings.

All this may sound so obvious that its significance is not seen. Let us then do a "double take." As we gather data on the results of Head Start and Follow Up, the efforts to save the dropouts in our educational scheme, it begins to become clear that the critical difference between middle-class children, who more often make it, and the impoverished lower classes is the ability to use language.[28] Not only are the middle-class children more articulate (and logical articulateness is what we mean by verbal intelligence) but they talk more *about* their feelings than lower-middle-class children do. Let it be clear that they do not necessarily express their emotions more than lower-class children do, perhaps less. But they talk more about them; they introspect their feelings more fully and more often. Thus they are guided into their cognitive growth.

[27]Carl Binger, "Living High on Wit, Wisdom, and Love," *Saturday Review,* July 25, 1970, p. 13.
[28]Basil Bernstein, "Social Structure, Language, and Learning," in A. Harry Passow, Miriam Goldberg, and Abraham J. Tannenbaum, eds., *Education of the Disadvantaged* (New York: Holt, Rinehart and Winston, Inc., 1967), p. 231.

The person who does not see that intelligence is a ship afloat on the currents of emotion is not aware of his or her dependence on feelings. A man sticks with his job or leaves it as a consequence of the feelings aroused in him day by day. A woman chooses her mate out of the feelings aroused in day-to-day interaction. We evolve ourselves and our spirit out of the feelings aroused by our day-to-day occupations over the years. If we but grunt our pleasures and displeasures we make decisions on feelings that have not been consciously examined and therefore channeled, directed, and controlled. If we experience in grunts we live a happy or an unhappy life, which is simply an automatic response to the love or lack of love experienced in our earliest years. To the degree that we are aware and masters of our fate we have learned to talk *about* our feelings in ways that lead to positive feelings and self-acceptance.

We must, of course, be careful in the choice of our conversant. The other person must not only be one we can trust but one who sufficiently accepts himself or herself not to be impelled to criticize and pass judgment on us. Sometimes responses from others are self-affirming; too often they are not. The negative responses of many parents—"You ought to . . ."; "Why don't you act like your brother?"; "Aren't you ever going to grow up?"—are, of course, particularly powerful, for we do not choose our parents, and their shaping of our self-concepts begins before we know what is happening. Our only choice is to search out our listeners as we begin to identify with peer groups. If we are born to parents who help us achieve self-acceptance, we are fortunate. If we are not, we usually stumble upon a person who listens with interest, not judgment. The person sufficiently self-aware of the impact of others on himself or herself and not too caught in self-condemnation seeks out accepting company. Thus, ultimately such a person learns to know and tolerate his or her feelings, then to follow the feelings that clarify his or her thought. As Ellis says, our reason and our feelings usually accompany each other, act in a circular cause-and-effect relationship, and in certain (though hardly all) respects "are essentially the *same thing*."[29]

DESPAIR—ANXIETY—HOPE

Throughout this book we have held to the view that our feelings are a basic force in our communication, and we have conceived of them as positive or negative. In several places we have identified *anxiety* as the

---

[29]Ellis, *op. cit.*, p. 38.

emotion or feeling that divides those two worlds, but we have not discussed the concept of anxiety. As we explore the anxious state we should distinguish anxiety from fear. Fear is the response to threat or danger. You are in danger when crossing a busy highway, trying to cope with a snarling dog, or facing a person who is shaking a fist in your face. A person who is not frightened by threat and danger is foolish.

But humans, alone among the animals, are extremely susceptible to a more common kind of foolishness, and that is anxiety. Anxiety is our worry about threats that do not exist. Anxiety is, as far as we know, a phenomenon of consciousness, a result of being able to talk to ourselves, to contemplate. Anxiety is the fussy "B" statement. If we are afraid of electrical storms, our house burning down, our lover being injured, getting cancer, or not getting a job when we graduate, when in reality there is no clear-cut threat, we are anxious.

One of the more fascinating experiences of a sports fan is in watching the rival teams wax and wane in their capacity to "put it together." Players and coaches talk about being "up" for a game. Part of the success is in being "ready," and that means doing the preparatory work for a game, but all good coaches can analyze the skills of the game. There is a certain something else about the coach who, year after year, with changing talent, produces teams that consistently come out on top. The difference between the physical skills of the best national teams is slight. Attitude, the belief in one's self, is very often the critical factor. Anxious players are self-conscious players. When we are at our peak we are lost in the act. The best coaches have a way of communicating confidence.

In recent years the concepts of "inner tennis" and "inner skiing" have come into common parlance.[30] The "inner gamesmen" talk about the battle between Self I and Self II. Essentially what they are getting at is "concentration," a kind of abandoned giving of oneself to the act, a living in the language of an experience. It is a conquering of anxiety.

In the *Saturday Review* long-time editor Norman Cousins recounts his experience of "fighting back" to health after he was wracked by an illness his physicians said was incurable.[31] Though his pain and inability to move told him he was in a serious state, he says he simply did not believe his condition was hopeless. Literally, he says, he willed to live and in giving himself to that will altered the flow of the endocrine glands, changing the chemistry of his body.

He speaks of the healing effect of believing in the medicine and in your doctor. Who has not felt the resurgence of life when he or she has

---

[30]W. Timothy Gallwey and Robert Kriegel, "Fear of Skiing," *Psychology Today,* November 1977, p. 78.

[31]Norman Cousins, "Anatomy of an Illness," *Saturday Review,* May 28, 1977, p. 4.

followed a doctor's prescription? We put ourselves in trusted hands and we can feel the glow of life take over. This account is not a denial of the power of drugs and other medications. We are focusing on the power of anxiety to erode our life forces and on the significance of the fact that the life processes rest on feelings. When we turn to a doctor, in large measure we do so because we cannot maintain the confidence necessary to recapture health without his or her support.

Anxiety is the terrible price we pay for consciousness. To understand it is to be able to look at it, talk about it, and in some measure to be its master.

CONCLUSIONS

Many years ago, in his studies about the character of intelligence, Spearman found a "g" (a general) factor that seemed to pervade. The intellectually sensitive person seems to discriminate among all sorts of data—verbal, spatial, mathematical. In like fashion it appears that the emotionally sensitive person discriminates among the emotional tones of human speech, music, and visual art. As you might suspect, those who are sensitive intellectually are most often those who are also sensitive to emotional meaning. Thomas Wolfe, canvassing his experience in the person of the fictional George Webber in *You Can't Go Home Again*, comes to the conclusion that vital interaction between our emotions and intelligence (fused in our self-talk) is the key to healthy growth.

> He had traveled through England, France, and Germany, had seen countless new "sights" and people, and—cursing, whoring, drinking, brawling his way across the continent—had had his head bashed in, some teeth knocked out, and his nose broken in a beer-hall fight. And then, in the solitude of convalescence in a Munich hospital, lying in bed upon his back with his ruined face turned upward toward the ceiling, he had had nothing else to do but think. There, at last, he had learned a little sense. He had learned that he could not devour the earth, that he must know and accept his limitations. He realized that much of his torment of the years past had been self-inflicted, and an inevitable part of growing up. And, most important of all for one who had taken so long to grow up, he thought he had learned not to be the slave of his emotions.
>
> Most of the trouble he had brought upon himself, he saw, had come from leaping down the throat of things. Very well, he would look before he leaped thereafter. The trick was to get his reason and his emotions pulling together in double harness, instead of between them. He would try to give his head command and see what happened: then if head said, "Leap!"— he'd leap with all his heart.[32]

[32]Thomas Wolfe, *You Can't Go Home Again*. By permission of Harper & Row, Publishers, Inc. and of William Heinemann Ltd.

THE UNKNOWN: A MEASURE OF ANXIETY

Following are 75 kinds of things people commonly worry about. Rate yourself from 0 to 4 on the degree to which you worry about each item. The scale is as follows:

0 = I do not feel uneasy about this.
1 = Rarely do I feel uneasy about this.
2 = Occasionally I feel uneasy about this.
3 = Often I feel uneasy about this.
4 = Usually I feel uneasy about this.

Example:
Strangers __3__

Things to fuss about:

1. Storms	____	16. Deep water	____
2. The dark	____	17. Commitment	____
3. Fire	____	18. Old age	____
4. Germs	____	19. Falling	____
5. Accidents	____	20. Cancer	____
6. Masturbation	____	21. Public humiliation	____
7. Failure	____	22. Suicide	____
8. Economic disasters	____	23. Examinations	____
9. Success	____	24. Guns	____
10. High places	____	25. Congested traffic	____
11. Bridges	____	26. Dying	____
12. A stroke	____	27. Sexual inadequacy	____
13. Crowded places	____	28. Arguments	____
14. Becoming insane	____	29. Illness	____
15. Air travel	____	30. Marriage	____

31. Snakes   ____   54. Open places   ____

32. Crawling creatures   ____   55. Social awkwardness   ____

33. Leaving home   ____   56. Noisy places   ____

34. My appearance   ____   57. Rodents   ____

35. Spending money   ____   58. Birds   ____

36. Debts   ____   59. Being trapped   ____

37. Social acceptance   ____   60. Anger   ____

38. Physical violence   ____   61. Leading others   ____

39. Being rejected   ____   62. Dependence   ____

40. Losing valuables   ____   63. Independence   ____

41. Moving to new places   ____   64. Social affairs   ____

42. Heart attack   ____   65. Relations

43. Elevators   ____   with authority   ____

44. Pregnancy   ____   66. Cats   ____

45. Atomic disaster   ____   67. Dogs   ____

46. Crossing streets   ____   68. Losing a job   ____

47. War   ____   69. Morals   ____

48. Public speaking   ____   70. Death of loved ones   ____

49. Making decisions   ____   71. Intelligence   ____

50. Hospitals   ____   72. Effectiveness   ____

51. Homosexuality   ____   73. Loneliness   ____

52. Attractiveness to   74. Capacity to love   ____
    opposite sex   ____   75. Persuasiveness   ____

53. Physical intimacy   ____   Total   ____

Now count the number of items to which you assigned numbers from 1 to 4 and put the total here:_____.

Divide that number by 75, which will give you the percentage of items you worry about. Put that number here: _____%

Do you worry about many things compared to other people?

Are you a worrywart compared to other people? How does your

total score compare with that of others? How does this bear on your scores in the Communication-Conflict Instrument?

If you sense that you dissipate too much energy in anxiety, see a counselor. As the authors move toward old age we regret the hours of confusion caused by anxiety.

EXERCISES

1. Thinking of the Ellis view, report what you said to yourself just prior to an emotional outburst in a conflict with another person. Analyze the statement as to whether it was rational or irrational.

2. Note the way you have, on a given occasion, said something you thought you ought to say even though you predicted accurately that it would arouse hostility in the other person. You had decided to avoid emotional involvement in the conflict. Note the role of the self-prediction and how it controlled your emotions in the incident. Discuss this with another person or write it out.

3. Discuss a typical verbal exchange with your father, stating the incident and the words exchanged. What were the emotions of the interaction? Describe the relationship of the two of you in the interaction.

4. Tell about an emotional experience of your life. Then explain the relationship that existed with the other person in the experience. Note that the two explanations are different ways of talking about the same thing.

5. Select two people and sit them face to face. Place a stick, ashtray, pen, ruler, or something else between them. Have neither of the two people say anything to each other. Note what they do with the object. Have each participant talk about the feelings he or she experienced during the situation.

6. Tell about an argument you were in, in which you felt that the other person was defensive. Tell how that person distorted what you said in order to protect himself or herself. Have the class determine whether you sound defensive in your explanation.

7. Recount an incident in which you discovered your own defensive behavior. Tell what condition it was that allowed you to see the defensive behavior.

8. Talk about a value that is very important to you. Then choose from the class a person who sincerely disapproves of or is indifferent to your value and ask him or her to explain why. Respond. Ask monitors who have been assigned to the task to evaluate the degree to which you were defensive in your response or in any way showed hostility.

9. Do the preceding assignment, recording your response on tape. Listen to the recorded response and evaluate your defensiveness or the absence of it.

10. One of the most desirable objectives of leadership in our times is to be cool under fire. Plan a scene with one of your classmates in which you are to present a point of view which, in turn, he or she is to vigorously attack. Your objective is to respond without feeling or expressing hostility. If you are

successful, how do you account for it? Did you divorce your ego from the attack? Or are you teaching yourself to accept yourself as an imperfect person?

11. Invite a member of the class who feels that he or she does not understand you to confront you and tell why you are difficult for him or her to understand. Respond, trying not to feel hostility or shame. Describe to the class the degree of your success.

12. Repeat the preceding assignment if you sense a reserve of confidence. The purpose of these assignments is to desensitize you to attack. But to endure more than your poise permits is to sensitize, not desensitize, to throw you back into the tendency to respond defensively.

13. The next time you get into an argument at home, try to respond without hostility or shame. Tell about the experience in class. What was the impact on you? On your family?

14. If you are secure enough to do it, give a speech in class about the discrepancy between your ideal self and your actual self. In this assignment there are these assumptions: (1) Not accepting our weaknesses is the cause of our defensiveness, and (2) defensiveness obstructs our growth. Behind all the conflicts between people are the conflicts within people.

15. Divide into groups of five or six. Listen to each of the group members tell about his or her feelings of the moment. Discuss the statements that sounded the most genuine. Whose (if any) statements seemed out of touch with the speaker's feelings? Discuss the nonverbal cues, if you can identify them, that will help you form your observations.
     This assignment is only for those who feel secure enough.

16. Break up into groups of four. Each person in turn tells each of the others what he or she likes and dislikes about that person. Note the level of relationship expressed in both the positive and negative statements that each makes. How well are you able to express both? What does your ability to express the one as compared to the other tell you about yourself? Write a paper or make an entry in your journal about the experience, the knowledge you gained about yourself and the others.

17. Write a statement about something you heard sometime in your life that had a great impact on you for good or ill. Label it "Something I Heard That Made a Difference in My Life." Read the statement to the class either over a public address system or from behind a screen. Have the class make comments. You will note that they will be emotionally involved, deeply so. You have removed the emotional constraints of the visual code. Discuss this fact.

18. Do the preceding assignment for forty minutes with a series of your classmates. Write a paper or journal entry about the impact of the day's class.

19. Break up into dyads, matching strangers. Each will be alert to the other person's nonverbal behavior. Get acquainted by exchanging the usual information about name, hometown, siblings, and so forth. Intersperse in the conversation statements about your feelings of the moment. Discuss with each other the degree of authenticity in the statement of feelings.

20. Form dyads of strangers in which each person is to try to learn from the other how he or she seems to manage the problem of social acceptance (how easily he or she establishes friendships, the embarrassment felt in establish-

ing new relationships, the need for social approval). Comment (see Chapter 5) on your feelings as you express them. Comment also on your feelings as you make inquiry about the other's feelings. Comment on your feelings as you respond to the inquiries of the other person. Comment on your feelings about the authenticity of your exchanges with each other.

8

Judgment

> But you'll be asking me why I'm writing you like this. Well...you're a sort of confessor to me, boss, and I'm not ashamed to admit all my sins to you. Do you know why? So far as I can see, whether I do right or wrong, you don't care a rap. You hold a damp sponge, like God, and flap! slap! you just wipe it all out. That's what prompts me to tell you everything like this. So listen!
>
> *Nikos Kazantzakis**

In a terrifying play called *The Shrike*, a wife, for her own purposes, commits her husband to a mental hospital.[1] The husband sees that he is being used but assumes that he can extricate himself from the situation. Everything he says, however, exacts a response from his fellow inmates at the hospital, from his "solicitous" wife who keeps visiting him, and from carefully coached friends she invites to see him that adds up to the judgment: "You are insane." As it dawns on the man that anything he says is going to be interpreted as irrational, he becomes desperate and, therefore, excessive in what he says. That, of course, provides the very evidence needed by his listeners to confirm their judgment. The final scene shows this once stable man reduced to blathering nonsense and helplessness. The shrike moves in for the kill.

The play is profoundly disturbing because we recognize it as an exaggerated model of what happens among people day in and day out. In our communication with each other, we habitually, often uncon-

---

*From Nikos Kazantzakis, Zorba the Greek; © 1952 by Simon and Schuster, Inc. Reprinted by permission of the publishers and of Dr. Max Tau, Oslo.

[1]Joseph Kramm, *The Shrike* (New York Dramatic Play Service, Inc., 1967). The shrike is sometimes called "butcherbird" because it impales its victims (grasshoppers, smaller birds, etc.) on thorns or barbs and then tears them to pieces. Significantly, their call is a shriek, but their song is a sweet warble.

sciously, sit in judgment, as the play vividly illustrates. However, *The Shrike* does not tell the full story of judgment. What happens to the person who convinces another that he or she is mad? Judgment, as we shall see, wreaks its vengeance on the person who pronounces it.

We are involved, in this chapter, with the most serious problem in human communication—judgmental speaking and its response, judgmental listening. If the communicative exchange is relatively free of judgment, information transfer, problem solving, and human growth evolve. If the interaction is guided by judgments of self and the other people involved, frustration, confusion, hostility, and threat usually result. Although the destructive results of judgment are easy to see, as the chapter will demonstrate, the erasure of judgment from our communication is extremely difficult to attain. What we are discussing in this chapter is probably the ultimate achievement in human maturity—the ability to live beyond judgment in our communication.

DESCRIPTIONS AND ANALYSES
OF JUDGMENT, CRITICISM, AND DISCRIMINATION

Some workable definitions are needed. The authors conceive of judgment as an attitude in communication at one end of a continuum, opposed, at the other end, by the attitude of noncritical discrimination. Criticism, which combines the qualities of both judgment and discrimination, stands halfway between them.

Judgment   Criticism   Discrimination

What do we mean by the term *judgment?* Quite literally, and probably best understood in its literal form, judgment is the work of a judge. A judge executes an act involving the moral assumptions that good and evil exist and that they exist in mortal conflict. Some acts are good and some are bad, and each tries to destroy the other. These assumptions, of necessity, employ the concepts of guilt and punishment. The judge on the bench holds the right and the power to exercise decisions about punishment, perhaps the imprisonment or freedom of another person. Judging a person, whether one holds the title of judge or not, then, is the act of passing an opinion on the value or worth of another person's behavior, or perhaps his or her very being. The judging act, therefore, assumes superiority of position, power, and integrity on the part of the judge. It should be noted that judges in courts of law carry out their work in prescribed decorum. They must not give way to the passion beneath judgment. They are permitted to exercise only two attitudes, firmness and gravity.

By contrast, most of our daily judgments of each other are saturated with emotions, and it is in understanding this that we arrive at a comprehension of the fundamental character of judgment. Quite simply, our judgments of another are very likely to be favorable *if we like the person.* If we dislike that person, our judgments will probably be unfavorable. And, as we all know, we are likely to be more temperate and compassionate in our unfavorable judgments of people we like than we are in our unfavorable judgments of people we dislike.

If the preceding is a fair description of the nature of judgment, what, then, do we mean when we speak of criticism and discrimination? In our view, discrimination, as opposed to judgment, is simply the response to perceptual data. One may note that another person is tall or short, fat or thin, light or dark, male or female, standing or sitting, talking or not talking. It is hard to conceive of communicating effectively without these perceptual discriminations. "Nonevaluative listening," so often discussed in recent explorations into communication, is not non-discriminating. The counselor recognizes the *differences* that the counselee is so desperately trying to separate out for himself or herself. Any good listener in any situation does this. If, however, we, as listeners, respect the inviolate integrity of the other person, we interfere with that person's observations and interpretations only insofar as he or she seeks our help. We allow the other person the first of all freedoms, the freedom to live without our claim on his or her observations. The other is allowed to see as he or she sees. When we respect the inviolate integrity of another person we help that person—if he or she asks for our observations—to gain data that will facilitate his or her own perceptions and decisions. We may say to the novice golfer, "Turning the right wrist like this, to the left, usually gets rid of the slice." We have listened; we have observed; we have stated our observation. In this instance, we have even gone so far as to offer advice. But we have not criticized. There is a different tone and a different impact when we say, "Come on, that's lousy golf," or, "Why don't you get rid of that slice?" or even, "You sliced again." That is criticism.

Let it be clear that judgment, criticism, *and even a simple statement* of our observations about another assumes a superiority over the other, if in varying degrees. They differ considerably, however, in emotional intensity and the feelings of relationship. "You're a liar!" is an explosive judgment. The person who makes such a judgment closes his or her ears to further credible examination of what the other says. The emotional entanglements are much more taut than they would be had he or she said, "That is not true; I wish you would reexamine that; look at it this way." This statement is critical but not highly charged, because the speaker has not passed sentence on the other person. Yet stating one's own observation arouses still different feelings. "I saw what happened this way . . ." says that I saw differently from you, but you may be right. Different as these three statements are, however, they have a common intent and effect. They all tend to assume control of the other person and thus assume varying degrees of responsibility for that person.

Judgment	*Criticism*	*Discrimination*
Great Authority		Little Authority
Strong Feelings		Weak Feelings

FIGURE 8-1

We would not want to suggest, by citing these observations, that we oppose all control (which is really impossible to eliminate). One's very presence in another person's life is a controlling factor. To eradicate completely the control of one person over another asks, quite literally, for the elimination of communication between people. (Even the memory of a person long dead has its controlling impact.) Just an observation, *even unstated,* that differs from the other's has its impact. It is an awareness of the immense power-of-being, of all people in whose presence we live, that we need among our understandings in order to sense the power of our judgments and criticisms.

The Power of Discriminative Perception, Said and Unsaid

Let us examine the subtle power of our expectations (of the other person) over that person's self-image. Strangely, most people think that what they think and feel, but do not say, does not get communicated. This notion is illustrated by the comment "I didn't say anything, but I thought plenty."

The most dramatic proof of the power of the unsaid is revealed in recent research on the expectations of the researcher.[2] In a series of studies it has been demonstrated that unconsciously the person conduct-

[2] J. D. Adair and Joyce Epstein, "Verbal Cues in the Mediation of Experimenter Bias," paper read at Midwestern Psychological Assoc. (Chicago, May, 1967); K. L. Fode, "The Effect of Non-Visual and Non-Verbal Interaction on Experimenter Bias," (Master's thesis, University of North Dakota, 1960).

ing an experiment tends to communicate to the subjects what he or she expects to find. If one experimenter is told that "your subjects are the bright ones" and the other that "your subjects have the lower IQ," the results will tend to show this difference, even though the subjects are all equally intelligent.[3] We assign no magic or mystery to these findings, though after ten years of exploration the research does not reveal the significant visual and verbal cues that do the communicating. The research does show that both are involved and that the more creditable and more competent researcher communicates his or her expectations more effectively than the less creditable and less competent researcher. The more unconscious the sender is of these expectations, the more subtly they are communicated.

So the father *shapes* his son by his unconscious fantasy of the boy's future. And if the father fears for his son's future, this is communicated too. How much of the anxiety of the earth is the product of parents' apprehension about the goodness of their children? How much of the aspiration of the human spirit is the consequence of the unfulfilled dreams of parents watching their child? How much of the anger of blacks is the unstated image of the black in the perceptions of the white who talks with him or her—or, again, the perceptions of the black person's parents? How many of the failures in life are the "self-fulfilling prophecies" of teachers and parents? How much is each of us sculpted by the expectations of other people?[4]

If we are indifferent to another person, especially if that person is related by blood or proximity in our life, we send a powerful message to that person about himself or herself. If indifference is replaced by fascination, consider the difference to the recipient. There is an immense power that each of us exerts over all others with whom we talk, hidden in our perceptions of the other person. When these are unstated, they make unconscious impact. When they are stated, they make conscious impact. It is hard to say which is the more powerful.

Inclusion Versus Exclusion

As we try to think through the meaning of these things, it seems to us that we must come to the conclusion that the most significant thing we

[3]Robert Rosenthal and Lenore Jacobson, *Pygmalion in the Classroom* (New York: Holt, Rinehart and Winston, Inc., 1968).

[4]B. F. Skinner, in *Beyond Freedom and Dignity* (New York: Alfred A. Knopf, Inc., 1971), holds to the view that humans are entirely controlled by genes and environmental reinforcement. The authors accept the significance and power of environmental reinforcement. But we do not see how one can hold so exclusively to the view of environmental control and at once set out to change the environment. Or, if the environment makes one

are discussing is the inclusion or exclusion power of the message. In judgment, said or unsaid, the person judged is excluded. The judged person is "sent to jail" or "charged a fine" or "executed." At best, the person has to change before, if ever, he or she is again included. The criticized person is not excluded, but is threatened with that possibility. He or she could fail. The observed person is under scrutiny, and surveillance arouses fear of being judged and excluded. Said and unsaid observations, criticisms, and judgments probably differ only to the degree that the receiver can tell clearly what he or she is receiving. But the essential point in our analysis is the inclusion or exclusion of the receiver of the message.

We asked Dr. Joseph Agnello, a stutterer who, despite crippling early years, has become a speech therapist and researcher, to tell us the great influences that have shaped his life thus far. He cited three.

> I spent three years in the first grade. I still remember the last day of the first year. One by one the other children were called to the front of the room and given slips that passed them into the second grade. The last two were not called; we sat there silently, me and the little girl whom we all knew to be an imbecile. I said to myself, "I am hopelessly stupid," and I wet my pants. Over the years I gradually changed my feelings of stupidity into the hostile conviction that people make me stutter. They like to do this to me. I said to myself, "People are all evil and enjoy my plight." The second great impression of my life came with the patience of a therapist, Dr. Charles Van Riper, who taught me to talk better and by his help taught me that there is love, devotion, and goodness in people. The third great change in my life came when I went to graduate school, and the voice scientist, Dr. John Black, listened respectfully to my talk. I said, "I have a brain, I can think."

If we examine the three incidents we see the issue at hand in bold relief. The first incident was judgmental and entirely destructive; it excluded the boy. The first positive change involved an inclusive act that said, "I can help and you can learn to talk." The listening of the graduate professor said covertly, "Speak, I want to hear." In neither of the two productive incidents of the stutterer's story is judgment or criticism in the foreground, if it exists at all. The main point we are making here is that, said or unsaid, our perceptions of the person we speak to have a significant impact on him or her. When those perceptions involve criticism or judgment, they can be devastating.

---

want to change it, on what basis can one assume that one's effort is wise? If one tries to persuade, one assumes that there are available alternatives that his or her arguments can influence. The argumentative act is an expression of the awareness of the existence of human choice.

THE NEED TO JUDGE

Why do humans find it so necessary to pass judgment on each other? Are most of us perversely aggressive, wanting to hurt others, or do we suffer delusions that we are God, believing it our assignment in life to make judgments? Certainly the need to judge others is deep in all of us, which is to say that the act of judging tells more about the giver than the receiver of the judgment. Out of the maze of World War II stories, one emerges that reveals the workings of the terrible drive to judge. It involves an encounter between General George Patton and one of his soldiers in a field hospital. A reporter explains what happened on that day in August 1943 when Patton walked into the medical tent of the 15th Evacuation Hospital.

Private Chares H. Kuhl was admitted to the 3rd Battalion, 26th Infantry aid station in Sicily on August 2, 1943, at 2:10 P.M. He had been in the Army eight months and with the 1st Division about thirty days. A diagnosis of "Exhaustion" was made at the station by Lieutenant H. L. Sanger, Medical Corps, and Kuhl was evacuated to C Company, 1st Medical Battalion, well to the rear of the fighting. There a note was made on his medical tag stating that he had been admitted to this place three times during the Sicilian campaign. He was evacuated to the clearing company by Captain J. D. Broom, M. C., put in "quarters" and given sodium amytal, one capsule night and morning, on the prescription of Captain N. S. Nedell, M. C. On August 3rd the following remark appeared on Kuhl's Emergency Tag: "Psychoneuroses anxiety state—moderately severe. Soldier has been twice before in hospital within ten days. He can't take it at front evidently. He is repeatedly returned." (signed) Capt. T. P. Covington, Medical Corps.

By this route and in this way Private Kuhl arrived in the receiving tent of the 15th Evacuation Hospital, where the blow was struck that was heard round the world.

"I came into the tent," explains General Patton, "with the commanding officer of the outfit and other medical officers.

"I spoke to the various patients, especially commending the wounded men. I just get sick inside myself when I see a fellow torn apart, and some of the wounded were in terrible, ghastly shape. Then I came to this man and asked him what was the matter."

The soldier replied, "I guess I can't take it."

"Looking at the others in the tent, so many of them badly beaten up, I simply flew off the handle."

Patton called the man a coward and slapped him across the face with his gloves.

The soldier fell back. Patton grabbed him by the scruff of the neck and kicked him out of the tent.

Kuhl was immediately picked up by corpsmen and taken to a ward.[5]

[5]By members of the Overseas Press Club, *Deadline Delayed* (New York: E. P. Dutton and Company, Inc., 1947). Reprinted by permission of Overseas Press Club.

General Patton's responses provide the data for noting the following about the need to judge:

1. The need to judge assumes the inferiority of the person being judged.
2. The need to judge assumes the moral degeneration of the person being judged.
3. The need to judge is triggered by the presence of the person that arouses the judge's anxiety.

General Patton, we discover late in the account, "went all to pieces." He explained his crying and "flying off the handle" as a consequence of seeing behavior diagnosed as "psychoneuroses anxiety state." One interpretation might be that seeing this behavior caused him to feel anxiety and stimulated the terrible fear that he might be reaching his own breaking point. We accept our weaknesses or blame ourselves or blame others. If we are essentially aggressive, we blame others. The need to judge, in the main, is an aggressive effort to throw off anxiety about the self.

The Genesis and Maintenance of Anxiety

In our efforts to understand the ubiquitous phenomenon of judgmental speech, we have found, as highlighted by the story of General Patton, that the agent is anxiety. We have noted that people who are at peace with themselves have no need to pass judgment on others and, along with this, that people who have achieved self-acceptance can calmly tolerate the judgment of others. Or, to say it again, if it were not for anxiety we would neither give nor be victimized by judgment.

What are the workings of anxiety? What is its origin? What is its relationship to listening? How is it that things happen to people as they grow up that seem to equip them to make judgments automatically? Harry Stack Sullivan refused to believe that this was simply a product of man's natural cussedness.[6] He did not find evidence in his clinical cases, he said, that people were "by birth" malevolent. He thought, instead, that something like this happens: The human infant is born into a physical world with which it is virtually helpless to cope. A "mothering one" (either its real mother or a mother-substitute) helps it meet its needs.

As the infant, then, becomes a child, a preadolescent, and an adolescent, he or she is *taught* anxiety by "significant others"—parents, friends, teachers, and so on. That is, the child *learns* from experience with these others whether to be anxious. At one point in his explanation, Sullivan asserts that the capacity to love (the capacity for intimacy) is directly

[6]Harry Stack Sullivan, *The Interpersonal Theory of Psychiatry* (New York: W. W. Norton and Co., Inc., 1953).

related to the degree to which the "significant others" in one's life have taught one not to be anxious. In other words, if an infant learns to expect tenderness but, as she grows, discovers that the "significant others" in her life are sitting in judgment on her, making arbitrary demands on her, blocking her efforts to develop her talents, she at once decreases her intimacy with them and becomes increasingly filled with anxiety. And as her anxiety level increases she grows more judgmental in her attitudes toward others. On the other hand, to the extent that the need for tenderness is met, the anxiety level lowers, as does the "need" to be judgmental in her attitudes toward others.

The observations of the authors would support this theory. For instance, the students we work with show some of the same patterns so often that one could almost make predictions like these: If a student is reluctant to risk his or her ideas with others, seeking safety in silence, or if a student presents himself or herself as a bold, aggressive judge of other people's ideas (so that fellow students finally accuse him or her of "playing God"), the chances are good that either or both of that student's parents listened to him or her primarily as critics.

THE RESULTS OF BEING JUDGED

The results of being judged have been suggested from the opening story of the chapter, but they need to be examined more fully. Let us come to focus with a typical case. A woman in one of our classes took an aggressive attitude among her peers. The more obvious cues suggested that she felt she was better than they. Sometimes she would laugh at another's ideas as ridiculous. One day, when a student was talking about uneducable children, she said with a sneer, "I hope we don't have any like that in here." By the time the semester was one-third gone she had antagonized almost all the class members to the extent that when she spoke we noted them trying to restrain themselves from saying what they were thinking. She was a bright woman, quite aware of how people were responding and unhappy with the image they had of her. In a diary, which was part of the class work, she wrestled with the question, How did I get the way I am?

At the beginning of the semester, she had written that communication between herself and her mother was very good. As the semester went along, she began to see that maybe her love of argument was a product of the model her mother had presented: "My mother always taught me to say what I had to say in the strongest possible way and to let someone else cut it down if they could." But always she would add that her mother had given her good training. Then one day she exploded, out of the blue, with this statement: "I never did anything right! She always criticized me. I even said to her one time, 'Why don't you praise me once in a while when I do something right?' And do you know what she said to me? She said, 'Because I expect it.'"

No explanation of what this meant in the life of this student seemed to be necessary. In a crystal-clear moment all understood. The child who has been listened to by a "critic" during the formative years may, as an adult, have a deep-seated need to "play God."

Fear wears a thousand faces—subtle, deceptive faces learned early in life. A strange form of psychic process begins in criticism received, transforms itself into anxiety, evolves into self-doubt, and forms a mask, out of the mouth of which pours criticism, which transforms itself into anxiety in another person—and on it goes.

As Sidney Jourard emphasizes, we each discover our identity in conversation with others. It follows that no person completely escapes the judgment that any other person places on him or her, spoken or unspoken.[7] Of course, the more we respect or fear the judge, the more we are impressed and imprisoned by the sentence. But we do not escape the judgment of another, even though we do not respect or like that person. We often try to escape into expressions of anger and contempt ("I don't give a damn what he says"), but our emotional outbursts—silent or overt—are proof that we did not escape.

And if the "repeated" criticism or judgment is more than we can bear, we repress it, pushing it down into our underworld, burying it below verbal recall. There, out of control, it does its mischief. All of us suffer uneasiness about ourselves that we cannot explain. Most of us suffer feelings of inarticulateness and lack of command in the presence of authority figures whose very presence arouses the echoes of unpleasant judgments of self that we cannot shake. Some of us occasionally need the help of a skillful counselor or conversant who induces us to speak and to gain control of the judgment festering in the unconscious.

Listening to the Double Bind

Listening to judgment, we have noted, can be confusing for a variety of reasons. Different people give different judgments. Unspoken judgments are hard to interpret and are often received without our knowing where or how we got them. But the most confusing states arise as a result of mixed judgments and criticisms from more than one person.

[7]Sidney M. Jourard, *The Transparent Self* (Princeton, N.J.: D. Van Nostrand Company, Inc., 1964).

The following is a classic story of a boy caught in the cross fire of the differing judgments of his parents:

> A boy of seven had been accused by his father of having stolen his pen. He vigorously protested his innocence, but was not believed. Possibly to save him from being doubly punished as a thief and as a liar, his mother told his father that he had confessed to her that he had stolen the pen. However, the boy still would not admit to the theft, and his father gave him a thrashing for stealing and for lying twice over. As both his parents treated him completely as though he both had done the deed and had confessed it, he began to think that he could remember having actually done it after all, and was not even sure whether or not he had in fact confessed. His mother later discovered that he had not in fact stolen the pen, and admitted this to the boy, without, however, telling his father. She said to the boy, "Come and kiss your mummy and make it up." He felt in some way that to go and kiss his mother and make it up to her in the circumstances was somehow to be completely twisted. Yet the longing to go to her, to embrace her, and be at one with her again was so strong as to be almost unendurable. Although at that time he could not, of course, articulate the situation clearly to himself, he stood without moving towards her. She then said, "Well, if you don't love your mummy I'll just have to go away," and walked out of the room. The room seemed to spin. The longing was unbearable, but suddenly, everything was different yet the same. He saw the room and himself for the first time. The longing to cling had gone. He had somehow broken into a new region of solitude. He was quite alone. Could this woman in front of him have any connexion with him? As a man, he always thought of this incident as the crucial event in his life. It was a deliverance from bondage, but not without a price to pay.[8]

One is tempted to believe that no child should have more than one parent. The conflicting judgments of one parent are hard enough to handle. Consider this: A boy runs out of school and his mother comes to pick him up.

> [She] opens her arms to hug him and he stands a little way off. The mother says, "Don't you love your mommy?" He says, "No." The mother says "But mommy knows you do, Darling," and gives him a big hug.[9]

As Ronald D. Laing says, the mother is impervious to what the boy says he feels, overruling the boy's testimony by telling him what he does feel and rewarding him for saying what he did not say. This is the double bind.

[8]Ronald D. Laing, *Self and Others* (New York: Random House, Inc.), 2nd rev. ed., pp. 143–144. Reprinted by permission of Random House, Inc. and of Tavistock Publications Ltd.

[9]*Ibid.*, p. 147.

Listening to Favorable Judgment

We have discussed the weight and power of the unfavorable judgments we hear. What about the favorable judgment, the rewards and praise—the positive reinforcement? Is this all good? In a very real sense, positive judgment is restricting too. A judgment of any description asserts power. And the person who learns to depend on the praise of others evolves into the other-oriented person, the faceless conformer who pervades our culture.[10] The freedom to become ourselves may be impaired as much by praise as by blame. A friend told us about an occasion when he said to his wife, "You know, I've noticed that when I call you endearing terms you shrug them off as if they were nothing—or you act as if you didn't even hear them. How come?" The two were on an all-day automobile trip alone. He was driving. There was a long pause and finally he was aware that his wife was crying. Hesitantly, she finally sobbed, "I know. And I know that you must be hurt by it. But when you say those things to me, I feel uneasy. I always think of what I really am, and how far that falls short of what you are saying about me, and I hate myself." The authors recall countless conversations with young people who were tearing at the chains their parents had placed on them by seemingly harmless praise of their values. "I know I can trust you" exerts a firm control over the one spoken to. In the eyes of the authors, favorable judgment is preferable to punishing judgment only in the fact that the relationship between speaker and listener is sustained by the former and destroyed by the latter. But judgment, pleasant or unpleasant, exerts a threatening control over the listener.

We all know the fright induced by listening to praise. "Can I live up to the praise?" is the question aroused. "If I win your praise, I can also lose your praise" is the knowledge gained. "As the giver of the judgment, even though you praise me, you assume the authority to change your approval." What is the meaning of reward if there is no power to withhold it, and even to punish?

Most people equate praise and confirmation. Praise from a person who feels only praise is not praise in the sense we are talking about here. It is acceptance. Unconditional praise is positive feeling for another—minus the control of praise. Sharing with another person one's unalterable favorable feelings about him or her is acceptance, and quite a different thing from favorable judgment. Acceptance on the part of a listener leaves the speaker free. Favorable judgment exerts a measure of control.

---

[10]David Riesman, in collaboration with Reuel Denny and Nathan Glazer, *The Lonely Crowd* (New Haven, Conn.: Yale University Press, 1950).

The Place for Praise

Our position on the impact of listening to judgmental responses—favorable or unfavorable—is one that counsels restraint, but we need to look at what to us seems to be an exception to the rule. What about people, especially children, who as a consequence of negative judgments have learned to conceive of themselves as stupid, ugly, or in some other way unacceptable? Those who use operant conditioning techniques can demonstrate radically favorable changes, for instance, in the slow learner whose bright behavior is reinforced. We have observed that positive reinforcement of bright behavior—where negative images are fixed—is more effective than unconditional acceptance, for one can be accepted even though one is stupid, and that helps little. Our position is this, that those who have developed negative self-images because they have been negatively reinforced need the opposite reinforcement. But—considering our description of the meaning of being judged—it should be recognized that we conceive of reward as an antidote for negative convictions about self, not food for the nourishment of life. Rewards are wisely used when an antidote is needed.

Summary

But the central point we want to make about the impact of being judged—good or bad—is this: Judgment arouses devastating doubts about the self that distort our ability to hear ourselves or others realistically. Jack Gibb, reporting the results of a detailed study of hours of taped discussions, concludes that the effect of judgment on the listener takes these forms: (1) It prevents the listener from concentrating on the message; (2) it causes the listener to distort what he or she receives; (3) it masks the listener's cues to the motives, values, and emotions of the sender. Gibb observes, moreover, that the loss of efficiency in listening is in direct ratio to the increase in defensive behavior. The more the defensiveness, the greater the distortion by the listener.[11] Yet defend we must when we are judged.

THE RESULTS OF MAKING THE JUDGMENT

Thus far, we have discussed the nature of judgment and the impact of listening to the judgments about ourselves made by others. Let us study the boomerang effect. What are the effects on the speaker of

[11]Jack Gibb, "Defensive Communication," *ETC.*, 22 (June 1965), 221-229.

adopting the role and speaking the lines of the judge? It is an age-old commonplace to remind people that every time they point a finger at another person they inescapably point three fingers at themselves. This is what seems to happen to the judgmental speaker. The more we "sit in judgment" on others, the more we are forced to judge ourselves. This is so because every conclusion one draws about another is a revelation of the self. After all, we cannot know anything about another that is totally foreign to the self. The person who consistently focuses on the errors of others reinforces and thus develops a prevailing uneasiness about himself or herself. He or she becomes more and more fearful of his or her own weaknesses. Sullivan has said it with a new twist of the biblical statement: "Judge not," says Sullivan, "lest ye be forced to judge yourself!"

A teacher in a modern novel is critical of some of his colleagues; he feels constantly antagonistic toward the principal and dwells on the hopeless stupidity of his students. Unavoidably, in that process he comes to think of himself as worthless.[12] His suicidal leap into the depths of a stone quarry is a logical way to end the story. Fortunately for most of us teachers, the impact of our judgments is not so devastating.

There is some empirical evidence, too, that the critical view of others turns back against the self and blocks growth. When one is trying, for example, to improve one's speech, the effect of a critical stance in listening to others is clearly negative. One of the authors ran a study for several semesters, searching for an understanding of the relationships between the way we speak and the way we listen. Here is how he did the study and what he learned.

In a beginning speech class, listeners were asked to write in a notebook whatever responses they wished to make at the close of each speech. It was understood that the comments were *not* to be shown to the speaker, that the responses were being made so that the listener, at a later date, might study the notes to see what kind of responses characterized his or her listening. At the close of the semester the notebooks were collected and each statement was classified into one or more of the following categories:

1. A statement of the main point the speaker made.
2. A citation of the part of the speech that seemed most interesting.
3. A restatement of what the speaker said.
4. Criticism of what the speaker said or the way he said it.
5. A creative response; a statement of the thoughts generated by the speaker.

[12]John Updike, *The Centaur* (New York: Alfred A. Knopf, Inc., 1963).

The instructor, of course, had evaluated the speakers as speakers throughout the semester, noting whatever they had gained in (1) fluency, (2) clarity of statement, (3) flexibility in handling situations, and (4) insightfulness—maturity in relating to self and others. Such measurement was, of course, subjective on the part of the instructor. The following is what seemed to emerge.

The student who showed decided growth in all criteria made responses in all five categories of listening behavior. For instance, a woman who seemed to make the greatest strides in the class showed 34 statements of the main point, 6 statements of high interest, 16 restatements of the speaker's thinking, 33 criticisms, and 6 creative remarks. On the other hand, the most rigid, unchanging behavior was noted in a woman whose listening responses were limited in variety and were essentially critical: 0 statements of the main point, 1 observation of a high point of interest, 3 restatements of the speaker's thinking, 31 criticisms, and 4 creative remarks. Strikingly, her criticisms were in the main positive. All the inflexible speakers demonstrated a predominance of criticism in their listening, and the degree of positiveness or negativeness in the criticism did not seem to be the significant factor. The point is that a clear dominance of critical response in listening correlated with rigidity. Yet while critical remarks characterized the listening of those who did not grow, many who were highly critical did grow, but in a distinctive way. They increased in fluency, clarity of statement, and sometimes flexibility in handling situations. They did not develop insight. Their growth, in other words, was in performance. Insight seemed to develop only in those who were relatively low in critical listening or in those who listened critically as only one of several dominant behaviors.

We expected to find that the decisive factor separating those who grew in insight from those who did not would be the creative response. Not so. The vital factor related to insight seemed to be the presence of restatements of the thinking of the speaker. A speaker who failed to develop powers of insight seldom restated the thinking of those he or she listened to. All speakers who seemed to mature as people as well as speakers showed a decided tendency to restate the thinking of the speaker they listened to.

These pilot studies suggest that the good speaker listens in many different ways and most particularly in the tendency to restate and translate the flow of the other person's thought. Speakers who changed the least tended to listen almost exclusively in a critical fashion.

The way our judging affects our daily work may be seen in the following, taken from studies in leadership and organization. It concerns a young employment interviewer just learning her job.

The third applicant wanted to be a foreman of the shipping gang. He was a burly 250-pounder who said that he used to work in the steel mills near Gary. He spoke loudly, with much self-assurance. "Some sort of bully—a leering Casanova of the hot-rod set," Jean thought. Jean always did dislike guys like this, especially this sort of massive redhead. Just like her kid brother used to be—"a real pest!" The more he bragged about his qualitifications, the more Jean became annoyed. It wouldn't do to let her feelings show; interviewers were supposed to be friendly and objective. She smiled sweetly, even if she did have a mild suspicion that her antagonism might be coming through. "I am sorry, we cannot use you just now," she said. "You don't seem to have the kind of experience we are looking for. But we'll be sure to keep your application on the active file and call you as soon as something comes up. Thank you for thinking of applying with us."[13]

There is no way of knowing how much the interviewer missed or distorted the potential of the applicant. But the point is clear: From the moment she judged the applicant "a massive redhead" like her brother, her capacity to search out his qualifications was limited.

But the loss in efficiency and productivity in the economy is a small part of the price we pay for sitting in judgment on each other. The incalculable price is the dwarfing and sterilization of our lives, the alienation, estrangement, loneliness, deep feelings of meaninglessness. Our tendency to take a critical view of those around us builds a cell for our own imprisonment. There we starve.

Perhaps we come too close here to preaching, but we feel impelled to add this. Every person who has cured himself or herself of despair has taken the medicine of service-to-others, not judgment. And it is not the service rendered that is the good, good as that is—for only those who have been given can give. It is the feeling stirred in the giver when he or she acts in service to others—beyond the world of judgment—that is the essential we are examining here. Conversely, the price the judge must pay for judging is diminished meaning in his or her own life.

A CASE FOR CRITICAL LISTENING

Because of the forces that twist the lives of so many people from the moment of birth, we do not live in the best of all possible worlds. We do have our exploiters. One of the authors learned this as a small boy when he bought a pair of rusty ice skates with rotten leather straps from an older boy. The younger boy said, "How much do you want for them?"

[13]Reprinted by permission from Robert Tennenbaum, Irvin R. Weschler, and Fred Massarik, "The Process of Understanding People," in *Leadership and Organization: A Behavioral Science Approach* (New York: McGraw-Hill Book Company, 1961).

"How much money do you have?" asked the older boy. "Fifty cents," answered the younger boy. "You can have them for fifty cents," said the older boy quickly. With the aid of old neckties to hold the skates on, the younger one learned his first lesson in skating, and in critical listening.

One student in a communication class selected as her project the study of gullibility, or insensitivity to the exploitive cues in nonverbal behavior. She was troublesome to both herself and her poor graduate student husband as she continually stumbled into expensive "bargains" with appliance salespeople. She had lived all her life, before going to college, in a small town on the shores of Lake Superior. She was not accustomed to the language of the industrial world and was completely unsuspecting in the face of aggressive salesmanship. We may be amazed that there could exist anyone so credulous, but several bad purchases in rapid succession had forced her into a study of herself and critical listening.

Critical listening is a self-protective device. And educators have tried a number of analyses designed to teach us how not to be taken in. There is "slanting" that we are warned to watch for, where the language and evidence are carefully selected to cover up the true nature of that which we are asked to accept. A quarter of a century ago every high school student was taught the propaganda devices of card stacking, plain-folks argument, bandwagon psychology, and the like. Every few years the educational system takes some new approach to the teaching of critical thinking, and it would require a lengthy discussion to mention the many categories of logical errors that have been taught to help us protect ourselves.

Although it is incidental to our main point here, the research on the learning of such analyses does not support the value of the training. Those who are trained to recognize "guilt by association" or any other category of persuasive trap learn to identify the category but show no less tendency to be impressed when it is used. The conclusions drawn are these. We are guided in our listening by our beliefs. That which fits our beliefs, we accept; that which does not, we reject. And we change our beliefs when acting on them frustrates us or gets us into trouble. It was the bad skating on those fifty-cent skates that taught a gullible boy to examine the speech of others skeptically. Critical listening is skeptical listening, and skeptical listening is suspicious in character. It looks for every clue of falsity and deception. When the automobile salesperson begins breathing hard we recognize the deep need of victory and should examine the potential arrangements with a skeptical eye and ear. But we have no ear, in the defensive set, for understanding the salesperson's needs as a person.

The doubts that arouse and guide critical listening are obviously justified in a ruthless world. But what about judgmental listening? This is something else. Survival is not enhanced for either the exploiter or the exploited when final judgment comes, unless one concludes that a break in civil communication is desirable.

Those who sit in judgment on each other are either at a standoff or in a state of battle. Judgmental listening that is condemning is the listening of enemies. Judgmental listening that is praising is the listening of friends in danger of mutual disillusionment. It is rather difficult to build a case for judgmental listening, but we do have to learn to be sufficiently skeptical and therefore critical in our listening in order to survive.

NONJUDGMENTAL DISCRIMINATION

It should be clear to the least suspecting reader that this book holds to the position that most people know how to communicate critically considerably better than they know how to listen and speak discriminatively but noncritically. Indeed, it is difficult for many people to understand the behavior of the noncritical response. To make doubly sure we know what we mean by a noncritical response, here are some final examples: "You make me think of the time I was trying to figure out where to go to college." "You are not looking foward to the end of school because you do not know what you are going to tell your parents when you get home." "Driving a Jaguar gives you the feel of the road, and this you prefer to the comfortable ride that masks that out." Nonjudgmental listening and its response try to capture and understand the basic intent of the speaker. And when the speaker is deeply moved, as when a counseling friend is sought out, the listener responds like this: "You have felt, for some time now, that the distance between you and your wife is growing, and you can't help wondering if it may be your fault. But when you think it through, you can't escape the conclusion that it is wrong to blame yourself. And this business of first thinking one thing and then the other is a constant frustration to you." The talent of capturing the nuances intended is just as difficult to develop as that of noting the error or weakness in another's argument—more difficult, because the culture does not train us to listen this way from early in life. But we have to have this kind of listening done for us only once to know the deep satisfaction of being understood. Anxiety fades and we feel whole. It turns out that for the other person, the listener in the exchange, the great value of trusting and listening accurately is that moment of insight provided for the self. As S. I. Hayakawa says, "It is only as we fully understand opinions and attitudes different from our own and the reasons for them that we better understand our own place in the scheme of things."[14]

How to Develop Nonjudgmental Discrimination

How can we develop our discriminative powers? The answer is simple, but the workings of the procedure are subtle. We learn discriminative communication by speaking openly and by being spoken to openly. Let us see how to do the latter first. In one study W. J. Powell found that the best way to get another person to talk openly is to talk about oneself to him or her.[15] In short, we teach what we do. The open and defenseless speech of the other person that follows will say both positive and negative things about the self. Telling the other person what you heard in his or her speech also causes that person to reveal himself or herself further. But the openness that follows, according to Powell's research, will tend to be more exclusively self-critical. Rewards, encouragement, and confirmation have no opening or closing effect.

But the reader may rightly ask, How does self-disclosure produce less judgment and criticism in observations? This effect can be seen best when we turn to examining the internal communication process of a person as that person—in his or her own speech—becomes more open. The following is a typical example of what people say when they are in the process of becoming less judgmental:

> As I bluntly told the other person my feelings and thought about him and what he was saying I always found he was surprised that I felt as I did about him. Then he would tell me how he had thought I had felt about him. This I found extremely valuable. His explanation showed me how I had concealed myself, but equally important, and at once, it showed some new feelings and attitudes of the other person, which I had not known. And so my prejudgments and my concealment began to break down together. Now I knew that both of us had judged each other wrongly. Strangely now I was out of judgment, trying to find out more about how the other person felt. *Instead* of listening *to* him now I was listening *with* him. I was experiencing what it was like to feel and to see as he does.[16]

If one examines the process suggested in the explanation, one sees that judgment and concealment work hand in hand. Conversely, dis-

[14]S. I. Hayakawa, *Symbol, Status, and Personality* (New York: Harcourt Brace Jovanovich, 1963), pp. 47–48.

[15]W. J. Powell, "A Comparison of the Reinforcing Effects of Three Types of Experimenter Response on Two Classes of Verbal Behavior in an Experimental Interview" (Ph.D. dissertation, University of Florida, 1963).

[16]From an interview with Mrs. Judith Lyons, a "crisis teacher," South Junior High School, Kalamazoo, Michigan.

criminative observation and openness go together. Thus by initiating self-disclosure we beget self-disclosure. With disclosure comes the information that lessens criticism and judgment.

One other thing. In the self-disclosure an appropriate emotion must be aroused in the listener, for, as we have learned, without emotions nothing changes. The "crisis teacher" just quoted, a black, when she speaks to a hostile white audience often begins like this: "OK, you don't like me or accept me, but I have a job to do. I have to help your kids and my kids have a school situation that is peaceful enough to allow some learning. You don't need to like me, but help me know what I have to know in order to do my job." Expressing other people's pent-up feelings with *appreciation* (as they would say them if they said them) vents the judgmental feelings, and facilitates discriminative listening and speaking.

You will also note in the last example a demonstrated courage Always there is risk in moving from judgment to discrimination, and courage must outweigh fear. We have to lower our defenses. Nonjudgment and courage are bedfellows, as are fear and defense.

Transition

The temptation to judge, as we have seen, is almost irresistible. And the inevitable consequence of judgment is the use of power to bring others to terms with that judgment. The next chapter is devoted to understanding the workings of power.

INSTRUMENT 8-1

THE INCLINATION TO JUDGE

Circle the number that reflects your response to each statement.

7 means "I feel very strongly this way."
6 means "I feel strongly this way."
5 means "I feel this way."
4 means "I do not feel this way."
3 means "I feel the opposite way."
2 means "I feel strongly the opposite way."
1 means "I feel very strongly the opposite way."

1. I respect most professors.

   7   6   5   4   3   2   1

2. I believe there is an afterlife.

   7   6   5   4   3   2   1

3. The belief that all sex is appropriate between consenting adults is dehumanizing.

   7   6   5   4   3   2   1

4. Communism and violence go together.

   7   6   5   4   3   2   1

5. Sex should be restricted to marriage.

   7   6   5   4   3   2   1

6. Commitment to the people you love is important.

   7   6   5   4   3   2   1

7. Free enterprise is the bedrock of American democracy.

   7   6   5   4   3   2   1

8. The penalty for rape should be capital punishment.

   7   6   5   4   3   2   1

9. Hard-core pornography should not be shown publicly in a college or university.

   7   6   5   4   3   2   1

10. We live in a wicked day.

    7   6   5   4   3   2   1

11. Those who do not believe in God will be destroyed.

    7   6   5   4   3   2   1

12. There will always be war among nations.

    7   6   5   4   3   2   1

13. The labor union movement is essentially destructive to the nation.

    7   6   5   4   3   2   1

14. The discipline of education is probably as important as anything one learns.

    7   6   5   4   3   2   1

15. Stricter divorce laws than we now have are desirable.

    7   6   5   4   3   2   1

16. The women's movement has in the main been injurious to both men and women.

    7   6   5   4   3   2   1

17. Achievement is the highest of all goals.

    7   6   5   4   3   2   1

18. I believe much can be known by astrology.

| 7 | 6 | 5 | 4 | 3 | 2 | 1 |

19. It has been found that children who obey their parents turn out best.

| 7 | 6 | 5 | 4 | 3 | 2 | 1 |

20. The contributions of practical people to society are greater than those of artists.

| 7 | 6 | 5 | 4 | 3 | 2 | 1 |

21. Much of the crime wave of recent years can be traced back to permissiveness in child rearing.

| 7 | 6 | 5 | 4 | 3 | 2 | 1 |

22. We are going through a time when the sex life of most young people is pretty loose.

| 7 | 6 | 5 | 4 | 3 | 2 | 1 |

23. Obedience is one of the most important things we learn in life.

| 7 | 6 | 5 | 4 | 3 | 2 | 1 |

24. Questioning all basic concepts (as many professors do) is essentially unhealthy.

| 7 | 6 | 5 | 4 | 3 | 2 | 1 |

25. The dress code in recent years has become informal to the point of carelessness.

| 7 | 6 | 5 | 4 | 3 | 2 | 1 |

Add the 6's and 7's circled and place the sum here: _____

Add the 3's, 4's, and 5's circled and place the sum here: _____

Add the 2's and 1's circled and place the sum here: _____

To the degree that you have a high number or percentage in the 6 and 7 class, you tend to want to judge according to the authority of the culture. Conversely, the degree to which you circled 2 or 1 indicates a tendency to judge by liberal standards. The degree to which you circled 3, 4, or 5 suggests a tendency not to be judgmental.

One of the authors had three 6's and 7's; seven 3's, 4's, and 5's; and fifteen 1's and 2's. He was not surprised to find himself on the liberal side, but was surprised that he was so judgmental. In less than 25 percent of the responses was he acceptant of either view.

One might argue that these are evaluations of behavior and beliefs, not of people. But most of us find it hard to accept people who hold views we reject. The chapter on ethics deals with this problem. What did you find out about yourself?

EXERCISES

1. Select an interesting campus controversy to discuss in class. Record the discussion. Replay it and have each person count the number of judgments, criticisms, and descriptive discriminations he or she made. What observations can be made?

2. Attend a campus event of interest to the class with two classmates. Agree ahead of time that one of you is going to report exclusively in judgmental terms. The second will report exclusively in critical terms. The third will report exclusively in descriptive statements. Have the class discuss whether each of the three of you stayed clearly within the classification of statements assigned to you. Discuss the different impact the reports made on both the speakers and the class.

3. Tell the class about an experience that had a powerful effect on you in which you were judged good or bad. Have several class members explain the significance of the experience to you as they heard it. Note the person or people who most clearly identify with your experience. Comment.

4. Canvass your life for the people who have aroused the most anxiety in you. Canvass your life for those who have helped you accept yourself. Note the differences in the level of criticism and judgment expressed in the communication of those who aroused your anxiety and those who made you feel comfortable with yourself. Write a paper or make a journal entry about your observations.

5. Have two classmates explain their attitudes toward race. Let the rest of the class rate the two on a scale between one and seven (one being the most racist) and evaluate the relative degree of racism. If there are black students in the class, have them comment on both the speeches and the class evaluations.

6. Describe to the class, as if it were an audience from Mars, the meaning of the following words: *prostitute, criminal, politician, college administrator, the Establishment, the Pentagon, dope pusher.* Have the class members each rate your explanation of each word on a scale between one and seven (one being the most judgmental) to indicate the degree of criticism in your explanation of the word. Discuss with the class the cues they used in evaluating you.

7. List some abstract words such as *democracy, beauty, justice, femininity, wisdom, freedom, hope, pleasure, worth.* Read these or other words like them slowly to the class with the instruction that each person is to write the word he or she hears and then as many other words as come to mind as fast as they occur. Let each person count the words as a measure of discrimination, and also count the number of judgmental or critical words as a measure of his or her tendency to judge. Discuss.

8. Set as a goal for a given day to go all day without making a single criticism or judgment about anybody or anything. Keep a record of the incidents in which you break the rule. Comment on those incidents in a paper or in your journal.

9. Set as a goal for a given day not to feel any criticism or judgment of your roommate. Note the way this forces you to see new potentials in him or her that you had not before observed. Note your new feelings and awarenesses about yourself.

10. Select a person with whom you have found it difficult to relate. Attempt for a day when you are around that person to resist any judgmental or critical feelings about him or her. Note the changes in his or her responses to you.

11. One of the deceptive features of our behavior when we think we have achieved an entirely descriptive view of a person or thing is a hidden or unconscious judgment that selects what we will describe. A way of becoming more aware of this self-deception is to practice slanting both positively and negatively in making comments. In order to sense this, make a series of negative and positive statements about a person, place, event, group, or institution. What did you learn?

9

Power

?

Those who question power do us a service, for such questioning
determines whether we shall use power or whether power shall use
us.

John F. Kennedy

What is won by force is as transient as the colors of a sunset.

Dean Acheson

In every communicative relationship there is a power problem. And
whether that relationship will work depends, in large part, on whether
the problem can be resolved for both parties. Letting it go unresolved
ensures that the communication will gravitate into conflict.

There is an exercise called "The Press"[1] that is used occasionally in
"human encounter" training groups. It is built on the assumption that
deep inside each of us lies the inescapable question, Who is going to
control whom? Two people are asked to stand facing each other in the
center of the room and are given the following directions: "One of you
place your hands on the other's shoulders and press him(her) to the
ground. You may use any method you wish to get him(her) down, but
you must put him(her) flat on his(her) back on the ground. He(she) may
cooperate or resist, depending on how he(she) feels. When that is completed, reverse roles and do the same thing the other way."

Some people are afraid of the exercise, others eager to try it. But
reluctant or eager, those who participate in it or observe it report that it
almost always stirs in them an awareness of an anxiety, stronger than they
knew, about where they stand in the power game. "Can I tolerate some-

[1] William C. Schutz, *Joy* (New York: Grove Press, 1967), pp. 157–167.

one exercising power over me?" "Will I insist on exercising power over the other?" "How do I feel about someone who exercises power over me?" "Do I have to exercise power to keep myself together?"

A person resolves such questions, Schutz[2] theorizes, in one of three ways. In one pattern, the person may submit to the exercise of power by others, moving away from responsibilities that would require him or her to exercise it. Typically, such a person plays the role of loyal follower. Schutz calls such people *abdicrats*. The key, he says, to their reaction is the feeling that others do not regard them as responsible adults and would not help them if they got into a spot in which they needed help. They feel hostility, but they engage in hidden responses rather than in open, active rebellion. A second characteristic pattern is found in people who are driven to exercise power in virtually all relationships. Everywhere such people look, they see hierarchies of power with themselves at the top. They are fighters, competitors. They can be labeled *autocrats*. Like abdicrats, they feel that others do not regard them as capable, responsible adults. But their response is in the mood, "I'll show them!" The third pattern, which Schutz calls the most appropriate response, presents people who are neither threatened by nor inclined to threaten others with power. Where it is appropriate, they can use it (e.g., in a crisis) without doing so compulsively. They can be just as comfortable not using it, where that is appropriate. By the same token, they are comfortable having someone else either use, or not use, the power with them where that is appropriate. In short, they are not driven as the other two types are. This type is labeled *democrat*.

We are impressed by this three-way analysis, for it shows how the behaviors interlock to make power a process. Those who abdicate, of course, excite the appetite of the power-hungry autocrats. The democrats know when the autocrats are becoming corrupt. Aroused, they act to restrain the domination excited by the weak.

However, the process is more complex than has been suggested so far, for the autocratic group is, in fact, two groups in constant warfare— the power-hungry people who have attained power and the power-hungry people who resist those in power. The latter think of themselves as democrats, and their standard justification is the "right of dissent" in a democracy. In truth, they are not democrats in the sense described by Schutz. They are professional dissenters, and they are as power oriented as those who have the authority. They play a "watchdog" role. We have such people on every faculty, in every student organization, in every

[2] William C. Schutz, *The Interpersonal Underworld* (Palo Alto, Calif.: Science and Behavior Books, Inc., 1958), pp. 28–30.

legislative group—the people who are power oriented but are more adept at resisting than at leading.

Difficult as it is for humans to handle power with wisdom, professional dissenters play an indispensable role in concert with the democrats at critical moments. But when organizations become rife with conflict, the problem is clearly one in which the two autocratic groups dissipate the energy of the organization in a relentless struggle. (The sections "Authority Conflict" and "Conflict with Others" in the chapter on conflict deal with the internal dynamics of both kinds of autocratic people.)

What seems clear is that the compulsive need to exercise power, or the persistent effort to somehow resist it or escape it, is developed early in life, taught by the way significant others have used power in their relationships with us. We will return to this and the foregoing later in the chapter.

But we have been using the key word, *power*, without a definition. What do we mean when we speak of power? We mean, simply, "the capacity to induce another person to act or change in a given direction."[3] Human life is inconceivable without it, yet power is dangerous because it is deeply involved in the way humans communicate. This, in the end, is the way our judgments and criticisms shape us and our communications. It may not be too much to hypothesize that power is the most important factor in any communication—whether between parent and child, teacher and student, employer and employee, friend and friend, or husband and wife.

When Lord Acton said "Power tends to corrupt," he meant, as we understand it, that power affects the listening of people—that positions of authority tend to desensitize those who hold them to the feelings of others, that probably the need to get to the top in an aggressive culture breeds a certain unawareness in those who compete. Moreover, in order to retain power a person at the top has to listen for the weaknesses of those who would displace him or her, thus learning how to handle them. What we are saying is that power separates people from others in their immediate life, indeed even from those who would support them in power, for those at the top must listen to their supporters suspiciously, too, in order to determine the limits of their loyalty. So corruption for those in power is due to the fact that their listening must conceive of those around them either as enemies or as tools for their own advancement. As a consequence, they are voluntarily starved of love, the emotion most needed in order to grow. Their ambitions, it turns out, cut their own lifeline.

What about the listening of those who are related to the power-

_____

[3]C. G. Browne and Thomas S. Cohen, *The Study of Leadership* (Danville, Ill.: Interstate Printers and Publishers, Inc., 1958), p. 375

hungry person? In the subordinate role, people listen for the emotional needs of the leader. They must hear his or her needs in order to give unwavering support. And if they idolize the leader, there need be no dishonesty on their part. Indeed, it is almost necessary that the closest followers of a power-oriented person believe in that person with little or no question, because such a person can ferret out distrust with remarkable accuracy. After all, the person who gains power does not do so without some ability. But the corruption for the followers does not come from the fact that they trust the leader; rather, it comes from the fact that they cannot listen to the leader as he or she is. The followers hear megalomania, pomposity, ruthlessness, and suspicion in a power-corrupted person as energy, greatness, strength, and brilliance. They cannot perceive him or her as a closed and dying person fighting for self-worth and fulfillment through power. Nor can they see the defenses of the power-hungry person. They interpret the inscrutable mask of the leader as character and strength. They do not perceive the mystery of the leader as a reflection of inability to hear himself or herself as unrevealing and unknown. And above all else, followers cannot see that the perfection of the leader, created out of the distortions just described, arises from their own need to have somebody strong to lean on—an escape from the greatest of all fears, a fear of trusting one's own appraisals. Run get the doctor; elect a strong president; tell me, teacher; interpret the news, Mr. Commentator.

While the preceding explanation may seem a bit too much for some people in authority or for those who, for whatever reasons, respect authority highly, it seems to us that the struggles between individuals, between religions, and between nations, and the overriding fear we have of each other as individuals, can be explained only by sensing the immense drive for power and prestige among those who perceive their own worth in terms of the control of others and, on the other hand, by observing the vast numbers of weak people whose needs complement and reinforce the needs of the power-hungry few.

Hypotheses about the Impact of Power on Communication

1. When used between people, power distorts perceptions of what each is saying to the other, causing them to omit, misinterpret, and garble.
2. Power relationships between people restrain them from saying what they would otherwise say, thereby robbing the listener of a chance to assess the unspoken feelings or ideas of the other appropriately.

If complete power corrupts completely, it is because the words said do not openly convey the meanings that maintain the power relationship.

Let us examine some of the ideas and data that make such hypotheses seem reasonable.

The Voice of Power in a Relationship

As Dr. Paul Watzlawick points out,[4] every communication occurs at two levels: (1) the content level and (2) the relationship level—the latter often involving power. Consider the following common interaction: Two college alumni who have not seen each other for several years meet on the campus. One recognizes the other, rushes over and extends his hand, and after conventional greetings, says,

> I've been with General Motors the last two years, but you know how wild it is in industry these days. IBM has been trying to get me to take an executive post in Seattle, and I had a phone call from another firm just Friday asking whether I would consider a move. . . .[5]

Analysis of the message from the sender's viewpoint:

> Content: I am providing you information about my present location, and I am purposely selecting some (only some) recent events in which I have been involved.
> Relational data: I want this renewed relationship between us to be one in which I impress you and thus bolster my ego. You must realize that I have moved ahead very fast in the business world. Our relationship ought to be one in which you listen to me, appreciate me, envy me. I'm not the kid you knew in college. I am a success. Therefore, it is right that you listen to me.

We teach each other on each meeting, says Watzlawick, what the relationship will be at any given moment. The kind of relationship that emerges can be classified into one of two categories.

Symmetrical   A symmetrical relationship is one that is based on a subtle struggle to establish or maintain equality. A college administration makes demands; students make counterdemands. One partner drops the name of an important person he or she has met recently; the other person drops an equally important name. The teacher asks a question; the student replies with a question about the question. A friend begins

---

[4]Paul Watzlawick, *An Anthology of Human Communication* (Palo Alto, Calif.: Science and Behavior Books, Inc., 1964). Much of the material in this section of the chapter is an interpretation of Watzlawick's concept of relationship.

[5]Notice that much of the "meaning" in this message is carried by the information the speaker decided to omit.

some sarcastic banter; her friend matches her. Whatever the situation, the partners to a communication that has been mutually defined as symmetrical make claim to equality.

And although we make much of the importance of equality in our culture, the symmetrical relation is a very unstable and difficult one to maintain. Any move to gain the upper hand is likely to result in an escalation of the effort at mutual influence. Thus each communicator becomes wary of the other. Garbling develops, and the partners either drift apart or grow belligerent. The power is there but undefined, and thus produces anxiety.

Complementary   A complementary relationship is one based on "the acceptance and enjoyment of difference." "There can be no giver without a receiver, no lover without a beloved, no mother without a child."[6] In one sense, most communications can be viewed as complementary. If there is to be a speaker, there must be a listener, and vice versa (see Figure 9-1).

Notice that both types of relationships are basically efforts to solve the power problem. In a *symmetrical* relationship, it is as though each person is saying, "Whatever you say, I will go you one better. You are not going to control me." In a *complementary* relationship, one of the partners is always saying, "Now look, here's the way it is." And it should be noted that the relationship is just as likely to be engineered by the submissive one as by the dominant one, the submissive one acting in such a way as to say to the other, "I can't solve this problem myself. You will have to help me find an answer. I am dependent on you." The other agrees. Indeed, it is the very fact that both parties to a complementary situation define the relationship in the same way that makes a complementary relationship possible (see Figure 9-2).

Instability in complementary and symmetrical relationships   If two people in an interaction are defining the relationship differently, there will be trouble. This seems to be precisely what happens in many of the "power contests" in communication. A mother and daughter can be

FIGURE 9-1   Diagram of a Symmetrical Relationship

[6]Watzlawick, *op. cit.*, p. 7.

FIGURE 9-2 Diagram of a Complementary Relationship

almost continuously at swords' points because the mother defines their relationship as complementary while the daughter defines it as symmetrical. Neither realizes the difference, and neither seems willing to make any shift. So they play the same record over and over again until they do not even hear the repetitiveness of their own messages.

Or again, if there is a "runaway" in either kind of relationship, trouble develops. Remember the times when "kidding around" ended in a fight? Those are examples of "runaway" symmetrical relationships. Consider an example of a "runaway" complementary relationship. Rollo May[7] tells of a young intern who was undergoing psychoanalysis because he had severe attacks of anxiety with repeated urges to drop out of medical school. Even when he had completed his medical studies and had received a letter from the hospital directors praising him for his work as an intern and offering him a choice position as resident, he was seized with another attack. In his therapy session shortly thereafter he reported this dream:

> I was bicycling to my childhood home where my mother and father were. The place seemed beautiful. When I went in, I felt free and powerful, as I am in my real life as a doctor now, not as I was as a boy. But my mother and father would not recognize me. I was afraid to express my independence for fear I would be kicked out. I felt as lonely and separate as though I were at the North Pole and there were no people around, but only snow and ice for thousands of miles. I walked through the house, and in the different rooms were signs tacked up, "Wipe your feet," and "Clean your hands."

The relationship was a "runaway" complementary one, as it turned out, between a man and his domineering mother. So completely had her power position been established that, though skilled and competent, he feared that his success would injure his relationship at home. In short, he was afraid that if he listened to the voices telling him he had power he would no longer be accepted at home.

[7]Rollo May, *Man's Search For Himself* (New York: W. W. Norton & Company, Inc., 1953), pp. 77–78. By permission of W. W. Norton & Co., Inc. and of George Allen & Unwin Ltd.

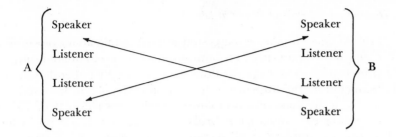

FIGURE 9-3 Diagram of a Symmetrical-Complementary Relationship

Symmetrical-complementary compromise   Our observations suggest that the "runaway" tendency of power in both symmetrical and complementary relationships means that in most long-term stable relationships a kind of symmetrical–complementary pattern develops (see Figure 9-3). One person is recognized as more powerful—to mutual advantage—in one regard, the other as more powerful in another way. In a conference, one person may speak more than another; yet if the conference is successful, it must be recognized that the good listener excited the best thinking of the speaker. One friend is best at initiating ideas; the other is better at executing ideas. The church is best at spiritual solace; the state is best at defense. Women are better than men at giving birth to children, though men have their part too.

Interdependence is the essential state of human relationships. Who can be teacher without student or doctor without patient? These basic observations have caused the authors to recognize their own children as their best teachers. The ultimate acceptance of the dignity of all parties must be communicated in any healthy relationship. Probably the very uniqueness of each person makes all relationships complementary yet interdependent. So the ultimate solution to the problem of power in relationships must probably find itself in the sense of union and mutual need, which leads to mutual agreement on the division of power. The equality of a symmetrical relationship is established by dividing up the power.

Let us summarize what we have said up to this point. Communications have both content and relational elements in them. The relational element is usually, if not always, more significant than the content element. It contains the efforts of both sender and receiver to exercise power. The contest is either symmetrical or complementary, or a mixture of the two.[8]

[8]For an illuminating discussion of how this struggle to control relationships works, see Jay Haley, *Strategies of Psychotherapy* (New York: Grune & Stratton, Inc., 1963), Chap. 1.

It would be a mistake, as suggested earlier, to talk about power as if it were simply an annoyance in communication, to be eliminated with the right prescription. The urge for dominance is deeply imbedded in animal life, including the human species. We should *expect* to have to communicate with the noise of power cluttering the airwaves. Alfred Adler, one of Freud's early associates, broke with Freud because he, Adler, finally came to conceive of all communication disorders as stemming from one's feelings of inferiority, rather than from sex. He saw these feelings of inferiority as a consequence of the restraints of the social order on our will to assert ourselves and exercise power.

Robert Ardrey also concludes that dominance (status) is a more powerful basic force than sex.[9] He says that every primate society so far observed can be explained best by examining its dominance system. He shows convincingly how the life of the baboon, water buffalo, cow, gorilla, lion, rhesus monkey, and a colorful variety of other animals all reveal "pecking order"—individuals in the species "lording it" over other individuals. Konrad Lorenz, the pioneering ethologist, believes that human life is an extension of this animal urge for dominance.[10] His description of life among the jackdaws is frighteningly "human." Desmond Morris, in *The Naked Ape,* needles all of us about failing to face up to our "nature." He points out that "it is a fact that the most level-headed intellectuals frequently become violently aggressive when discussing the urgent need to suppress aggression."[11] So deep, we are saying, is the need of most people to stamp their values on somebody else—often just to erase their own doubts—that a listener can only expect to do most of his or her listening in the presence of that power.

The Conforming Listener

In any culture, perhaps, and certainly in an aggressive culture such as ours, most listening induces conformity. What we are learning about conformers seems to justify the following conclusions. The use of power in communication (1) makes them more cautious and thereby leads them to reduce the range of messages they get, (2) makes them more self-centered in their responses, and (3) renders them more inaccurate in reading the incoming messages. Let us have a look at some of the evidence on which these conclusions are based.

[9]Robert Ardrey, *African Genesis* (New York: Dell Publishing Company, Inc., 1961).

[10]Konrad Lorenz, *On Aggression* (New York: Harcourt Brace Jovanovich, 1966).

[11]Desmond Morris, *The Naked Ape* (New York: McGraw-Hill Book Company, 1967), p. 146.

If a listener has a strong need to conform, it follows that he or she should listen for things supporting what he or she is "supposed" to think, and should suppress "undesirable" responses. A study using college students as subjects bears this out.[12]

There is another way, however, in which the conforming listener distorts messages. As suggested earlier, most people learn from early childhood that the *source* of what they hear is more important than the *message*. The source represents for them expertise, wisdom, special knowledge—power. So when they listen they tend to hear primarily the details that will be consistent with the image they have of the person sending the message.[13] Thus teaching children to rely on the source of what they hear is the equivalent of urging them to listen for the tones of authority. So the findings of Myron Burger's study with neuropsychiatric patients should not surprise us: The stronger the source, he discovered, the more conforming the responses of the listener.

Why does it happen with such remarkable frequency that a stutterer can talk fluently to animals? The most commonly accepted explanation holds that the threat of power represented by the judgment of people is the disorganizing influence. If this is so, is it not also reasonable to suppose that normal speakers, trying to assert their own significance in the face of an effort by another to control them, should be disorganized in their processes even though they do not end up stuttering? "Moral threat," Brock Chisholm has said, "is the enemy of imagination." Douglas Heath found that intellectual performance suffered in the presence of anxiety and that "more disorganization" occurred in the situations and on the issues and with the people that produced the most anxiety for the individual.[14]

The self-image of the conformer   But there must be a part of the story yet untold. Are listeners helpless in the face of power? Why do they not reject the hand that would cripple them? The answer seems to lie somewhere in the need to defend the ego. When one is trapped in the conviction that one is inadequate, one spends one's energies trying somehow to affirm oneself and, thus, has little chance to interpret incoming messages clearly. Conversely, the better one feels about oneself— that is, the less one feels under threat by an authority figure, the better one can perform as a listener.

[12]Kay Smith and Barrie Richards, "Effects of a Rational Appeal and of Anxiety on Conformity Behavior," *Journal of Personality & Social Psychology,* 5 (1967), 122–126.

[13]Myron Burger, "Source/Message Orientation, Locus of Control, and Conforming Behavior in Neuropsychiatric Patients" (Ph.D. Dissertation, Purdue University, 1965).

[14]Douglas H. Heath, "Individual Anxiety Thresholds and Their Effect on Intellectual Performance," *Journal of Abnormal and Social Psychology,* 52 (1956), 403–408.

Consider a case in point. At the University of Michigan students saw a film and were then asked to write what they had seen and heard.[15] Those who rated themselves as good witnesses tended to be more correct and covered the material more completely than those who rated themselves poorly. But the most impressive finding in the study was this: If the person asking the students to respond showed that he or she regarded them as good witnesses, they usually believed they were good witnesses, and thus performed well. Listeners get more and get it more accurately when the other person is able to help them feel good about themselves. "Runaway" power tends to do just the opposite. Any effort to change (persuade, influence, etc.) another, one writer has pointed out, implies that the other person is inadequate. Built into the desire to control is the assumption that the other person is not taking adequate action on his or her own. It reflects, therefore, on his(her) quality—and he(she) is quick to sense this.

Almost as if it was designed to illustrate the point, one of the saddest of stories appears among Robert Frost's letters to his friend Louis Untermeyer.[16] Frost's only son, Carol, had had a long struggle with progressive paranoia, becoming increasingly suspicious of people. As his desperation deepened, his father took time out from a lecture tour to go to New England to talk with him. All night they talked, Frost trying to convince his son that he had the capacities to develop a rich and meaningful life. In the rueful letter written later to Untermeyer, Frost notes that the last thing said between them was the son's poignant remark to his father, "You always have the last word." Two days later, Carol shot himself.

What makes this story so powerful is that in spite of Frost's sensitivity and insight his son *perceived* him as the one asserting superiority in their relationship, and apparently learned to listen more and more to the messages that told him of his own vulnerability and weakness—turning away from those that spoke of his abilities.

Somewhere in Russian literature is the story of a child who, in his boisterous play, broke a treasured vase. His enraged uncle sentenced him to a period in the closet for punishment. In an eloquent passage that follows, the boy, now alone in the closet, plots all the satisfying ways in which he can get revenge on his uncle and, for that matter, on all adults who hold power over his life.

Such delightful fantasy is not for children alone. The "games" that

[15]James Marshall, "The Evidence," *Psychology Today*, February 1969, pp. 48–52.

[16]Louis Untermeyer, *The Letters of Robert Frost to Louis Untermeyer* (New York: Holt, Rinehart and Winston, 1963), p. 322.

grownup children play are hidden just as imaginatively. When we have to come to terms with the power of others, we think one thing and say another. Speaking dishonestly, we create dishonesty in the opposition, and thus we feed each other's doubts about both self and the other. Defensiveness soars on both sides, and communication worsens.

Leaders, Followers, and Resisters

As you have probably observed, leaders send more messages than followers do, for language is people's essential tool for making impact on others.[17] But the nature of one's power determines the character of one's language. If one is appointed by higher authority, one will tend to ask for the opinions of others. Conversely, if one emerges as a leader in a group, one will tend to give one's own opinions. The fact that a person has bid for leadership means he or she has a dream.

The leader who stays in power tends to be essentially optimistic and satisfies the emotional needs of the group to which he or she is responsible. And one of the things the leader must be careful about is not to assert authority any more than is absolutely necessary; otherwise he or she becomes disliked and cannot satisfy the needs of the followers. Our own explorations with the Communication–Conflict Instrument indicate a $-.82$ correlation between managing conflict effectively and asserting control. Only the most conforming people accept the heavy-handedness of a leader.

People of low status and power tend to overestimate a leader's capacity to assert power.[18] The closer one moves into the seat of power in an organization, the more one recognizes that it is belief in the leader that is the source of his or her power. Every use of power by the leader is in the end a test of belief in him or her.

Spread in varying degrees across the spectrum of human personality is resistance to authority. As will be discussed more fully in the next chapter, we all vary in the value we place on control. Those who are highly task oriented but are aroused to dislike people when they exercise the power of authority are the first to challenge authority. Because they are also highly related to the values of the group, a great number of the lower-status group members support the resister. Thus the leader who asserts authority arouses people to test that authority. The quickest way to lose power is to overplay one's hand.

[17]Wally D. Jacobson, *Power and Interpersonal Relations* (Belmont, Calif.: Wadsworth Publishing Company, Inc., 1972), p. 141.
[18]*Ibid.*, p. 143.

We have already had a look at the theory that the struggle for dominance is deeply imbedded in all of animal life and, thus, in human life. We have tried to show that either getting on top or accepting the inferior role distorts messages, for the self-image must be preserved. All this can be seen in a somewhat different perspective by examining the role of status in human organization—for example, in a business organization. Let us take an oversimplified organizational chart like the one in Figure 9-4.

Several things are known about the flow of communication in such a structure:

1. Communications will flow laterally (e.g., between people on the same level—between workers or between foremen) more readily than they will flow either downward to the workers or upward to high-level management.
2. There will be more messages sent downward than upward.
3. Those who are low on the authority ladder will be more cautious about the messages they send upward than those who are high on the ladder.
4. People who are high on the status ladder will think they are being heard more accurately than will really prove to be the case.
5. People who are low on the ladder will distort the messages they receive from above in such a way as to fit their purposes.
6. The "lows" will try to move toward the "highs" and away from the "lowers."[19]

Take a look at the following table, which shows the flow of communication, in each of several media, among forty academic employees in a typical university hierarchy.[20]

Communication Types	Up	Down	Lateral
Telephone	19.7%	26.1%	54.2%
Individual conference	23.7	49.8	36.4
Staff conference	21.4	32.3	47.4
Reading	30.7	20.6	48.7
Writing	26.3	33.3	40.4

Notice that lateral communication is by far the most frequent of the three directions of flow except for individual conferences. People tend

[19]A very similar list appears in Barnlund's summary of research on the matter. See Dean C. Barnlund, *Interpersonal Communications: Survey and Studies* (New York: Houghton Mifflin, 1968).

[20]Charles Goetzinger and Milton Valentine, "Communication Channels, Media, Directional Flow and Attitudes in an Academic Community," *Journal of Communication,* 12 (1962), 23–26.

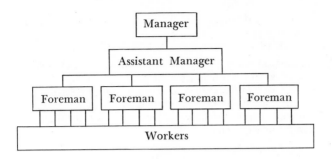

FIGURE 9-4

to shy away from talking to others on either end of a "power" relationship. Notice, too, that in individual conferences the communication is initiated downward (i.e., by the power holder) more than twice as often as upward. Notice, above all, that the differences in quantity of contact are the greatest where power is exercised directly, by speech, and least where the message sender has little direct control over the receiver, as in writing. Add this to the preceding: Eighty percent of the communicating done in the business is oral, only twenty percent written.

It is little wonder, then, that a high degree of lateral communication has been found to be associated with poor morale and poor productivity.[21] Apparently, the more communication is cut off between superiors and subordinates, the less likely the job is to get done. And conversely, the poorer the job performance, the less superiors and subordinates tend to be in communication. Just as the ineffectual human is out of contact with himself or herself, so the ineffectual organization is out of contact with its leaders.

Subordinates, we have noted, talk more to those above them than to those below them. But there is more to it than this. Generally, people are trying to rise in the organization. The harder they try for higher positions, it has been found, the less accurately they will communicate problem-related information to their superiors.[22] For example, they will communicate more pleasant matters and withhold unpleasant ones. They will talk more about their achievements than about their errors or difficulties. For like reasons, the teacher fails to know the student. Similarly, the parent loses contact with the child.

So part of the distortion in upward and downward communication in an organization comes from the selective character of the speech of

[21]*Ibid.*, p. 25.
[22]William H. Read, "Upward Communication in Industrial Hierarchies," *Human Relations*, 15 (1962), 3–15.

the person in the inferior role. Discussing defensive management in business, Gibb has this to say:

> Any restriction of the flow of information and any closed strategy arouses energy devoted to circumventing the strategy and fosters counterstrategies that are at least as imaginative and often more effective than the original inducing strategy. A familiar example is the strategy of countering the "top brass" by distorting the upward-flowing data; feelings of hostility are camouflaged by deferential politeness. . . .[23]

If the superior typically recognizes the distortion, and allows for it, it does not, in the end, turn out to be so distressful. But this is not the way it usually works. In a typical study on this question, it was discovered that school administrators, in self-deception for whatever reason, considered both upward and downward communication in the schools over which they had charge more effective than the teachers with whom they were communicating did.

It is probably safe to assert that all of us, superior or subordinate, will listen as we must in a hierarchy of organization in order to satisfy our need to be comfortable with that constant companion—ourselves.[24] We probably have a more difficult time as subordinates. In the universally famous Charlie Brown of the Peanuts cartoon, we all see ourselves struggling to cope with our superiors and would-be superiors. We identify with honest Charlie, who somehow seems to survive and escape utter despair despite his complete lack of the usual human defenses against power-oriented messages. Low-status people confront a self-esteem problem every time they listen or speak to a person of higher status, and since all organizations are pyramidal it is in the nature of things that there will always be more Indians than chiefs. Thus most people are subordinates; hence the universal problems of Charlie Brown. As people develop low self-esteem, they become more susceptible to persuasion or, to put it another way, more vulnerable to the exercise of power by superiors.[25] On the other hand, if those power figures reward subordinates' responses to their communications, thus ascribing worth to them, they will think better of themselves and will maintain that change for a significant period. But if coercion is used by the power figure, even if it is

[23]Jack Gibb, "Fear and Facade: Defensive Management," in Richard Farson, ed., *Science & Human Affairs* (Palo Alto, Calif.: Science & Behavior Books, 1965), pp. 197–214.

[24]Arthur R. Cohen, "Upward Communication in Experimentally Created Hierarchies," *Human Relations*, 11:1 (1958), 41–54; W. Charles Redding and George A. Sanborn, *Business and Industrial Communication: A Source Book* (New York: Harper & Row, 1964), p. 119.

[25]Carl Hovland, Irving Janis, and Harold Kelley, *Communication and Persuasion* (New Haven, Conn.: Yale University Press, 1953), p. 187.

perceived as good by the subordinate, the subordinate's self-esteem drops.[26]

Power Shifts in the Family Hierarchy

If we have been using the business and industrial organization as chief whipping boy in our efforts to explain the impact of status on communication, it is not because it is the only place where status is a potent producer of distortion. The school is a hierarchy too. And, perhaps most significant of all, the very structure of the family is arranged in a "pecking order."

But it is also obvious that the pecking order in the home is not what it used to be and that, as the bold contemporary folk song has it, "The times they are a-changin'" in ways that will reshape all our institutions. One psychologist theorizes that we can trace a considerable amount of this status change to the emancipation of women.[27] When the husband lost control over his wife, says Rudolf Dreikurs, he and his wife both lost control over their children. As he sees it, the chief reason for the highly publicized "breakdown of communication" between the generations is this massive revolt against the old status system of a paternalistic society. Children are demanding that they be treated more as equals. They visualize a symmetrical–complementary relationship when they converse with adults, though the adult world still thinks in terms of the old social order—a complementary relationship with adults dominating. We agree with Margaret Mead's pronouncement that now not only do children fail to follow the models of parents but they also tend to reject their teachers, with whom the culture has tried to replace the parent model. If, in the new situation, a teacher wants to teach with significant influence, he or she must listen and know young people. It is not that we, the wrinkled ones, are not wanted. The young are desperate for teachers, and they appreciate listening teachers as never before. Without viable models, they are searching for those who will help them find their own identity. But older ones must know that whatever person now evolves, it will not be a copy of the past. The question is, What will it be and will it be cohesive? There is, to put it bluntly, a heaving in the hierarchy.

[26]John Schopler, Charles L. Gruder, Mickay Miller, and Mark Rousseau, "The Endurance of Change Induced by a Reward and a Coercive Power Figure," *Human Relations*, 20 (1967), 301–309.

[27]Rudolph Dreikurs, *Democracy in the Home and School* (New York: Grune and Stratton, 1960).

It is possible to live a lifetime without even wondering why we have the impulse to exercise power over others in our communication—or the reverse. That urge comes so early in life, so unconsciously, as a consequence of our smallness as a child in a world of large, insensitive, and sometimes frightening adults. Erik Erikson sees each adult as carrying the burden of childhood:

> Every adult, whether he is a follower or a leader, a member of a mass or of an elite, was once a child. He was once small. A sense of smallness forms a substratum in his mind, ineradicably. His triumphs will be measured against this smallness, his defeats will substantiate it. The question as to who is bigger and who can do or not do this or that, and to whom—these questions fill the adult's inner life far beyond the necessities and desirabilities which he understands and for which he plans.[28]

This situation has its roots deep in our earliest recollections and is more profound than we like to admit. The problem is dramatized by a most devastating example of an excessively powerful father. Adolph Hitler's father was a drunkard and a tyrant who abused and ruled the family. And even though he died while Hitler was only a boy, he apparently set forces in motion in his son that would incite him to listen too exclusively to the messages that reinforced his own devastating power. Hitler says in the first chapter of *Mein Kampf* that no one, not his father "nor any power on earth," could make an official out of him. The irresponsible and abusive power of the father turned, as we all unhappily know, to total tyrannical power in the son.

Consider the very opposite example, Helen Keller. Someone has suggested that the reason Keller turned out to be a zestful and vivacious traveler in life, in spite of her "handicaps," was that the people who would have wielded power over her early in life could not get through. She could neither see nor hear.[29] She therefore escaped the power-exposure experience of most of us, and did not have to be defensive. Thus she became an open, sensitive communicator.

But few of us are deafened early in life. As Erikson says, none of us normal hearers escapes the impact of the power impulses of others. This does not mean, however, that all normal hearers, even those who have had bad communications in the early years, are doomed for a lifetime.

---

[28]Erik Erikson, *Childhood and Society*, 2nd ed. (New York: W. W. Norton & Company, 1963), p. 313.

[29]Apparently, she had tactile communication, the warmth of touch, from the beginning of life; otherwise she would not have grown to be the affectionate and concerned person she was.

Elizabeth Barrett Browning's life is a classic story to the contrary. We present it here as the picture of a highly intelligent woman who misunderstood how she was listening until she was changed with the help of a listening friend. Had it not been for Robert Browning's discovery and courtship of her, she probably would not have found her lilting song; for before she was a famous writer she was an invalid with sinking fortunes—a virtual prisoner of her father. Her father, if historical research is correct, was a tyrant who kept his children under his thumb even when they were adults.

Mr. Barrett, the father, whose own father, note, had deserted his mother when the son was only two years old, showed kindness and generosity toward his children as long as they obeyed his commands.[30] But he made one unyielding demand of his three daughters, namely, that they must not marry. So when Elizabeth Barrett fell in love with Robert Browning, she was thrown into direct conflict between her father and her suitor.

At the beginning of her correspondence with Browning, she tries to defend her father and refuses to admit that she blocks out threatening messages from him. She argues that he has responsibilities; that his harshness just seems so to outsiders; that, in any case, she has gotten used to his chains and has her own freedoms within them. At one point she writes:

> But what you do not see, what you cannot see, is the deep, tender affection behind and below all those patriarchal ideas of governing grown up children "in the way they must go!" And there never was a truer affection in a father's heart . . . no, nor a worthier heart in itself. . . . He loves us through and through . . . and I, for one, love him![31]

After fourteen months, Browning dares to bring up the subject in a letter to Elizabeth. He says, in effect, that he cannot imagine a father with genuine interest in his children who could still deny an invalid daughter the happiness she might get from the occasional visit of a friend.

Somewhat later, Elizabeth Barrett writes in quite a different vein about her father. She comes to see his "love" for what it is—the vindictive, demanding manipulation of a man terrified of his own insecurity. She decides that if she is to know life for herself she will have to throw

---

[30]R. V. Sampson, *The Psychology of Power* (New York: Pantheon Books, 1965), pp. 59–69. In the introduction to the book, Sampson offers the startling proposition that "to the extent that we develop our capacity for power we weaken our capacity for love; and conversely, to the extent that we grow in our ability to love we disqualify ourselves for success in the competition for power."

[31]*Ibid.,* p. 7.

off the tyranny of his demands. Her Rubicon is crossed when she agrees to elope with Robert Browning. By this time she is ready to steel herself to the violent consequences. She imagines how she will ask her father to pardon her for seeking happiness in her own way. And she predicts that when she does he will show himself as he really is (". . . and he will wish, in return, that I had died years ago!"). She was, as it turned out, right. Despite her tenderness and sensitivity, her father refused to forgive her and broke off their relationship, never to speak to her again.

The story is a parable of the way listening to a power figure early in life can shape us. Yet at the same time it is a story that tells us that with the aid of another we can escape that tyranny.

At the Most Practical Level

Throughout this chapter we have discussed the impact of power on communication as it affects the very evolvement of our lives. What we may have overlooked is the way these power relationships affect communication in everyday experiences—those in which somebody's error makes us say, "But why didn't you listen?"

Consider one such case. New employees in a Long Island plant were trained in the use of the grappling irons they had to use on the job. The instructor told them that when they needed an iron it could be taken from the rack on the wall at the left of the forge; that when they were done using an iron it should be placed on the rack at the right of the forge, where it would be left to cool. The cool irons would then be moved to the rack at the left and would be available for use. One of the new employees, the story goes, placed his red-hot grappling iron on the rack at the left. The next man who came along took it from the rack (where, he had been led to believe, there were only cool hooks), and it burned him so badly that he could not disengage his hands. He fainted with the burning iron in his hand.

In the investigation following the incident, the man who had erred vowed that no one had told him about those racks. But it was established that he was present at the training session at which all new employees heard the directions, and the instructor recalled that he appeared to be listening intently when the instructions were given.[32]

Many things could have gone wrong here, of course. The worker who made the error might have been sitting in a place where external noise prevented him from hearing the explanation accurately. He could have misinterpreted. He could have been daydreaming at that moment.

---

[32]Ralph G. Nichols and Leonard A. Stevens, *Are You Listening?* (New York: McGraw-Hill Book Company, Inc., 1957), pp. 144–145.

He could have been fascinated with his new physical surroundings. But he also *could have tuned out* the voice of authority. His lifetime experience could have taught him to counter inwardly another person's effort to control him by simply ignoring the message. In short, his failure to hear the directions about the grappling hooks could have been of a piece with his failure to catch his third grade teacher's instructions for the next day's arithmetic assignment.

There seem to be a remarkable number of instances in which the person who does not hear shows a history of "authority problems."

Possible Solutions

Are we faced with an insoluble problem? How can people be authentic, be themselves, if they are confronted by authority? Yet, on the other hand, do we not have to have authority? How can we escape the evils encased in the words *superior* and *subordinate?*

At least two approaches offer hope. One is a changed attitude toward child rearing. "We treasure a promise of things to come," says Erikson, "the simple daily observation that wherever the spirit of partnership pervades a home and wherever childhood provides a status of its own, a sense of identity, fraternal conscience, and tolerance results." The other is to increase, by every means possible, opportunities to communicate. *Communication and power are, in one sense, deadly enemies.* Let us illustrate by citing commonly known examples in which power is wielded through noncommunication. In primitive cultures, the medicine man held all the secrets. As "medical" information began to be communicated, the power of the medicine man faded. Feudal lords could keep peasants in bondage until the word got around that a person's worth is not to be measured by his or her birth and that peasants need not remain peasants. In twentieth-century American culture, the power of whites to enslave blacks, the power of parents to dominate children, the power of teachers to make pawns of students—all of these types of power have been reduced through the increase of communication, both about the situation and between the parties involved.

The only alternative to power-over is the power to do. And becoming sensitive to one's own feelings is the door to finding one's own talents and powers. It turns out, as the preceding life stories illustrate, that the exercise of power is an evasion of the most difficult of tasks—listening to the self, taking the risky road to self-evolvement. It is so much easier to imagine one's own superiority by controlling the growth of those around one.

The thrust to project ideas, to control the environment, to organize the social world, to be aggressive, to assert the "male" side of our nature at the expense of listening, imagining, creating, and nurturing the "female" side of our nature is the peculiar imbalance that inhibits our abilities to cope with the peculiar problems of the twentieth century. It is not that power-over is inherently bad. One cannot avoid the power to influence. Even one's silent presence is itself a power. The problem is not to find a way to eliminate power but to take out of life the desire to exploit one's fellow human beings. As usual, the answer is not an easy either/or proposition. Rather, it is a case of walking the narrow ridge, holding in precarious balance all the parts of our nature. To assert power, yes; but to develop the power to *do* first. Those who develop the power to do, which comes from open communication with oneself, usually find that they can have influence without subjecting others to their needs.

TOMORROW'S PROBABLE POWER PROBLEM

Since former Secretary of State Henry Kissinger has left the seat of power in international affairs, he has discussed in a number of forums a strange new power problem emerging in the world. It takes form in highly industrialized nations and at this writing is most intense in the western nations of Europe—France, Italy, Spain, and others. Despite the fact that only 200 miles to the east, in Russia, they can see the depressed economic and psychological state of highly authoritarian rule, middle-class workers are aligning themselves with communism. Kissinger reasons this way: In a highly complex industrial system each industry itself is a huge organization in which the major decisions, which of course affect everybody, are made by a handful of people. Thus the average middle-class citizen feels powerless; he or she has no direct input to the decision-making process. The average citizen resents the authority of the system and is identifying with the chief opponent of the system.

Indeed, Kissinger sees the hijacking of airplanes and acts of terrorism by small bands of people as having essentially the same motivation. It is a kind of romantic bid for power. But the stimulus is the feeling of being powerless in a huge system that makes decisions that affect the way one lives. Kissinger believes the industrial nations are threatened by the blind fury of well-fed people.

He goes further. He thinks the fury is more than resentment about one's dependent state. Thus far, the whole design of an industrial structure has focused on the production of plenty. Humans cannot live fully if they live only to live well. Kissinger says the industrial world needs two things very badly: (1) a cause, a goal, a reason for living beyond living well, and (2) leaders who can point the way.

A well-fed human has a half-fed life. The centrality of the power problem in a well-fed life emerges from the fact that almost every person's terrible need is to feel worthy. When the body is well fed, the needs of the self become powerful forces. The great drive for self-actualization is more than a need to grow into one's fullness. It is also the need to be comfortable with the one person one has to live with—the self.

The God in humans can turn into a demon if sufficiently frustrated by a self that behaves in meaningless daily routines.

We closed Chapter 2 by noting that the building of an authentic self-concept is every person's first order of business. Here we can see that perhaps the same objective should be high on the agenda of every national state. Maybe one of the chief responsibilities of leaders in the culture is to give the people a dream for their lives in the culture. It is the decline of community in Europe that is turning the mass of successful people against the system.

As we write, the primary motivation in the college population is "my career." Thinking about this, we note that the mean scores of the Communication–Conflict Instrument in at least three samples of the college population reveal that the focus is on one's self and on the other individual's values. Students apparently are involved in private relationships. Feelings, community value, and control value are depressed. The rebellion of the 1960s is gone, but the smoldering ashes are there. Let someone spark the task energy and we will have a new rebellion.

If we examine industrial and political leadership with our usual doubt, we are likely to see it as self-serving and/or corrupt. In terms of what Kissinger is observing, this is but the cause of their greater failure—the failure to help the well-fed masses discover personal fulfillment within the bonds of their common dreams.

SUMMARY

Wherever there is power—as there always is—the communicator has problems. The power signals involved may not be noticed if one looks only at the communication "content," but they exist in abundance when the "relationship" is examined. The relationship can be either *symmetrical* (based on equality) or *complementary* (based on inequality), and is usually more stable when it is a mixture of both. The more either partner is determined to exercise power, the more likely it is that a "runaway" in either kind of relationship will evolve. If that happens, or if the partners refuse to accept each other's way of defining the relationship, we are on our way to conflict.

In the presence of power, certain things happen to us: (1) The range of messages to which we are open is reduced; (2) our responses as listeners become self-centered and insensitive; (3) our accuracy in reading incoming messages is reduced. More basically, connections can be seen between the exercise of power on people and a thwarting of their development as persons.

If the effectiveness and clarity of communication is to be improved, attitudes toward child rearing will have to put more emphasis on helping the child find, and believe in, his or her identity. In a free environment, as one learns the power to do one is less driven to exercise power over others.

INSTRUMENT 9-1

POWER ORIENTATION

Circle the number in each statement that best reflects your response:

5 means "I almost always feel this way."
4 means "I usually feel this way."
3 means "I often feel this way."
2 means "I occasionally feel this way."
1 means "I almost never feel this way."

A

1. I grow angry when people exploit me.
   5   4   3   2   1

2. Majority rule is the heart of democracy.
   5   4   3   2   1

3. Dissent is basic to decent government.
   5   4   3   2   1

4. Almost all people in powerful positions become corrupt in gaining their positions.
   5   4   3   2   1

5. I tend to become related to groups that are concerned with justice.
   5   4   3   2   1

6. I can get emotional about the injustice all around us.
   5   4   3   2   1

7. I experience considerable tension when I speak in public.
   5   4   3   2   1

8. I do not believe in any kind of censorship.

| 5 | 4 | 3 | 2 | 1 |

9. Eternal vigilance is the price we pay for freedom.

| 5 | 4 | 3 | 2 | 1 |

10. I find people who are elected to power positions more effective and more responsible than people who are appointed to power positions.

| 5 | 4 | 3 | 2 | 1 |

Add the circled numbers and place the sum here:_____

B

11. People do not very often exploit me.

| 5 | 4 | 3 | 2 | 1 |

12. I enjoy exercising power.

| 5 | 4 | 3 | 2 | 1 |

13. I like to make decisions.

| 5 | 4 | 3 | 2 | 1 |

14. I feel good in leadership roles.

| 5 | 4 | 3 | 2 | 1 |

15. I like to develop strategy.

| 5 | 4 | 3 | 2 | 1 |

16. I am a better talker than I am a listener.

| 5 | 4 | 3 | 2 | 1 |

17. You have to expect to be disliked by some people if you are going to be an effective leader.

| 5 | 4 | 3 | 2 | 1 |

18. My public statements are energetic but not highly emotional.

| 5 | 4 | 3 | 2 | 1 |

19. Most people are ineffective.

| 5 | 4 | 3 | 2 | 1 |

20. The notion of democratically operated business and industry is unrealistic.

| 5 | 4 | 3 | 2 | 1 |

Add the circled numbers and place the sum here:_____

C

21. I find it difficult to stand up for my own rights.

| 5 | 4 | 3 | 2 | 1 |

22. I steer clear of conflicts with people.

| 5 | 4 | 3 | 2 | 1 |

23. I am essentially a quiet person.

| 5 | 4 | 3 | 2 | 1 |

24. I am not much interested in political affairs.

| 5 | 4 | 3 | 2 | 1 |

25. For me good friends are much more important than positions of power.

| 5 | 4 | 3 | 2 | 1 |

26. I am rather easily embarrassed.

| 5 | 4 | 3 | 2 | 1 |

27. I usually refuse leadership roles.

| 5 | 4 | 3 | 2 | 1 |

28. I am a better follower than I am a leader.

| 5 | 4 | 3 | 2 | 1 |

29. I am nervous in associating with people in authority.

| 5 | 4 | 3 | 2 | 1 |

30. I am more of a spectator than a participant in social life.

| 5 | 4 | 3 | 2 | 1 |

Add the encircled numbers and place the sum here: _____

D

31. Decisions arrived at democratically are more likely, in the long run, to fit the needs of society than decisions made by individuals.

| 5 | 4 | 3 | 2 | 1 |

32. Essentially private enterprise is ruthless.

| 5 | 4 | 3 | 2 | 1 |

33. Social welfare programs are more basic to democracy than majority rule.

| 5 | 4 | 3 | 2 | 1 |

34. A tax supported national health program is more basic to democracy than the election of officials.

| 5 | 4 | 3 | 2 | 1 |

35. The true measure of democracy in an organization is the degree to which decisions are made in the interest of the greatest number of people.

| 5 | 4 | 3 | 2 | 1 |

36. I am attracted to the notion that a democracy would do much better if it made decisions only when at least 75 percent agreed rather than by majority vote.

| 5 | 4 | 3 | 2 | 1 |

37. People are far more equal in ability and worth than the range of income in America would suggest.

| 5 | 4 | 3 | 2 | 1 |

38. The protection of self-esteem and the creation of equal living conditions are the most basic objectives of democratic rule.

| 5 | 4 | 3 | 2 | 1 |

39. Respect for all people, even your enemies, is more basic to democracy than freedom of speech and the press.

| 5 | 4 | 3 | 2 | 1 |

40. I am more attracted to the power of love than the power of just laws.

| 5 | 4 | 3 | 2 | 1 |

Add the circled numbers and place the sum here:_____

> A, Dissenting Autocrat =
> B, Autocrat   =
> C, Abdicrat   =
> D, Democrat   =

One of the authors has the following scores to consider: A, 29; B, 26; C, 22; D, 43. He feels that the order of the scores is correct—he is democrat, dissenter, autocrat, and abdicrat. He is interested in the power world from a very idealistic (democratic) view, and he is both on the side of those in power and against them. His abdicating score seems a little high, and (not revealed in these scores) he flutuates back and forth between being an active agent in the "Establishment" and being a dissenter.

What do your scores make you want to say about yourself?

Do you like what your scores suggest about you?

How do you compare to others?

Caution! If you compare your scores with those of another person, you should not, in our judgment, compare the A scores (or the B, C,

or D scores) but should note the pattern. Which of yours is highest?
Which is lowest? Are your scores close or scattered over a wide range?

EXERCISES

1. Write a paper or make a journal entry in which you explain the difference
   in tension level between the times when you are alone and those when your
   roommate is present though silent.
2. Arrange to be alone for a day in order to sense the meaning of eliminating
   the power impact of another person's presence. Write a paper or make a
   journal entry about the experience.
3. Explore a relationship in your life in which you think there is no exercising
   of power either by you or by the other person. Give a talk on your observations and conclusions.
4. Describe your power relationship with your roommate. How is the power
   exercised? Is it a mutually agreeable relationship?
5. Give a talk describing incidents in which you have enjoyed teasing people.
   Discuss this in terms of the use of power.
6. Think of a relationship in which you use humor that has as its target the
   other person. Talk about it.
7. Humor was once thought to be exclusively tension reducing. More recent
   research shows that jokes are tension building if one person or group is an
   object of the humor. Analyze your favorite jokes for their power content.
8. Divide into groups in which you discuss any agreed-upon problem, the
   solution to which will be compared with that of each other group. After
   fifteen minutes of discussion decide which member of your group will be
   asked to join a different group for the remainder of the assignment. Discuss
   the power dynamics that emerge in excluding this person.
9. Talk to the class, sitting on the floor. Then stand, so that now you tower
   over the class; continue your talk. Place a desk between you and the class
   and continue. At the close, discuss your different feelings about yourself
   and the class in the three different physical modes.
10. Write a paper or make a journal entry or tell the class about the power
    relationships between you and your father, mother, sisters, and brothers.
    Listen carefully to the comments your classmates make.
11. In order to increase your awareness of the way power messages are sent
    nonverbally, identify (a) a relationship in which you see yourself as operat-
    ing on a level of equality with the other person, (b) another relationship in
    which the other person is dependent on you, and (c) still another relation-
    ship in which you are dependent on the other person. Observe such things
    as the following about the nonverbal behavior of each person in each of the
    three relationships: the freedom to touch the other, the ease of looking into
    the eyes of the other, the freedom to interrupt, the division of time in which
    to talk.
12. Come to class prepared to talk about a situation in which you consciously
    dominated another person. What was the effect on both you and the other
    person?

13. Explore your life for incidents in which you have been forced to think and behave in accordance with another person's influence. Evaluate the impact of these incidents on your daily behavior. Talk to your class about this and note the response.

14. Form groups of six or seven and choose one member to report to the class. The reporter will discuss the selection process. Did the reporter vie for leadership? Did he or she compete with others? Did others assume leadership and force the reporting role on the one chosen? What was the character of the humor? Who avoided the discussion? How did he or she do it?

15. Discuss the leadership patterning that has emerged in your class. List three people who have exercised the strongest leadership. List three whom you would most prefer as leaders. List three who have made a considerable impact but have said little. List three who have frightened you by their behavior. List three whose leadership has irritated you. Report your observations in a paper, journal entry, or talk.

16. List the people in your life who have had the greatest influence on you. List those who have had the greatest influence on your growth. List those whom you love the most. List those for whom you feel a rather prevailing hostility. Compare the names on the four lists. What conclusions do you draw? Write a paper, make a journal entry, or give a report to the class.

17. Make a speech about power and American society.

18. Make a speech on power and race in America.

10

Conflict

Mankind is poised midway between the gods and the beasts.
Plotinus

It is the business of the future to be dangerous. . . . The major
advances in civilization are processes that all but wreck the
societies in which they occur.
*Albert North Whitehead**

Too often, the study of communication is conceived of as the remedy for
conflict. Not so. Conflict is indigenous to life, human and otherwise.
Chickens have their pecking order. A herd of milk cows string out in
order as they come to the barn for milking. The leader is always the
same. A ewe will mate only with a ram of comparable dominance. How
chickens, cows, and sheep know who is most dominant, and the order of
dominance, is anybody's guess. Probably they settle these matters in
fights when they first meet.

Human beings have more difficulty, for obviously the meaning of
dominance is tangled with self-esteem, and our capacity to hurt each
other in order to care for our esteem is ingenious. This is not surprising,
however, for the overall conclusion of studies of the moral development
of children shows that a young child sees transgression and punishment
as two sides of the same thing and equates rightness with severity of
punishment.[1] We come from dark beginnings.

But what are we talking about? What are the dimensions of human
conflict?

*From *Adventures of Ideas* (New York: The Macmillan Company, 1933).

[1]Justin Aronfreed, *Conduct and Conscience* (New York: Academic Press, 1968), pp.
257–258.

Robert Stoller, a psychoanalyst and a professor at UCLA, has evolved a theory that sees hostility as the basis even of sexual excitement.[2] The reasoning runs like this: Most of us are hounded by fears of failure in life. Usually, just coping produces great frustration. Stoller says that if you examine the "scripts," the fantasies people experience, that "trigger sexual excitement" they usually involve some aggressive and hostile feelings, not necessarily directed against one's lover. The theory holds that the human's intense sexual interest, then, is a way of turning feelings of frustration and defeat into ritual triumph. Part of Stoller's documentation consists of noting the *hostile* themes that run through pornographic literature. He goes on to say that certainly most of us recognize that humans are not a very loving species.

In contemplating this position, one of the authors recalls the flourishing scroll over the arch above the pulpit in the church he attended as a boy: "God is love."

Surely there is something that we desperately want, and have not attained, if we define God as love. And in the Old Testament, which contains much that had been handed down from parent to child for generations, the Creator is described as a wrathful and jealous God. In the ethics of *Exodus* we read, "Eye for eye, tooth for tooth, hand for hand, foot for foot, burning for burning, wound for wound, stripe for stripe."

Later, in *Numbers,* we read that when the people of Israel complained "it displeased the Lord—and his anger was kindled; and the fire of the Lord burnt among them and consumed them . . ." If the God of our beginning view of the universe was so cruel, certainly cruelty is deep in the human spirit, at least in our culture.

It would seem to us that glands alone are enough to explain sexual excitement and that, deep as hostility is in the human spirit, certainly sexual response cannot be free of aggression. But the real question is, Why so much hostility? Why is hostility so deep in the human family? We turn again to Ernest Becker, who says the answer is this, that the desperately conflictual character of the human spirit drives us to worship love in order to manage, if not resolve, the great schism and disharmony of our inner lives.[3] Division echoes throughout our being. *Birth, growth, decay, and death put life and death against each other*—and we, by our awareness, must live with struggle. All of our philosophy and everything we do is in some way an accommodation to the life–death theme.

Humans (whom somebody has called the eyes of the universe) are

---

[2]*Time,* January 3, 1977, p. 76.

[3]Ernest Becker, *The Structure of Evil* (New York: Free Press, 1968); *The Denial of Death* (New York: Free Press, 1973); *Escape from Evil* (New York: Free Press, 1975).

aware that they are born and that they must die. In our very bodies, aside from our wishes, a constant struggle between being and not being goes on. We are afraid of our destiny.[4] Indeed, in order to be cheerful, to have courage, to be free of anxiety, to hope—so that our living days may be good and filled with pleasure, yes, even ecstacy—requires that we be able to lift ourselves up by our very bootstraps.

Almost all of us are attracted to the pleasures of good food and drink. But enjoying ourselves too much speeds us on our way to our end. High achievement is in some measure needed to satisfy self-esteem, yet an overemphasis on achievement challenges the heart and the vascular system, so that almost all who work hardest to be comfortable with themselves die early. "It's hell if you do and hell if you don't."

Enough! Conflict and stress are a part of life, and we are not fully human or even going to reach our best without the courage to meet life *on its own terms.* It is not the purpose of this chapter to explore the dark sources of human conflict or to discuss in depth the role of conflict in human experience. That would better be the burden of a book on the subject.

The purpose of the preceding discussion is to put the topic in perspective. *Being what it is, conflict is not resolved. It is managed, well or badly.* With the preceding backdrop, then, what we want to do is (1) define the concept of conflict; (2) show how conflict works and how to manage it constructively, personally, and socially; and (3) discuss the several forms it takes in our communication with ourselves and others.

A DEFINITION OF CONFLICT

We do not care to be fussy about a definition. But it is easy to talk too loosely about the concept, as we will see. Let us first look at two extreme positions about what we should call conflict. Many of our students want to call any difference that irritates people with themselves or others a conflict. This places conflict too close to the frustration of almost all experience and thus makes it nothing very distinct because it becomes almost everything. Say you are trying to twist off the lid of a jar of pickles and, at a critical point, the lid breaks loose faster than expected and you spill pickle juice on your roommate's term paper, which he was ready to hand in this afternoon.

He explodes, "What the hell? You . . . clod!"

The top of the jar broke off and you cut your finger. You begin to bleed like a stuck pig. You explode with a few choice words in an ugly

[4]Ernest Becker, *The Denial of Death* (New York: Free Press, 1973).

tone, partially directed at your roommate. He does not like that, feeling that he is being blamed for your mishap. It may end here or, if both of you have lived in considerable tension in recent days, you may have it out.

Now this is a "blowup," and at first blush it has all the earmarks of a conflict. You are fighting, and people fight when they are in conflict. Indeed, a situation like this or a series of them probably would lead to what we, the authors, would call a conflict. But we would rather call the event described a fight or an altercation. The chances are that the event will actually have little to do with your relationship. In fact it may become a favorite story of the two of you, providing much joshing and many a laugh.

On the other hand, Lewis Coser, a serious student of conflict, defines conflict as the destructive interaction that takes place when people are intent on injuring each other.[5] For us, this goes too far in the opposite direction, confining our topic to the most vicious interactions that culminate in lawsuits, murder, and war.

Thus we define conflict somewhere between those extremes, as *differences involving real or perceived incompatible positions.* This is the perspective of Rensis and Jane Gibson Likert, who say, "Conflict is viewed as the active striving for one's own preferred outcome, which, if attained, precludes the attainment by others of their preferred outcome, thereby producing hostility."[6] If two people want to be president of a given institution, that is a conflict. If a husband and wife both want to go to college and there is money only for one, that is a conflict. If two people believe there is only one way to get to heaven and they believe in different ways, that is a conflict, especially if each believes that it is his or her responsibility to persuade the other. The key words in our definition are *differences, incompatible,* and *perceived.*

Difference there must be to have conflict because it is difference that depresses people's feelings and turns them to mutual efforts to control the other. But the difference must be an "incompatible difference" or a "perceived incompatible difference." In the case of the husband and wife who both want to go to college the incompatibility is real. Only enough money is available for one. Which one will go? The incompatibility rests on "restricted resources." Many wars have been fought for food, supplies, and material resources. At present the world is in deep conflict over a dwindling oil supply. What one nation (or person) has, the other cannot have. That is real incompatibility.

[5]Lewis Coser, *The Functions of Social Conflict* (New York: Free Press, 1956), p. 8.

[6]Rensis Likert and Jane Gibson Likert, *New Ways of Managing Conflict* (New York: McGraw-Hill Book Company, 1976), p. 7.

We are *not* suggesting that real incompatibilities must lead to destructive conflict. Two people may have only one life jacket when their boat is swamped and sunk. The life jacket will hold up only one person. But one may swim while the other rests on the jacket, and they may reverse these roles until help comes. If neither can swim, the incompatibility reaches a critical point where one gives up his or her life for the other, thus managing the incompatible difference in probably the best of several undesirable ways. Or one may grasp the jacket and push the other away, managing the conflict, from our perspective, in probably the worst of all possible ways.

But there are "perceived" as well as real incompatibilities. When two people each consider it their moral responsibility to convert the other to the right belief, *that* is not a shortage of resources but a perceived incompatibility.

One would think that real shortages would cause the more destructive conflicts. The records show, however, that perceived incompatibility is likely to produce more destructive conflict than shortages of resources. Marital discord is more a matter of the dislike, or suspicion, or distrust one partner develops for the other than of a scarcity of money or space or goods. The most devastating wars have been fought among the wealthy nations.

Perhaps we should clarify the distinction between *constructive* and *destructive* conflict at this point. When the managing of the differences, though perhaps bitter, is essentially still a search to find a mutually agreeable accommodation, the process is what we would call constructive. In the literature of human struggle this is called a fight in which the rules are those of a *non-zero-sum game*.[7] When you add up the wins and losses of the contestants you get some figure *other* than zero, preferably greater than zero. That is, it becomes possible for both to win.

Let us get back to the couple who both want to go to college. If the wife attends one year and then the husband one year, neither gains what the other loses. They both gain; they split the cost. Indeed, by taking independent study in their year off both may finish in three years and reduce the total cost of their education by one-fourth. *Non-zero sum* means that the handling of the problem at hand is done in a way that is *not a putdown* for one of the contestants.

Thus one does not determine whether the conflict between people is a *non-zero sum* in terms of economic cost but in terms of the cost to the self-concept of the people involved. If two people settle their differences in a constructive way they save the relationship, and this is done if the dignity of each is preserved.

[7]Anatol Rapaport, *Fights, Games and Debates* (Ann Arbor: University of Michigan Press, 1960).

A destructive conflict, in contrast, is played out in rules that call for a *zero-sum game*—what one wins, the other loses. This is the character of our sports. Football games are not designed to permit two winners. Even if the score is 64 to 63, one is the winner and the other is the loser. If the couple trying to decide who goes to school flip a coin to decide, the winner takes all. One gets the education, the other does not. In such decisions the enhancement of one is the diminution of the other; the relationship is injured, if not destroyed. A *zero-sum* set of rules lies behind destructive conflict.

HOW CONFLICT WORKS IN INTERPERSONAL COMMUNICATION

There is little in the workings of conflict that you have not felt. Thus the stages will be immediately recognized. We will therefore set them out in outline form without discussion.

When there are no differences to trouble a relationship, feelings are positive, generating energy to maintain the relationship. However,

1. If feelings about the other person become indifferent, one begins to put less energy into maintenance of the relationship, and the relationship begins to become vulnerable.
2. As the feelings toward each other turn to the more negative, one of the two people will become more self-assertive.
3. Assertive behavior arouses counterassertive behavior.
4. Thwarted assertive behavior arouses frustration.
5. Frustration arouses frustration.
6. The expression of frustration stimulates aggressive behavior.
7. Aggressive behavior arouses counteraggressive behavior.

The Critical Point

If the differences lead to stage 6 or 7, we are at a point of critical decision. Will we go for management of the differences within the relationship or management dictated by individualistic urges? In short, will there be just winners, or winners and losers?

Productive management of interpersonal conflict   Above all, productive management involves an awareness that the biggest issue at stake is the self-esteem of the people involved. When each contestant is trying to preserve the dignity of the other,

1. One or both will refuse to put the conflict into a win–lose form. Though the disputees will be trying to get something for themselves, they will want to keep the need for victory and triumph out of mind. As long as people are angry or dominated by other aggressive feelings, the best they can do is

restrain themselves. If one does not nurture negative feelings by going over them repeatedly and justifying them, he or she can gain some perspective in time and perhaps even feel some compassion for the other person's position. Such a person may come to ask for forgiveness for his or her own part in the conflict. When one is trying to keep the conflict from reaching the win–lose stage one will, thus, do all one can to keep the dialogue open.

2. At least one will verbalize his or her need to preserve the relationship. In the presence of strong, conflicted feelings this is not easy to do, but it is possible and healthy to do.

3. One or both disputants will be empathic and will give evidence that they understand the other person's feelings *with appreciation* even though they find the other person's actions unacceptable. Insofar as we know, this position has not been tested by research in personal quarrels, but studies of social conflict, as we will see, show this.

4. If the empathic posture is maintained, each will restrain himself or herself from interrupting the other, even when the effort is painful.

5. Each will do all he(she) can to be as clear as possible about his(her) own position, even as he(she) struggles to understand the other person's position.

6. Absolute honesty is an indispensable ingredient of the conflict that is going to be managed constructively.

7. One must stay clear of making a critique of the other person's behavior. Having already studied the destructiveness of judgment, we need not examine the reasoning. *But we should look at the communicative result of placing the blame on a person for past acts.* Nothing immobilizes the other person's ability to see how to act constructively more than to be held responsible for what he or she cannot change.

   "You got me into this!" Well, even if it is true, what can one do about that now?

   "Why didn't you . . . You hurt me . . . You started this . . ." All our ways of condemning another person are good ways to feel righteous but bad ways of helping the other person to be of aid in maintaining a constructive management of the distress.[8]

It should be obvious that there are seven or more ways of moving into a conflict with approaches that will allow the deterioration or breaking of the relationship: These are the opposite of the preceding seven approaches—beginning with the need to win.

Stages of a Conflict in a Group

Some research has been done on the stages of a conflict in decision making in small groups.[9] The dynamics are obviously quite different

---

[8]Nevitt Sanford and Craig Comstock, eds., *Sanctions for Evil* (San Francisco: Jossey-Bass Inc., Publishers, 1971).

[9]Donald G. Ellis and B. Aubrey Fisher, "Phases of Conflict in Small Group Development: A Markov Analysis," *Human Communication Research*, 1 (1975), 195–212; B. Aubrey

from those of struggles between two people, for in a group actions and arguments are designed not only to persuade the opponent but also to gain the support of others. However, noting the way the battle in groups goes is of use in understanding conflict.

1. Usually the first negative statement is tentative, followed by a positive observation. All the members are testing, trying to determine the climate of the group.
2. As soon as a critical statement is followed by another critical statement one can be relatively sure two things are happening: Some members are willing to accept the challenge of those they perceive as opponents and some are indicating which of the two sides they are going to be on. During this period, while information may be used, the essence of the output is emotionally charged language. Consider the difference in the cargo of the two following statements:
   "Our first responsibility is to get rid of the one-third who should not have been admitted in the first place."
   "One-third of our freshmen this year fell below the national norms on the English test."
3. Once the sides have been established, a battle ensues in which the feelings are vented.
4. Then perhaps one person will propose a solution and a reasoned exploration of the available evidence will be examined.
5. Though now guided by feelings, the solution will be shaped by examination of the data.

Of course, if at stage 3 the perceptions of each side become reinforced by "rump sessions" of the battling subgroups, the two groups may come to feel an identity of values in the subgroup and a difference between the values of the two subgroups. In this case the group splits or remains in constant conflict. Churches are famous for the fight-and-split pattern. But the split is not possible in some relationships, for both parties are too dependent to allow the division. Management and labor, or the disputing parties in a school district, are common examples.

Institutionalized Conflict

Perhaps the most fascinating illustrations of institutionalized conflict exist in our political parties, and these splits seem to run through almost all the governments of the world. In the very few, small social orders, like that of the Zuñi Indians, where leadership is abhorred, institutionalized factions are not likely to develop. At the other end of

---

Fisher, "Decision Emergence: Phases in Group Decision Making," *Speech Monographs,* 37 (1970), 53-66; Edward A. Mabry, "Sequential Structure of Interaction in Encounter Groups," *Human Communication Research,* 1 (1957), 302-307.

the spectrum, in totalitarian states, the second or third party exists undestroyed only by going underground.

There is nothing in the Constitution of the United States that calls for political parties. But from the beginning the strong central government advocated by Hamilton and the more decentralized perspective advocated by Jefferson emerged. *Today we accept the two-party system as much as the Constitution itself.* It is difficult for us to conceive of democratic government without a continual struggle. To create the perspective that we are one people, each party refers to itself in relation to the other as the "loyal opposition."

Authority is necessary in order to have organization, but it unfortunately provides us with the source of much evil. We tried to fathom this fact in the chapter on power. Apparently, the need for power and the corruption of power are so great that we cannot exist in groups without a constant struggle for power and against the power of others. The literature is replete with evidence that *groups hang together as much because they fear other groups who do not share their common values as by mutual attraction.*[10] What would America do if one night the crust of the earth shifted dramatically and Russia sank into the sea?

The Likert Profile of Conflict Characteristics

Having said that, we need to look at the recent research of the Likerts, who have studied the management of social conflict in many kinds of organizations, including business and industry, where the dollar is the basic motivation.[11] The Likerts have placed all activities they have studied on a continuum marked by four points (see Figure 10-1). The most authoritarian management, of course, runs a "tight ship." The least power-oriented management works toward goals arrived at by widespread involvement.

For the sake of clarity, we have rearranged the profile characteristics, showing how the process of social conflict works when it leads to loss in business and how it works when it leads to productivity.

This is how it goes when an organization is unproductive:

1. The number of communication channels is limited.
2. Both parties try to make these channels ineffective.
3. Both try to further limit the number of channels.
4. Thus both parties are trying to close off communication.

---

[10]Raymond W. Mack and Richard C. Snyder, "The Analysis of Social Conflict—Toward an Overview and Synthesis," *Journal of Conflict Resolution*, 1 (1957), 212-248; Lewis Coser, *The Functions of Social Conflict* (New York: Free Press, 1956).

[11]Likert and Likert, *op. cit.*, pp. 34-42.

FIGURE 10-1

5. They do not empathize with each other.
6. They do not try to state the position of the other party to its satisfaction.
7. They reject third (neutral) party involvement when they are in a deadlock.
8. They induce feelings of hostility in each other.
9. They discourage cooperation.
10. They reject the concept of decision by joint effort.
11. Each party tries to impose its solutions on the other.
12. Which is to say, they resort to the instruments of power.
13. They use their energy trying to outwit the other—in strategy.
14. This calls for deception.
15. What they agree to they try to keep from implementing.

Organizations operating in "System 4," which the Likerts found to be the productive ones, showed the *opposite* of the fifteen conflict characteristics just cited.

Now note the motivations at work in the masses of workers when top management tries to operate a tight ship.[12]

1. The key is that an informal organization develops among workers that opposes management goals.
2. It operates covertly, underneath the surface.
3. Subordinates feel no need to send accurate information to their superiors.
4. In fact, they have a strong need to distort information,
5. because they feel hostile toward the decision makers.
6. They feel no responsibility for the health of the total organization,
7. or its goals.
8. On the other hand, the decision makers feel no responsibility for trying to induce cooperation among workers.
9. They reject teamwork.
10. Too much distrust develops for teamwork to be possible.
11. The motives of both parties are carried out in the "manner" of fear and threat.
12. The ultimate objective of both parties becomes their own survival and safety,
13. because the motives of both are the injury of the other.

[12]*Ibid.*, pp. 19–26.

Conspiracy. From Carl Zigrosser, *Prints and Drawings of Kathe Kollwitz* (New York: Dover Publications, Inc., 1951, 1969). Reprinted through the permission of the publisher.

In both the analysis of organizational conflict and the motives of workers (which in fact cannot be separated from the motives of management) when there is conflict, two things stand out in the Likerts' research. First, the focus of attention of both parties is the injury of the other. Second, both analyses, essentially, are a study of communication between fighting parties. The basic character of productive and destructive conflict stands out clearly, like a sore thumb.

THE FORMS OF COMMUNICATION CONFLICT

There are probably an infinite number of torques that produce conflict for people, with themselves and with each other. Use of the Communication-Conflict Instrument has shown that the stresses are between behavior and values or among values. Several patterns have shown up, but we restrict the discussion to the most common ones.

Self–Other Value Conflict

This is probably the most common pattern we have observed in the college population. Its peculiar feature is a very great emphasis *both* on one's own values and on respect for the individual values of the person one is relating to.

In Figure 10-2 we have marked only the essentials of the pattern. The peculiarity of the person in this conflict is that *he(she) becomes immobilized when difference arises between himself(herself) and another person.* In

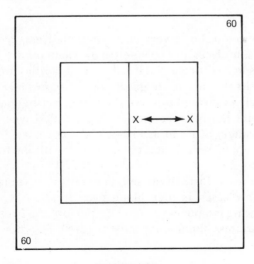

FIGURE 10-2

talking with the student, say, about a class project or topic for a term paper, we note that he or she will elicit suggestions and at once resist (in a pleasant way) any development on the part of the other person. As a consequence both the student and the conversant become highly frustrated and tense. We have noted that the student will usually be highly interested in discussions and classes in self-assertiveness.

One of the authors began to see the nature of this stress with clarity when such students explained that they kept the conflict at a minimum by extremely careful selection of the people or groups they associated with in depth. As long as such a person is involved with people very much like himself(herself), that person can keep the stress within manageable limits.

You will note that we have placed the behaviors at a point just above the anxiety level and have indicated a range of task orientation-energy. The more task oriented the person, the greater the intensity of the conflict. It is little wonder that most students with the self–other conflict tend to be low in task energy. The reverse is too stressful.

The authors dislike leaving this discussion where it is and would like to suggest ways of resolving the self–other value stress. The simple truth is that we do not know the answer. It is obvious that it is more comfortable to be more empathic or more aggressive, one of the two patterns discussed at the close of Chapter 4. And we would suspect that as years go by people who have developed the conflict pattern under discussion do resolve the stress by some such alteration in their values. But we do not know for sure, nor, if this is done, do we know how it is done.

Self Attack

Not as common, but a very clear state of stress, is the situation in which the person places an extremely high value on the individuality of the other person and negates self-values that conflict with those of the other person. In the torque suggested by the scores of Figure 10-3, the person is clearly motivated to serve the group he(she) belongs to and to please the people he(she) relates to. This person's drive to control others is low, as is his(her) belief in asserting his(her) values. It is not strange that the behavior score indicates compromise, with the tendency to submit or withdraw.

Where is the conflict? In the self, and it shows up in resentment, and indeed, in severe cases, in high blood pressure.

The following is a poem written by a person who lives this conflict. It shows his awareness about what must be done in order to manage the conflict constructively.

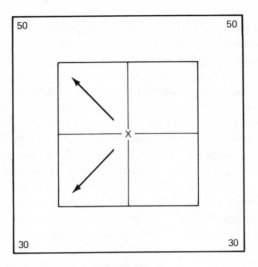

FIGURE 10-3

forces fused together
from years of fear,
from feasible and unfeasible
foolishness,
from societal foolery and
from fathoms and fathoms of
fouled up flash
comes down and clamps down
so tough

'til you
forget/remember that you are a
force too.[13]

Authority Conflict

There are probably as many themes in authority conflict as there are categories of personality, for all conflicts in one way or another involve the control of one person by another. But one of the most striking ones is that of the revolutionist, for in all social upheavals the leadership of the conflict is composed of those who resist the powers that be—the Establishment. The earmark of the militant is rejection of the value of control, and therefore the resistance to the exercise of authority by others. But

[13]By permission of Dr. Earl M. Washington, Department of Communication Arts and Sciences, Western Michigan University.

resistance is the exercise of power, to "overcome the evils of authority." In a democratic culture authority is conceived of as having been washed of its evil when it is spread evenly among the people. Thus, the resister can, as indicated in Figure 10-4, conceive of his or her resistance as guided by the ideal of low control of anybody by anybody. *However, one cannot break down the exercise of control in any way except by the exercise of control.* A million people, all with equal authority and power, have no authority and power except to vote for *somebody, who, by the accumulated authority, now exercises power.* Thus a person with the scores that indicate him or her to be resistant to authority either assumes the leadership against those in charge or follows somebody else of like value who assumes the leadership. Obviously, such a person is much more comfortable if he or she just follows another with like ideology, for *the role of exercising control when one has a low regard for control involves, at best, confused feelings.*

Let us illustrate. One of the authors is acquainted with a professor whose scores on the Communication-Conflict Instrument are almost identical to those in Figure 10-4. He is an elected chairperson of a large department, having permitted himself to be elected to his administrative responsibilities because, as he states, he has a deep-seated distrust of the administration. As he is an administrator, however, he is forced to relate to an administration with which he does not feel comfortable. In his departmental meetings he is comfortable in following the wishes of the majority, but there is also a highly vocal and relatively large minority who distrust him very much as he distrusts Central Administration.

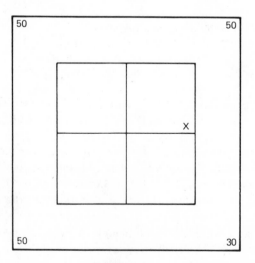

FIGURE 10-4

After he had worked out the departmental schedule and teaching assignments in, as he saw it, as democratic a way as possible, one professor insisted on discussing his schedule, complaining vigorously that he had not been permitted to teach a course he wanted very much to teach. In talking about the incident with the author, the chairperson said,

I cannot allow him to teach the creative writing course. He just is not competent. In fact, he is not competent or responsible enough to teach anything but the first course, if that. It's my responsibility to see that the department retains its quality.

He was angry and read me the riot act just before the meeting started. I was so damned angry I could scarcely conduct the meeting, but I could not just explode and tell him to go to hell.

It is not difficult to see why the chairperson says,

I will allow myself to hold this job just one more year. I do that only because we have too few who are electable who can stand up against the administration. But there is always somebody biting at your heels.

Besides, my own teaching and writing are suffering because the administrative tasks demand so much of my time and energy.

We do not know how this man will decide to act. But it should be clear that much of his internal conflict is the consequence of the fact that the chairpersonship places him in a position where his behavior, getting the job done effectively, makes him behave in ways that his values reject. He knows it, talks about it freely, wants to get out of the position, and feels guilty because he does.

Anybody who is *revolted* by the injustice of whatever conditions he lives in, and either accepts them or does anything about them, is almost certain to experience the pains of authority conflict. Discharging authority and fighting authority call upon the same behavior.

This point should be made clear before we leave this discussion. It does not follow that a low control value puts one into this conflict. We have given the Communication-Conflict Instrument to almost 50 Trappist monks from several American monasteries, and almost all of them scored very low in the value of control. Insofar as we have been able to understand the Trappist monk, he does not exercise control nor believe in its value. His life is devoted to spiritual explorations. The significant difference between the monks' scores and the pattern of Figure 10-4 is that their behavior is a fusion of positive feeling and low task energy. In short, the key to whether the very low control score is a reflection of an authority conflict depends on whether the person is task oriented. A low score in control and a high score in task orientation forms the conflict—one does what one despises.

Power Conflict

The difference between the pattern of scores noted in Figure 10-5 and the patterns of Figure 4-9 is a matter of degree. Here the drive to control by virtue of both behavior and value is so great that lack of personal restraint throws the person into conflict with others. Leadership of all forms requires some aggressiveness, but at a given point aggressiveness causes resistance in others, not followership. Moreover, you will note that the concern for the values of others is less than the concern for self-values. Thus the person has little sensitivity to the responses of others. We have not come upon a great number of students who show this set of urges, but some do. They are obviously extremely individualistic.

We hasten to add that, as in all the conflict states, one should not conceive of any particular style of conflict as neurotic or bad. As long as a given style receives support from others it fits the great mosaic of humanity.

Confusion of Values

One of the more common patterns of conflict states is a basic conflict of values, as indicated in Figure 10-6, in which the values are all attractive. But the fact is that community and the other person's values together are dead set against one's own unique values and the value of controlling others. Usually this situation of conflicting values is also marked by the compromise position in feelings and energy expenditure.

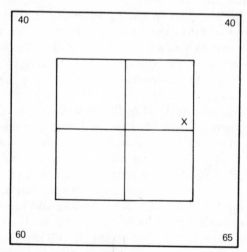

FIGURE 10-5

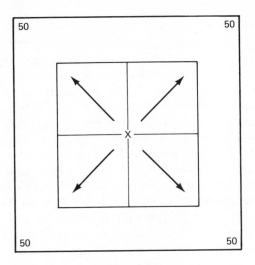

FIGURE 10-6

Thus the equal torque of incompatible values produces inconsistent responses in behavior. An almost unchanging environmental situation may produce productive cooperation, attack, withdrawal, or submission. Usually, people with these torques give most trouble to themselves and, having just as much inclination to agreeable and cooperative behavior as the opposite, engage in very good relationships with many people. They seldom, however, become prevailing leaders as they are not sufficiently predictable to be appointed or elected to highly responsible positions. In saying this we do not want to leave the impression that this syndrome of conflicts marks a person as a failure. Among all the groups we have worked with, including students and professional and business groups, there are people whose values are confused.

We have described the preceding pattern as a conflict of confused values because the person shows irritation and stress. If, however, a person with these apparently confused values is relatively positive in feelings and is decidedly *task oriented*, the total impact is no longer one of distress but marks the person as one who functions in decision making, by choice, according to his or her perception of the demands of the situation. Such a person is driven not by an ethical philosophy, as a person is who places a great significance on a given value, but by the peculiar circumstances of the situation. We think we have observed that a person who believes in *situation ethics* makes a very good second-level leader in organizations because he or she finds accommodations that work. First-level leaders, however, are usually more oriented toward one or two (compatible) value schemes. Charisma is, in part, a consequence of having a dream.

WHAT ARE PATTERNS FOR?

Millions upon millions of snowflakes fall to earth every year. Under microscopic study we find that each is unique. Yet there are several kinds of snow, too—light, small, large, fluffy, wet, sleety. In like fashion, the complexities of the human spirit mark each of us as unique, yet within categories. Thus these five patterns are but several central tendencies. Yet without patterns we have no way of comprehending. All we can see are many different scores. It was only as the authors matched human behaviors against patterns of scores that they were able to attach meaning to the scores. With the two patterns described in Chapter 4 and the five discussed here (with variations within them, as in the last one discussed), we describe enough general tendencies for you to place some meaning on your own scores and better understand the communication conflicts of humanity.

CONCLUSION

We have defined conflict as differences within or between people, differences that are incompatible in character. We have described these incompatibilities as real or perceived. It is the perceived ones that are the more difficult to deal with, for they are the consequences either of our behavioral habits in conflict with our values, or of conflicts among our values.

In describing the forms of conflict we have tried to make clear that the issue is not what is right or wrong, good or bad, except *in the way those differences are managed.* The issue in management is, Are we dead set on injury to someone else? If so, that is destructive conflict.

After the most destructive wars (personal or national), the incompatibility is still there to be managed. Then, without destructive passions or vindictiveness, we are left with the task of seeing what to do about the ongoing problem. If after the victory we do not restrain ourselves, we set the conditions for more destruction.

An attorney in one of the authors' conflict classes said,

> One of my biggest problems as an attorney with business partners breaking up or marriage partners breaking up is to get the parties to recognize that the "break" does not end the relationship. It just alters it. I have a hard time getting them to see that when you go at the "change of relationship" with vengeance you only make the new relationship being developed more difficult to manage.

COMMUNICATION-CONFLICT INSTRUMENT[14]

This is the only somewhat involved instrument in this book. Having read Chapters 1 and 4, however, you will find that the parts fall into place rather easily. It has six primary parts, which measure feelings, task energy, and the four value orientations. On the basis of the pattern of the scores on those six parts, it also measures six communication–conflict states: management of conflict, creative interaction, empathy, inclination to control, authority conflict, and interpersonal conflict. These are explained in the interpretation of the instrument.

Each statement has a range of responses from 1 to 7. Follow the directions on the answer sheet.

Here is an outline of the order of materials related to the instrument.

1. The preceding explanation
2. A scanner sheet for machine scoring is needed. Your college will have its own.
3. The sixty questions.
4. Instrument scoring information
5. An analysis of Jane Doe's scores, as an example, on an interpretation form.
6. Your interpretation form
7. Interpretation of the instrument

All of us have our own peculiar insights about how we feel, think, and act in life. This task involves describing the way you see yourself feeling and behaving. Each item describes a specific feeling, view or behavior, but does not ask that you judge whether it is desirable or undesirable. Simply indicate the degree to which you see yourself holding this perspective or behavior most of the time. Do not think about what you might happen to feel, think, or do in a particular social situation; rather think about how you most typically respond.

Please do not spend too much time on any one item. Try to answer as *honestly as possible*. All answers are STRICTLY CONFIDENTIAL. There are no right or wrong answers. Some statements may be difficult

[14]© Western Michigan University, 1977 Communication Arts and Sciences.

because you are not sure of your response. On these questons, however, please try to determine which way you are leaning and answer in that direction. In short, avoid "4" answers if at all possible.

DIRECTIONS
Read these answer categories carefully. Then answer each question according to how you feel or think it should be answered.

Place mark on scanner sheet

	ALMOST NEVER	RARELY	SELDOM	SOMETIMES	OFTEN	USUALLY	ALMOST ALWAYS
EXAMPLE:							
I respect people who say what's on their minds.	1	2	3	4	5	6	7

Questions

1. My thoughts are more important to me than those of other people.	1	2	3	4	5	6	7
2. My feelings are more positive than the feelings of most people I know.	1	2	3	4	5	6	7
3. Authority should be in the hands of the few most competent people.	1	2	3	4	5	6	7
4. I am very work oriented.	1	2	3	4	5	6	7
5. The best way to live is in service.	1	2	3	4	5	6	7
6. I work harder than most people I know.	1	2	3	4	5	6	7
7. It is important that I spend a share of my working hours alone each day.	1	2	3	4	5	6	7
8. I am more successful in what I do than most people I know who are my age.	1	2	3	4	5	6	7

(Communication Conflict Instrument Questions, cont'd.)

	ALMOST NEVER	RARELY	SELDOM	SOMETIMES	OFTEN	USUALLY	ALMOST ALWAYS
9. I speak with authority.	1	2	3	4	5	6	7
10. I spend much of my time being entertained by mass media.	1	2	3	4	5	6	7
11. I feel a great sense of attachment and loyalty to my community.	1	2	3	4	5	6	7
12. I have a very high regard for my uniqueness.	1	2	3	4	5	6	7
13. I like to give orders to people.	1	2	3	4	5	6	7
14. I feel sorry after I tell a person off.	1	2	3	4	5	6	7
15. I am more involved in leadership roles than most people I know who are my age.	1	2	3	4	5	6	7
16. I enjoy participating in community service projects.	1	2	3	4	5	6	7
17. I am irritated by people.	1	2	3	4	5	6	7
18. I would like myself more if I spent more of my energy in community service.	1	2	3	4	5	6	7
19. My life is fully committed to those I love deeply.	1	2	3	4	5	6	7
20. I have great faith in the gradual improvement of humanity.	1	2	3	4	5	6	7
21. I allow the needs of people with whom I am related to take precedence over my own needs.	1	2	3	4	5	6	7
22. I am able to listen to others even when I am annoyed by them.	1	2	3	4	5	6	7
23. I spend more time in meetings than most people I know.	1	2	3	4	5	6	7
24. I would give up my life for world peace.	1	2	3	4	5	6	7

(Communication Conflict Instrument Questions, cont'd.)

	ALMOST NEVER	RARELY	SELDOM	SOMETIMES	OFTEN	USUALLY	ALMOST ALWAYS
25. I believe that personal independence is a chief mark of the good life.	1	2	3	4	5	6	7
26. I believe my principles are superior to those of our society.	1	2	3	4	5	6	7
27. My feelings are a valid compass for directing my life.	1	2	3	4	5	6	7
28. I tend to subordinate my needs to the needs of others.	1	2	3	4	5	6	7
29. I admire a volunteer nurse more than I do a community leader.	1	2	3	4	5	6	7
30. I appreciate everybody I know.	1	2	3	4	5	6	7
31. I think wars among nations will be eliminated.	1	2	3	4	5	6	7
32. I know I am helping others.	1	2	3	4	5	6	7
33. I am highly tolerant of other people's negative feelings.	1	2	3	4	5	6	7
34. I like to tease people.	1	2	3	4	5	6	7
35. I get more accomplished than most people do.	1	2	3	4	5	6	7
36. Welfare programs tend to weaken society.	1	2	3	4	5	6	7
37. I dream of becoming a powerful person in society.	1	2	3	4	5	6	7
38. I work out my differences with others in a cooperative way.	1	2	3	4	5	6	7
39. I get extremely angry with some members of my family.	1	2	3	4	5	6	7
40. A competitive system brings out the best in people.	1	2	3	4	5	6	7
41. Most people are out to get the most they can for the least effort.	1	2	3	4	5	6	7

(Communication Conflict Instrument Questions, cont'd.)

	ALMOST NEVER	RARELY	SELDOM	SOMETIMES	OFTEN	USUALLY	ALMOST ALWAYS
42. I believe in saying what I feel in dealing with other people.	1	2	3	4	5	6	7
43. I like to watch contact sports.	1	2	3	4	5	6	7
44. I like competitive games.	1	2	3	4	5	6	7
45. I care for the person I am talking to.	1	2	3	4	5	6	7
46. I can get very angry with people.	1	2	3	4	5	6	7
47. I am more ambitious than most people I know.	1	2	3	4	5	6	7
48. I like controversy.	1	2	3	4	5	6	7
49. I believe in making my own decisions, even when other people think I am wrong.	1	2	3	4	5	6	7
50. I would rather watch a game or movie than be in it.	1	2	3	4	5	6	7
51. I am committed to the groups I join.	1	2	3	4	5	6	7
52. I believe that most people are as trustworthy as I am.	1	2	3	4	5	6	7
53. I think the fittest should survive.	1	2	3	4	5	6	7
54. I have feelings of despair.	1	2	3	4	5	6	7
55. The world lacks powerful leaders.	1	2	3	4	5	6	7
56. I see the uniqueness in each individual I experience.	1	2	3	4	5	6	7
57. If I had to I would die for my best friend.	1	2	3	4	5	6	7
58. My chief concern is for my individuality.	1	2	3	4	5	6	7
59. My fantasies are important to my growth.	1	2	3	4	5	6	7
60. I admire a forceful person more than a cooperative person.	1	2	3	4	5	6	7

(*Communication Conflict Instrument Questions, cont'd.*)

61. Highest Educational level:
    1. Less than high school diploma
    2. High school diploma
    3. One (1) year of college
    4. Two (2) years of college
    5. Three (3) years of college
    6. Bachelor's degree
    7. Masters degree
    8. Masters degree plus work
    9. Doctoral degree
62. Sex:
    1. Male
    2. Female
63. & 64. Age in years:___ ___. (First digit in box 63; second digit in box 64. For example, if your age is 25, put the 2 in box 63, and the 5 in box 64.)

SCORING INFORMATION

Following are the questions that bear on each of the primary six variables.
Feelings: 2, 13, 17, 34, 39, 43, 44, 46, 48, 54
Task: 4, 6, 8, 9, 10, 15, 23, 35, 47, 50
Community: 5, 11, 16, 18, 20, 24, 29, 32, 51, 52
Other: 19, 21, 22, 28, 30, 33, 38, 45, 56, 57
Control: 3, 14, 31, 36, 37, 40, 41, 53, 55, 60
Self: 1, 7, 12, 25, 26, 27, 42, 49, 58, 59

In order to score correctly, all the following questions must be scored in reverse: 10, 13, 14, 17, 31, 34, 39, 43, 44, 46, 48, 50, 54. (One is seven, two is six, three is five, etc.)

The preceding data will give you scores for the six basic variables.

In order to score for the six communication–conflict constructs one uses the following formulas:

Management of conflict = the sum of the scores for feelings, task, community, and other; subtract from that sum the sum of the scores for control and self.

Creative interaction = the sum of the scores for feelings, other, and self; subtract from that sum the sum of the scores for task, community, and control.

Empathy = the sum of the scores for feelings, other, and community; subtract from that sum the sum of the scores for task, self, and control.

Authority conflict = the sum of the scores for task, community, and self; subtract from that sum the sum of the scores for feelings, other, and control.

Interpersonal conflict = the sum of the score for self and 200; subtract from that sum the sum of the scores for feelings, task, community, other, and control.

Aggression conflict = the sum of the scores for all the questions except 4, 6, 7, 8, 10, 12, 18, 23, 27, 31, 32, 35, 43, 47, 50, 54, 58, and 59. Of the forty-two questions used in this measure, the following questions are scored in reverse: 2, 5, 11, 16, 19, 20, 21, 22, 24, 28, 29, 30, 33, 38, 45, 51, 52, 56, 57. Item 14, also, is reversed, but that was done for the scoring of the previous constructs. Questions 3, 9, 13, 19, 21, 22, 28, 33, 34, 37, 46, 48 are doubled in quantity because they more powerfully reflect the construct than the other thirty questions used in this measure.

INTERPRETATION FORM (Sample)

Name ____Jane Doe____

Age _____22_____

Sex _____F_____

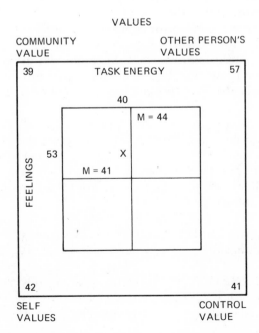

Jane's feeling score is 53. Since her score could have been from 10 to 70, the 53 falls in the block above the mean for college students, which is 41. Had she had a score of 41 it would have been placed on the heavy midline of the vertical range (feelings).

Jane's task energy score being 40 is placed in a block below (to the left of) the mean for task, which is 44. Thus her behavior is placed on the grid at the point where the feeling score and task energy score intersect. That places her in the upper left quadrant near the center, the compromise point.

Jane's "other" value score is her highest value, which supports her behavior score. Indeed, the sum of her community and other scores is greater than the sum of her self and control value scores. Thus her behavior tends to be held within the upper two quadrants.

Note the tension between Jane's self and other values. By studying many individual cases we learned that a 42–57 tension reflects an empathic relationship, which makes it possible for Jane to work productively with others. She can be aggressive or submissive according to her evaluation of the situation. She will not withdraw, except under pressure.

The other two value scores, 41 and 39, are rather neutral positions, known from individual interviews and a scanning of scores. If you look at the means at the end of the interpretation of the instrument, you will note that Jane is at the mean for control value and just below the mean for community value.

Jane's task energy and control value score tells us that she will not assert aggressive leadership. The self–other value torque indicates that Jane can and will assume a supportive position in interaction, in a creative way.

This pattern of scores is rather typical of the college student who has good relationships, is interested in human relationships, conceives of a life career in some service work, but has few or no ideological (social) principles at this point in life. Jane is not an individualist, but she is not community oriented either. She is person-to-person oriented.

Now note the scores this gives Jane:

Management of conflict	=	105.00	The mean is	89.00
Creative interaction	=	32.00	The mean is	12.00
Empathy	=	26.00	The mean is	−01.00
Aggression conflict	=	190.00	The mean is	203.00
Authority conflict	=	− 30.00	The mean is	05.00
Interpersonal conflict	=	+ 12.00	The mean is	31.00

Thus Jane manages conflict better than most college students. Her high empathy score tells us the reason why. The only kind of conflict Jane is likely to stumble into is an interpersonal one, but she is less likely to do so than the average college student.

Jane belongs to the large class of people who fit into the helping professions. She is not leadership oriented. This does not mean that she cannot lead; it means, at this time, that she does not have the drive to lead.

INTERPRETATION FORM

Name _____

Age _____

Sex _____

VALUES

COMMUNITY VALUE

OTHER PERSON'S VALUES

TASK ENERGY ACTIONS

M = 44

FEELINGS

M = 41

SELF VALUE

CONTROL VALUE

INTERPRETATION

The communication–conflict instrument is built on a theoretical foundation that holds that there are three interrelated dynamic forces in human life that shape our interactions with others. They are the bonding-dissolving forces of our feelings, the basic life force of our energy (which varies, of course, from person to person), and the abstracts we call values, which "guide" our feelings and energy.

The following are descriptions of patterns of interaction for which we have discovered means of scoring. (We are working on others.) There are three communication patterns that bring results that are productive, getting things done with satisfaction for all concerned. They are conflict management, creative interaction, and empathic interaction. There are also three kinds of interaction that tend to result in unproductive conflict, conflict that gets things done with little satisfaction. They are authority conflict, interpersonal conflict and aggression conflict.

Three Productive Styles of Interaction

1. Conflict management   In talking with people there are always differences in point of view and in personal needs, ranging from minor incompatabilities to serious conflict. Your conflict management score is a measure of your capacity to manage these interactive conflicts effectively. Good management means differences are handled smoothly to the satisfaction of both yourself and the others you relate to. Poor management means you experience stress in interaction with others that ends in an exchange of punitive words and unsatisfactory decisions or in withdrawal from the other person with ill feelings. We have found that people who get the lowest scores here tend to avoid conflict. They escape.

The dynamics of conflict management are as follows. Positive feelings, high task energy, and high value for the group and for each person in the group work together to make a person effective in dealing with the inevitable conflicts of interaction. But we all have a need to have the world we live in the way we want it to be and we all have our personal needs, dictated by our values. As these two values come to dominate our behavior, they detract from our effectiveness in conflict management. Your score in conflict management is a reflection of the way these dynamics work in you, as perceived by you.

2. Creative interaction   In groups there is sometimes a person or two who can see still another way of going about things when the ways thus far discussed fail to meet approval or cause deep distress for people. Such people very often fail in many of their suggestions. But they do not mind, nor do they back off. They try another way. They are brainstormers—there is always still another way to skin a cat. When people use this as their method of operating when there is conflict, they have a favorable internal climate of feeling, are highly task oriented, and place a high value on their unique skills. Conversely, they are not so community oriented that they cannot bend the rules to get the job done.

They obviously do not need to control, but, if they have to offend another person in order to work through the mass of conflicts, they do.

Your creative interaction score is a reflection of your tendency to function as just described.

An extremely high score means considerable individualism and perhaps nonconformity. A very high degree of nonconformity is obviously attended by high interpersonal conflict.

3. Empathic interaction By definition, empathy is your (1) understanding of the other person's feelings (2) with appreciation. We cannot appreciate what we do not understand. We are likely to fear and feel threatened and thus attack what we do not understand. Yet merely understanding the other person's feelings can lead to exploitation. Thus to be empathic we have to understand the other person with appreciation of his or her feelings.

In order to be empathic, our own feelings and task energy must be such as to make us concerned for the relationship with the other person. Our self–other value relationship makes it possible for us to "step into the other person's shoes." Finally, the more we value community and the less we value control, the more empathic we are.

Your empathic interaction score is a measure of one of the chief traits contributing to the ability to manage conflicts productively.

Three Unproductive Styles of Interaction

The following are common unproductive methods of dealing with conflict that lessen one's ability to manage situations in ways satisfactory to all concerned.

1. Authority conflict All institutions establish certain people in roles of authority—the father, the mother, or both in the home. Industry has its array of bosses, the nation has its president, king, or prime minister. Even gangsters organize under a leader.

Yet all of us as individuals, by virtue of our own sense of individuality, assert our own personal authority too. Thus all of us vacillate, in varying degrees, between asserting our own authority and accepting the institutionalized authority. The more we are rebels by nature, the more we insist on exercising our own personal authority.

The authority conflict score is a measure of the degree to which you fear and resent the persuasion and decisions made by institutionalized authority. The dynamics at work are as follows. High task orientation, a sense of community responsibility, and a high concern for your own personal values motivate you to assert yourself. Negative feelings, low concern for the other person, and low regard for control tend to make you resist authority.

Power and authority are problems for all of us. If we give in to authority that, in our judgment, exploits us, we feel weak. If we place a high value on all people, including ourselves, as free agents, we have a low value for control. Yet if we resist authority we are exercising an effort to control. Thus high task energy and low control value are the basic sources of vacillation about authority.

You may find it hard to determine whether this statement describes authority conflict as socially good or bad. This is intentional, for the situation itself determines the wisdom of resistance to institutionalized authority. Without resistance to authority there would be no reform. But the fact remains that when institutionalized authority is resisted smooth management of conflict is not facilitated; and people who have a proclivity to resist authority are thus diminished in the ability to manage conflicts without disruption.

A high score reflects uneasiness with institutionalized authority. A low score indicates a tendency to accept the authority in charge.

2. Interpersonal conflict   Conflict with another person is essentially a clash in personal values. Thus, the higher your concern for your own values relative to the other three values, feelings, and task energy, the higher the tendency to kindle interpersonal conflict. Also, the higher your control value the more you are inclined to struggle with a person. The lower your control value the more likely you are to walk away from a person with whom you are in conflict. Thus the degree of control value is a measure of interpersonal conflict *style*. The essential dynamic of interpersonal conflict is the incompatibility of two people's values. In short, the more self-oriented we are, the more we clash with others.

Your interpersonal conflict score is not a measure of the number of open confrontations you have with people. It is a measure of your tension with people. How often that tension breaks out in overt stress with others varies with events and pressures.

3. Aggression conflict   Leadership is one's effort to get another person or other people to follow. The essential instrument of leadership is speech and therefore the person talking in a group is for that moment the leader. The value behind leader energy is the control of others and of the situation. The more we insist on having things done our way in the interaction with others, the more we are assertive and aggressive, at some point causing resistance in others. The dynamics are as follows. When we try to lead we have great task energy, a controlling vision of the way things ought to be, which is almost always mixed with a high concern for our own values. The resulting aggressive effort is restrained only if our feelings, community and other person values are great. But resistance to our leadership is likely to lessen these tempering forces. Then we may become even more aggressive.

The higher your aggression conflict score the greater your tendency to dominate when resisted. The lower your score, the more likely it is that you will search for other postures, compromise, or submission to the wishes of the other. In the definitions of this test, empathy and efforts to control are, in the main, opposing behaviors, but not mutually exclusive. One can be persistent and empathic at once, but to do so one walks a narrow line and the tension is likely to erode one's empathic response.

Summary

For your own perspective you will want to examine most particularly your highest and lowest scores for the measures of feelings, task, community, others, control, and self. Then consider your scores that facilitate communication, scores 1, 2, and 3. Finally, note which of the three kinds of unproductive conflict cause your interaction to be less productive than it might be.

It should be noted that an important relationship exists between the conflict management score and each of the other constructs. In short, the management score is the critical one. A person, for instance, may have a relatively high authority, interpersonal conflict, or aggression conflict score, but also a high management of conflict score. This means the conflict remains intrapersonal and only potentially interpersonal. But if the management of conflict is low, then the kind of conflict one feels is likely to break out in overt behavior.

An examination of these dynamics helps you see in what ways to change, if you desire to change.

Conflict is a basic ingredient in all communication. Each of us has to decide how we want to manage it.

Following are the means (N = 231) for college students and other relevant data for the measures just discussed.

	Mean	Standard Deviation
1. Feelings	42.10	7.40
2. Task energy	45.23	7.26
3. Community value	42.07	8.21
4. Other value	48.64	7.61
5. Control value	40.03	6.44
6. Self value	48.94	6.91
7. Conflict management	89.08	22.82
8. Creative interaction	12.35	16.57

9. Empathic interaction	−1.38	20.04
10. Authority conflict	5.48	14.42
11. Interpersonal conflict	30.87	21.13
12. Aggression conflict	203.41	23.02

EXERCISES

1. Keep a journal for at least a week, making entries every day concerning (1) the conflicts you have with other people and (2) the conflicts you have with yourself. Then examine these entries. Is there a central theme? Whom do you have conflicts with? How much do you suffer in the conflict? Do you operate constructively or destructively?

2. Jot down, for several days, the substance or topic of any fantasies you catch yourself engaging in that involve conflict or power. Do you talk to yourself when alone? What is your role in this talk? Does it involve conflict?

3. Jot down the theme of any troublesome night dreams you have. Analyze them. Do they involve frustrations or conflicts? With what and whom? What can you do about the source of stress?

4. The following is an exploration of conflict in your class. It is not a game in the usual sense but an effort to control the destiny of the class for a time, and the uses of your energy.

   a. Divide yourselves, in any arbitrary way, into two equal-sized groups.

   b. In the following class meeting the groups will meet for the amount of time your instructor decides is appropriate and decide on an assignment for the class related to a study of conflict. The assignment, to illustrate, could be further reading on some aspect of the discussion of conflict, the taking of a value test, a conflict test, the writing of one of the journals described in suggestions 1 and 2, the reading of a book such as *The Intimate Enemy*, by George Bach and Peter Wyden (Avon, 1968), or *Rules for Radicals*, by Saul D. Alinsky (Vintage Books, 1972), or *The Angry Book*, by Theodore Rubin (Collier Books, 1969), a speech, a term paper, or the like.

   c. In whatever manner your group decides upon or your instructor prescribes, you will present your argument for the assignment to the instructor.

   d. Your instructor will decide which of the two groups has prescribed
      I. the most useful assignment
      II. in the best-defended way
      The instructor will announce the decision and you will follow his or her instructions.

Note the following:

A. The feelings you have in the group about yourselves and the other group and about the instructor.

B. The strategies used by yourself and others.

C. Your feelings about the assignment.

D. The energy expended.

E. The trust in each other.

F. The aggressiveness of some people and the compliance of others.

G. The tactics of competitive leadership.

5. This suggestion is for the person who is deeply interested in trying to understand the human condition. The Likerts, cited ealier in the chapter, believe the research reveals that the business of using parliamentary procedure, in which the decisions of a group are determined by a majority vote, usually leads to unproductive solutions because the behavior that it prescribes is based on *zero-sum principle*—the winner, even if by one vote, rules. They suggest arriving at decisions by consensus. Do not misread this. There is going to be conflict in trying to gain consensus, and much frustration. But a group decides not to act until a consensus is reached. This is the way the Quaker Church operates. One might read about the Quaker experience. What do you think about this? Almost any efficiency-oriented administrator will say this is pure nonsense. But what about the terrible loss resulting from destructive conflict in business, government, and education? Why not proceed without decisions on matters in which you cannot get consensus?

6. For the research-minded person, Prisoner's Dilemma is a classic game. It goes this way. You and a buddy have robbed a bank and have been picked up. *You are put in separate cells and cannot talk to each other.* The DA visits both of you and makes the following proposition:

   1. Turn state's evidence and you will get off scot-free. Obviously, that is pretty attractive.
   2. But if you do that your buddy will be put in the cooler for ten years.
   3. Unless he too turns state's evidence, in which case both of you will be stashed away for 5 years.
   4. If neither of you will talk, you will both be put away for two years. Your decision depends on your ethics and your appraisal of the decision your buddy is likely to make. This experiment has been done many times. The rule is that a person who plays the game over and over soon "locks in" on the same decision each time. Will you find this to be true? If so, can you discover any explanation of why a person soon settles for one decision?

Ethics

11

Authentic communication is a mutual struggle for common ground
between two distinct and inviolable identities—a loving contest in
which each man surrenders his weapons to the other.

*Floyd W. Matson and Ashley Montagu**

The trouble with communication is that it works!

Words "bite like a saw into white pine."[1] An exchange of views never
leaves the participants unchanged, and some encounters "make all the
difference" in a person's life. Psychologist Sidney Jourard once painted a
picture of what can happen in interpersonal exchanges in these terms:
"Some people invite you to live; some invite you to die." A commonsense
observation of what happens in everyday life seems to bear him out.
Some interpersonal exchanges have the effect of opening doors to
growth and creative energy. Other exchanges sow the seeds of despair
and defeat.

Does it matter how one human being communicates with another?
Is it possible to decide that one case of communication is healthier than
another? Do I, as a communicator, have any responsibility to the person
I talk to? If words are so powerful, are there some principles for their
use, a guide to what is right and wrong?

*Floyd W. Matson and Ashley Montagu, *The Human Dialogue* (New York: The Free
Press, 1967), page 7. By permission of The Free Press.

[1] William Stafford, "Lit Instructor," in *Traveling Through the Dark* (New York: Harper &
Row Publishers, Inc., 1967), p. 38

A SNAPSHOT OF PAST THOUGHT

Writers at least as far back as Aristotle have been struggling with those questions. One thing virtually all of them agree on is that any communicator does have a responsibility toward those with whom he or she communicates.[2] Beyond that, there is impressive agreement on specific ways in which you can tell whether a communicator is ethical or unethical.[3]

Here is a sampling:

A speaker is unethical if he or she

tells deliberate lies.

knowingly distorts the truth.

pretends to know something he or she does not know.

uses emotional appeals that cannot be supported by reason.

conceals his or her real purpose.

uses tactics designed to block the listener's chance to think clearly about the topic.

As a group, these statements say, in effect, "All individuals ought to be responded to in ways that would not deceive them and would strengthen their ability to reason for themselves rather than block that ability." Machiavelli catalogued, and accurately described, many ways in which a prince could influence and control his subjects. But the question he was raising was, What works? and not, What is healthy for all the participants?

The tests of ethics just listed were thought of almost entirely in connection with public speaking because this was the kind of communication the ancients were most interested in. But in a world built on a bill of rights and concern for human potential we now have to ask whether those tests are adequate for describing healthy or unhealthy *interpersonal communication*. Our answer is that all of them apply when we move from public speaking to interpersonal communication, but that our new understandings of the latter require an important shift of emphasis.

[2]See such sources as the following: Henry N. Weiman and Otis Walter, "Toward an Analysis of Ethics for Rhetoric," *Quarterly Journal of Speech*, 43 (1957), 266–270; Karl Wallace, "An Ethical Basis for Communication," *The Speech Teacher*, 4 (1955), 1–9; Franklyn S. Haiman, "A Re-examination of the Ethics of Persuasion," *Central States Speech Journal*, 3 (1952), 5–10; Lane Cooper, *The Rhetoric of Aristotle* (New York: Appleton, 1932).

[3]For an especially clear and thorough description of the ways in which communication ethics can be examined, see Richard L. Johannesen, *Ethics in Human Communication* (Columbus, Ohio: Charles E. Merrill Publishing Co., 1975).

AN INTERPERSONAL ETHIC

The tests we have cited have to do chiefly with the content of a message—does it contain lies and distortions? Are the tactics used in presenting it misleading? Is there pretense, exaggeration? *An interpersonal ethic accepts these tests, but is more concerned with the attitude a speaker and a listener show toward each other.* What is wrong with a lie? It is just a different set of words from those that tell the truth. The *ultimate* issue in communication, we are saying, is not the validity of words but the validity of the relationship between the people exchanging words. The reason truth, as we know the truth, is important is that people cannot build bridges between them that crumble when tested.

The *interpersonal* ethic is concerned with the loyalty you have toward the person with whom you are communicating. That ethic can be stated as follows:[4]

> *A's communication is ethical to the extent that it accepts B's responses; it is unethical to the extent that it is hostile to B's responses, or in some way tries to subjugate B. The ethic can best be put to a test when A discovers that B rejects the message A is sending.*

Concretely, if parents or teachers or friends or coworkers try to convince you that something is true, or that a conclusion should be accepted, and you find that you cannot agree with them, how they treat your response to them will reveal whether they are willing to take responsibility for their communication with you.

A Dig Beneath the Surface

Does such a test make any sense? Let us try to sketch in the background for it. At one of the many really arresting spots in *The Brothers Karamazov* Dostoevsky has Ivan, an intellectual, trying to convince his younger brother Alyosha, a cleric, of the rightness of his life view. Ivan conjures up a problem to make his point. He says to Alyosha,

> Imagine that you are creating a fabric of human destiny with the object of making men happy in the end, giving them the peace and rest at last, but that it was essential and inevitable to torture to death only one tiny creation . . . and to found that edifice on its unavenged tears, would you consent to be the architect on those conditions? Tell me, and tell the truth.

"No, I wouldn't consent," says Alyosha. It is tempting to want to stop

---

[4]Much of the material discussed in this chapter comes from the authors' first attempt to find an adequate interpersonal ethic. See Paul W. Keller and Charles T. Brown, "An Interpersonal Ethic for Communication," *Journal of Communication*, 18 (1968), 73–81.

and pursue the values that are brought into question by Alyosha's firm answer. But we want to use the scene as the basis for a paraphrase we would pose regarding communication:

> Imagine that you have the welfare of another person at heart, and that you are convinced that you know what would be good for him in a given situation. Suppose that you recommend to him the "right" course of action, explaining your reasons fully, developing the reasonable foundations for your view patiently. And suppose that when you are finished—perhaps after repeated conversations—he rejects your proposal. Would you accept his response without rancor, without an undercover resolution to set him right—in short, would you accept his response as the authentic reaction of a free individual?[5]

We take it that the most common way to react, when you think you know what is good for someone else and that person keeps turning down your proposals, is either to turn your back on him or her ("If that's the way he(she) feels, let him stew in his own juice") or to bite your tongue and determine that you will change his or her mind one way or another. If the measure we are proposing of what is ethical is accepted, however, neither of those reactions will pass the test.

Who Should Be Free?

The point we are trying to make is that a communication might pass all of the tests previously proposed—it might be without lies, without distortion, without deceit, without unsupportable emotional appeals— and still prove unethical. For the ethic we are proposing is imbedded in the assumption that *whatever enhances that which is uniquely human in participants is ethical; whatever dehumanizes is unethical.*[6] This assumption finds expression in one of the values held most dear in a democratic society, namely, that conditions *of free choice* be created and maintained in which it becomes possible for *the individual to realize his or her potential.* This is achieved to the extent to which others with whom he or she communicates *do not* try to control, coerce, manipulate, maneuver, or exploit him or her.

Not only is coercive communication unethical because of the injury it does the other. It is unethical for the user also, because it gradually cuts a person off from his or her own creative growth. The constant effort to exercise power over others makes one increasingly dependent on getting defeated responses from others. If the desired responses are not forthcoming, the effort to persuade must be redoubled. And this

---

[5]*Ibid.,* p. 74.
[6]Johannesen, *op. cit.,* Chap. 4.

preoccupation closes the door to one's own personal development. The power of personal competence is given up for the exercise of power over other people.

How Free Is Free?

Any unit of communication, by virtue of its psychological nature, involves *mutual control*. We take this to be self-evident: When a message is sent, the speaker intrudes into the life space of the listener. To the extent that anything is communicated, the speaker determines that the listener shall hear, think, and perceive one thing rather than another. At the same time, the listener to such a message inescapably influences the speaker by virtue of the way he or she either rewards the speaker or withholds rewards. In short, our communicative habits, as speakers, are molded and shaped by the responses we get from our listeners.[7] Thus, even in a one-sided situation in which one person does most of the talking, the speaker and the listener control each other. When we exchange the speaking and listening roles in a conversation, we simply exercise different kinds of control over each other.

Now if this two-way control system is constantly at work in communication, and if it is true that its influence on both the sender and the receiver of messages is profound, then the values each of the communicators regards as important become extremely significant, for both the speaker and the listener are, in part, at each other's mercy.

Why Does Everything Have to Be So Complicated?

If we try to discover through the traditional ethical tests what values communicators hold, the problem turns out to be more intricate than it appears on the surface. Take, for example, the notion that in order to be ethical an argument must be valid. In cases of differences between arguments, who is to say which argument, evidence, or conclusion is valid? What is the truth, and how do we know when we know it? How can we be responsible for believing what is not true? Were people unethical when they believed the earth was the center of the universe? Today there is some suggestion that there are velocities that exceed the speed of light. What are the dangers of taking flu shots or being X-rayed?

Let us make the question even tougher. Is it not true that even a deliberate lie, or the withholding of what is believed, may be justified by the most careful exercise of conscience? Deliberate distortion is surely

---

[7]William Verplanck, "The Control of the Content of Conversation: Reinforcement of Statements of Opinion," *Journal of Abnormal and Social Psychology*, 51 (1955), 668–676.

dangerous, but who has not painfully chosen, as the lesser of two evils determined by conscience, to skirt the facts?

And is it not possible that unconscious distortion is carried in every communication? *How else can we explain the uniqueness of each person's perceptions?* "It's a wise cove as knows wot's wot," says one of Stevenson's pirates.

If both the speaker and the listener are mutually controlling each other's responses, how does either one decide who is right and what is true when they differ?

Where do the waters of the Caribbean Sea and the Gulf of Mexico begin and end? Now tell the truth.

It would seem to us that the loyalty of one person to another is more fundamental than the truth, and that it is easier to answer the question, How do I feel about you? than the question, What is the truth?

How do I, the speaker, react to my listener's reaction?

How do I, the listener, react to the speaker?

If my listener does not respond in a way that satisfies my goal, or vice versa, if the speaker does not respond in ways that satisfy me, am I angered? Am I despondent, and thus tempted to play for sympathy? Do I, in short, refuse to accept the responses of the other person as those of a free individual? Whatever enhances the basic freedom of response in the individual, we are suggesting, is more ethical; whatever either overtly or covertly attacks that energy is less ethical. A person, we are saying, is likely to know more about his or her feelings than about the truth.

SUPPORT FOR THE ARGUMENT

The idea of an ethic concerned specifically with interpersonal communication is not new. A number of years ago Thomas Nilsen tried to identify some of the most important values in a democracy.[8] His list included the following:

Belief in the intrinsic worth of the human personality.
Belief in reason as an instrument of individual and social development.
Self-determination as the means to individual fulfillment.
Fulfillment of one's potential as a positive good.

Particularly important in Nilsen's list, for our purposes, is his belief in "self-determination as the means of individual fulfillment." It is this

[8]Thomas R. Nilsen, "Free Speech, Persuasion, and the Democratic Process," *Quarterly Journal of Speech*, 44 (1958), 235–243.

kind of freedom that we have been urging in our proposed test of the ethics of communication. We proceed on the assumption that to discourage a listener from the conviction that he or she has powers for making choices is to downgrade his or her humanity. As Erich Fromm puts it, freedom can be thought of as "the ability to preserve one's integrity against power." Moreover, he says,

> Freedom is the necessary condition of happiness as well as of virtue; freedom, not in the sense of the ability to make arbitrary choices and not freedom from necessity, but freedom to realize that which one potentially is, to fulfill the true nature of man according to the laws of his existence.[9]

It is easy enough to pay lip service to such a concept of freedom, but willingness to use it in communicative behavior is by no means automatic. There is something in the very effort to persuade that seduces a person into an authoritarian ethic. Fromm's analysis of the way this works is worth quoting:

> Unless the authority wanted to exploit the subject, it would not need to rule by virtue of awe and emotional submissiveness; it could encourage rational judgment and criticism—thus taking the risk of being found incompetent. But because its own interests are at stake the authority ordains *disobedience* to be the main sin. The unforgivable sin in authoritarian ethics is rebellion, the questioning of the authority's right to establish norms and of its axiom that the norms established by the authority are in the best interests of the subjects.[10]

But there is in the ethic we have been proposing something that goes beyond simply the question of whether one is granted freedom or is inhibited from exercising that freedom in a given instance. It has to do with the effect of having another person react toward you with hostility or reserve or vindictiveness, over and over again, when you make a choice that is not consistent with the desires of the other person. Learning theory suggests that if individuals are rewarded in an interpersonal situation for making their own decisions they are likely to habituate that kind of independence in decision making; that is, *they learn to take responsibility in expressing their potential.* If they are not rewarded, they are likely to learn dependence on others for their decision making, and come thereby to live at a level below their potential. Nilsen has expressed it this way:

> When being persuaded a man is not only influenced directly or indirectly in his choice of a course of action, he is influenced in his *method of making the*

[9]Erich Fromm, *Man for Himself* (New York: Rinehart, 1947), p. 247.
[10]*Ibid.*, p. 12.

choice. The problem of ethics enters when what we do affects the lives of others. How we influence others to make choices about things of importance to them is obviously affecting their lives in a significant way.[11]

All of this emphasizes the *long-term injury done when there is a threat to "self-determination as the means to individual fulfillment,"* and shows that our temptation to use that threat is the core of the ethical problem in persuasion.

THE INTERPERSONAL ETHIC RESTATED

How does the speaker react to the listener's reactions? And how does the listener react to the speaker? If the listener reacts in such a way as to enhance the self-determination forces within the other person, his or her communication can be considered more ethical. If the listener reacts in such a way as to inhibit the self-determination forces within the other person, his or her communication can be considered less ethical, regardless of the purity of the devices used in the communicative effort.

FACTORS THAT MAKE
AN INTERPERSONAL ETHIC HARD TO APPLY

For some people the kind of ethic just described has a Pollyannaish sound to it, and it is clear that not many people find it easy to live by. A colleague of one of the authors says,

> I always tell my students that I want them to probe, and disagree, and come to their own conclusions. I tell them that I enjoy most the student who has a mind of his own. I tell them that if they aren't disagreeing they are probably dead. But then when one of them disagrees with me in class, I get all defensive and try to overwhelm them with my expertise.

That seems fairly typical. We know that people have it in them to either nurture or debilitate their fellows, but the temptation to dominate the other seems incurable for most of us. Why is this so?

The Power Problem

In every communicative relationship, as suggested in Chapters 4, 9, and 10, there is a power problem that must be resolved. If the relationship is to thrive, the people in it must feel comfortable with their

---

[11]Nilsen, *op. cit.,* p. 243.

definition of the way power will be used. They must be willing to use it where that is appropriate, or to have it used with them where that is appropriate.[12] If the power problem is never resolved, one person in the relationship will probably end up dominating the other (a husband, for example, may "force" his wife to take care of him by using his dependence on her as a way of dominating her).

It is a universal experience to urge another person to do what you want him or her to do, and to wonder only later whether that was good for the other person. One of the pictures that surely captures the human condition is the one that shows sports fans claiming, in frenzied terms both verbal and nonverbal, that "we are number one." There is in most of us (whether by nature or by cultural influence is a subject of debate) the desire to be "top dog," to control and to diminish others. Increasingly we are trying to understand why this urge is so strong in us. Ernest Becker sees it as primarily a response to our inability to accept our own death.[13] We have, he says, a need to transcend our mortality—to prove we are better than others, to leave a legacy that will be perpetuated after we are gone. We have, to use his terms, an irrepressible drive toward the heroic.

Whatever proves to be the mystery underlying the urge, the need to dominate, to exercise power over another, is all around us. We silently cheer Tom Sawyer because he is so beautifully ingenious in finding ways to control his autocratic aunt. She, symbolizing the forces that intrude on all of us day in and day out, gets her comeuppance because Tom is able to outsmart her over and over again.

But as Rollo May has pointed out, there are significant differences in the kinds of power one chooses to exercise.[14] May finds at least the following kinds of power available to each of us:

Exploitive—the rapist, the slave driver, etc. (power against)
Manipulative—the persuader, the evangelist, etc. (power over)
Nutrient—the parent, the teacher, etc. (power for)
Integrative—cooperative effort (power with)

Only the last of these omits the effort to dominate the other person. And clearly most instances of power take one of the earlier forms.

---

[12] William Schutz, *The Interpersonal Underworld* (Palo Alto, Calif.: Science and Behavior Books, Inc., 1958), Chap. 2.

[13] Ernest Becker, *The Denial of Death* (Glencoe, Ill.: Free Press, 1973).

[14] Rollo May, *Power and Innocence* (New York: W. W. Norton, 1972), Chap. 5.

The infant cannot be considered highly ethical just because of its innocence. Ethical tests cannot be applied until a person is aware of his or her responsibilities and makes choices regarding them. And since parents are bigger and have lived longer than children, there is a stage at which the ethical tests between parent and child must be different. But what we note is that moral development can grow as a life matures. On the basis of studies done in the 1960s, Lawrence Kohlberg[15] thought it possible to describe the stages of moral development rather accurately.

First stage: Obedience and punishment orientation   Seventy percent of the seven-year-old boys in the Kohlberg study were found to make statements like "If he doesn't help his family, his wife will probably divorce him and take away his children." Only 10 percent of the thirteen- to sixteen-year-olds made such statements. This earlier stage, says Kohlberg, represents a meager kind of ethical reasoning since it takes its guidance from outside the chooser. ("Don't do it, because if you do you will get punished.")

Second stage: Naively egoistic orientation   As people grow into stage two, when they try to make decisions they think only of their immediate interests and focus primarily on their needs in that situation. They assume that whatever will take care of those interests and needs is the ultimate guide. They omit concern for the future or for the wider consequence of their choice. ("It's according to what he wants most. If his family is most important to him, he ought to go and help them. If all the people in this neighborhood matter more to him, he ought to stay and protect them.")

Third stage: the "good boy" orientation   At this stage choice is still based on egocentric principles ("What would be good for me?"), and it emphasizes the expectations of society for the chooser. He or she will do something, or not do it, on the basis of what people would say.

Fourth stage: Orientation toward authority and social order   At this stage choices will be made in keeping with whatever person or group is charged with maintaining the social order. ("The *school principal* has a right to know where you are, because parents or friends may ask her and they will hold her responsible.") Note that the decisions at this stage are still being made on the basis of outside forces.

[15]Irvin L. Child, *Humanistic Psychology, and the Research Tradition: Their Several Virtues* (New York: Wiley, 1973), pp. 32–41.

Fifth stage: Social-contract orientation Decisions at this stage grow out of the *perceptions the chooser has* of people's obligations toward one another in a society. In this sense the level of choice rises because it comes more from inside the decision maker and represents an evaluation of the effect of the choice on other people. ("A man ought not to walk out on his wife and children because they have invested something in the life of the family and he owes them something in return.")

Sixth stage: Principles of conscience orientation Reasoning at this stage flows from conscience. It reflects what the person regards as "right" or "wrong" *not just because of conventional standards, and not just because of social contract, but because the nature of life requires it.* It puts emphasis on meeting the needs of both the individual and the community. ("It's wrong to place the interests of a few people, even close relatives, above the general welfare of people at large. The warden is the person this whole neighborhood counts on for safety, and his first duty is toward them, even though he ought to help his family if he were free to do so.") It is the most mature phase in ethical reasoning. Kohlberg found hardly any trace of this kind of reasoning at age 7 or 10, and only a hint of it at age 13 and 16. He guesses that it is rather rare in the population at large.

We present the Kohlberg analysis because it shows the kind of change that takes place as people accumulate experience. In short, people are not caught helplessly in an ethical straightjacket. They can, and do, grow in their ways of thinking about right and wrong. But Kohlberg's analysis shows that the struggle is a long and hard one. He estimates that very few people operate at a moral level above the third stage: One decides what is good for oneself that others will not criticize. If Kohlberg is right, it is understandable that the kind of interpersonal ethic we have suggested is hard to achieve.

A Salute to the Devil

If the struggle to put the power impulses to service for interpersonal health has its grim, difficult side, it also has its hopeful side. May describes some of the absolutely necessary expressions of power needed in order to live. He sees the *"power to be"* as universally necessary. Once a person can exercise that power, it is necessary to express the power of *self-affirmation.* And once that is adequately expressed, the individual is ready for the expression of the power of *self-assertion.* Unless power can be maintained *against* opposition, says May, it is not power and will never be experienced as real by the person being opposed.[16]

[16]May, *op. cit.,* p. 145.

Up to this point May has us walking primarily through inner choices and expressing our own identity. But in the next step—the movement into *aggression*—he has us invading the world of other people for the purpose of influencing them, changing them, controlling them. *This is the point at which the interpersonal ethic either works or fails.* Can we arrest our impulse to engage in destructive aggression?[17] Can we harness the desire to dominate the other person without regard for what it will do to his or her growth potential? The interpersonal ethic is difficult but optimistic. It assumes that self-knowledge and self-control are active options in the life of a person who seeks wholeness.

IMPLICATIONS OF THE INTERPERSONAL ETHIC

Those who try to live by such an ethic are faced with serious problems and exceptional rewards.

The Threat and Reward of Integrity

They have to be able to rely on their own level of self-esteem, because if their views or ideas are rejected they will tend to believe that their intelligence, skill, or personal worth are being questioned. If they ride herd on others, never allowing doubt to creep in, they escape having to face such deflation. The ethic now proposed asks people to respect themselves enough to be able to respect the autonomy of others.

A friend of one of the authors has the job of keeping supporters of the institution he works for happy. He must cultivate both their emotional support and their financial support. Often he works patiently to get them to contribute their money or to accept a new program being developed at the institution. And often they reject his appeals. If they are angry enough, they vow that they will never donate another cent. If they are only disturbed, they smile at his idealized views. How does he respond? With the hard sell? No. He grants them the right of self-determination that he is anxious to protect for himself. He is sure to expose them to his views and his feelings, but he is ready to grant them theirs. His tone of voice, muscle tension, and demeanor all underscore the freedom he is willing to grant the other. And his experience shows long-term success. Somewhere he has developed the power of self-assertion without having to move beyond it to destructive aggression.

Psychologist William Glasser, working with the girls at the Ventura School for Girls in California, discovered that most of the case histories

---

[17]*Ibid.*, pp. 156–163. In these pages May distinguishes between constructive and destructive aggression.

of girls confined there revealed such a low sense of personal esteem that *when these girls met opposition from anyone else* they felt driven to try to destroy them. He discovered, further, that the girls had developed their low self-esteem against a background of overwhelming criticism and assignment of failure by their parents and teachers. He concluded that "schools without failure" could have a profound influence on the level of self-esteem developed in students and thereby allow them to deal with disagreement more constructively.

The ultimate reward for allowing others to be free of your demands is a gradual lessening of any threat to your own self-esteem. And vice versa. *The ultimate punishment for insisting on controlling others is vulnerable self-esteem*—dependence on the approval of others.

Feelings of Powerlessness

An interpersonal ethic like this one takes control out of your hands and therefore can threaten not only your ability to function as you wanted to but your values as well. In the 1960s, when students joined blacks and other minorities in the cry for freedom, when "the student as nigger" was an inflammatory symbol, one teacher who had arranged his classes in such a way as to reduce his control to the minimum was heard to say, "Sometimes it seems the class is all flow and no form." And he was willing to have that message translated to mean "I feel helpless." As we want to say later in the chapter, such a feeling does not have to emerge when this ethic is applied, but the risk is certainly there.

An associated risk is that accepting the other's responses as genuine can mean that people who are very important to you may not accept the values you are convinced they should adopt. You are a parent who has always worked hard and who regards hard work as the mark of a successful person. Your college-age daughter has dropped out of school at the end of her sophomore year and has moved back home. She settles in to "get her head together." You try to convince her that she ought to set some goals for herself and go after them. She replies that such a view is what is corrupting our society, that we have lost touch with nature, with what is real in the world. You modify your hopes and keep passing along to her news of job openings. You tell her she might be surprised how much satisfaction she could get out of having an income of her own. Working would give her a chance, you say, to find out what she really wants to do. She smiles and thanks you for your concern, but reminds you that Siddhartha corrupted himself when he gave in to the temptation to think that work would lead him to the meaning of life. One day she leaves you a note saying she is on her way to the hills north of San

Francisco to live with a group of friends who have found their answer in Buddhism.

To react as the ethic we have proposed suggests would require accepting her response as the authentic response of a self-determining person—but it would mean foregoing any control you had dreamed of exercising over her values. Thus the temptation is great to want somehow to impose your values on those who count most to you. But such an imposition, if it succeeds, imposes dependency and, in the end, weakness on the person being dominated. Those who believe in freedom for all know this, but they may suffer feelings of weakness and powerlessness when they cannot have their way—*knowing* that it is the right way.

THE SIXTY-FOUR-DOLLAR QUESTION

When the interpersonal ethic proposed here first appeared, a thoughtful colleague of one of the authors wrote to express his concern. He put it into the form of a hypothetical problem:

> Suppose you lived in a community dominated by racist attitudes. Suppose you felt the injustice of such attitudes, and took on the responsibility of talking earnestly with influential people in the community who used racist approaches to bring financial gain and political power to them. Suppose you got a civil reception whenever you talked to them, but that they spurned every suggestion you made. How could you *not* feel hostility toward them and secretly determine that you would force them to see their error, by one means or another? And even if you could discipline yourself to cover your feelings toward them, should you, in good conscience, do so? Isn't there a need for "righteous indignation"? Doesn't human nature, marred as it is with selfishness and greed, require forcing the exploiter to stop his exploiting, and to do it with cunning and force if necessary? Does not your ethic require you to abandon urging what is right?

Many students exposed to the idea of the ethic have reacted in much the same way. It is as though they are saying, "Would not such an ethic take away the sharp edge of conscience? Would it not finally be a disservice to society?" Such questions cannot be ignored.

There are at least three ways of answering them.

One Way

The ethic does *not* require its users to give up their convictions or to abandon urging the right, as they see the right. Indeed, if one of the participants to an exchange gives up what he or she thinks is right out of fear that the other would be displeased, the ethic is not working—the other person has applied pressure that will not allow him or her to be authentic. To be authentic, one who feels that racism is deeply unjust must continue to express opposition to racist policies and do all he or she can to persuade others to change. Such a person is not rendered inactive.

A Second Way

Nor is one asked to give up one's own value system unless one of his or her values is to despise those who have different values. One *is* asked to respond to the racist in ways that would recognize that the racist is a genuine human being with ways of looking at the world that make sense to him or her.

In his chapter on "Dialogue Perspectives,"[18] Richard Johannesen shows how monologue in communication can be thought of as representing the "poor ethic" and dialogue the "good ethic." In monologue, he points out, the person "seeks to command, coerce, manipulate, conquer, dazzle, deceive, or exploit." In contrast, in dialogue there is a "spirit of mutual trust and an absence of defensive attitude or self-justification." Johannesen's model for the dialogue ethic is taken from the thought of Martin Buber. Buber's idea of dialogue is one of the wellsprings of the ethic we have described, but it is significant that it does not require giving up values. At one point Buber says,

> Further, if genuine dialogue is to arise, everyone who takes part in it must bring himself into it. And that also means that he must be willing on each occasion to say what is really in his mind about the subject of the conversation. And that means further that on each occasion he makes the contribution of his spirit without reduction and without shifting his ground. Even men of great integrity are under the illusion that they are not bound to say everything "they have to say." But in the great faithfulness which is the climate of genuine dialogue, what I have to say at any one time already has in me the character of something that wishes to be uttered, and I must not keep it back, keep it in myself. It bears for me the unmistakable sign which indicates that it belongs to the common life of the word. Where the dialogical word genuinely exists, it must be given its right by keeping nothing back.[19]

We are here arguing that acceptance of the "enemy" is a requirement of persistence of argument *within* the ethic.

[18]Johannesen, *op. cit.*, Chap. 5.
[19]Martin Buber, *The Knowledge of Man* (New York: Harper & Row Publishers, Inc., 1965), pp. 85–86.

In addition, there is a real persuasive payoff if you can accept the person whose values are repugnant to you. If Carl Rogers is right, a person is most likely to change when he(she) is confirmed just as he(she) is.[20] Confronting the racist authentically—*including one's own anti-racist convictions*—permits the racist to put his or her world together in the presence of new perceptions *because he or she does not need to defend his or her selfhood from an attack by you. If there is a chance of persuading a person, it is because the person is permitted to retain his or her self-esteem.* Acceptance of the "enemy" provides the best chance for influencing him or her. We all hang our lives on our values (as we learned in Chapter 4). We may come to see a value as false if our self-esteem is not threatened.

But, we should add, the best chance for influencing a person is not a guarantee. What if one fails? Then what? This is the ultimate test. If one cannot accept an opponent when one cannot influence that opponent, one does not believe in the interpersonal ethic.

An ethic is not a rule of life that we use when all is going our way. The issue of ethics in such a climate is not even pertinent. One's ethic is the rule of life one calls upon when things do not go as one desires.

THE ETHIC ILLUSTRATED

The kind of ethic we have proposed does not require giving up action in regard to what one believes is right, but it does call for acceptance of one's opponents. Mahatma Gandhi's efforts to throw off the weight of English dominance in India provide a good example of this point. Gandhi assumed that there is no such thing as absolute truth and that therefore no one has the right to take the life of another over a difference in viewpoint. He felt required to honor the integrity and authenticity of anyone he found as an opponent, and he contented himself with the goal of trying to persuade that opponent. He even admitted the possibility that he might be led to change his own mind in the course of the struggle. *But this did not lead him to inaction.* He drew up action plans incessantly. He shared them openly with his opponents. He marched, demonstrated, wrote, boycotted wherever he felt it necessary, but he continued to respect the responses of his opponents. He was able to demonstrate that it is possible to hold fast to your own values while honoring the personhood of another.

[20]Carl Rogers, *On Becoming a Person* (Boston: Houghton Mifflin Co., 1961), pp. 63-64.

CONTEMPT AND ETHICS

It seems to us that the power of the objections to an interpersonal ethic rests in the fact that one wants to reserve the right to despise certain people. Certainly the ethic cannot be applied in communication with people we detest.

Breathes there a person who has not given up on somebody else? How can we be expected to respect the opinion of a person whom we do not respect? It is hard enough for most of us to apply the interpersonal ethic with people we love. All of this, however, does not so much raise a question about the ethic as it challenges our insistence on reserving the right to despise, hate, and try to defeat and obliterate the narrow-minded ones who are so revolting—and unethical.

Almost all of us reject the "right" of the self-righteous. But it is very difficult to give up our godly indignation. Very few of us can distinguish between our moments of close association with God and the moments when we sit in God's Chair.

SUMMARY

We have been examining a common problem in human existence: how to know when the way one is communicating with another is "healthy" and when it is not. Everyone, as we have seen, has a need to exert power. But there seems reason to believe that we can, if we wish, harness this need so that when we move from *self-assertion* to *aggression* we do not have to move into *destructive aggression*. This kind of control can be learned as we move through the stages of moral development from the primitive response to punishment and authority to a mature sense of community in which we seek our own wholeness in sensitivity to the wholeness of others.

The goal toward which such development moves is expressed in this test: "Whatever develops, enlarges, enhances human personalities is good; whatever restricts, degrades, or injures human personalities is bad."[21] The test is rigorous because it covers sins of both omission and commission in everyday life. It even reaches into such things as

> a failure to speak when someone needs encouragement; a hasty response that suggests indifference; an arbitrary order that wounds someone's ego; a seemingly innocent remark that hurts someone's pride; a word of disapproval in a context that magnifies the disapprobation; gossip; a half-truth, or the full truth at the wrong time and place.[22]

[21]Thomas R. Nilsen, *Ethics of Speech Communication* (Indianapolis, Ind.: Bobbs-Merrill Co., Inc., 1966), p. 9.
[22]*Ibid.*, p. 6.

ETHICAL SELF-EVALUATION

Circle the number that is closest to the way you feel.

5 means "I almost always act this way."
4 means "I usually act this way."
3 means "I often act this way."
2 means "I occasionally act this way."
1 means "I almost never act this way."

1. When a clerk makes an error in my favor, I keep quiet.

   5   4   3   2   1

2. When I am given a test in private I cheat if it will improve my grade.

   5   4   3   2   1

3. In an argument I twist the facts to my advantage when I am angry.

   5   4   3   2   1

4. I tell the truth as I know it.

   5   4   3   2   1

5. I exaggerate the facts when it is to my advantage.

   5   4   3   2   1

6. When a person invites me to dinner and I do not want to go, I make excuses.

   5   4   3   2   1

7. I flatter people to get my way.

   5   4   3   2   1

8. I keep information from my spouse/lover about some of my activities.

   5   4   3   2   1

9. I get involved in sexual relationships that I keep secret from the people I am most closely related to.

   5   4   3   2   1

10. I have ways of cheating at the grocery store.

    5   4   3   2   1

11. I hide blemishes in my car when I am trading it in.

    5   4   3   2   1

12. After an automobile accident I give somewhat false statements to the police.

5	4	3	2	1

13. I pad my expense accounts.

5	4	3	2	1

14. My tax accounts are as dishonest as I dare make them.

5	4	3	2	1

15. I try to impress my friends.

5	4	3	2	1

Add the circled numbers and place the sum here:_____

The highest score possible is 75; the lowest, 15. The lower you score, the more ethical you are. The higher the score, the more you are a "scoundrel" by your own evaluation. One of the authors scored 37, which makes him neither saint nor sinner. He will probably spend eternity in Purgatory.

EXERCISES

1. Describe an incident in which you found yourself reacting with hostility to others because they had rejected the ideas you were urging them to accept. For example, you may have tried to get your parents to accept a boyfriend, or a girlfriend, about whom they were dubious. They listened, but held fast to their doubts.

   Ask yourself the following questions: How did my hostility affect my relationship with my parents? How did it affect our later communication on this topic? What did it do to my self-image?

   Visualize how you might have made a "better" response.

2. Think of someone in your community (or among your acquaintances) whom you have tried to persuade without success. Design a way of confronting him or her without diminishing the mutual respect between you.

3. Develop your own ethic for interpersonal communication. Be prepared to explain it orally and compare it with the one described in this chapter.

4. Be prepared to comment, in terms of the ethical approaches the chapter presents, on each of the following:
   a. Those who participated in Gandhi's resistance movement were known as *Satyagrahi*. Before people could be accepted as *satyagrahi* they had to accept the principle that in the search for truth they would not do injury to others. Beyond that, "the satyagrahi must re-examine continuously his own position—for his opponent may be closer to the truth than he.... The objective of satyagrahi is to win

the victory over the conflict situation—to discover further truths and to persuade the opponent, not to triumph over him" (Joan V. Bondurant, *Conquest of Violence*).

    b. "What should be our policy toward non-Marxian ideas? As far as unregenerate counter-revolutionaries and wreckers of the socialist cause are concerned, the matter is easy: We simply deprive them of their freedom of speech. . . . Within the family it is harder. There we must show them how they are mistaken" (from the writings of Chairman Mao).

5. List the ways in which you exercise control over the other person when you are the listener. Prepare to talk about what the list reveals about you.

6. Think of a time when you had to give up, or cover up, one of your values in order to meet the expectations of another person. After the experience was over did you regret the coverup? Did you feel that the relationship with the other person was just as firm as ever? Did you feel that your coverup had changed the relationship? How did you conclude that you would act if and when such a situation came up again?

7. In an exercise with one other person, try to persuade him or her to accept certain of your ideas or views. The other person will respond to you with such statements as "No, thank you"; "I can't accept that"; "Sorry, I just can't see it"; "Never"; and so forth. See if you can remain interested in the other person as a person, giving him or her full exposure to your views without trying to put him or her down.

8. Think of the moments in which you have wanted to be "heroic." Try to understand what made the feeling so strong in you. How completely did it dominate your energy and attention? Talk about what you think this effort tells you about who you are and what you want out of life.

9. It is popular to say, "A gun is neither good nor bad. It is how it is used that counts." Can the same thing be validly said about communication? Justify your answer.

10. Think of the environment in which you live (town, campus, farm, etc.). What stage of moral development (as Kohlberg discusses it) is generally represented in its population?

12

From Monologue to Dialogue

> Every man is a potential adversary, even those whom we love. Only through dialogue are we saved from this enmity . . .
>
> *Reuel L. Howe**

> If you and I were to change places, I could talk like you . . .
>
> *The Book of Job*

A woman amused the other students in one of our classes by telling about meeting a "guy" at a folk festival who was the best conversationalist she had ever known. It turned out that she could not remember anything in particular that he had said or that in fact he had even talked very much. She had been the one who talked, and she really did not remember what she had talked about. But she yearned to meet this person again and feared that she would not, as it was one of those events to which people came from long distances. "I have never been as free and as exhilarated in my talk with anyone. And you are wrong, I only had one drink all night. I ranged free and easy. I was so fluent and said things that were meaningful. My life seemed just right that night. There was no show-off—and that's not me. I knew he understood and that we understood much together. There was a strange intimacy—and yet there was no intimacy at all. This is one of the most beautiful and most precious memories of my life."

It turns out that occasionally complete strangers quickly develop openness and intense relationship, largely perhaps because they know that they will not meet again and thus are not risking entanglements and

*From Reuel L. Howe, *The Miracle of Dialogue*. By permission of The Seabury Press, Inc.

FIGURE 12-1

commitments. This may be what happened here. But it is well that the woman remembers the incident cited, for she will know that moment when she is met, confirmed, and listened to in depth only a few times, even if she lives to be an ancient lady. Many, many times she will talk to impress, and her auditor will indulge her, especially if he is male. (She is an extremely attractive person.) Many times she will argue and be caustic. (She is an aggressive person, too.) How much of her verbal demand is the consequence of hungering for a person who understands her one can only speculate. How many people never know what it is to be listened to at all and spend their lives talking to themselves in the presence of other people?

The levels of interpersonal communication exist on a continuum between self-talk, at one end, and depth of understanding of others—real dialogue—at the other. This chapter concerns those levels.

In even the most superifical exchange, however—in which one or both people are talking almost entirely for their own benefit—each person is to some extent, aware of his or her involvement with the other. The diagram in Figure 12-1 is an inaccurate perception of the way interpersonal communication works. This diagram fails to account for the basic ingredient of communication, a relationship. This last chapter, exploring in depth the perspective of the first chapter, concerns that ubiquitous and enveloping, if vaporous, feature of communication, which is added in Figure 12-2. Perhaps the significance of human relationship to the way we talk and listen is best borne out by studies of the likenesses and differences among the several schools of psychotherapy.

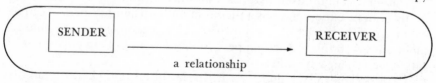

a relationship

FIGURE 12-2

In discussing this, Dean Barnlund says that "relationship is therapy."[1] By relationship he means the affective state, the emotions aroused by the communicants, which, as suggested in Figure 12-2, determines the level of the communication. We discussed the role of emotions in communica-

[1]Dean Barnlund, *Interpersonal Communications: Survey and Studies* (Boston: Houghton Mifflin Company, 1968), p. 673.

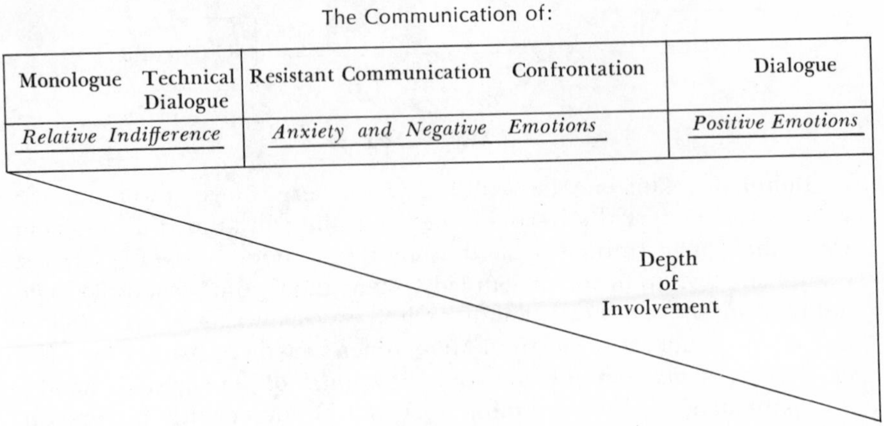

The Communication of:

Monologue Technical Dialogue	Resistant Communication Confrontation	Dialogue
Relative Indifference	*Anxiety and Negative Emotions*	*Positive Emotions*

Depth
of
Involvement

FIGURE 12-3

tion in Chapter 7. In this chapter we refer to the emotions only insofar as an examination of them lets us see into the character of the differences among the levels of communication. Or, to turn it another way, the level a person seeks in a communication is the consequence of the emotions aroused in the communication, ranging as they do over the continuum from indifference to the other person to deep concern for that person.

The conceptual framework of this final chapter may be visualzed as shown in Figure 12-3.

MONOLOGUE

Communication marked by indifference for the other person results in a speech in which the intended receiver is the self. The other person serves almost exclusively as a stimulant. Just as an amputated leg or arm can be experienced as a phantom limb, so another person can be experienced as a part of one's own communication system—a kind of phantom.[2] And this is what happens in monologue, a kind of communication we learn early in life.

The Russian psychologist A. R. Luria found that children talk six times as much in the presence of others as when alone. Apparently, internal speech is excited by the presence of another child. Internal speech, or *verbal thought* if you like, develops as the child internalizes the

[2]Ludwig von Bertalanffy, "The Mind-Body Problem: A New View," in Floyd W. Matson and Ashley Montagu, eds., *The Human Dialogue* (New York: The Free Press, 1967), p. 233.

partner who is not present, a feat that depends on, as a first stage, imagining that one is talking to another person—best done when one has somebody present. In this way children turn themselves into the recipients of their own messages. Recently we asked a four-year-old girl to repeat a comment that was unclear. She looked startled for a moment and then replied, "Oh, I was talking to myself."

But children are not the only ones who do this. Professors (the better ones, who are essentially our more mature children) behave similarly quite often in their lectures. Their faces may go vacant, eyes lose focus; perhaps the head will tilt back while they explore some thought just at the edge of awareness. All creative people have this self-orientation. While monologue, by definition, means a minimum of involvement with the other, self-listening is at a maximum, and this, as suggested earlier, is extremely valuable.

On the other hand, the listening of monologue may be for the purpose of self-adoration rather than for the exploration of one's thoughts. When this happens a self-reflective smile (a dead giveaway) dominates the speech, especially at the end of sentences. The articulation of such speech, almost always unduly precise, expresses language to match, usually ornate. This behavior is all highly infuriating to others, often arousing a caustic response.

However, we all do this "face work," and when it is half hidden it is socially acceptable.[3] Indeed, one's feelings about oneself, one's position with one's conversants, and one's status at large are always involved in one's communication. We may lapse into silence, overrespond, joke, mimic, argue, ignore, belittle, bitch, praise, blame, or laugh in order to draw attention to ourselves. This is inevitable, for we are all self-conscious; in fact this is one of the chief accomplishments of language. The laws of human interaction do not rule out "face work"; they can and do order it into the background.

Yet some people insist on talking openly for their own amusement and amazement, and it is this that is infuriating. If they do this in most of their interaction, they gradually evolve into socialized isolates; that is, they spend much of their time with people but are actually alone. Any honest emotional exchange initiated by another causes them to grow silent or flippant, in some way to evade the relationship suggested by conversation.

Narcissistic monologue is largely self-destructive, but exploratory monologue has its important value for both the individual and society, as noted previously.

[3]Erving Goffman, *Interaction Ritual* (New York: Doubleday & Company, Inc., 1967), pp. 5-45.

TECHNICAL DIALOGUE

The listening of technical dialogue is more fully alert to the presence of the other person than that of monologue. Indeed, the interaction is mutual, which is not the case in monologue. One person speaks, the other answers, and the first makes a rejoinder. Each recognizes that "it takes two to tango," that without the other person the communication intended is incomplete. As one might expect, the content of technical dialogue is characterized by two basic elements: (1) The topic of discussion concerns objective things, and (2) the emotions expressed concern relationships with things, not with the other person.

Concerning the former, the topic, we humans live in a physical and social environment that, of necessity, must command much of our attention. Hence the talk about weather, crops, taxes, the price of automobiles. Considering people's inescapable need for food, clothing, and shelter, economic discussion is basic and fundamental to all other needs. Much as we may deplore materialism, exploration into the flights of spirit is not possible or sensible when the conditions for existence are distressing or out of order. Even the most spiritually oriented person recognizes the significance of technical dialogue to civilization. And indeed, it was the ability to accumulate technical information that led to the Industrial Revolution, beginning in England about 1760 and reaching its peak in the automation of recent years. Thus the plethora of goods of the Western world. Advertising, which provides many of the stimulants for technical dialogue at this point in history, keeps us all alert to the latest improvements in a multitude of things, some valuable, some not. Of course, it is the scientific dialogue beneath the technical advance that gave us not only the comforts of our age but, unhappily, atomic bombs, deadly germs, and devastating gases. The development of these kinds of destructive goods shock the student of communication into recognizing the limitations of technical dialogue.

But the purpose of technical dialogue is not to hold the world together but to accumulate information about the environment so that people may deal with it to their common advantage. Both the Brown-Carlsen test and the Educational Testing Services STEP Test of Listening, as well as the Science Research Associates tests and others, are designed to measure a person's ability to participate effectively, as a listener, in technical dialogue. Indeed, humanity's phenomenal success in mastering the physical environment is the consequence of an educational system, of which the listening tests are an example, that is designed almost exclusively to improve the capacity to participate in technical dialogue. As early as the fourth grade reading tests are constructed to see how accurately the child remembers specific data in a story or essay. The lecture, the teaching machine, even the book, which dominate our educational scheme, are designed in the interest of developing the power to participate in technical dialogue. Tests and examinations measure the ability to listen to technical dialogue. Thus it is the skill of listening, not intelligence or reading ability, that correlates most highly with the capacity to make good grades in school.[4]

Competence in technical dialogue is indispensable to an industrial culture.

The second characteristic, as noted, is that the emotions expressed in technical discourse are associated directly with things and only indirectly with other people. Many, perhaps most, social relationships evolve out of exchanges with people with whom we work, and these friendships are based on the mutually agreeable feelings aroused by conversations about the work. Take away the work and the people are strangers to each other. Where technical dialogue dominates a person's communication, it becomes extremely difficult for that person to understand himself or herself and even the members of his or her family.

Harold McCurdy compares the communication between most people with efforts to communicate with possibly intelligent creatures on some far-off planet in some galaxy 18 or perhaps 800 light-years away.[5] Let us take that imginary trip in the interest of getting a feel for the reason people depend so much on technical dialogue to care for their need to relate to others.

Sebastian von Hoerner calculates that perhaps 6 percent of the planets of the universe have conditions similar to our own and that therefore it it is likely that our intelligence is matched or surpassed by some creature on some far-off planet. But even if this is so, physical contact is impossible. Only by means of messages traveling at the speed of light can we reach some intelligent being in outer space, and even then the people on earth who might send such messages will have died before an answer can return. Perhaps unknowingly we are even now receiving such messages from some point in space, messages initiated before Columbus discovered America. Some basic code known to all forms of intelligence, perhaps a mathematical code, is the only possible way of saying "hello" across cosmic space. This may all seem somewhat odd and irrelevant to a discussion of the emotional involvements in technical dialogue unless one senses that what McCurdy is trying to say, by analogy, is that within the human family the ability to reach across psychic inner space is as difficult as reaching across outer space. So much

[4]Charles T. Brown, "Three Studies in the Listening of Children," *Speech Monographs*, 32 (June 1965).

[5]Harold McCurdy, *Personality and Science* (Princeton, N.J.: D. Van Nostrand Company, Inc., 1968), p. 49.

of each person's meanings consists of private translations for which there often seems to be no code. This is why, at least in part, we place such a premium on technical dialogue. A discussion of the new colors of the latest automobile models is safe and easy and gives some feeling of belonging.

RESISTANT COMMUNICATION

By resistant communication we refer to communication that is dominated and directed by objections to what the other person has said. If the relationship between the people involved is essentially affectionate, the resistant exchange fastens upon facts and rational argument: "I don't see why you insist on seeing France as the ideal democracy. A really democratic president seldom stays in power there for more than a few months. Only a dictatorial personality like De Gaulle . . ." And the other person answers, "Now wait a minute. The instability of French government is the perfect reflection of democracy. If a people are free their government must change as they change. . . ." The listening of resistant communication, at the most rational level, is a search for the logical weakness in the other person's argument. It is much like the listening of technical dialogue (focused at language levels three and four), differing in that it does not share in mutual observations but presents the other person with the differences in their logic and information. If one or both of the conversants is open and calm but alert, one or both may alter his or her position. If emotional resistance comes into play, the arguers usually cease only when exhausted, both still of the same opinion with which they began.

We all know the urge to criticize. It characterizes the mid-level of communication, the ambivalent state between the extremes of indifference and total involvement. If technical dialogue is our most common way of relating indirectly, resistant dialogue is our most common way of relating directly. Here we are, each unique and treasuring our uniqueness, yet needing so badly to be related to others. Half knowing that we will change if we listen, we talk to change the other person for the sake of that needed relationship. Usually it does not work, for the other person has the same needs and uses the same strategy. Thus we are all highly threatened by listening to views that are different from our own. In case you think we make too much of the threat of open listening, let us remind ourselves that the only way some anthropologists find cultures alike is in the terrible resistance each has for the messages of the other. And the social disease of war, organized resistance against the way of "those others," is society's mirror of the individual's fear of listening to another person with different views. Each of us learns through work in a decision-making committee dealing with a controversial issue—shall we abolish grades, dormitories, the ROTC—to sense how difficult it is to find agreement or even compromise. It is common knowledge that 80 percent of all problems in social organizations—whether in industry, education, or government—are personnel conflicts, conflicts of judgment, observations, motivations. More than half of the couples who marry will part in conflict. Resistant communication is the level of involvement that is halfway between indifference and acceptance. It is the state in which we "can't live with them or without them"; it is a consequence of people being unable to listen to each other.

Each of us, in fulfilling our needs, wants to be accepted by others whom, in turn, we want to influence. Here may be the basic source of conflict. We want to help others but also to be helped by others. We wish to assert ourselves but also to comply with the wishes of others. We need to esteem ourselves, but we hear the criticism of others, which we cannot completely ignore or negate. We have to involve ourselves with the lives of other people, many of whom in many ways we cannot trust. Somehow each person must resolve all these conflicts in order to feel united, not anomic. No wonder we resist, for every consequential message upsets the delicate balance within us. As it turns out, when one settles into resistant listening one usually searches out and joins up with other people of the same disposition, listening appreciatively to those with similar complaints. Thus the unstable resistant internal order is confirmed. Misery loves company.

The speech of the persistently resistant communicator is marked by interruptions, corrections, vocalized pauses—um, ah, uh—repetitions, periods of silence, changes in loudness, jerky spurts, and fast talking.[6] For the person who persists in resistant listening, the muscular tension eventually results in stiffness of body and posture, awkwardness of gait, clenched jaws, lips that form a thin red line, and a face that is an "immobile mask, frozen in false smile or anxious frown or counterfeit dignity."[7]

Resistant communication settles for the negative side of the emotional scale. Thus the behavior of such a person is aggressive, dominating, and critical.[8] Yet, as suggested earlier, the state is basically unstable. It is likely, therefore, to retreat to technical dialogue or to move even

[6]Barnlund, op. cit., p. 367.

[7]Sidney M. Jourard, Disclosing Man to Himself (Princeton, N.J.: D. Van Nostrand Company, Inc., 1968), p. 49.

[8]Gay Boyer, "Over-30 Despair: The Reality Gap," Careers Today, February (1969), p. 69.

more negatively to confrontation with those who send the disturbing messages.

CONFRONTATION

When we confront a person the messages we have been receiving from him or her are so upsetting that we wish at last, at least, to stop them. "I've had enough; shut up and listen!" If our feelings about the other person are a mixture of love and hate, we are moved to persuade that person in order to make him or her more acceptable. If, however, our feelings are essentially hateful, we hear the other person as evil, someone to be thwarted, punished, or exterminated symbolically or even literally.

While the persuader in resistant communication hopes to win over the other person, the confronter hopes to embarrass or, in one way or another, destroy the other person. Confrontation is excited by intense passion, which controls the communication. And note this: The most important character of such passion is the complete identity between self-behavior and self-ideals. This takes away the source of our more usual restraints. At once we perceive a complete incompatibility between the other person's behavior and his or her avowed ideals. Thus the purpose of confrontation, conscious or otherwise, is to force others to confront themselves, to see themselves as they are. With such an intent, we can listen only to that which reinforces our own absolute rightness and unquestioned judgment. Hence the vindictiveness and lack of restraint, indeed the affirmation of passion. As is demonstrated every day in the street and on the evening telecast, the vicious talk of angry people in confrontation often leads to physical violence, to behavior much like that ascribed to the person they want to destroy.

Since the spread of radio and television, social confrontation has become a powerful tool for social change. At the time when we wrote the first edition of this book, in the early 1970s, we were in the midst of the black and student uprisings. For the past five years, however, aside from the nationwide confrontation of Richard Nixon we have had little in the way of social confrontation except by small, militant groups.

It is our observation that the society is always changing, just as a person is. As a consequence of the now generally accepted immorality of the Vietnam War, the new awareness of the suppression of women and blacks, and the shocking revelation of gangsterism in government, we have a president who won an election with moral arguments. At this writing, Congress is writing a self-initiated, stringent ethical code. The Establishment is self-conscious and is confronting itself. Even business and industry is listening to its workers, as has seldom been the case in the past.

Confrontation is the communication tactic that commends itself when the other party has lost its sensitivity, and it becomes a social phenomenon when those in authority do not listen to the impact of their behavior and decisions. As we noted in the power and conflict chapters, the word comes down from Washington, and the executive offices of all the institutions, very readily. Almost all people have their ears open to their "superiors." However, almost always there is a feeling among those in charge that they are listening to those in lower echelons. The fact that they are listened to tends to deceive them into believing that the reason this is true is that they have listened to, and have understood, their listeners. Breathes there a teacher who has not been embarrassed to find, upon congratulating himself or herself on his or her effectiveness, that students conceive of the course as off course. The role of sending messages tends to blunt the power to receive messages. Even in healthy organizations the communication audits show that the word tends not to get to the top as readily as it gets down. Water will not flow uphill. It has to be pumped. Confrontation pumps the word to the top.

It is not clear to us where in the maze of social institutions listening at the top is causing frustration. But given the nature of speech flow in social structures, we know it is and thus periodic social confrontation is inevitable.

At this time, when authority is in a more responsive state, confrontation communication is being exercised more in one-to-one relationships, less in organizations. The still-increasing divorce rate is probably our best index of this phenomenon. We find among our students a great loneliness, as discussed in the chapter on the self-concept. Moreover, the times have led students to a special concern about their careers and their futures in general. Private concerns are the focus of their attention, and therefore confrontation communication is being exercised more in the private sector than in the public sector.

The consequences of confrontation, private or social, are these: (1) Recognition comes to the person who has not been listened to; (2) emotional turmoil ensues; (3) objectives are clarified; (4) new leaders evolve (in social confrontation); and (5) changes take place. The relatively invisible person gains recognition for his or her existence by the very act of confrontation. The chapter on emotion explains in some detail the role of emotional turmoil in changing what is heard. If the contestants are reasonably well matched, the language becomes increasingly exclusive and abusive. Listening deteriorates, and verbal abuse may lead to physical violence. Ultimately, out of the chaos some semblance of order arises after exhaustion has been reached on one side or the other, or both. In the struggle, objectives that were clouded become clearer. Frustration changes perception. In the end, as things improve, one will note that the listening indicates understanding of the position of the other person.

DIALOGUE

Let us make clear at the outset of an examination of dialogue that dialogue is not some ideal that belongs to a nonexistent peaceful world. Even the gentle Martin Buber said that he often struggled with his partner in order to alter that person's view.[9] Dialogue goes directly and honestly to the difference between "me and thee," and this requires an immense toughness of self—for it does combat without going on the defensive. And so there is a considerable difference between the struggle of dialogue and that of confrontation. In confrontation, the purpose is the humiliation of the other person. When, however, conflict develops between people in dialogue, the other person is confirmed. The other is looked upon as responsible and competent even though he or she may not be persuaded.[10] Even downright rejection of a view can still stay within the framework of dialogue. To reject ideas or behavior in another while confirming him or her as a person is, of course, difficult, requiring a deep faith in self. And yet this is the true test of one's ability to carry on dialogue. It is one thing to feel in such a way as to say "I don't like you" and quite another thing to say "I am getting angry with you." The former judges you and excludes you and initiates the termination of dialogue—the work of anxiety. Saying "I am getting angry," however, makes an authentic statement about one's feelings, recognizes the status of the relationship, and musters the courage to continue the dialogue. It does not cover up, as in the distortion "I like you" (when actually I don't), nor does it polarize the feelings of the two conversants, as is likely when one puts labels on the other person that he or she can do nothing about. The upshot is that the deepest level of human interaction has a profound faith in the intentions and the ideal self-concept of the other person—attained when things and events are seen as he or she sees them.

Why is this empathy difficult to achieve in the face of conflict?

Above all else, the need of every person is to be confirmed as he or she is. How else can we hope to be more? Without a future what is hope? And what is life without hope? But no person is capable of doing his or

[9]Martin Buber, *The Knowledge of Man* (New York: Harper & Row, 1965), p. 179.
[10]Jourard, *op. cit.*, p. 123.

her own confirming. In our search for confirmation, however, we deceive ourselves if we dare not differ with others, for we are different. And so, only as we are confirmed in our uniqueness are we confirmed at all. Our greatest assurance depends on support for what we are when we dissent from another person's opinion. But as Buber points out, this is probably the Achilles' heel of the human race.[11] Almost all humans are stingy with support except when they are agreed with—when they are confirmed in their uniqueness. So the great moments in dialogue are hard to come by. Let it be clear that we are not saying that people have to be in conflict with each other in order to have dialogue. What we are saying is this: (1) We really have no test of the ability to carry on dialogue if the talk has no threat in it, and (2) one actually does not know the deepest level of dialogue except when one is comfortably related to a person from whom one differs greatly.

The first point should be obvious. The test of anything is its ability to endure under stress. The second point is not so obvious. The injunction to "love thine enemy" gets at the issue. This command is essentially an invitation to know the deepest experiences in relationship—drawing heavily on one's courage. The ultimate in *self-confirmation,* thus, takes place when one trusts one's enemy.

By definition, the defensive posture is the acceptance of self-doubt. The political leader, for instance, who insists that "we will bargain only from a position of strength" reflects fear, not strength. The perception of the self as strong when one is weak is a deception that comes because one blames the other for one's feelings. Such a person conceives of the enemy as wholly distrustful, thus freeing himself or herself from responsibility for his or her own feelings. If one really wants to talk openly and defenselessly with an enemy, one must develop sufficient trust in oneself to produce responsible behavior in the other—which means that one faces possible treachery, having dropped one's guard. Conversely, by maintaining one's guard one excites the defensiveness of the enemy and thus ensures the failure of dialogue.

Perhaps the hardest of all lessons to learn is that defensive listening (which, as we all know, establishes pseudo-dialogue) is irresponsible behavior. Defensive behavior insists that the responsibility for one's feelings is in the other person. Let it be clear that the lowering of our defenses, especially once mutual defense has developed, may be a miscalculation. But then the escalating of our defenses may also be a mistake. There is no guaranteed safe path for people in conflict. The question is, Shall we depend on our capacity to survive in dialogue or in defense? Defense and dialogue are mutually exclusive behaviors, and

---

[11]Martin Buber, "Distance and Relation," *Psychiatry,* 20 (1957), 97–104.

there is danger in either course because no person has complete control over another person.

Consider what we are saying as it applies to the healing professions. The basic character trait of the effective psychotherapist is the ability to trust in his or her own health while listening to a sick patient. And this is possible only if the therapist believes the relationship will stir the potential health of the patient. Two swim as one only as each gives up one swimming arm to embrace the other. The therapist confirms the sick person and thus initiates the healing, but this is not achieved without risk. And so the great test of the professional listener is the capacity to maintain the relationship when his or her partner is sinking.

In similar fashion, the great test of a love relationship is the ability of partners to listen to each other when in conflict. Can the one embrace the other when differences arise? Each is tested. "Do I have enough tolerance for myself to embrace a person whose very being I learn stimulates my awareness of those qualities I dislike in myself?"

Our capacity to carry on a dialogue with a politician, a policeman, a teacher, a teenager, a foreigner, a whore, a homosexual, a thief, a murderer, an insane person, or even a professor is the capacity to tolerate the feelings about the self aroused when we identify with the other person—to understand life from the other's point of view. After all, life can be lived the other person's way: He or she is living proof. It is the fear aroused by contemplating this prospect that cuts off the dialogue.

Abraham Maslow asserts that safety holds priority over growth, which means that in the presence of threat defense is inevitable. One can hardly argue with him in the face of the evidence. But this is the reason that few humans experience much dialogue in the course of a lifetime.

Dialogue, then, above all else, is based (1) on faith in the self (2) entrusted to the other person in the exchange of communication.

Second, dialogue means that one has deep concern for the other person.[12] If a dialogue exists between two people, each considers the other an inviolate entity, a person to be concerned about. Neither will use the other for his or her own personal gain. The relationship is prized above any control or advantage.

It is the break in such a relationship, when it is romantic, that is the source of all sad love songs, expressing the sickening emptiness that is felt when a deep faith in a relationship with another has withered. The relationship of dialogue is one in which each person assumes responsibility for the relationship and, indeed, for the other person.

[12]Milton Mayeroff, On Caring (New York: Harper & Row, Publishers, Inc., 1971).

THE LANGUAGE OF DIALOGUE

To fix the concepts and initiate the attitudes of dialogue, it may be helpful to speak of the role and quality of the language used. In so doing we should be careful to recognize that there are no gimmicks that work; the language that works is guided by appropriate intent.

Yet the language that works is a guide to us in moments when dialogue is threatened. We had a call from a man this morning whose first response to a proposed meeting was, "Well, it is a little premature. You and I have not yet discussed ____." In our urge to maintain the best of relations we responded, "Perhaps I have forgotten something that should be taken care of first. What do you think we ought to do before the meeting?" This response was guided by the need to preserve the dignity of our conversant. Thus the language was, we hope, appropriate. We have noted that the language of people who are able to talk to many people at deep levels is replete with phrases such as "I may be wrong, but here is the way I see it . . . It could be . . . What would you think . . . I think what I am trying to say . . . Isn't there something missing here . . . What you say might be so . . . I don't think I know if . . ." The statement is tentative, open to alteration. For some people these phrases seem unsure and in direct opposition to the description of the courage of dialogue. But the peculiar thing about the language of confidence is that on the surface it sounds weak. It is tentative in order to ensure accommodation to the other person. Conversely, language that says "This is the way it is. There are no ands, ifs, or buts . . ." on the surface sounds as if it comes from the mouth of a strong person. Such sure language allows, if possible, only one interpretation. But again, it is the flexible person, seeing the possibility for several or many interpretations, who is strong, strong enough to accommodate, perhaps, a less flexible conversant.

Yet we hasten to add that strength is not wishy-washy accommodation to anything. It is not fearful confusion. And this should be added: The fearful conformist may use the language phrases of the strong person as a camouflage. "I really don't know what to think" may mean that the speaker cannot tolerate the responsibility for taking a position—in which the nonverbal cues give us our best clues—but it is also the language of the person who truly has an open mind willing to listen and to find a position, qualities that are necessary to preserve a healthy relationship. When we are too sure of our words we are not listening to them or to the words of others. We are listening to fears, which are demanding firm and legal definitions. Legal language is abstract, logical, and technically correct. But the language of dialogue is spontaneous, free, noncritical, tentative, reflective, searching—based on faith and tolerance. When people meet in dialogue their language is not an analysis of the rights and privileges of each other but a mutual participation of the lives involved.

Telling Back

Carl Rogers has lifted into prominence the value of telling back to the other person what we, the listener, think that person has said. It is a way of giving the speaker a chance to correct our listening impressions, of correcting communication as the communication proceeds. But this takes courage, for our own first interpretations always come from our own needs. In changing the language to fit the needs of our conversant we are changing ourselves—because speaking, as we discovered in Chapter 5, has a self-hypnotic effect. Yet if we can restate other people's statements to their satisfaction we tell them that we are trying to listen as they want to be listened to and thus, out of appreciation, they in turn become sensitive to our needs and try to make no greater demand than their judgment tells them we can stand. So, in effect, careful restatement by the listener creates in both parties the conditions for dialogue.

This telling back technique has been developed and discussed most widely in connection with psychotherapy. It is, however, an equally valuable instrument among healthy people in conflict—particularly where the conflict has hardened into confrontation.

A friend of one of the authors tells of an occasion when his teenaged son, in the course of a disagreement, called him a "phoney." The father replied calmly, "You say I am a phoney."

"Yes," said the son.

"This is not pleasant to hear, but if that is the way you see me, I can understand why you don't want to go on vacation with me. But I don't know why you see me as a phoney."

The son began to explain, "You try to press your damned middle-class values on me. You've booby trapped me into needing to live on a luxury income."

"You're saying I am a phoney because I am exposing you to a way of living that will put you into the rat race. You would like to be free."

"Yes," said the son softly, with relief, knowing he was understood.

"I am sorry, and I don't know what to do about it. I almost feel like I am condemned for existing. I don't know how to make you entirely free of me . . ."

On the son's choice the two went on vacation together—and a good one, the turning point in a deteriorating relationship. In the young man's search for independence he had come to perceive his father as "the enemy." The father's statement of this perception in language that confirmed the son helped them both understand each other better.

As anybody who has tried this knows, the emotion of the restatement is highly important. It would have done no good if the father had said "You say I am a phoney" with feelings of resentment, anger, or disbelief. This would have been defending against the blow. The son would have struck again or, if frightened, would have searched for cover. But the calm, and perhaps sad, "You say I am a phoney . . . I don't know how to . . ." was an acceptance of the intent of the son—the way the son had to be heard if he was to be understood. In return for being understood the son lowered his defenses against the father and in his new openness perceived the father more nearly as the father perceived himself.

He also saw how the father could accept himself even when confronted by the label "phoney," the implicit challenge in every confrontation: "I am going to make you see yourself as you are." To be understood and accepted by a person we attack is to create the conditions in ourselves to understand that person. These are the magical results of the restatement. But once again, the magic becomes a fraudulent gimmick unless the language is guided by the intent to confirm and respect the one who is attacking us. The magic is our real, not feigned, confirmation of our confronter, who is confirmed even as he or she attacks us.

When all is said and done in the search for the way we poor humans thrash about for understanding of each other, it comes down to this: The madness in our effort is generated by desperate doubt about our own worthiness. Conflict in a dialogue stimulates this basic anxiety. Depending, as we must, on language to be human, we build a life out of a stack of abstract values by which we direct ourselves. Thus we rest our lives on our values, the vaporous wings of a prayer. These values must be confirmed by others; otherwise they die and we die. Research has demonstrated time and again that each of us is unique in our perceptions, there being no more alikeness among friends than among strangers or enemies. Friends are united and confirmed in their common ideals. Society exists in common aspirations. Therefore dialogue between people both develops and depends on trustful openness among people in search for common ideals and hopes. This is the human story.

It came to us as something of a shock to find near the close of a course that many students do not grasp the concept of dialogue as difficult to attain but see it as an unrealistic ideal. One very bright and sensitive student wrote a paper called "Dialogue," composed of five devastating love scenes, abusive and exploitive, much in the vein of *Who's Afraid of Virginia Wolfe*. As one of the authors began to explain that these were defensive battles in which neither tried to understand the other the student said, "Yes, I know. Over and over I tried to write experiences where trust, depth of understanding, and empathy took place, but they all came off false. Then I looked over all my relationships and I studied all the talk on campus. There are no beautiful conversations. If I am going to write dialogue, I said, I have to write it like it is."

Professor and student talked past each other for several exchanges until it dawned on the professor that the student, and at least the more articulate students in the class, conceived of "dialogue" as any conversation, and that confrontation was the closest thing to honest conversation that is ever achieved in this life. "Dialogue" as used in this chapter is for many students, we have learned, an unattainable ideal. We have described dialogue as a reaching for the most basic satisfaction in life, without which full humanness is not attained. The students knew this. They understood the description of dialogue that you have just read. But for them it was like an atheist's description of God.

We can still feel the eyes of the student who wrote the abusive dialogues pleading for understanding.

CONCLUSION

Faith has a contempt for fear and is therefore risk-taking. In monologue, risk-taking involves deep trust of the self but little risk with others. As alienation from others decreases, we pass through the stages from technical to resistant to confronting communication. When we risk full involvement with another person we enter into dialogue and belong, find self-esteem, and perhaps fulfillment.

INSTRUMENT 12-1

AN INDEX OF YOUR TALK

Assign a rank from 1 to 5 to each of the ten groups of phrases, 1 being most like you and 5 being least like you. Ignore the code letter to the left as you rank the phrases.

		1	Rank
M	To find peace.		____
R	To find a position in which I can do what I want to do.		____

T To find the information necessary to be effective. _____

D To find the meaning of life. _____

C To find a way to eliminate treachery in Washington. _____

2

M To have people notice what I do. _____

R To have people persuaded to see as I see. _____

D To have people I can help. _____

T To have people to study. _____

C To have people I do not like put in their place. _____

3

T To be a salesperson. _____

R To be a U.S. senator. _____

D To be a counselor. _____

C To be a labor leader. _____

M To be a teacher. _____

4

T To go to a museum. _____

R To visit the House of Representatives. _____

D To visit a sick friend. _____

C To go to a prize fight. _____

M To hike in the woods alone. _____

5

R To be a great leader. _____

M To be a great person. _____

D To be a great friend. _____

T To be a great artist. _____

C To be a great evangelist. _____

6

D   To be forgiving.   ——

M   To be attractive.   ——

C   To be self-assertive.   ——

T   To be informed.   ——

R   To be absolutely right.   ——

7

M   To tell a friend what I have done today.   ——

D   To listen as I would like to be listened to.   ——

R   To do what I want to do.   ——

C   To tell the board of trustees what to do.   ——

T   To tell a person how to do something.   ——

8

R   To help people get off my back.   ——

T   To help a person understand how to do something.   ——

D   To help the underprivileged.   ——

C   To help tell a person off.   ——

M   To help myself be more effective.   ——

9

M   To become a self-actualized person.   ——

R   To beat the system.   ——

C   To argue effectively.   ——

D   To become a more useful person.   ——

T   To be well informed.   ——

10

M   To be liked.   ——

D   To be helpful.   ——

C   To be outspoken. ____

R   To be free from other people's expectations. ____

T   To be skilled. ____

Place the numbers for the five categories in the following chart.

M (Monologue)	T (Technical)	R (Resistant)	C (Confronting)	D (Dialogue)
1 ____	____	____	____	____
2 ____	____	____	____	____
3 ____	____	____	____	____
4 ____	____	____	____	____
5 ____	____	____	____	____
6 ____	____	____	____	____
7 ____	____	____	____	____
8 ____	____	____	____	____
9 ____	____	____	____	____
10 ____	____	____	____	____
Total ____	____	____	____	____

What does this say to you?

EXERCISES

1. During the next week engage in a conversation in which you restrict yourself to one of each of the five levels of communication. After each conversation write a statement or make a journal entry concerning the experience. Make an oral report concerning the five experiences, noting particularly the sense of well-being felt in each of the experiences.

2. Think of a relationship in which you have been tempted to confront a person. Confront the person, trying to make the experience as healthy as possible for both yourself and the other person. Report the results. It is quite obvious that this is an assignment in which injury is possible. However,

our experience has been that confrontations that have gotten us into trouble have not been the ones that are cool and collected but, rather, those in which we confronted each other in uncontrolled anger. When we confront without anger we have no desire to destroy, so that the person usually feels that he or she has been helped by the confrontation.

3. List the people who have been most meaningful to you in your life. Discuss these people in terms of the words *confrontation* and *dialogue*.

4. Report your experiences in risking trust, both successful and unsuccessful.

5. Discuss this theme: The worst things that happen in our lives involve breach of faith.

6. Discuss this theme: Every failure in a human is, in the end, a breach of faith in oneself.

7. In Chapter 5 we discussed, as the highest achievement of language, moments of identification or "peak" relationship with a person, nature, some thing or idea. Report a peak experience, then explain it in terms of the concept of trust.

8. Identify a close relationship that has flattened out or deteriorated. During the next week try to make some specific contacts with that person intended to renew the relationship. Analyze the experience. Report to the class (or write a paper or make a journal entry) about the experience.

9. Form dyads in class and discuss any matter of mutual concern. Try to be as completely present to the other person as you know how to be. In more usual language, try to give the other person your undivided attention, your most empathic attention. Exchange your feelings about the results.

10. Do the preceding assignment with a trusted friend or a person in distress who wants to talk with you.

11. Make a speech in which you discuss the national political climate in terms of trust and distrust.

12. Analyze a campus confrontation in terms of the discussion in the chapter. Make a report.

13. Discuss a modern movie in terms of the concepts of confrontation and dialogue.

14. If the equipment is available, make a movie based on the most significant concept you have developed in the course.

Selected Readings

ARGYLE, MICHAEL, *The Psychology of Interpersonal Behavior* (Baltimore, Md.: Penguin, 1967).

Argyle is a British social psychologist with a special interest in the way what he calls "social techniques" determine interpersonal responses. His book contains an interesting examination of nonverbal signals, as well as understandings of communication available in the observation of small groups.

BARNLUND, DEAN C., *Interpersonal Communication* (Boston: Houghton-Mifflin, 1968).

An excellent collection of empirical and theoretical studies on communication is presented here. The book is significant as a source because the items in it were chosen out of a "meaning-centered" view of communication.

W. BENNIS, E. SCHEIN, F. STEELE, and D. BERLEW, *Interpersonal Dynamics: Essays and Readings on Human Interaction*, 3rd ed., (Homewood, Ill.: The Dorsey Press, 1973).

For the most part the essays collected in this volume are written from the context of humanistically-oriented psychotherapists. Sections in the book are devoted to emotional expression in interpersonal relationships, some interpersonal aspects of self-confirmation, and various avenues to personal change involving interpersonal relationships.

BERNE, ERIC, *Games People Play* (New York: Grove Press, 1964).

Intimacy in human interaction is seen, in this book, as rare. The next best alternative, the author thinks, is to engage in communicative "games" (transactions). Berne explains how "parent," "child," and "adult" ingredients function in each person. The hope of the book is to raise the reader's level of awareness concerning the "games" he or she uses. It can also serve as an introduction to transactional psychology.

BUBER, MARTIN, *I and Thou,* 2nd ed. (New York: Scribner's, 1958).

This is Buber's classic statement of what he considers to be the highest relationship conceivable between human beings. It is an important item in the bibliography because it describes communicative relationship in terms that go considerably beyond the usual view of communication as a superficial mechanistic process.

BURTON, JOHN W., *Conflict and Communication: The Use of Controlled Communication in International Relations* (London: Macmillan & Co., Ltd., 1969).

While the author's theories and experiments focus on international conflicts, his ideas could easily be applied to conflict in a dyad with third-party intervention. Two chapters explore the establishment and "control" of communication in conflict. The book is filled with provocative ideas for the student of interpersonal conflict.

D'AMBROSIO, RICHARD, "No Language but a Cry," *Good Housekeeping,* August, 1970, p. 64ff.

The article reports a therapist's struggle, over a period of years, to help an autistic child break through the wall of silence into a world of oral communication. The importance of the report lies in the clues it provides for an understanding of what produced such compulsive silence in the child. Everyone exhibits a degree of silence in communication. Perhaps the factors at work in intensive form here are also at work, to a lesser degree, in "normal" communication.

DAVITZ, JOEL R., *Communication of Emotional Meaning* (New York: MacGraw-Hill, 1964).

A collection of empirical studies is presented involving examination both of how emotional messages are sent and how they are received. Such questions as, "What sort of communicator is best able to read emotional messages accurately?" and "Is there any relationship between the capacity to express emotion and the capacity to interpret it?" are examined. The research presented is unique.

EISELEY, LOREN C., *The Immense Journey* (New York: Random House, 1957).

An anthropologist would not seem a logical choice for inclusion in a bibliography on communication, but Eiseley belongs for at least two reasons: (1) His book is itself a demonstration of the way poets, and exceptional prose writers, can unlock the language so it reveals what was hidden before, and (2) The book discusses the ways in which a person can find an identity with the distant past, with the future, and with the unifying experiences available in life.

ELLIS, ALBERT, *Reason and Emotion in Psychotherapy* (New York: L. Stuart, 1962).

Psychotherapists, in Ellis's view, can work most successfully if they help the client identify the statements he or she makes to him- or herself that form the basis for the emotions he or she experiences. Once identified, the state-

ments can be judged more or less "rational" and, through this new awareness, the client can gain healthy control over the emotional dimension of his
or her life. The book is unique in its effort to tie together silent speech and
emotion.

ELLIS, ALBERT and HARPER, ROBERT A., *A New Guide to Rational Living* (Englewood Cliffs, N.J.: Prentice-Hall, Inc., 1975).

This is an up-dated version of the volume in which the authors explain the
principles of "rational-emotive therapy." It presents emotion as inescapably
tied to self-talk, and therefore open to the same kind of control we can
exercise with any other form of self-talk. An interesting feature: the book is
written entirely in E-Prime—that is, without use of any form of the verb "to
be."

ERIKSON, ERIK, *Childhood and Society*, 2nd ed. (New York: W. W. Norton, 1964).

Part 4 of Erikson's book is entitled, "Youth and the Evolution of Identity."
Along with the chapter that precedes it, on the development of personal
identity, it represents a provocative picture of the ways in which communication and identity are related.

ERIKSON, ERIK, *Identity: Youth, and Crisis* (New York: W. W. Norton, 1968).

As the title suggests, this book flows out of the one cited above, with particular emphasis on crises in the search for identity.

FRANKL, VIKTOR, *Man's Search for Meaning* (New York: Washington Square Press,
1966).

Frankl's book is included in the bibliography because (1) it is an unusual
sample of a human being verbalizing his own experience, (2) it poses a view
of life in which "the search for meaning" is central, and (3) it is a demonstration of the power of inner-speech (listening to self).

FROST, JOYCE HOCKER and WILMOT, WILLIAM W., *Interpersonal Conflict* (Dubuque,
Iowa: Wm. C. Brown Co., Publishers, 1978).

It is a relatively rare thing to find a book surveying the connections between
conflict and communication written by communication scholars. This is
such a book. It approaches conflict as a potentially positive factor in human
interaction, and suggests ways to understand and deal with it.

GOFFMAN, ERVING, *The Presentation of Self in Everyday Life* (New York: Doubleday,
1959).

Goffman studies the events of interpersonal behavior from a sociologist's
point-of-view. He concentrates, in this book, on the idea that in any effort to
communicate each person involved "defines" him- or herself as he or she
wishes the other to see him or her. People are rarely aware that they are
doing this, he thinks, but it can be clearly seen when one analyzes communicative experience. Goffman's book goes into detail in describing how
those definitions are made and what effect they have on the interaction.

GRIER, WILLIAM and COBBS, PRICE, *Black Rage* (New York: Basic Books, 1968).

Two black psychiatrists draw heavily on case histories of blacks struggling to
establish their personal identities in a white society in this unusual report.
The reader becomes aware of the intensity of the impact of the environ-

ment on what an individual says to him- or herself, and on how he or she interprets the messages from outside.

HALL, EDWARD T., *The Silent Language* (Garden City, N.Y.: Doubleday, 1959).

Hall explores, from the viewpoint of an anthropologist, the nonverbal clues that supplement spoken language. He calls attention to physical signs and attitudes, which are profoundly meaningful, but usually overlooked in human communication. His material, more extensive than could be found in most sources, is drawn from both interpersonal and intercultural contexts.

HAYAKAWA, S. I., *Language in Thought and Action*, 3rd ed. (New York: Harcourt Brace Jovanovich, Inc., 1972).

Here is a clearly-written, anecdotally-documented, explanation of the principles of "general semantics." Hayakawa shows how language, thought, and human behavior are bound to interact.

JACOBSON, WALLY D., *Power and Interpersonal Relations* (Belmont, Calif.: Wadsworth Publishing Co., Inc., 1972).

This is one of the most extensive descriptions we have seen of the variety of ways power is expressed in human interaction. Documentation of the conclusions drawn in the book is superb (as is the bibliography at the end of the book).

JOURARD, SYDNEY M., *The Transparent Self* (Princeton, N.J.: Van Nostrand, 1964).

Out of his background as a clinical psychologist the author discusses the experiences that have convinced him that revealing oneself to another person is a doorway to an understanding of the self. Some of the book is addressed to nurses, and some to professional counselors, but the early chapters are provocative for anyone trying to understand the communication process.

JOURARD, SYDNEY M., *Disclosing Man to Himself* (Princeton, N.J.: D. Van Nostrand, 1968).

Jourard develops further the idea he introduced in *The Transparent Self*, namely, a person only becomes known to him- or herself when he or she is able to allow him- or herself to be known to another. Self-knowledge, then, becomes in part a social experience in which those who invite revelation by the other play an important role.

KENISTON, KENNETH, *The Uncommitted* (New York: Harcourt Brace Jovanovich, Inc., 1965).

What sort of influences, discernible in the life history of college students who have "dropped out" of society, have proven to be most influential in shaping the decision of those students? Keniston culls through an imposing number of in-depth interviews and questionnaires and draws some conclusions of special interest to anyone trying to understand how communication (or the lack of it) plays an important formative role.

KENISTON, KENNETH, *The Young Radicals* (New York: Harcourt Brace Jovanovich, Inc., 1968).

In contrast to those college students who "drop out" of society (and are described in *The Uncommitted*), there are those who are motivated to take an active role in reform or revolutionary movements. Keniston sought, again, to identify the forces in the early life of these young people that turned them in the direction of involvement. In the process he sheds additional light on the role of communication in human development.

LANGER, SUZANNE K., *Philosophy in a New Key* (Cambridge, Mass.: Harvard University Press, 1942).

This is a philosophy with language at its core. Langer argues that the human has an "organic need" to symbolize. Symbolizing, in her view, does not simply fulfill social purposes, nor is it a secondary function. The human needs it, she says, to make sense of his or her world. Without it, all would be chaos. The major part of the book ties various symbol systems into that over-arching idea.

LORENZ, KONRAD, *On Aggression* (New York: Harcourt Brace Jovanovich, Inc., 1966).

Perhaps the best known of all ethologists writes here a book showing how pervasive and basic aggressive behavior appears to be among many types of animals. He goes on to conjecture that the human's class of life may be a defensible analog to what is being found in animals. If so, he implies, there are things we can learn about why and how people use power in their interpersonal experiences.

McLUHAN, MARSHALL, *Understanding Media: The Extensions of Man* (New York: McGraw-Hill Book Company, 1965).

A profound change in the destiny of the human took place, as McLuhan sees it, when the electronic media ushered in an age of instant communication. This book describes the fundamental features of this new age and discusses the revolution in communication that he anticipates.

MASLOW, ABRAHAM H., *Religions, Values, and Peak-Experiences* (Columbus, Ohio: Ohio State University Press, 1964).

A number of books exist in which Maslow explains his theory of self-actualization. This is one of them. He deals particularly, here, with those "unifying," transcendent experiences that come unpredictably to self-actualizing people. And a part of his analysis has to do with the role of inner-speech and inner freedom in making the transcendent experience possible.

MASLOW, ABRAHAM H., *Toward a Psychology of Being* (Princeton, N.J.: D. Van Nostrand, 1962).

The book is especially useful to anyone probing the relationship between values and interpersonal communication. Maslow makes an effort to identify the values, and the levels at which they must be satisfied, if a person is to reach self-actualization.

MATSON, FLOYD W. and MONTAGU, ASHLEY (eds.), *The Human Dialogue: Perspectives on Communication* (New York: The Free Press, 1967).

An excellent collection of basic essays on communication is presented here. The topic is looked at from perspectives in psychology, sociology, philosophy, and anthropology. Entries come from such sources as Gordon Allport, Buber, Camus, Fromm, Festinger, Maslow, George Herbert Mead, Rogers,

Weiner, and many others. The introductory essay, by the editors, is a milestone statement regarding communication as the shaper of individual and social destinies.

MAY, ROLLO, *Love and Will* (New York: W. W. Norton & Co., Inc., 1969).

The exercise of will is often described as opposing love. Rollo May disagrees. He shows in this book how the most authentic impulses in life (the evidences of the *daemonic*) have to be held in tension with the relationship impulses in us. Without will, he says, love is not possible; without love, will is destructive. The book has an excellent chapter on dialogue, but the whole book can be read as a treatise on communication.

MAY, ROLLO, *Power and Innocence: A Search for the Sources of Violence* (New York: W. W. Norton and Co., Inc., 1972).

A psychotherapist investigates the factors that produce violence between humans. He finds that it is often the absence of a fundamental power—the power to be—that lies behind the expression of violence by individuals, and he shows how nurturant, humane forms of power can become creative sources of energy. The role of self-talk and dialogue is implicit throughout the book.

MAYERHOFF, MILTON, *On Caring* (New York: Harper & Row, 1971).

This is an extended, informal essay on the effect of "loving" ("caring") in interpersonal relations. The author concludes, essentially, that "caring" means you are concerned both for the growth of self and the growth of the other. Implications for communication are abundant.

MEAD, GEORGE HERBERT, *Mind, Self, and Society* (Chicago: The University of Chicago Press, 1934).

This has become a classic statement of the view that "meaning" is a social phenomenon. Mead asserts that one must call out in him- or herself the same "verbal gesture" that he or she calls out in the other before meaning can be assumed to exist in the interaction. The role of "I" in human thinking is explored more fully than is usual in the literature.

NYE, ROBERT D., *Conflict Among Humans: Some Basic Psychological and Social-Psychological Considerations* (New York: Springer Publishing Co., Inc., 1973).

Although Nye's book treats conflict in a limited sense (that is, as occurring in situations dominated by hostility), it makes a pioneering contribution by identifying factors that must be understood if conflict is to be successfully dealt with. A very useful feature of this book is its extensive bibliography.

PATTON, BOBBY R. and GIFFIN, KIM, *Interpersonal Communication in Action* (New York: Harper & Row, 1977).

The book is designed as a text for the beginning course in interpersonal communication. It reflects a strong orientation toward conceiving communication as a problem in relationships. There are, therefore, very useful sections discussing interpersonal perception, ways in which communicative relationships are defined, the bases of trust, and similar topics.

ROGERS, CARL, *On Becoming a Person* (Boston: Houghton-Mifflin, 1961).

This collection of essays contains a number of chapters dealing with the problems anyone faces in the effort to come to believe in his or her inner world. It asks, "How can a person deal with the expectations others have for his or her life in such a way as to enhance his or her growth in the process?"

ROKEACH, MILTON, *The Nature of Human Values* (New York: The Free Press, 1973).

Perhaps the major study of values, beliefs, and attitudes in the past twenty-five years is summarized and up-dated in this volume. Special attention is given to how values come into being, and how they change. Survey results allow comparison among religious groups, age groups, economic groups, etc. Values are shown to be inseparable from personal identity, and therefore crucial to an understanding of communication.

ROKEACH, MILTON, *The Open and Closed Mind* (New York: Basic Books, 1960).

Rokeach and his associates develop in this book a series of hypotheses related to the characteristics of people who exhibit "open" orientations and those who exhibit "closed" ones. The functions of belief systems and disbelief systems are integrated into the theory Rokeach presents. Both the hypotheses and the experiments reported are unique in the study of psychological openness.

ROSENTHAL, ROBERT and JACOBSON, LENORE, *Pygmalion in the Classroom* (New York: Holt, Rinehart and Winston, 1968).

How do the expectations of a superior regarding the behavior of subordinates affect the self-image of those subordinates? Much has been theorized on that topic. The authors of this book offer documented evidence to support the conclusions they regard as valid. The book speaks directly to the issue of the effect of power exercised by the teacher in the classroom.

SAMPSON, RONALD V., *The Psychology of Power* (New York: Pantheon Books, 1966).

An English psychologist takes a look, here, at the effect of power used in interpersonal relationships. He hypothesizes that such power stands in antithesis to "love." A special feature of the book is the author's analysis of the role power played in the formation of John Stuart Mill and Elizabeth Barrett Browning.

SARGANT, WILLIAM W., *Battle for the Mind* (Garden City, N.Y.: Doubleday, 1957).

A fascinating examination is made, by Sargant, of various forms of psychological suggestion. Chiefly the emphasis is on studying religious ecstasy, the background of "conversion," mass evangelism, etc. Out of such a study come some hypotheses about what kind of psychological states produce optimum "openness" and what kind of overload makes it hard for the individual to handle incoming messages. This is a book about "brainwashing."

SCHUTZ, WILLIAM C., *The Interpersonal Underworld* (Palo Alto, Calif.: Science & Behavior Books, 1966).

Schutz searches out the forces that seem to dominate the silent world of people in interaction. He identifies them as the desire for (1) inclusion, (2) affection, (3) control. His book is devoted to explaining how these forces affect interpersonal responses, and how they are related to each other.

SHOSTROM, EVERETT L., *Man, the Manipulator: The Inner Journey From Manipulation to Actualization* (Nashville, Tenn.: Abingdon Press, 1967).

This book separates and analyzes the power-to-be and the power-over behaviors in all of us.

SPITZ, RENÉ, *The First Year of Life* (New York: International Universities Press, 1965).

Spitz, and his collaborator, Godfrey Cobliner, have made in-depth studies of the first year in the life of human infants, with the focus on what kinds of communication seem to occur between mother and child. Understandings about early life as a source of either security or fear in the communicative experiences of later life emerge from the studies.

SULLIVAN, HARRY STACK, *An Interpersonal Theory of Psychiatry* (New York: W. W. Norton, 1953).

Sullivan develops his conviction that human growth and the psychological illnesses that beset the human can best be understood in terms of interaction among people. His book makes a special contribution when it theorizes about how anxiety is implanted in the life of an individual, what effects it appears to have on human interaction, how it influences the learning and adapting process, and especially how it is associated with the effort to communicate.

WATZLAWICK, PAUL; HELMICK, JANET; and JACKSON, DON D., *Pragmatics of Human Communication* (New York: W. W. Norton, 1967).

This is a pioneering book in that it sees communication as a problem in relationship, and explores the impact of such relationship on the development of the person. The communicative relationships defined are analyzed in some detail, using Edward Albee's *Who's Afraid of Virginia Woolf* as a sample of interaction.

WIENER, NORBERT, *The Human Use of Human Beings* (Boston: Houghton Mifflin, 1950).

One of Wiener's major contributions to an understanding of communication is in what he has to say about feedback and self-correcting systems. He discusses both of those concepts in this book, which is an effort to apply the principles of cybernetics to human behavior.

WILMOT, WILLIAM W., *Dyadic Communication: A Transactional Perspective* (Reading, Mass.: Addison-Wesley Publishing Co., 1975).

Few books have displayed the restraint necessary to study communication only in the context of the dyad. This book exercises that restraint, and the result is a profitable gain in depth. Wilmot is both systematic and imaginative as he explores the nature of communication between two people. The book promises a clarifying and sharpening function for those interested in communication theory.

Index

A

Abdicrats, 213
Acheson, Dean, 212
Acton, Lord, 214
Adler, Alfred, 220
Adventure of Birds, The (Ogburn), 1
Affection, 12
Aggression
ethical factors, 285
and sexuality, 241
Aggressive producer type, 104-5
Agnello, Dr. Joseph, 193
Albee, Edward, 14, 174
Amplification system, 168
Anger
and listening, 175-76
and self-talk, 171
Anshen, Ruth, 119*fn*
Anxiety, 180-82
and judgment, 195-96
self-evaluation instrument, 183-85
Ardrey, Robert, 220
Argyle, Michael, 142, 144, 315
Aristotle, 7, 21, 95, 275
Athens, 125
Attachment, 1

Attention, 63-64
Authority
and conflict, 248, 253-55
solutions to, 231-32
Autocrats, 213-14

B

Bach, George, 22
Bales, Robert, 101
Balzac, Honoré, 48
Barber, James David, 94-95
Barnlund, Dean, 295, 315
Barrett, Edward Moulton, 229
Battle for the Mind (Sargent), 169
Bavelas, Alex, 130
Becker, Ernest, 241, 282
Behavior, 87-95
and general semantics, 111-12
Behavior in Public Places (Goffman), 8
Belief, 132-34
Belonging, 37-38
Bennis, Schein, 315
Bennis, W. G., 17
Berelson, Bernard, 97
Berne, Eric, 315

Beyond Freedom and Dignity (Skinner),
    192*fn*
B-feelings, 16
Bickel, Alexander, 37
Binger, Carl, 178
Birds, 1
Birdwhistell, Ray, 141
Blake, Robert R., 9
Blum, Gerald, 168, 172, 175
Body chemistry
    and listening, 169-70
    and stress, 242
Body image, 43
Body movement, 143-49
Bohr, Niels, 87
Bonding
    and feeling, 10-16
    instinct, 1
    and values, 96-100
Bondurant, Joan V., 293
Bourland, D. David, 137
Brandeis, Louis D., 49
Bridges, Not Walls (Stewart), 13
Bronowski, Jacob, 99, 100, 101
Brothers Karamazov, The (Dostoevsky),
    276-77
Brown, Charles T., 128*fn*
Brown, Roger, 16
Brown-Carlsen test, 298
Browning, Elizabeth Barrett, 229-30
Browning, Robert, 229-30
Bruner, Jerome, 128
Buber, Martin, 22, 288, 304, 305, 316
Burger, Myron, 221
Burton, John W., 316
Buss, Arnold, 171, 175

C

Canada, 31
Caring Relationship Inventory (Shostrom),
    10
Carter, Jimmy, 89-95, 113
Center of the Cyclone, The (Lilly), 45
CIA, 23
Childhood
    ethical development, 283
    peak experiences, 36-37
Children
    effects of power on, 228-30
    rejection of authority, 227
    verbal thought, 296-97
China, 31
Chisholm, Brock, 221
Chomsky, Noam, 62
Christian religion, 48

Cobbs, 317
Columbus, Christopher, 299
Commitment, 85
Communication
    central role of feelings, 83-84
    chain of command, 224-27
    conflict processes, 247-51
    and emotion, 164-82
    ethical factors, 274-90
    fear of, 43-44
    forms of conflict, 251-57
    impact of power on, 212-16
    and interaction, 4-5
    interactive functions, 73-77
    listening, 61-71
    nonverbal messages affecting, 143-53
    orientation test, 105-7
    patterns, 102-5
    and relationship, 2-4
    resistant, 300-302
    role of symbols, 5
    and self-concept, 44-50
    significance, 2
    silent and overt speech, 58-61
    social function, 5-6
    speaking, 71-73
Communication-conflict instrument,
    259-72
Compassion, 174-75
Confidentiality, 22-24
Conflict, 240-72
    of authority, 253-55
    characteristics, 248-51
    constructive and destructive, 244
    defined, 242-45
    in a group, stages of, 246-47
    institutionalized, 247-48
    pervasiveness, 240-42
    of power, 256
    prevalence, 301
    productive management of, 245-46
    over self-other values, 251-52
    of values, 256-57
Conformers, 220-23
Confrontation, 302-4
Congruence, of nonverbal messages,
    153-54
Conscience, 284
Contempt, 290
Couch, Arthur, 101
Courage, to listen, 173-74
Coolidge, Calvin, 94
Coser, Lewis, 243
Cousins, Norman, 181
Credibility, 21
Criticism
    and judgment, 189, 190

and listening, 203–5
and resistant communication, 300

D

D'Ambrosio, Dr. Richard, 75, 316
Danforth Foundation, 38
Davitz, Joel R., 177, 316
Death
    and conflict, 241–42
    and heroism, 282
De Gaulle, Charles, 300
Democracy, 279
Democrats, 213–14
Dependency, 15
De Quincy, Thomas, 109
Descartes, René, 7
Despair, 180–81
D-feelings, 14–16
Dialogue
    confrontation, 302–4
    ethical issues, 288
    language of, 307–10
    nature of, 304–6
    resistant, 300–302
    technical, 298–300
Dictionaries, 114
Discrimination
    and judgment, 189, 190
    nonjudgmental, 205–7
    power of, 191–92
Dominance, 220
Dostoevsky, Feodor, 276
Double bind, 197–98
Dreikurs, Rudolf, 227

E

Edison, Thomas, 85
Educational Testing Service STEP Test of
    Listening, 298
Einstein, Albert, 6, 86, 87
Eiseley, Loren C., 316
Eisenhower, D. D., 91
Ekman, P., 147
Ellis, Albert, 8, 170, 171, 180, 316–17
Ellis, Havelock, 173
Emerson, Ralph Waldo, 124fn
Emotion, 164–82
    anxiety, 180–82
    control of, 177
    and distorted listening, 167
    facial expressions, 147–48
    and feelings, 166–67
    and identity and empathy, 176–77

and intelligence, 182
and judgment, 190
language without, 165
and memory, 167–68
role of self-talk, 170–76
and speech, 177–80
theory of, 168–69
and words, 165–66
See also Feelings
Empathy, 12–13
    and emotions, 176–77
    and listening, 70–71
    and peak experience, 37–38
Encounter groups, 21, 212–13
Energy, 84–87
Epictetus, 164
Erikson, Erik, 228, 231, 317
Eros, 13fn
Ethics, 274–90
    in cases of conflicting values, 287–89
    and contempt, 290
    development of, 283–84
    power problem, 281–82
    and self-determination, 277–81
    self-evaluation exercise, 291–92
    tests of, 275–76, 277
Ethos, 21
Europe, 232, 233
Exodos, 24
Expectations, 191–92
Eyes, nonverbal messages, 143–47
Eysenck, H. L., 107
Eysenck, Sybil B. G., 107

F

Facial expressions
    nonverbal messages, 147–48
    and monologue, 297
    sensitivity test (FMST), 157–61
Family, hierarchy of power, 227
Farther Reaches of Human Nature (Maslow),
    32
FBI, 23
Fear
    distinguished from anxiety, 181
    and listening, 175
    and self-concept, 42–44
Feedback
    role of eyes, 143–44
    and translation, 129–30
Feelings
    and bonding, 10–16
    defined, 8
    and emotions, 166–67
    of inferiority, 220

Feelings (continued)
  in interaction, 8–10
  of powerlessness, 286–87
  projection of, 29
  and quality of relatedness, 16–19
  and relationship, 6–8
  significance in communication, 83–84
  See also Emotion
France, 300
Frankl, Victor, 125, 126–27, 317
Freedom, ethical issues, 277–78, 279–80
French Revolution, 48
Freud, Sigmund, 13*fn*, 220
Friesen, W., 147
Fromm, Erich, 280
Fromm-Reichmann, Freida, 1, 19–20
Frost, Joyce Hocker, 317
Frost, Robert, 222

G

Gandhi, M. K., 289, 292
General semantics, 111–18
Gergen, Kenneth, 172
Germany, 31
Gestalt Prayer, 49
Gibb, Jack, 200, 226
Gibran, Kahlil, 73
Giffin, Kim, 8, 320
Glasser, William, 51, 285–86
Goals, and self-concept, 28
Goethe, J. W. von, 172
Goffman, Erving, 8, 10, 141, 317
Greece (ancient)
  classification of feelings, 83
  importance of myth, 125
  view of emotion, 168
  view of human life, 7
Grier, William, 317
Groups, conflict in, 246–47
Gulliver, J. P., 69

H

Hall, Edward T., 12, 149–50, 164, 318
Hamilton, Alexander, 248
Hands, nonverbal messages, 148
Haptics, 152–53
Harper, Robert A., 317
Harvard Law Review, 49
Hayakawa, S. I., 112, 205–6, 318
Head Start program, 179
Heath, Douglas, 221
Hegel, George, 86
Helmick, Janet, 322

Hendrix, Jimi, 67
Hierarchy of needs, 32–33
Hitler, Adolf, 228
Holmes, Sherlock, 155
Hoover, Herbert, 95
Hora, Thomas, 28
Howe, Reuel L., 294
Hughes, J. P., 62
Humanistic psychology, 31–32
Human-potentials movement, 49

I

I and Thou (Buber), 22
Identification, 126–28
Identity
  and communications, 74–76
  and emotions, 176–77
Inclusion, 13
Incompatibilities, 243–44
India, 289
Industrial Revolution, 298
Inferiority, 220
Information
  acquiring through listening, 71
  power of, 87
  and repatterning of thought, 76–77
Integrity, 285–86
Intelligence
  and achievement, 86–87
  "g" (general) factor, 182
  interplanetary code, 299
  and self-concept, 43
Interdependence, 15–16
Intimacy
  and affection, 12
  proxemics, 149–51
Intimate Enemy, The (Bach), 22
Involvement, 8–9
"Is," 114–15

J

Jackson, Don D., 322
Jacobson, Lenore, 321
Jacobson, Wally D., 318
James, William, 14, 63, 149
Japan, 31
Jefferson, Thomas, 248
Jesus, 98–99
Job, 294
Johannesen, Richard, 288
Johari Window, 46–47
Johnson, Lyndon B., 95

Joplin, Janis, 67, 110
Jourard, Sidney, 46, 152, 197, 274, 318
Judgment, 188–207
  described, 189–91
  vs. discrimination, 205–7
  effect on judge, 200–203
  effect on judged, 196–200
  and expectations, 191–92
  inclusion or exclusion based on, 192–93
  need for, 194–95
  self-evaluation instrument, 207–9

K

Kazantzakis, Nikos, 188
Keller, Helen, 122, 228
Kendon, Adam, 143, 144
Keniston, Kenneth, 318
Kennedy, John F., 212
Kindred spirit, 19–21
Kinesics, 143–49
Kinlife, 13–14
Kissinger, Henry, 232, 233
Knapp, Mark L., 143
Kohlberg, Lawrence, 283–84
Korzybski, Alfred, 111–12, 113, 116
Kunen, James, 129

L

Laing, Ronald D., 198
Langer, Susanne K., 120, 319
Language
  and association, 64
  and attention, 64
  of belief, value, and self-concept,
    132–34
  of dialogue, 307–10
  without emotion, 165
  of eyes, 145–47
  and general semantics, 111–12
  levels of, 120–31, 136–37
  and meaning, 110–11
  structural problems, 114–18
  of values, 124–29
Lasswell, H. S., 89
Leadership
  and power, 223
  styles, 91–94
Learning, 85–86
Leary, Timothy, 8, 9
Leathers, Dale, 147
Leonardo da Vinci, 99–100, 101, 145
  illus., 148

Levy, R., 177
Lies, 275, 276, 278–79
Life
  conflict with death, 241–42
  role of power, 220
Likert, Jane Gibson, 243, 248–51
Likert, Rensis, 243, 248
Lilly, John, 45
Lincoln, Abraham, 69–70, 71
Listening, 61–71
  and body chemistry, 169–70
  confidence for, 131
  of conformers, 220–23
  and control of emotions, 177
  critical, 203–5
  to the double bind, 197–98
  and emotion, 167–77
  to favorable judgment, 199–200
  functions, 70–71
  to oneself, 64, 65–67
  to others, 68–70
  rating scale, 107–9
  resistant, 301
  as silent speech, 58–59
  in technical dialogue, 298–99
  three basic conditions, 63–64
Lives of a Cell, The (Thomas), 15
Logic, vs. feeling, 7
Loneliness, 47–50
Lonely Crowd, The (Reisman), 47
Lorenz, Konrad, 220, 319
Love
  and anxiety, 195–96
  and listening, 172–73
Ludwig, Emil, 155
Luria, A. R., 296

M

Machiavelli, N., 275
McCroskey, James C., 43–44
McCurdy, Harold, 299
McLuhan, Marshall, 110, 319
Maddocks, Melvin, 58
Man's Search for Meaning (Frankl), 125
Mao Tse-tung, 293
Maslow, Abraham, 1, 14, 31–32, 33, 34,
    35, 37, 127, 306, 319
Matson, Floyd W., 274, 319
Mattis, Steven, 177
May, Rollo, 13*fn,* 125, 218, 282, 284–85,
    320
Mayerhoff, Milton, 320
Mead, George Herbert, 3–4, 320
Mead, Margaret, 227

Meaning, 110–34
    general semantics, 111–18
    nonverbal messages, 140–56
    test instrument, 134–35
    and translation, 118–31
    transmission, 62–63
Mediation, 119*fn*
Mehrabian, A., 151, and *fn*
Mein Kampf (Hitler), 228
Memory, and emotion, 167–68
Mexico, 31
Mill, John Stuart, 165
Monologue, 296–97
    ethical issues, 288
Montague, Ashley, 274, 319
Moral self, 44
Morris, Desmond, 220
Mortensen, C. David, 82
Moses, Dr. Paul, 151
Mouton, Jane S., 9
Murray, Henry A., 4
Myth, 125–26

N

Naked Ape, The (Morris), 220
Nazi concentration camps, 125, 126–27
Negative emotions, 10, 18–19, 175–76
Nietzsche, Friedrich W., 125
Nilsen, Thomas, 279, 280–81, 290
Nixon, R. M., 95, 302
Nonverbal messages, 140–56
    eyes, 143–47
    face, 147–48
    hands, 148
    inconsistent with speech, 153–54
    inescapability of, 141–42
    posture, 148–49
    proxemics, 149–51
    reading of, 155–56
    touch, 152–53
    voice, 151–52
Non-zero-sum game, 245
Numbers, 241
Nye, Robert D., 320

O

Ogburn, Charles, 1
Ogden, C. K., 119*fn*
Old Testament, 241
Openness, 22–24
Organizations, conflict in, 248–51, 301

Osgood, Charles, 119 and *fn*
Overstreet, Bonoroo, 42

P

Patton, Bobby, 8, 320
Patton, Gen. George, 194–95
Pavlov, I., 70*fn,* 168
Peak experiences, 35–38
    and identity, 127–28
Pei, M., 62
Perception
    commonality of, 11
    and conflict, 243, 244
    discriminative, 191–92
    and self-esteem, 29–30
Perls, Fritz, 49
Piaget, Jean, 120
Pillsbury, W. B., 63
Plotinus, 240
Polarizing trap, 115–16
Political parties, 247–48
Positive emotions, 9–10, 18–19, 172–75
Posture, 148–49
Powell, W. J., 206
Power, 212–34
    chain of command, 224–27
    conflict over, 256
    conforming to, 220–23
    of discriminative perception, 191–92
    in early life, 228–30
    and ethics, 277–78, 281–82
    in everyday experiences, 230–31
    in family hierarchy, 227
    future problems, 232–33
    hopeful side, 284–85
    impact on communication, 212–16
    information as, 87
    and leadership, 223
    and relationships, 216–19
    role in life, 220
    and self-esteem, 34
    solutions to problems of, 231–32
    temptation of Christ, 98–99
    types, 282
Powerlessness, 286–87
Power orientation, self-evaluation instrument, 234–38
Praise, 199–200
Predictability, 21–22
"Press" exercise, 212–13
Privacy, 49
Projection, 112–13

Proxemics, 149–51
Psychotherapy, 306

R

Reference, 119*fn*
Relationships
    during college years, 38
    communications and identity in, 74–76
    defined, 6–8
    development stages, 11
    quality of, 16–19
    and self-identity, 24
    social function of communications, 5–6
    symmetrical and complementary,
        216–19
    three main factors, 2
    voice of power in, 216–19
Rembrandt, 155–56
Richards, I. A., 119*fn*
Riesman, David, 47
"Right to Privacy, The," (Brandeis), 49
Rogers, Carl, 40–41, 137, 289, 308, 320
Rokeach, Milton, 132*fn*, 321
Roosevelt, Franklin D., 92, 95
Rosenfeld, H., 149
Rosenthal, Robert, 321
Russia, 31

S

Sampson, R. V., 229*fn*, 321
Sapir, Edward, 156
Sargent, William, 168, 321
Saturday Review, 181
Schutz, W. C., 13, 213, 321
Schweitzer, Albert, 124, 126
science, language of, 123
Science of Language, The (Hughes), 62
Science Research Associates tests, 298
Secrecy
    function, 22–23
    and power, 87
Self
    attack on, 252–53
    vs. other, 251–52
    social, 43–44
Self-awareness, 155–56
Self-concept
    communication processes that affect,
        44–50
    disparities that create fear, 42–44

evaluation instruments, 51–56
growth process, 31–39
importance, 28–29
language of, 132–34
of nations, 233
present vs. ideal self, 39–42
and world problems, 30–31
Self-determination, 279–81
Self-disclosure, 46–48
Self-esteem, 28–51
    and chain of command, 226–27
    and commitment, 85
    and conflict management, 245–46
    and eye contact, 144
    and "grumbles," 33–35
    and interpersonal ethics, 285–86
    low, causes of, 41
    and need hierarchy, 32–33
    and perception, 29–30
    role of values, 33
Self-feelings, 14
Self-identity, 24
Self-image, 221–23
Self-listening, 64, 65–67
Self-talk, 170–76
Sensitivity groups, 21
Sex, and eye contact, 144
Sexual excitement, 241
Shostrom, Everett, 10–11, 13*fn*, 14, 322
Shrike, The (Kramm), 188–89
Signs, 171
Silence, and listening, 58–59
Skinner, B. F., 120, 122, 192*fn*
Snyder, Ross, 173
Social self, 43–44
Socrates, 3
Spearman, C., 182
Speech
    defined, 62
    and emotion, 177–80
    functions, 71–72
    inconsistent with nonverbal messages,
        153–54
    resistant, 301
    silent and overt, 58–59
Spitz, René, 146, 322
Statements, translation between, 119–20
Steele, Berlew, 315
Steiner, Gary A., 97
Sterne, Laurence, 140
Stevenson, Robert Louis, 279
Stewart, John, 13
Stoller, Robert, 241
Story of Language, The (Pei), 62
Stress, 252

Sullivan, Harry Stack, 3, 195, 201, 322
Symbols
    role in communication, 5
    vs. signs, 171

T

Tarte, R. D., 168
Telling back, 308–9
Tennyson, Alfred Lord, 134
Terman, Lewis, 43
Thomas, Lewis, 15, 85
Thoreau, Henry David, 74
Thought, repatterning, 76–77
Tolstoi, Leo, 133
Touch, 152–53
Tournier, Paul, 164
Translation, 118–31
    within and between language levels,
        120–23
    role of feedback, 129–31
    between statements, 119–20
    and values, 124–29
Truman, Harry S, 22, 93
Trust, 21–24, 84
Truth, value of, 99

U

United States Congress, 302
United States Constitution, 248
University of Chicago, 146, 173
University of Delaware, 146
University of Michigan, 222
Untermeyer, Louis, 222

V

Values, 95–102
    and bonding, 96–100
    confusion of, 256–57
    ethical conflicts, 287–89
    function, 95–96
    language of, 132–34
    and self-determination, 286–87

    and self-esteem, 33
    self-other conflicts, 251–52
    ultimate, 100–101
Van Gogh, Vincent, 3
Verbalization
    and emotional control, 178–79
    resistance to, 72–73
Vietnam War, 302
Voice, 151–52
Voice of Neurosis, The (Moses), 151
von Hoerner, Sebastian, 299
Vygotsky, Lev, 64

W

Walker, E. L., 168
Wallace, Henry, 22
Watergate, 31
Watzlawick, Paul, 123*fn*, 140, 216, 322
Whitehead, Albert North, 240
Who's Afraid of Virginia Wolfe (Albee), 14,
    309
Wiener, Norbert, 322
Williams, M., 151
Williams, Tennessee, 38
Wilmot, William W., 317, 322
Wilson, Sloan, 174
Wilson, Woodrow, 95
Wittgenstein, Ludwig, 110, 127
Wolfe, Thomas, 182
Woodworth, R., 63
Words, and emotion, 165–66

Y

You Can't Go Home Again (Wolfe), 182

Z

Zero-sum game, 245
Zestful participant type, 103–4
Zoo Story, The (Albee), 174
Zuñi Indians, 247